Business Economics in Corporate

Business Economics in Corporate

Dr. Ashok Purohit

RANDOM

RANDOM PUBLICATIONS

NEW DELHI (INDIA)

Business Economics in Corporate

ISBN 978-93-5111-941-8

Published in 2016 in India by

RANDOM PUBLICATIONS

4376-A/4B, Gali Murari Lal, Ansari Road
New Delhi-110 002
Phone : +9111-43580356, 011-23289044, 011-43142548
e-mail: sales@randompublications.com,
info@randompublications.com, randomexports@gmail.com

Type Setting by : Friends Media, Delhi-110089
Printed at : Sanat Printers

Preface

Business economics entails the understanding of the global economy and its connection to organizations, individuals and society. The wide selection of career options related to business economics requires a deep understanding of mathematics, finance and business communication.

The term 'business economics' is used in a variety of ways. Sometimes it is used as synonymously with industrial economics/industrial organisation, managerial economics, and economics for business. Still, there may be substantial differences in the usage of 'economics for business' and 'managerial economics' with the latter used more narrowly. One view of the distinctions between these would be that business economics is wider in its scope than industrial economics in that it would be concerned not only with "industry" but also businesses in the service sector. Economics for business looks at the major principles of economics but focuses on applying these economic principles to the real world of business. Managerial economics is the application of economic methods in the managerial decision-making process.

Local economies realize distinct benefits from the activities of local small businesses. Small businesses, in turn, can realize competitive advantages by employing a local focus in their service and marketing activities. Major benefits of business in the local economy include a boost in employment and discretionary income in the community, tax income increases for local governments and a loyal customer base for businesses.

Almost all business decisions, in one way or other, relate to business and economic variables. The behaviour of these variables is uncertain. Therefore, business decisions are taken in an environment of uncertainty and thus risk is involved. This fact of uncertainty and complexity of modern, business makes the function of decision-making and future planning complicated. To take appropriate business decisions, management of a business organisation must have clean understanding about internal issues of the organisation and general business environment.

– Author

Contents

Preface .... *v-vi*

1. Introduction **1**

Economic System 2
Evolutionary Economics 8
The Advantages of Businesses in the Local Economy 9
Benefits of Businesses for the Local Economy 10
The Benefits of Studying Economics 10

2. Consumer Behaviour in Market **15**

Consumer Buying Behaviour 15
Consumer Buying Behaviour 18
Buying Motives and Consumer Behaviour 18
Meaning and Concept of Consumer Behaviour 29
Business vs Consumer Markets 30

3. Capital Marketing in Business Economics **69**

Capital Market: Meaning, Features and Importance of Capital Market 69
Definition of 'Capital Markets' 71
Capital Market Theory 73
Market Value of Invested Capital (MVIC)? 78

4. Production Analysis **92**

Definition of Production Management 92
Scope of Production Management 93
Production System 98
Types of Production Systems 98

5. Analysis Cost **140**

Cost Function 141
Determinants of Cost 145
Fixed, Variable, Total, Average and Marginal Costs 145
Classification of Costs 151

6. **Demand Analysis** **166**

An Overview 166
Transportation of Demand Analysis 168
Demand and Need 172
The Curve Demand 174
Determinants of demand Analysis 177

7. **Market Situations and Pricing** **192**

Meaning of Price 192
Prices and Marketing 194
Importance of Prices in the Economy 194
Market Price under Monopoly 198

8. **Evolution of Strategic Business Management** **233**

Introduction 233
The Selected Strategy of Business 237
Competitive (Business Level) Strategy Management 240
Societal Strategy Management 245

9. **Corporate Communication** **266**

Corporate Strategy 270
Corporate Culture and Technology Use at Netcon Division 281
Case One: Kent 282
Case Three: Scott 285
Virtues of Corporate Life 290

Bibliography **309**

Index **311**

1

Introduction

Business economics is a field for individuals interested in applying economic theory and analysis in business decision making. Read on to learn what it takes to launch a career in business economics and whether this industry is right for you. Business economics is a field in applied economics which uses economic theory and quantitative methods to analyze business enterprises and the factors contributing to the diversity of organizational structures and the relationships of firms with labour, capitaland product markets. A professional focus of the journal Business Economics has been expressed as providing "practical information for people who apply economics in their jobs."

SUBJECT MATTER

Business economics is concerned with economic issues and problems related to business organization, management, and strategy. Issues and problems include: an explanation of why corporate firms emerge and exist; why they expand: horizontally, vertically and spacially; the role of entrepreneurs and entrepreneurship; the significance of organizational structure; the relationship of firms with the employees, the providers of capital, the customers, the government; the interactions between firms and the business environment.

AMBIGUITY IN THE USE OF TERM

The term 'business economics' is used in a variety of ways. Sometimes it is used as synonymously with industrial economics/industrial organisation, managerial economics, and economics for business. Still, there may be substantial differences in the usage of 'economics for business' and 'managerial economics' with the latter used more narrowly. One view of the distinctions between these would be that business economics is wider in its scope than industrial economics in that it would be concerned not only with "industry" but also businesses in the service sector. Economics for business looks at the major principles of economics but focuses on applying these economic principles to the real world of business. Managerial economics is the application of economic methods in the managerial decision-making process.

INTERPRETATIONS FROM VARIOUS UNIVERSITIES

Many universities offer courses in business economics and offer a range of interpretations as to the meaning of the word. The Bachelor of Business Economics (BBE) Programme at University of Delhi is designed to meet the growing need for an analytical and quantitative approach to problem solving in the changing corporate world by the application of the latest techniques evolved in the fields of economics and business. The programme at Harvard University uses economic methods to analyze practical aspects of business, including business administration, management, and related fields of business economics. The University of Miami defines business economics as involving the study of how we use our resources for the production, distribution, and consumption of goods and services. This requires business economists to analyze social institutions, banks, the stock market, the government and their relationships with labour negotiations, taxes, international trade, and urban and environmental issues.

Courses at the University of Manchester interpret business economics to be concerned with the economic analysis of how businesses contribute to welfare of society rather than on the welfare of an individual or a business. This is done via an examination of the relationship between ownership, control and firm objectives; theories of the growth of the firm; the behavioural theory of the firm; theories of entrepreneurship; the factors that influence the structure, conduct and performance of business at the industry level. Italian Universities borrow their concept of business economics from the tradition of Gino Zappa, for example a standard course at the Politecnico di Milano involves studyingcorporate governance, accounting, investment analysis, budgeting and business strategy. La Trobe University of Melbourne, Australia associates business economics with the process of demand, supply and equilibrium coordinating the behaviour of individuals and businesses in the market. Also, business economics extends to government policy, economic variables and international factors which influence business and competition.

ECONOMIC SYSTEM

An economic system is a system of production and exchange of goods and services as well as allocation of resources in a society. It includes the combination of the various institutions, agencies, entities (or even sectors as described by some authors) and consumers that comprise the economic structure of a given community. A related concept is the mode of production.

The study of economic systems includes how these various agencies and institutions are linked to one another, how information flows between them, and the social relations within the system (including property rights and the structure of management). Among existing economic systems, distinctive methods of analysis have developed, such as socialist economics and Islamic economic jurisprudence. Today the dominant form of economic organization at the world level is based on market-oriented mixed economies. Economic systems is the category in the Journal of Economic Literature classification codes that includes the study of such systems. One field that cuts across them is comparative economic systems.

Subcategories of different systems there include:

- Planning, coordination, and refor
- Productive enterprises; factor and product markets; prices; population
- Public economics; financial economics
- National income, product, and expenditure; money; inflation
- International trade, finance, investment, and aid
- Consumer economics; welfare and poverty
- Performance and prospects
- Natural resources; energy; environment; regional studies
- Political economy; legal institutions; property rights.

COMPONENTS

There are multiple components to economic systems. Decision-making structures of an economy determine the use of economic inputs (the factors of production), distribution of output, the level of centralization in decision-making, and who makes these decisions. Decisions might be carried out by industrial councils, by a government agency, or by private owners.

In one view, every economic system represents an attempt to solve three fundamental and interdependent problems:

- What goods and services shall be produced, and in what quantities?
- How shall goods and services be produced? That is, by whom and with what resources and technologies?
- For whom shall goods and services be produced? That is, who is to enjoy the benefits of the goods and services and how is the total product to be distributed among individuals and groups in the society?

Thus every economy is a system that allocates resources for exchange, production, distribution and consumption. The system is stabilized through a combination of threat and trust, which are the outcome of institutional arrangements.

An economic system possesses the following institutions:

- *Methods of control over the factors or means of production:* This may include ownership of, or property rights to, the means of production and therefore may give rise to claims to the proceeds from production. The means of production may be owned privately, by the state, by those who use them or be held in common.
- *A decision-making system:* This determines who is eligible to make decisions over economic activities. Economic agents with decision-making powers can enter into binding contracts with one another.

- *A coordination mechanism:* This determines how information is obtained and used in decision-making. The two dominant forms of coordination are planning and markets; planning can be either decentralized or centralized, and the two coordination mechanisms are not mutually exclusive and often co-exist.
- *An incentive system:* This induces and motivates economic agents to engage in productive activities. It can be based on either material reward (compensation or self-interest) or moral suasion (for instance, social prestige or through a democratic decision-making process that binds those involved). The incentive system may encourage specialization and the division of labour.
- *Organizational form:* There are two basic forms of organization: actors and regulators. Economic actors include households, work gangs and production teams, firms, joint-ventures and cartels. Economically regulative organizations are represented by the state and market authorities; the latter may be private or public entities.
- *A distribution system:* This allocates the proceeds from productive activity, which is distributed as income among the economic organizations, individuals and groups within society, such as property owners, workers and non-workers, or the state (from taxes).
- A public choice mechanism for law-making, establishing rules, norms and standards and levying taxes. Usually this is the responsibility of the state but other means of collective decision-making are possible, such as chambers of commerce or workers' councils.

TYPES

There are several basic questions that must be answered in order for an economy to run satisfactorily. The scarcity problem, for example, requires answers to basic questions, such as: what to produce, how to produce it, and whogets what is produced. An economic system is a way of answering these basic questions, and different economic systems answer them differently. Many different objectives may be seen as desirable for an economy, like efficiency,growth, liberty, and equality.

Economic systems are commonly segmented by their ownership structure and property rights and by their dominant mechanism of resource allocation. Economies that combine private ownership with market allocation are called "market capitalism", and economies that mix private ownership with economic planning are called "command capitalism". Likewise, systems that mix public or cooperative ownership of the means of production with economic planning are called "planned socialism", and systems that combine public or cooperative ownership with markets are designated as "market socialism". Some perspectives build upon this basis and consider other variables, such as class processes within an economy. This leads some economists to categorize, for example, the Soviet Union's economy as state capitalism based on the analysis that the working class was exploited by the party leadership.

In a capitalist economic system production is carried out for private profit, decisions regarding investment and the use of the means of production are determined by business owners in the marketplace. The means of production are owned primarily by private enterprises and decisions regarding production and investment determined by private owners in capital markets. Capitalist systems range from laissez-faire, with minimal government regulation and state enterprise, to regulated and social market systems, with the stated aim of ensuring "social justice" and a more equitable distribution of wealth or ameliorating market failures.

In socialist economic system (socialism), production is carried out to produce goods and services directly for use; decisions regarding the use of the means of production are adjusted to satisfy economic demand, investment is determined through economic planning procedures. The means of production are either publicly owned, or are owned cooperatively by their employees. A socialist economic system that features social ownership but is based on the process of capital accumulation and utilizes capital markets for the allocation of capital goods are designated asmarket socialism.

The basic and general economic systems are:

- Market economy ("hands off" systems, such as laissez-faire capitalism)
- Mixed economy (a hybrid that blends some aspects of both market and planned economies)
- Planned economy ("hands on" systems, such as state socialism, also known as "command economy" when referring to the Soviet model)
- Traditional economy (a generic term for older economic systems)
- Participatory economics (a system where the production and distribution of goods is guided by public participation)
- Gift economy (where an exchange is made without any explicit agreement for immediate or future rewards)
- Barter economy (where goods and services are directly exchanged for other goods or services)
- Post-scarcity economy (a hypothetical form where resources aren't scarce, such as Marx's concept of a Communist society)

Capitalism

Capitalism generally features the private ownership of the means of production (capital), and a market economy for coordination. Corporate capitalism refers to a capitalist marketplace characterized by the dominance of hierarchical, bureaucratic corporations.

Mercantilism was the dominant model in Western Europe from the 16th to 18th century. This encouraged imperialism and colonialism until economic and political changes resulted in global decolonization. Modern capitalism has favored free trade to take advantages of increased efficiencies due to national comparative advantage and economies of scale in a larger, more universal market. Some critics have applied the term neo-colonialism to the power imbalance between multi-national corporations operating in a free market vs. seemingly impoverished people in developing countries.

Mixed Economy

There is no precise definition of a "mixed economy". Theoretically, it may refer to an economic system that combines one of three characteristics: public and private ownership of industry, market-based allocation with economic planning, or free-markets with state interventionism. In practice, "mixed economy" generally refers to market economies with substantial state interventionism and/or sizable public sector alongside a dominant private sector. Actual mixed economies gravitate more heavily to one end of the spectrum.

Notable economic models and theories that have been described as a "mixed economy" include:

- Georgism - socialized rents on land
- Mixed economy
- American School
- Dirigisme
- Nordic model
- Japanese system
- Social market economy also known as Soziale Marktwirtschaft
- Social corporatism
- Socialist market economy
- Progressive utilization theory
- Indicative planning also known as a planned market economy
- State capitalism

Socialism

Socialist economic systems (all of which feature social ownership of the means of production) can be subdivided by their coordinating mechanism (planning and markets) intoplanned socialist and market socialist systems. Additionally, socialism can be divided based on their property structures between those that are based on public ownership, worker or consumer cooperatives and common ownership (*i.e.*, non-ownership). Communism is a hypothetical stage of Socialist development articulated by Marx as "second stage Socialism" in Critique of the Gotha Programme, whereby economic output is distributed based on need and not simply on the basis of labour contribution.

The original conception of socialism involved the substitution of money as a unit of calculation and monetary prices as a whole with calculation in kind (or valuation based on natural units), with business and financial decisions replaced by engineering and technical criteria for managing the economy. Fundamentally, this meant that socialism would operate under different economic dynamics than those of capitalism and the price system. Later models of socialism developed by neo-classical economists (most notably Oskar Lange and Abba Lerner) were based on the use of notional prices derived from a trial-and-error approach to achieve market clearing prices on the part of a planning agency. These models of socialism were called "market socialism" because they included a role for markets, money and prices.

The primary emphasis of socialist planned economies is to coordinate production is to produce economic output to directly satisfy economic demand as opposed to the indirect mechanism of the profit system where satisfying needs is subordinate to the pursuit of profit; to advance the productive forces of the economy in a more efficient manner while being immune to the perceived systemic inefficiencies (cyclical processes) and crisis of overproduction so that production would be subject to the needs of society as opposed to being ordered around capital accumulation.

In a pure socialist planned economy that involves different processes of resource allocation, production and means of quantifying value, the use of money would be replaced with a different measure of value and accounting tool that would embody more accurate information about an object or resource. In practice, the economic system of the former Soviet Union and Eastern bloc operated as a command economy, featuring a combination of state owned enterprises and central planning using the material balances method.

The extent to which these economic systems achieved socialism or represented a viable alternative to capitalism is subject to debate. In orthodox Marxism, the mode of production is tantamount to the subject of this article, determining with a superstructure of relations the entirety of a given culture or stage of human development.

Other Aspects

Corporatism refers to economic tripartite involving negotiations between business, labour, and state interest groups to establish economic policy, or more generally to assigning people to political groups based on their occupational affiliation. Certain subsets of an economy, or the particular goods, services, techniques of production, or moral rules can also be described as an "economy".

For example, some terms emphasize specific sectors or externalizes:

- Digital economy
- Green economy

- Information economy
- Internet economy
- Knowledge economy
- Natural economy
- Virtual economy
- Circular economy

Others emphasize a particular religion:

- Arthashastra - Hindu Economics
- Buddhist economics
- Islamic economics
- Distributism - Catholic ideal of a "third way" economy, featuring more distributed ownership in a mixed economy

EVOLUTIONARY ECONOMICS

Karl Marx's theory of economic development was based on the premise of evolving economic systems; specifically, in his view, over the course of history superior economic systems would replace inferior ones. "Inferior" systems were beset by "internal contradictions" and "inefficiencies" that make them "impossible" to survive over the long term. In Marx's scheme, feudalism was replaced by capitalism, which would eventually be superseded by socialism. Joseph Schumpeter had an evolutionary conception of economic development, but unlike Marx, he de-emphasized the role of class struggle in contributing to qualitative change in the economic mode of production. In subsequent world history,Communist states run according to Marxist-Leninist ideologies have either collapsed or gradually reformed their centrally-planned economies towards market-based economies, for example with perestroika and the dissolution of the Soviet Union, Chinese economic reform, and ĐoiMoi in Vietnam.

Mainstream evolutionary economics continues to study economic change in modern times. There has also been renewed interest in understanding economic systems as evolutionary systems in the emerging field of Complexity economics.

CONTEXT IN SOCIETY

An economic system can be considered a part of the social system and hierarchically equal to the law system, political system, cultural, etc. There is often a strong correlation between certain ideologies, political systems and certain economic systems (for example, consider the meanings of the term "communism"). Many economic systems overlap each other in various areas (for example, the term "mixed economy" can be argued to include elements from various systems). There are also various mutually exclusive hierarchical categorizations.

THE ADVANTAGES OF BUSINESSES IN THE LOCAL ECONOMY

Local economies realize distinct benefits from the activities of local small businesses. Small businesses, in turn, can realize competitive advantages by employing a local focus in their service and marketing activities. Major benefits of business in the local economy include a boost in employment and discretionary income in the community, tax income increases for local governments and a loyal customer base for businesses.

LOCAL EMPLOYMENT

One of the most personal advantages of businesses in the local economy is the boost in employment in the region. Employment levels influence a range of other standard-of-living metrics, such as disposable income, home foreclosure rates and new small business startups. Employing people in the local community can stimulate word-of-mouth advertising for a company as well, assuming the company treats its employees well enough to get positive mentions.

LOCAL TAX INCOME

Businesses pay a significant portion of all taxes in the United States, including income tax, property tax and employment tax. Having more businesses in the local economy can boost tax income for local governments, bringing in more money to repair roads, develop schools and improve public services.

ACCESS TO SERVICES

Along with the standard-of-living increases inherent in raising local employment, the presence of many business types can raise the standard-of-living further by providing a wider range of services and amenities in the local area. Adding a movie theater to a small town, for example, can add an entertainment option to local residents while bringing in money from outlying communities.

POLITICAL ADVANTAGES

Businesses with strong ties to a local community can lend a hand in community-focused political actions. Businesses can help to fund and organize campaigns for lobbying, letter-writing and other political activities to influence legislators on issues that affect the local community. A local business can help to convince a presidential candidate to hold a campaign speech in the town, for example, by making sizable campaign contributions.

LOYAL CUSTOMERS

Businesses with a local focus have the advantage of cultivating a loyal customer base, especially when their services are not threatened by big-box chain stores in the area. While this may not influence company growth, it ensures a certain level of financial sustainability, and helps to ensure the company maintains a positive reputation in at least one region.

BENEFITS OF BUSINESSES FOR THE LOCAL ECONOMY?

Local businesses have been a staple of economies all around the world ever since people first began trading for goods and services. With the increase of large corporations and chain stores, many local businesses have closed down or sold their assets and ceased operations. This is a problem on a number of levels, but economically, local businesses provide many advantages to the economy where they operate. Because of their advantages, it is important to patronize local businesses whenever possible to help preserve the local economy in your area.

SUPPORT STAFF

One major advantage of local businesses to the local economy is that they typically employ a wide variety of supporting services that must also be obtained locally. For example, if a local business needs to add to its facilities, it will hire a local contractor. Local businesses might also require the services of a tax preparer, cleaning service or other local businesses, which increases the amount of work for everyone in the local economy.

LOCALLY MADE GOODS

Small businesses also typically offer more locally produced goods than large chain stores do. If you have a product that you want to sell, like produce, you may find a local farmers' market that will allow you to sell it. A chain store might purchase all of its strawberries from California or Florida, while you can sell yours right near your home. Because of this, individuals in the local economy are able to sell their goods and services at a local business, which benefits everyone in that area.

KEEPING MONEY IN THE AREA

Another advantage of local businesses is that more of the money spent at a local business stays in the local area. A study done in 2003 in Austin, Texas, by the American Independence Business Alliance found that out of every $100 spent at a nationwide chain store, only about $13 stayed in the local economy. However, out of every $100 spent at a locally owned and operated business, about $45 stayed in the local economy. This provides a huge boost to other local businesses, workers and families in the local area.

THE BENEFITS OF STUDYING ECONOMICS

Where can students study economics? Over 95 departments across the UK offer an Economics degree. Some of these are straight ('single') Economics degrees. Normally they are simply called Economics, but sometimes they are more specialist, *e.g.* Agricultural Economics or Business Economics. Other degrees combine Economics with another subject ('joint degrees'). The titles of these joint degrees includes: Economics and Management; Economics and Finance; Economics and Philosophy; Economics and Accounting; Economics and Business; Economics and History; and Economics and Politics.

What will economics students do at university? Most economics students will experience a generic first year at university which builds a solid foundation. The most important modules for a first-year economics student are Introductory Microeconomics, Introductory Macroeconomics and Quantitative Methods for Economics (statistics/mathematics). The concepts taught in these three modules will be used throughout an economics undergraduate degree. In their second, and particularly third, year at university, economics students will have a number of optional units. Students will be able to specialise in Development Economics, Managerial Economics, Labour Economics, Monetary Economics and so on. If students are on a joint degree they will have modules in their other subject in all three years, some of which will be compulsory. Students on either single or joint economics degrees may also be able to do an optional module in another subject area such as a modern language.

"Until studying a course like economics not a lot of people are aware of how the world works, including industries, businesses and governments. You realise that it's very important to be educated in this type of thing even if it gets to the stage where you become annoyed with family and friends for moaning about taxes!" The workload at university is generally heavier than at A-level. Students can expect around 10 – 15 hours of contact time a week, consisting of a mixture of lectures and tutorials/seminars/workshops. In addition to this, students will be expected to put in a minimum of 20 hours per week of independent study. The number of contact hours will normally fall between years one, two and three but the amount of independent study will rise (at least it should do!).

Why do students enjoy economics? Economics is the perfect combination of numbers and words, problems and essays, calculations and interpretations. It is both an art and a science subject. Students have the opportunity to build models which give insights into the real world, and then to critique these models on the basis of their assumptions. There is rarely a right answer in economics but any argument put forward must be backed up by quantitative evidence. Students ultimately enjoy economics because it allows them to employ and develop analytical and evaluative skills. "My decision to pursue an Economics degree has been the single most valuable investment I have made to date. It sharpened my ability to critically assess information, deliver disciplined and well structured arguments and become a more confident team player." What do students need to have studied to read economics at university?

Some universities have A-level Maths as a prerequisite for their economics degrees. Even if it is not required, A-level Maths is still very useful for university level economics, especially those degrees with a heavy number of quantitative modules. Those institutions that do not require A-level Maths still require a good GCSE in Maths. Furthermore, some universities may look more favourably on candidates with other quantitative subjects, such as Physics or Accounting. No university requires students to have studied A-level Economics, but it helps if they have. Aside from the subjects studied, students should only choose to read economics at university: if they enjoy keeping up with current affairs; if they are comfortable working with numbers; and if they are willing to write a number of essays.

But how can a student, who has never studied economics before, prepare for their degree? One way is through work experience, especially when this involves handling money or making any form of economic choice. Reading economic articles in newspapers and/or subscribing to The Economist will give students an edge over their peers when it comes to writing their first essay. Students could also read a couple of the books on their course's reading list, particularly those that give lots of background information (*e.g.* "Fool's Gold" by Gillian Tett). Alternatively, a lot of the popular economics literature, such as theUndercover Economist or Freakonomics, will show students that economics can be used to explain virtually any phenomena.

"Economics places a key role in all aspects of life and is an important subject worth knowing more about."

To get an idea of the level of maths involved in their economic modules, students should have a flick through a first year textbook and have a go at some of the problems set. Finally, students should brush up on their statistics either by going back to their notes or, if they did not study maths, by working through some problems in an A-level statistics textbook. Statistics is vital for students to understand econometrics, a technique used by many authors in a number of economic journals.

And what can students do after an Economics degree? Economics graduates are well equipped, having analytical and problem-solving skills, numerical and computer skills, as well as the ability to work well either alone or within a team. All of these skills are very transferable allowing economics graduates to branch into anything from investment banking and financial services, business and public-sector management and research, to working with charities, teaching or the media. There is little restriction on what students can do afterwards.

ADVANTAGES OF STUDYING ECONOMICS

If you make a point of keeping up to date with current events around the globe and love anything to do with startups, businesses, or economics, it is probably a good idea to look into an economics degree to enhance your future with an economics career. There are numerous career options for economics majors students.

At its heart, economics is a human-oriented subject, though it may look to be all about money on the surface. Economics can, in fact, be defined as the study of how people allocate and utilise resources on an individual and collective basis. This human-centric element renders the Economics major courses available very wide-ranging, indeed. There are many different ways to approach this diverse subject and a host of advantages of studying economics. In fact, there are both Bachelor of Arts and Bachelor of Science degrees available for undergraduates pursuing Economics major courses.

WHAT IS ECONOMICS?

Economics is a social science that explores an entire range of issues that influence financial decisions. Economics looks at how individuals and organisations use, produce, consume, and distribute the world's goods and services. Knowing about money is not enough: areas like sociology, law, psychology, politics, geography, and history should be examined as well. Any knowledge in these expansive fields would further enhance and increase the benefits of studying economics, since these subjects are all inter-disciplinary and understanding one subject would potentially deepen the understanding in another.

Microeconomics and macroeconomics are the two main types of economics. As the names imply, microeconomics focuses on the economical behaviour of individuals (*e.g.* companies, families, consumers), while macroeconomics looks at economies on the global or national scale, with a focus on such issues as inflation, unemployment, and fiscal policy. Both types of economics subjects have wide-ranging applications in the real world, thereby further broadening the career options for Economics majors graduates.

Indeed, the skills acquired by students of Economics major courses extend far beyond the knowledge gained; students also develop transferable soft skills, including analytical problem-solving skills, and the ability to communicate quantitative data as well as qualitative research findings. The advantages of studying Economics differ from the advantages of studying other humanities subjects, since Economics allows students to learn how to analyse very specific figures which enable them to predict future economically-oriented events. This can render Economics graduates a marketable, employable asset that differentiates them from other graduates.

WHAT TO EXPECT FROM AN ECONOMICS DEGREE

An Economics degree offers students an amalgamation of lectures, smaller-group seminars, written assignments, project reports, and perhaps examinations. A Bachelor of Science in economics will focus more on mathematics and statistics. The latter two subjects have broad-reaching application within a practical context, and most prestigious corporations and financial institutions require employees to have a solid grasp of mathematical principles. Thus, in such cases, the benefits of an Economics degree are particularly noticeable.

A Bachelor of Arts in Economics will still entail a mathematical element; however, it takes a more qualitative approach and incorporates related theoretical fields such as psychology or sociology. Degrees in areas like Behavioural Economics do not necessarily limit the career paths for Economics majors students though, because companies are increasingly recognise the need for creativity and innovation, in order for their consultants and analysts to come up with solutions within a dynamic, financial context.

Whether you decide to pursue a BA or BSc, a degree in Economics will ask that you understand both Economic theory and how to engage in empirical investigation. A knowledge of statistics will help you investigate issues in public policy, business, or financial industries. If you do not have a ready aptitude for maths and information technology, or an ability to tackle problems, then the thrill and the benefits of studying economics may be far more diminished for you. In such a situation, economics may not be the right choice for you, and there are many other academic programmes discussed here which may be more suited to you. However, if you do have those qualities, and enjoy keeping up to date with current affairs as well, then this subject may be the key to a plethora of career options for you Economics majors graduates out there. A degree in Economics will certainly not preclude you from continuing onto an academic career; it is a very respectable degree that many professors and researchers are passionate about. It can also frequently be offered as part of an Honours programme and combined with many other subjects, including modern languages, politics, sociology, computer science, law, and engineering, among others.

2

Consumer Behaviour in Market

CONSUMER BUYING BEHAVIOUR

Possibly the most challenging concept in marketing deals with understanding why buyers do what they do (or don't do). But such knowledge is critical for marketers since having a strong understanding of buyer behaviour will help shed light on what is important to the customer and also suggest the important influences on customer decision-making. Using this information, marketers can create marketing programmes that they believe will be of interest to customers.

As you might guess, factors affecting how customers make decisions are extremely complex. Buyer behaviour is deeply rooted in psychology with dashes of sociology thrown in just to make things more interesting. Since every person in the world is different, it is impossible to have simple rules that explain how buying decisions are made.

But those who have spent many years analysing customer activity have presented us with useful "guidelines" in how someone decides whether or not to make a purchase. In fact, pick up any textbook that examines customer behaviour and each seems to approach it from a different angle. The perspective we take is to touch on just the basic concepts that appear to be commonly accepted as influencing customer behaviour.

TYPES OF CONSUMER PURCHASE DECISIONS

Consumers are faced with purchase decisions nearly every day. But not all decisions are treated the same. Some decisions are more complex than others and thus require more effort by the consumer. Other decisions are fairly routine and require little effort. In general, consumers face four types of purchase decisions:

- *Minor New Purchase*: These purchases represent something new to a consumer but in the customer's mind is not a very important purchase in terms of need, money or other reason (*e.g.,* status within a group).
- *Minor Re-Purchase*: These are the most routine of all purchases and often the consumer returns to purchase the same product without

giving much thought to other product options (*i.e.*, consumer is brand loyalty).

- *Major New Purchase*: These purchases are the most difficult of all purchases because the product being purchased is important to the consumer but the consumer has little or no previous experience making these decisions. The consumer's lack of confidence in making this type of decision often (but not always) requires the consumer to engage in an extensive decision-making process..
- *Major Re-Purchase*: These purchase decisions are also important to the consumer but the consumer feels confident in making these decisions since they have previous experience purchasing the product.

For marketers it is important to understand how consumers treat the purchase decisions they face. If a company is targeting customers who feel a purchase decision is difficult (*i.e.*, Major New Purchase), their marketing strategy may vary greatly from a company targeting customers who view the purchase decision as routine. In fact, the same company may face both situations at the same time; for some the product is new, while other customers see the purchase as routine. The implication of buying behaviour for marketers is that different buying situations require different marketing efforts.

WHY CONSUMERS BUY

Customers make purchases in order to satisfy needs. Some of these needs are basic and must be filled by everyone on the planet (*e.g.,* food, shelter) while others are not required for basic survival and vary depending on the person. It probably makes more sense to classify needs that are not a necessity as wants or desires. In fact, in many countries where the standard of living is very high, a large portion of the population's income is spent on wants and desires rather than on basic needs. In this tutorial when we mention the consumer we are referring to the actual buyer, the person spending the money. But is should also be pointed out that the one who does the buying is not necessarily the user of what is bought and that others may be involved in the buying decision in addition to the actual buyer.

While the purchasing process in the consumer market is not as complex as the business market, having multiple people involved in a purchase decision is not unusual. For example, in planning for a family vacation the mother may make the hotel reservations but others in the family may have input on the hotel choice.

Similarly, a father may purchase snacks at the grocery store but his young child may be the one who selected it from the store shelf. So understanding consumer purchase behaviour involves not only understanding how decisions are made but also understanding the dynamics that influence purchases.

WHAT INFLUENCES PURCHASING

As we discussed the decision-making process for consumers is anything but straight forward. There are many factors that can affect this process as a person works through the purchase decision. The number of potential influences on consumer behaviour is limitless. However, marketers are well served to understand the KEY influences. By doing so they may be in a position to tailor their marketing efforts to take advantage of these influences in a way that will satisfy the consumer and the marketer (remember this is a key part of the definition of marketing).

For the purposes of this tutorial we will break these influences down into three main categories: Internal, External and Marketing. However, those interested in learning more about customer buying activity may want to consult one or more consumer behaviour books where they will find additional methods for explaining consumer buying behaviour. For the most part the influences are not mutually exclusive. Instead, they are all interconnected and, as we will see, work together to form who we are and how we behave. For each of the influences that are discussed we will provide a basic description and also suggest its implication to marketers. Bear in mind we only provide a few marketing implications for each influence; clearly there are many more.

INTERNAL INFLUENCES

We start our examination of the influences on consumer purchase decisions by first looking inside ourselves to see which are the most important internal factors that affect how we make choices.

Perceptual Filter

Perception is how we see ourselves and the world we live in. However, what ends up being stored inside us doesn't always get there in a direct manner. Often our mental makeup results from information that has been consciously or subconsciously filtered as we experience it, a process we refer to as a perceptual filter. To us this is our reality, though it does not mean it is an accurate reflection on what is real. Thus, perception is the way we filter stimuli (*e.g.,* someone talking to us, reading a newspaper story) and then make sense out of it.

Perception has several steps:

- *Exposure*: Sensing a stimuli (*e.g.,* seeing an ad)
- *Attention*: An effort to recognize the nature of a stimuli (*e.g.,* recognizing it is an ad)
- *Awareness*: Assigning meaning to a stimuli (*e.g.,* humorous ad for particular product)
- *Retention*: Adding the meaning to one's internal makeup (*i.e.*, product has fun ads)

How these steps are eventually carried out depends on a person's approach to learning. By learning we mean how someone changes what they know, which in turn may affect how they act. There are many theories of learning, a discussion of which is beyond the scope of this tutorial, however, suffice to say that people are likely to learn in different ways.

For instance, one person may be able to focus very strongly on a certain advertisement and be able to retain the information after being exposed only one time while another person may need to be exposed to the same advertisement many times before he/she even recognizes what it is. Consumers are also more likely to retain information if a person has a strong interest in the stimuli. If a person is in need of new car they are more likely to pay attention to a new advertisement for a car while someone who does not need a car may need to see the advertisement many times before they recognize the brand of automobile.

CONSUMER BUYING BEHAVIOUR

Possibly the most challenging concept in marketing deals with understanding why buyers do what they do (or don't do). But such knowledge is critical for marketers since having a strong understanding of buyer behaviour will help shed light on what is important to the customer and also suggest the important influences on customer decision-making. Using this information, marketers can create marketing programmes that they believe will be of interest to customers.

As you might guess, factors affecting how customers make decisions are extremely complex. Buyer behaviour is deeply rooted in psychology with dashes of sociology thrown in just to make things more interesting. Since every person in the world is different, it is impossible to have simple rules that explain how buying decisions are made. But those who have spent many years analyzing customer activity have presented us with useful "guidelines" in how someone decides whether or not to make a purchase. In fact, pick up any textbook that examines customer behaviour and each seems to approach it from a different angle. The perspective we take is to touch on just the basic concepts that appear to be commonly accepted as influencing customer behaviour.

BUYING MOTIVES AND CONSUMER BEHAVIOUR

Buying Behaviour is the decision processes and acts of people involved in buying and using products.

Need to understand:

- Why consumers make the purchases that they make?
- What factors influence consumer purchases?
- The changing factors in our society.

Consumer Buying Behaviour refers to the buying behaviour of the ultimate consumer.

A firm needs to analyse buying behaviour for:

- Buyers reactions to a firms marketing strategy has a great impact on the firms success.
- The marketing concept stresses that a firm should create a Marketing Mix that satisfies customers, therefore need to analyse the what, where, when and how consumers buy.
- Marketers can better predict how consumers will respond to marketing strategies.

STAGES OF THE CONSUMER BUYING PROCESS

Six Stages to the Consumer Buying Decision Process. Actual purchasing is only one stage of the process. Not all decision processes lead to a purchase. All consumer decisions do not always include all 6 stages, determined by the degree of complexity...discussed next.

The 6 stages are:

1. *Problem Recognition*: Difference between the desired state and the actual condition. Deficit in assortment of products. Hunger—Food. Hunger stimulates your need to eat.
2. Can be stimulated by the marketer through product information—did not know you were deficient? *I.E.*, see a commercial for a new pair of shoes, stimulates your recognition that you need a new pair of shoes.
3. *Information search*:
   - Internal search, memory.
   - External search if you need more information. Friends and relatives. Marketer dominated sources; comparison shopping; public sources etc.

     A successful information search leaves a buyer with possible alternatives, the evoked set. Hungry, want to go out and eat, evoked set is:
   - Chinese food
   - Indian food
   - Burger king
   - Klondike kates etc
4. *Evaluation of Alternatives*: Need to establish criteria for evaluation, features the buyer wants or does not want. Rank/weight alternatives or resume search. May decide that you want to eat something spicy, indian gets highest rank etc.
5. If not satisfied with your choice then return to the search phase. Can you think of another restaurant? Look in the yellow pages etc. Information

from different sources may be treated differently. Marketers try to influence by "framing" alternatives.

6. *Purchase decision*: Choose buying alternative, includes product, package, store, method of purchase etc.
7. *Purchase*: May differ from decision, time lapse between 4 and 5, product availability.
8. *Post-Purchase Evaluation*: Outcome: Satisfaction or Dissatisfaction. Cognitive Dissonance, have you made the right decision. This can be reduced by warranties, after sales communication etc. After eating an indian meal, may think that really you wanted a chinese meal instead.

TYPES OF CONSUMER BUYING BEHAVIOUR

Types of consumer buying behaviour are determined by:

- Level of Involvement in purchase decision. Importance and intensity of interest in a product in a particular situation.
- Buyers level of involvement determines why he/she is motivated to seek information about a certain products and brands but virtually ignores others.

High involvement purchases—Honda Motorbike, high priced goods, products visible to others, and the higher the risk the higher the involvement.

Types of risk:

- Personal risk
- Social risk
- Economic risk

The four type of consumer buying behaviour are:

1. *Routine Response/Programmed Behaviour*: Buying low involvement frequently purchased low cost items; need very little search and decision effort; purchased almost automatically. Examples include soft drinks, snack foods, milk etc.
2. *Limited Decision Making*: Buying product occasionally. When you need to obtain information about unfamiliar brand in a familiar product category, perhaps. Requires a moderate amount of time for information gathering. Examples include Clothes—know product class but not the brand.
3. Extensive Decision Making/Complex high involvement, unfamiliar, expensive and/or infrequently bought products. High degree of economic/performance/psychological risk. Examples include cars, homes, computers, education. Spend alot of time seeking information and deciding. Information from the companies MM; friends and relatives, store personnel etc. Go through all six stages of the buying process.

4. Impulse buying, no conscious planning.

The purchase of the same product does not always elicit the same Buying Behaviour. Product can shift from one category to the next.

For example:

- Going out for dinner for one person may be extensive decision making but limited decision making for someone else. The reason for the dinner, whether it is an anniversary celebration, or a meal with a couple of friends will also determine the extent of the decision making.

THE EXTENT IN POLICY DECISION-MAKING

Today's market is characterized by highly competitive organizations which are all vying for consumer's loyalty. Profit-oriented firms are faced with the challenge to maintain their own competitive edge in order to survive and be successful. Strategies are carefully planned and executed to gain the ultimate goal of all: company growth. However, internal factors are not the only elements which influence growth. There are also external factors and components working within the organization which shape the direction of the organization. Among this is the consumer - the fuel of the organization.

The dynamics of contemporary living define most of the aspects of human life today. From traditional ways to technologically driven mechanisms, life indeed is no longer the same decades and centuries ago. The recent developments and revolutionary processes resulting to increased convenience of people in various applications contributed to the topical standards of living. Along with the changing business world, customers change as well, becoming more demanding, knowledgeable and highly sophisticated. Before, it is enough if they have purchased a product or service the best way and condition possible. Now, the process of commercial interaction does not end that way. There are more complex steps to be completed to be able to achieve satisfactory results. In turn, company management had shifted their focus on their clients or customers so as to stay successfully in business. This transition meant that organizations have to completely reformulate their conventional business aims and purposes from being process-focused to customer-centred.

In the business, the consumers eventually developed as a result of the radical emergence and amalgamation of innovative and manipulative processes in the global marketplace. Established characteristics in terms of their behaviour and identity are important aspects to consider in studying the significant role they play in any economic endeavor. Furthermore, the subject of consumerism in given societies is becoming popular and a sought-after area of research. In connection, the presence of consumer policies and laws in the global market serve as controlling mechanisms to regulate the diversity of the international economic battlefield. This makes the buying experience even more multifaceted and interactive.

Advertising is the common playground where consumers ensnare themselves with products/services available in the market. The adverse effects of advertising are perceived to be reinforcing elements in the development of consumerist behaviour and culture. This is where the aspect of policy decision making is applicable. The creation of regulating policies in connection to advertising and its effects to consumerism and consumer behaviour is quantified.

This document aims to critically analyse the extent of the relationship of consumerism, consumer behaviour and identity with respect to policy decision-making of the state and business organizations predominantly in terms of the advertising medium. Specifically, it opts to qualify the extent of consumerism in relation to consumer behaviour and culture. Guidelines in advertising are the parametres to be used in policy decision-making. Additionally, it will provide several conceptual backgrounds about the said areas of the general consumer. To fully substantiate the arguments and findings in this research, information taken from vast sources of literature is used as supporting documents. There are also specific examples to be used to show the claims.

Initially, the understanding buyer behaviour is one of the more perplexing tasks confronting every manager. The difficulty arises from the heterogeneity of buyers, from their being groups of individuals who differ from one another. But differences notwithstanding, consumers do share attitudes, opinions, reactions, and desires at various times. Business experience, marketing research, theoretical constructs and models, and trial-and-error methods help to find some of the common denominators.

Believing on the idea that the consumers are the fuel of every profit and/or non-profit organization, studying their behaviour and identity remains parallel and important in every decision-making activity. Consumers have always been regarded as vital factors in relation to different organizational operations and functioning. They live and act in a constantly changing cultural, social, technological, legal, and economic environment. Shaped by the environment, marketing institutions, and activities in return have a major/minor impact on it. Their behaviour and identity, on the other hand, significantly determine the business future in a particular part of country and given culture. As we all know, as region varies on its own, so does the consumer behaviour and identity of such group of people in a region. Through observations of the consumer behaviour, the category in competition, organization, and the marketing strategies of businesses are well evaluated. Consumer behaviour is influenced by different aspects in its environment. It can be viewed with different factors such as the cultural, personal, psychological and social factors of the consumers.

The study of consumer behaviour is one of the most interesting and challenging as well as important aspects in marketing management. Practically, essential decisions that are taken in developing an effective marketing mix for specific product/service are based in the systematic knowledge of the consumers that make up its permanent target market. Believes that understanding the behaviour of the consumer is the most basic step in helping marketing authorities to visualize and predict future trends, reactions, and changes in the marketing mix. It may also serve as a reference in determining the potentials of new products and its adoption. Consumer behaviour is said to be closely associated to marketing research – another important field that deserves further comprehensive investigation.

Each organization provides some products/services that are used by consumers, even though they may not always recognize as products/services by the consumers as such. For example, it seems fairly obvious that the college students who drink a cola produced by a specific beverage company are the consumers of that beverage product. In a general sense, we can all think of public high school students as the consumers of a state's educational product; voters can be thought of as consumers of a political candidate's leadership and administration product; and, the members of a religious group might be viewed as consumers of a church's spiritual product. Thus, the study of the behaviour of consumers involves an examination of a wide range record of everyday human buying behaviour.

Consumer behaviour as defined by is "the activities that people engage in when selecting, purchasing, and using products and services so as to satisfy needs and desires". continued: "...such activities involve mental and emotional processes, in addition to physical actions". In general perspective, consumer behaviour studies individuals, groups or organizations with regards to obtaining, using and disposing of products and services. It also accounts the decision processes that lead and follow these behaviours. Consumer behaviour investigates consumers' actions, as well as the reasons for those behaviours. In order to fully understand the broad spectrum of consumer behaviour, identified its macroscopic and microscopic perspectives.

Consumer behaviour in a macro level categorizes marketers to look for demographic shifts as well as the general public's values, beliefs and practices which affect their interaction with the economic marketplace. Meanwhile, the micro level indicates consumer behaviour focused on human behaviour and the motivations underlying these behaviours. These concepts are drawn out from sociological and psychological perspectives as proven results of studies in the said aspect.

There are many factors that determine these activities, and the product/service is just one of them. There are some frameworks that helps explain customer behaviours. Among these are brand orientation model and integrated framework for cross-cultural consumer behaviour. Others, on the other hand, are expressed through demographic research, such as the relationship of culture on consumer behaviour. These models and studies are applicable to consumer behaviour in general products/services. But delving into such topic discussion will make this report technical and might astray away from its real objectives.

In the recent years, the study of consumer behaviour and consumer decision-making has become a sought-after research field. Topics in the various fields of consumer science are considered hot stuffs in scholastic as well as marketing management sectors. Theoretically, consumer science includes the former discipline of home economics – the foundation of basic consumption. The consumer science discipline also evolves around consumer behaviour and decision making concerning the necessities of live and survival. Among these are foods and nutrition, clothing and textiles, housing and interior merchandise in everyday living. Believe that the providence of the aforementioned goods will result to physical, psychological, socio-psychological and financial satisfaction in a complex micro and macro environment. Of specific importance, observed that buying and consumer decision-making are complicated as based on the result of external influences that have to be handled within an internal frame of reference that has come about through consumer socialization.

The complex phenomenon of consumer behaviour is dependent to some considerable factors in the working environment of people. It is somewhat innate or even cultural in its foundation, external or internal in nature, or just a by-product of the common circumstances in the purchasing experience.

Advertising is among the external factors that plays a great role in the buying experience of people. For the record, an average American household exposure to television advertising is about an estimated 7 hours per day times 9 to 16 minutes of non-program material per hour. Additionally, advertising traditions hold that the average consumer is exposed to over 1,500 radio, television, newspaper, magazine, and/or billboard advertisements per day. As a result, it could be said that advertising and its component influence the behaviour of consumers. The promises of advertised products/services are subject to trial and materialization by the consumer. Thus, purchasing the said product/service is the sole way to prove its claims.

The daily exposure of people to all the different kinds of media makes it accessible and convenient for them to recognize the presence of the latest product/service in the market. With the assistance of ads, consumers are engaged in buying experience. As a part of their consumer behaviour stimulation, there are internal assessments that are occurring within the limits of the human nature. In Taiwan, and colleagues studied the behaviour of consumers in relation to the medium. They indicated that the elements of advertising, the manner of presentation, or a certain ad for instance, greatly affect the culture, concept and emotions, and other human attributes of a certain setting. More often than not, advertising contributes to the development of changes in connection to the existing behaviour and identity of the consumer. It may also lead to the practice of consumerism. According to, most advertising agencies keep on striking into insights on how to gain a deeper understanding on the reason why consumers behave the way they do. Further, advertising practitioners found assessment in probing the thoughts of every individual by using focus groups as variables in eliciting ideas for new products and promotional campaigns to be established. In advertising, I believe that people who are only exposed to recurring ads focus and elaborate on tangential cues such as the credibility of the source. For instance, a controversial political figure endorsing a product/service will simply be viewed as trash among its critics. Thus, the purchase of the product/service is almost impossible. This certain example is related in the process of forming brand attitude among the ordinary consumer that falls under the capacity of the advertising medium.

Largely, researchers linked consumer decision making in the study of perception. The study of perception is largely bounded on what humans consciously or subconsciously add to or subtract from their raw sensory inputs to produce a private and selective picture of the world. In general term, it is the process that involves the individual's decision in selecting, interpreting, and organizing stimuli into a meaningful and coherent picture of the world. A stimulus is any unit of input to the senses – may it be products, packages, brand names, advertisements, and commercials. In studies of consumerism, it has become almost a cliché to claim that the purchase, use and display of goods in some way expresses social identities and is rooted to the persuasive effects of advertising. The relationship of consumerism and customer behaviour plus advertising has been long overdue. Its interconnection opened up various horizons for academic marketing and management probing.

Consumerism is already deep-rooted part of every given culture. It has become so disturbing on a global scale. Defining consumerism is always equated into a negative image. However, with this report, consumerism will be tackled in connection to the rights of consumers as well as its association to consumer behaviour and identity towards policy decision-making. Traditionally, consumerism is known as the purchasing of products beyond the basic requirement of consumption.

Indicates:

- "In a Buddhist view of mutual co-arising and radical interrelatedness the cause of consumerism is boundlessly plural—a virtual infinity of conditions affecting and being affected by countless other conditions. The desires of individuals have been conditioned by the way parents raised them, by the historical conditions… by the use of media, and so on."

Furthermore, consumerism is related to environmental conditions that are persuasive. These conditions are contributory factors along with politics, economics, social institutions, industrial technology, and ideological tendency. Take for example, the consumerist behaviour of Filipino people during the holiday season perfectly show the factors affecting the practice.

With the various criticisms in consumerism, it has been connected with media applications such as advertising. In advertising, consumerism is a powerful mechanism that is driven by considerable sums spent on advertising. These are designed to generate both a desire to follow trends and the consequential personal self-reward scheme based on personal procurement. The basic idea of materialism and consumerism is one of the by-products of overt advertising.

The presence of consumerism in various cultures is studied in relation to policy decision making. The regulations made by the state are directed to the welfare and being of every buying individual. Laws on consumer rights are created to protect people against abuses in the economic marketplace. There are given considerations that are taken at hand when passing and eventually implementing such laws. The extent of consumer behaviour and identity as well as the relationship of culture are fully considered in realizing its intended purpose. For instance, the advertising medium proliferate consumerism. Every advertisement is produced with the aims to procure interest among the buyer and persuade him/her to have the product/service. The aesthetics of advertising easily provoke a culture of consumerism. Paradoxically, quaintness in advertising shows consumerism correcting itself, disassociating itself from its own conceited techniques, hiding consumerism from the consumer and ostensibly rejecting the commercialism on which it is based. Thus, animated or unrealistic presentation of some advertisements could easily attain its goal - persuasion.

In reference to my personal experiences, advertising materials that are too-good-to-be-true are appealing to me. The tendency is that I am persuaded to try on the product/service being advertise. My buying behaviour was stimulated by the ad. Therefore, it creates an identity that can lead to addiction and constant purchase beyond my normal consumption. As a result, I am practicing a culture of consumerism. As of the moment, there are government policies that control media like advertising standards. Countries like UK, Canada, and some developing nations maintain protocol in using the said medium. It is always subject to regulation and continuous assessment. The measurement of its extent of applicability in connection to the personal characteristics of consumers is strictly implemented. Its degree of interdependency to consumer behaviour and the present existing culture is not fully taken into considerable contemplation. This is the reason why the extent of policies must be measured in connection to consumer behaviour as well as identity.

The emphasis on consumerism and an increasing awareness of environmental and ethical issues all have their implications for marketing strategists. Many firms are blending communications activities with public purpose policy decision making. Of course, innovation and the production of the new are intrinsic to consumerism and tend to structure the conceptual field of the study of consumerism. The connection of creating advertising policies to the release of new products/services is undeniable. Thus, advertising is among the medium where policies must be evaluated.

New connections between the cultural and the political, the visual and the material, advertising and personal belonging, consumerism and the rights of citizenship has been premeditated issues tackled by each government worldwide. Within European nation-states, individuals' access to citizenship rights has increasingly been framed through discourses of consumerism. The presence of communal and societal awareness and battle against consumerism is another turning point for legislative undertakings of the state's authorities. People in various countries individually contribute to the cessation of consumerist behaviours or practices. The sense of national belonging and citizenship to consumerism and focus on choice as a prime mechanism in the production of consumer-citizenship identities linked the idea of individual behaviour and culture. Thus, the fight against consumerist attitudes is unyielding.

With the present realities, the intervention of state policies in the subject of consumerism is appropriate. State policies must deal with the basics of consumer behaviour. Considering the various factors affecting the decision making of consumers, the government is expected to regulate advertising processes in all sorts of medium – print or broadcast. While advertising is a recognizable media to proliferate economic activity, policies created must deal with the common protection of consumers. However, the degree of effect to consumerism is boundless due to the fact that consumers possess the freedom to choose.

This is aside from the truth that every consumer differs in behaviour and identity. In advertising standards created, implemented, and promoted by authority, it is highly needed that every advertisement must present only what is real and substantial to consumers. The ethics of advertising is necessary for every media regulating system.

Advertising policies and standards posed by authorities must be in accordance to the general moral discretion of the society and organizations. Thus, advertisements of organizations must maintain its commitment to corporate social responsibility. Prior to its public release, every advertisement must be taken into legal scrutiny in order to identify its effect in establishing the culture of consumerism. The protection of consumers' rights and welfare is the main concern of the state as well as the business organization.

Furthermore, the measurement of the extent of consumerism, consumer behaviour and identity in policy decision making of government is rooted on the natural laws of what is acceptable and not. As previously stated, ethics in advertising is the name of the game.

For instance,:

- "... The Federal Trade Commission should become concerned with regulating... type of potentially unfair advertising.... the FTC prohibits a company from stating that its product will cure an illness when such is not the case, the FTC might begin prohibiting a company from stating that its product will encourage sexual satisfaction, make one more masculine/feminine, or promote a happier homelife when such is not the case".

There are more concerns that the government and lawmakers need to qualify in relation to advertising regulation. But then again, the dynamic state in every given situation of human life is a significant factor in determining the extent in policy decision making and taking.

Materialism in modern life is rooted in the innate freedom and quest for satisfaction of people. In the U.S., personal freedoms and life satisfaction or the need to optimize on life's happenings are both integral elements in lifestyles. By this fact, the tendency to acquire a consumerist behaviour is ubiquitous. It is indeed true. There are internal processes that occur during a buying experience. This is simply apparent due to the personal characteristics of certain consumers especially to the environment. and colleagues stated that "the standards and values that stem from the environment greatly influence consumer behaviour, affecting purchasing and consumption activities, and the business organizations concerned."

The cultural context of consumer behaviour can be defined as "the totality of the customs, arts, sciences, religions, politics, and economics that distinguishes one society from another, and that influences the individual consumer's behaviour". The presence of subculture among the main culture makes the difference.

Subculture is usually defined as a category of people who share a sense of identification that is distinguishable from that of the culture as a whole. This shared sense of identification may result from a shared set of values, from a common history, or from similarity in socio-demographic attributes. Social class is perhaps the type of subculture that is most often used by consumer psychologists. The attribute that distinguishes between levels of social class is the relative level of social benefits. In connection to principles of consumerism, it could be assumed that this process is now a subculture.

All in all, the premise on economic interpretation of consumerism as the belief in the freedom to choose among consumers should indicate the economic structure of a society. This must be the basis of evaluating the extent of policy decision making of the states as well as business organizations. The relationship of consumerism, consumer behaviour and identity in connection to activities, policies, and actions taken by the state and business organization must be based and dependent on the consumer's behaviour and identity. The practice of consumerism, consumer behaviour and identity will always be pertinent to the buying experience of consumers. Thus, proper regulation of such laws implemented must be strictly determined and observed. This will eventually serve the welfare of the ultimate beneficiaries – the consumers.

MEANING AND CONCEPT OF CONSUMER BEHAVIOUR

Through the application of sociology, psychology and demographics, marketers can begin to understand why consumers form attitudes and make decisions to purchase. Consumer-behaviour studies inform marketers, advertisers and public agencies how product and service selection is influenced by personality, perception, values and beliefs. For marketing, these influences are studied in the context of demographics, which includes ethnicity, age, marital status, size of family, income, education and employment.

PERCEPTION

Perception is how information is collected and categorized. Perception is affected by the amount of exposure to a stimulus and by individual interpretation. For example, a consumer who hears—once—that dairy herds contribute to greenhouse gas would not take the statement seriously. If the same consumer encountered that information often and from many sources, then the consumer's attitude towards dairy products might change enough to influence how often the consumer chose yogurt as a breakfast food.

PERSONALITY

Personality is a weak component of consumer behaviour. Personality means a pattern of behaviour founded on an individual's outlook and internal traits. In this use, outlook means point-of-view and traits mean the consumer's usual manner of responding to the environment. An example of outlook is the effect of a recessionary economy on consumer confidence. Examples of traits are introversion or extroversion, ambition or complacency, aggressiveness or timidity and compulsiveness or pragmatism. A consumer whose decision to purchase is influenced by extroversion or compulsiveness, might choose to be less innovative during an economic downturn because confidence is lower.

VALUES

Values are the consumer's set of standards about conduct that arise from learned culture. A "terminal value" is a long-term goal or role model, as when a consumer strives for a particular lifestyle, such as healthful diet and exercise. An "instrumental" value is a flexible and negotiable action that is exercised daily, such as when a consumer makes a decision to purchase either organic or non-organic products.

BELIEFS

In consumer behaviour study, "beliefs" are specific beliefs about products in the marketplace. Consumer belief is a combination of knowledge, emotions and actual actions to purchase or not purchase. For example, if a consumer has a negative or prejudiced set of beliefs about Yugoslavia, then marketing an automobile manufactured in Yugoslavia would have to focus on changing those beliefs.

ATTITUDE

Consumer attitude is a combination of perceptions, values and beliefs. The consumer must first perceive the product and then focus values and beliefs onto the product and make a decision to purchase or not to purchase. Beliefs are more vulnerable to marketing than values are, because beliefs are subject to knowledge and emotion. For example, positive facts can inform a consumer's knowledge about automobile manufacturing in Yugoslavia. A marketer might decide what demographic group can best afford a Yugoslavian automobile and then generate positive emotion by associating the automobile with music towards which that demographic group feels positive.

BUSINESS VS CONSUMER MARKETS

For marketers, the selling environment of business markets present uniquely different circumstances when compared to selling to consumers.

At the beginning of this tutorial we saw two ways in which consumer and business markets differ:

- Business markets are more likely to be price driven than brand driven, and
- Demand in business markets tends to be more volatile than consumer markets.

However, the two markets are dissimilar in other ways requiring marketers to take a different approach when selling to business customers than to consumers.

These differences include:

- How Decisions Are Made
- Existence of Experienced Purchasers
- Time Needed to Make Buying Decision
- Size of Purchases
- Number of Buyers
- Type of Promotional Effort Needed to Reach Buyer

BUYING DIFFERENCES

Buying Centre Decisions

In the consumer market a very large percentage of purchase decisions are made by a single person. As we discussed in the Consumer Buying Behaviour tutorial, there are situations in which multiple people may be involved in a consumer purchase decision, such as a child influencing a parent to choose a certain brand of cereal or a husband and wife deciding together to buy a house, but most of the time purchases are individual decisions.

The business market is significantly different. While single person purchasing is not unusual, especially within a small company, a significant percentage of business buying, especially within larger organizations, requires the input of many. In the marketing literature those associated with the purchase decision are known to be part of a Buying Centre, which consists of individuals within an organization that perform one or more of the following roles:

- *Buyer*: Responsible for dealing with suppliers and placing orders
- *Decider*: Has the power to make the final purchase decision
- *Influencer*: Has the ability to affect what is ordered such as setting order specifications
- *User*: Those who will actually use the product when it is received
- *Initiator*: Any Buying Centre member who is the first to determine that a need exists
- *Gatekeeper*: Anyone who controls access to other Buying Centre members

For marketers confronting a Buying Centre it is important to first identify who plays what role. Once identified the marketer must address the needs of each member, which may differ significantly.

For instance, the Decider, who may be the company president wants to make sure the purchase will not negatively affect the company's bottom line while the Buyer wants to be assured the product will be delivered on time. Thus, the way each Buying Centre member is approached and marketed to requires careful planning in order to address the unique needs of each member.

Experienced Purchasers

As noted in the discussion of the Buying Centre, organizations often employ purchasing agents or professional buyers whose job is to negotiate the best deals for their company. Unlike consumers, who often lack information when making purchase decisions, professional buyers are generally as knowledgeable about the product and the industry as the marketer who is selling to them.

Decision Making Time

Depending on the product, business purchase decisions can drag on for an extensive period. Unlike consumer markets where impulse purchasing is rampant, the number of people involved in business purchase decisions results in decisions taking weeks, months or even years.

Size of Purchases

For products that are regularly used and frequently purchased, businesses will often buy a larger volume at one time compared to consumer purchases. Because of this business purchasers often demand price breaks for higher order levels.

Type of Promotions

Companies who primarily target consumers often use mass advertising methods to reach an often widely dispersed market. For business-to-business marketers the size of individual orders, along with a smaller number of buyers, makes person-to-person contact by sales representatives a more effective means of promotion.

CONTINUOUS CONSUMER PANELS

The process of obtaining information about the behaviour of consumers throughout a prolonged time period involves a research approach known as the continuous consumer panel. This is different from making a number of surveys at intervals in the sense that a relatively static group of consumers provides information about their individual behaviour on a continuing, day-to-day basis. Consumer panels are used for a variety of purposes, including the testing of new products, measurement of broadcast media audiences, and determining purchase behaviour.

The method of obtaining information is by a self-administering form which is usually referred to as a diary. Consumers daily record all purchases made by family members, often supplemented by information about price, place of purchase, and so on. Reports are sent periodically to the research organization, where specific items of information are transferred to tabulating cards for sorting and analysis. Consumers are usually compensated in cash or premium merchandise for their cooperation.

As compared with store audits, purchase panels provide a wider range of data, including characteristics of consumers making or not making purchases of certain types or specific brands of products. One of the main advantages is the ability to measure both gross and net changes in consumer purchases of a particular product during a time period. This can be illustrated as follows: During one six-month period, consumers purchased 1 million units of product *X*. Purchases in the next period dropped to 800,000 units, indicating a *net* change of 200,000 units. If 200,000 of the 800,000 units were purchased by people who did not make any purchases during the first period, the *gross* change would be 400,000 units. Since the research organization has complete information on the socioeconomic characteristics of all households in the sample, elaborate analyses can be made of purchase diary information in relation to such characteristics.

Warranty Card Analysis

Store audit and consumer panel procedures are widely used in the case of convenience goods but have not been widely applied to shopping or specialty goods where sales are much more infrequent at the retail level or involve significant seasonal variations. To determine the movement of such commodities to consumers, manufacturers of many forms of appliances make detailed statistical analyses of warranty cards. Such cards are usually given to the consumer at the time the product is delivered or installed, and must be filled out and mailed to the manufacturer in order to register the beginning of the warranty period. Customers must furnish their name and address, model and serial number of the unit, place of purchase, date of delivery or installation, and, often, other information of marketing significance.

In the Automatic Blanket and Fan Department of the General Electric Company, for example, about 1 million returned warranty cards are processed annually. A postal-size card is used, which is designed with holes around the edges that can be notched for machine sorting.

The card is so designed that the consumer can provide a variety of information merely by placing check-marks in boxes and by filling in certain data, such as name, address, and date and place of purchase. From the flow of these cards, the department can accurately estimate its sales at the retail level for current periods, determine the average store-shelf life of products, and ascertain other consumer information, such as sex of buyer, reason for purchase (own use, gift, etc.), and advertising media that prompted the sale.

By periodically checking the total production of a given model during a long time period, and later comparing this with the total number of warranty cards eventually returned, and how many at different intervals after purchase, the department establishes formulas which enable it to estimate sales on a current basis, depending upon the number of warranty cards returned during a given week or month. Through this type of analysis, the manufacturer knows the rate of consumer sales from week to week and can judge whether consumer sales are up to expectations and, consequently, whether to maintain production at expected levels or to increase or curtail manufacturing activity, revise prices, or enter into different types of promotional activity.

Obtaining Marketing Information from the Consumer

It often happens that the marketing information needed to solve a particular problem cannot be obtained from published sources, cannot be developed from analyses of a firm's internal records, and cannot be supplied by agencies in the channel of distribution. In such cases it is often necessary to resort to surveys of consumer opinion. Various applications of the findings of consumer research, in connection with the study of consumer motivation. Little attention was given, however, to the complexity of planning and administering a comprehensive consumer survey. An operational chart indicating the sequence of activities in a well planned consumer investigation is provided. Such an investigation begins with a statement of the marketing organization's problem, which may be of the form, "What can we do to increase the share of the market now enjoyed by our frozen orange juice?" Through discussions with the client, the research organization attempts to obtain pertinent data on the product, its position in the market, and the client's aims and philosophy of doing business. This is ordinarily supplemented by information from available research studies on related problems and a study of the position of competitive products in the markets.

After a review of such information, research personnel develops ideas or hunches by observations of their own behaviour or attitudes in relation to the problem at hand, perhaps by enquiring why they do or do not like or use orange juice or the particular client's brand of orange juice. On the basis of such hunches, information is obtained about other people's behaviour or motivations. This may be done by conducting long and detailed interviews with a variety of consumers to ascertain their feelings, by using various kinds of direct or projective techniques developed in psychology or psychiatry to test consumer reactions to ideas relevant to the investigation, or by employing some form of statistically sound surveys to ascertain the relative significance of different buying motives.

From the information gleaned from such preliminary study, the researchers can proceed to develop the experimental design for a complete investigation of the problem. This usually involves the formulation of some hypotheses, of the following illustrative character: "Consumers would like to buy frozen orange juice in larger cans." It is then necessary to determine just what types of analyses are required in order to confirm or refute such hypotheses, to determine interviewing and sampling procedures, and to formulate the pattern of tabulations for the data to be collected.

At this point, the research organization is ready to undertake a field survey. A questionnaire is developed and usually pretested on a small group of consumers to determine whether the wording is clear and whether the questions are understood by respondents as intended by the research objectives. Decisions must be made about the type of sample to be surveyed, including such matters as the number of respondents, kind of respondents (*e.g.*, only housewives), how the sample is to be distributed geographically, and when consumers are to be reached (season of year, day of week, time of day). Interviewers must then be obtained and instructed in their work. When the questionnaires are completed by the interviewing staff, they are edited for legibility and meaning and the responses are grouped into categories for coding and tabulation.

When tabulations are completed, researchers analyse the data to ascertain their meaning in relation to the hypotheses. After interpretation of the results, specific conclusions are formulated in terms of various courses of action that might be taken by the client. Recommendations are statements of the course of action that the research organization thinks the client should take and the results that are to be expected if such courses of action are followed. From the foregoing, it is apparent that consumer research is a complicated undertaking. It is not the mere collection and analysis of facts, but it involves also the attempt to predict the results of a recommended course of action.

TYPES OF CONSUMER PURCHASE DECISIONS

Consumers are faced with purchase decisions nearly every day. But not all decisions are treated the same. Some decisions are more complex than others and thus require more effort by the consumer. Other decisions are fairly routine and require little effort. In general, consumers face four types of purchase decisions:

- *Minor New Purchase*: These purchases represent something new to a consumer but in the customer's mind is not a very important purchase in terms of need, money or other reason (*e.g.*, status within a group).
- *Minor Re-Purchase*: These are the most routine of all purchases and often the consumer returns to purchase the same product without giving much thought to other product options (*i.e.*, consumer is brand loyalty).
- *Major New Purchase*: These purchases are the most difficult of all purchases because the product being purchased is important to the consumer but the consumer has little or no previous experience making these decisions. The consumer's lack of confidence in making this type of decision often (but not always) requires the consumer to engage in an extensive decision-making process..
- *Major Re-Purchase*: These purchase decisions are also important to the consumer but the consumer feels confident in making these decisions since they have previous experience purchasing the product.

For marketers it is important to understand how consumers treat the purchase decisions they face. If a company is targeting customers who feel a purchase decision is difficult (*i.e.*, Major New Purchase), their marketing strategy may vary greatly from a company targeting customers who view the purchase decision as routine. In fact, the same company may face both situations at the same time; for some the product is new, while other customers see the purchase as routine. The implication of buying behaviour for marketers is that different buying situations require different marketing efforts.

WHY CONSUMERS BUY

Customers make purchases in order to satisfy needs. Some of these needs are basic and must be filled by everyone on the planet (*e.g.*, food, shelter) while others are not required for basic survival and vary depending on the person. It probably makes more sense to classify needs that are not a necessity as wants or desires. In fact, in many countries where the standard of living is very high, a large portion of the population's income is spent on wants and desires rather than on basic needs. In this tutorial when we mention the consumer we are referring to the actual buyer, the person spending the money. But is should also be pointed out that the one who does the buying is not necessarily the user of what is bought and that others may be involved in the buying decision in addition to the actual buyer. While the purchasing process in the consumer market is not as complex as the business market, having multiple people involved in a purchase decision is not unusual. For example, in planning for a family vacation the mother may make the hotel reservations but others in the family may have input on the hotel choice. Similarly, a father may purchase snacks at the grocery store but his young child may be the one who selected it from the store shelf. So understanding consumer purchase behaviour involves not only understanding how decisions are made but also understanding the dynamics that influence purchases.

WHAT INFLUENCES PURCHASING

As we discussed the decision-making process for consumers is anything but straight forward. There are many factors that can affect this process as a person works through the purchase decision. The number of potential influences on consumer behaviour is limitless. However, marketers are well served to understand the KEY influences. By doing so they may be in a position to tailor their marketing efforts to take advantage of these influences in a way that will satisfy the consumer and the marketer (remember this is a key part of the definition of marketing). For the purposes of this tutorial we will break these influences down into three main categories: Internal, External and Marketing. However, those interested in learning more about customer buying activity may want to consult one or more consumer behaviour books where they will find additional methods for explaining consumer buying behaviour. For the most part the influences are not mutually exclusive. Instead, they are all interconnected and, as we will see, work together to form who we are and how we behave. For each of the influences that are discussed we will provide a basic description and also suggest its implication to marketers. Bear in mind we only provide a few marketing implications for each influence; clearly there are many more.

INTERNAL INFLUENCES

We start our examination of the influences on consumer purchase decisions by first looking inside ourselves to see which are the most important internal factors that affect how we make choices.

Perceptual Filter

Perception is how we see ourselves and the world we live in. However, what ends up being stored inside us doesn't always get there in a direct manner. Often our mental makeup results from information that has been consciously or subconsciously filtered as we experience it, a process we refer to as a perceptual filter. To us this is our reality, though it does not mean it is an accurate reflection on what is real. Thus, perception is the way we filter stimuli (*e.g.*, someone talking to us, reading a newspaper story) and then make sense out of it.

Perception has several steps:

- *Exposure*: Sensing a stimuli (*e.g.* seeing an ad)
- *Attention*: An effort to recognize the nature of a stimuli (*e.g.* recognizing it is an ad)
- *Awareness*: Assigning meaning to a stimuli (*e.g.*, humorous ad for particular product)
- *Retention*: Adding the meaning to one's internal makeup (*i.e.*, product has fun ads)

How these steps are eventually carried out depends on a person's approach to learning. By learning we mean how someone changes what they know, which in turn may affect how they act. There are many theories of learning, a discussion of which is beyond the scope of this tutorial, however, suffice to say that people are likely to learn in different ways.

For instance, one person may be able to focus very strongly on a certain advertisement and be able to retain the information after being exposed only one time while another person may need to be exposed to the same advertisement many times before he/she even recognizes what it is.

Consumers are also more likely to retain information if a person has a strong interest in the stimuli. If a person is in need of new car they are more likely to pay attention to a new advertisement for a car while someone who does not need a car may need to see the advertisement many times before they recognize the brand of automobile.

Marketing Implications

Marketers spend large sums of money in an attempt to get customers to have a positive impression of their products. But clearly the existence of a perceptual filter suggests that getting to this stage is not easy. Exposing consumers to a product can be very challenging considering the amount of competing product messages (ads) that are also trying to accomplish the same objective (*i.e.*, advertising clutter). So marketers must be creative and use various means to deliver their message. Once the message reaches consumer it must be interesting enough to capture their attention (*e.g.*, talk about the product's benefits). But attending to the message is not enough.

For marketers the most critical step is the one that occurs with awareness. Here marketers must continually monitor and respond if their message becomes distorted in ways that will negatively shape its meaning. This can often happen due in part to competitive activity (*e.g.*, comparison advertisements). Finally, getting the consumer to give positive meaning to the message they have retained requires the marketer make sure that consumers accurately interpret the facts about the product.

Knowledge

Knowledge is the sum of all information known by a person. It is the facts of the world as he/she knows it and the depth of knowledge is a function of the breadth of worldly experiences and the strength of an individual's long-term memory. Obviously what exists as knowledge to an individual depends on how an individual's perceptual filter makes sense of the information it is exposed to.

Marketing Implications

Marketers may conduct research that will gauge consumers' level of knowledge regarding their product. As we will see below, it is likely that other factors influencing consumer behaviour are in large part shaped by what is known about a product. Thus, developing methods (*e.g.*, incentives) to encourage consumers to accept more information (or correct information) may affect other influencing factors.

Attitude

In simple terms attitude refers to what a person feels or believes about something. Additionally, attitude may be reflected in how an individual acts based on his or her beliefs. Once formed, attitudes can be very difficult to change. Thus, if a consumer has a negative attitude towards a particular issue it will take considerable effort to change what they believe to be true.

Marketing Implications

Marketers facing consumers who have a negative attitude towards their product must work to identify the key issues shaping a consumer's attitude then adjust marketing decisions (*e.g.*, advertising) in an effort to change the attitude. For companies competing against strong rivals to whom loyal consumers exhibit a positive attitude, an important strategy is to work to see why consumers feel positive towards the competitor and then try to meet or beat the competitor on these issues. Alternatively, a company can try to locate customers who feel negatively towards the competitor and then increase awareness among this group.

Personality

An individual's personality relates to perceived personal characteristics that are consistently exhibited, especially when one acts in the presence of others. In most, but not all, cases the behaviours one projects in a situation is similar to the behaviours a person exhibits in another situation. In this way personality is the sum of sensory experiences others get from experiencing a person (*i.e.*, how one talks, reacts). While one's personality is often interpreted by those we interact with, the person has their own vision of their personality, called Self Concept, which may or may not be the same has how others view us.

Marketing Implications

For marketers it is important to know that consumers make purchase decisions to support their self concept. Using research techniques to identify how customers view themselves may give marketers insight into products and promotion options that are not readily apparent. For example, when examining consumers a marketer may initially build marketing strategy around more obvious clues to consumption behaviour, such as consumer's demographic indicators (*e.g.*, age, occupation, income). However, in-depth research may yield information that shows consumers are purchasing products to fulfill self-concept objectives that have little to do with the demographic category they fall into (*e.g.*, senior citizen may be making purchases that make them feel younger). Appealing to the consumer's self concept needs could expand the market to which the product is targeted.

Lifestyle

This influencing factor relates to the way we live through the activities we engage in and interests we express. In simple terms it is what we value out of life. Lifestyle is often determined by how we spend our time and money.

Marketing Implications

Products and services are purchased to support consumers' lifestyles. Marketers have worked hard researching how consumers in their target markets live their lives since this information is key to developing products, suggesting promotional strategies and even determining how best to distribute products. The fact that lifestyle is so directly tied to marketing activity will be further examined as we discuss developing target market strategies.

Roles

Roles represent the position we feel we hold or others feel we should hold when dealing in a group environment. These positions carry certain responsibilities yet it is important to understand that some of these responsibilities may, in fact, be perceived and not spelled out or even accepted by others. In support of their roles, consumers will make product choices that may vary depending on which role they are assuming. As illustration, a person who is responsible for selecting snack food for an office party his boss will attend may choose higher quality products than he would choose when selecting snacks for his family.

Marketing Implications

Advertisers often show how the benefits of their products aid consumers as they perform certain roles. Typically the underlying message of this promotional approach is to suggest that using the advertiser's product will help raise one's status in the eyes of others while using a competitor's product may have a negative effect on status.

Motivation

Motivation relates to our desire to achieve a certain outcome. Many internal factors we have already discussed can affect a customer's desire to achieve a certain outcome but there are others. For instance, when it comes to making purchase decisions customers' motivation could be affected by such issues as financial position (*e.g.*, Can I afford the purchase?), time constraints (*e.g.*, Do I need to make the purchase quickly?), overall value (*e.g.*, Am I getting my money's worth?), and perceived risk (*e.g.*, What happens if I make a bad decision?).

Marketing Implications

Motivation is also closely tied to the concept of Involvement, which relates to how much effort the consumer will exert in making a decision. Highly motivated consumers will want to get mentally and physically involved in the purchase process. Not all products have a high percentage of highly involved customers (*e.g.*, milk) but marketers who market products and services that may lead to high level of consumer involvement should prepare options that will be attractive to this group. For instance, marketers should make it easy for consumers to learn about their product (*e.g.*, information on web site, free video preview) and, for some products, allow customers to experience the product (*e.g.*, free trial) before committing to the purchase.

EXTERNAL INFLUENCES

Consumer purchasing decisions are often affected by factors that are outside of their control but have direct or indirect impact on how we live and what we consume.

Culture

Culture represents the behaviour, beliefs and, in many cases, the way we act learned by interacting or observing other members of society. In this way much of what we do is shared behaviour, passed along from one member of society to another. Yet culture is a broad concept that, while of interest to marketers, is not nearly as important as understanding what occurs within smaller groups or Sub-Cultures to which we may also belong. Sub-cultures also have shared values but this occurs within smaller groups. For instance, sub-cultures exist where groups share similar values in terms of ethnicity, religious beliefs, geographic location, special interests and many others.

Marketing Implications

As part of their efforts to convince customers to purchase their products, marketers often use cultural representations, especially in promotional appeals. The objective is to connect to consumers using cultural references that are easily understood and often embraced by the consumer. By doing so the marketer hopes the consumer feels more comfortable with or can relate better to the product since it corresponds with their cultural values. Additionally, smart marketers use strong research efforts in an attempt to identify differences in how sub-culture behaves. These efforts help pave the way for spotting trends within a sub-culture, which the marketer can capitalize on through new marketing tactics (*e.g.*, new products, new sales channels, added value, etc.).

Other Group Membership

In addition to cultural influences, consumers belong to many other groups with which they share certain characteristics and which may influence purchase decisions. Often these groups contain Opinion Leaders or others who have major influence on what the customer purchases. Some of the basic groups we may belong to include:

- *Social Class*: Represents the social standing one has within a society based on such factors as income level, education, occupation
- *Family*: One's family situation can have a strong effect on how purchase decisions are made
- *Reference groups*: Most consumers simultaneously belong to many other groups with which they associate or, in some cases, feel the need to disassociate

Marketing Implications

Identifying and understanding the groups consumers belong to is a key strategy for marketers. Doing so helps identify target markets, develop new products, and create appealing marketing promotions to which consumers can relate. In particular, marketers seek to locate group leaders and others to whom members of the group look for advice or direction. These opinion leaders, if well respected by the group, can be used to gain insight into group behaviour and if these opinion leaders accept promotional opportunities could act as effective spokespeople for the marketer's products.

Purchase Situation

A purchase decision can be strongly affected by the situation in which people find themselves. In general, a situation is the circumstances a person faces when making a purchase decision, such as the nature of their physical environment, their emotional state, or time constraints.

Not all situations are controllable, in which case a consumer may not follow their normal process for making a purchase decision. For instance, if a person needs a product quickly and a store does not carry the brand they normally purchase, the customer may choose a competitor's product.

Marketing Implications

Marketers can take advantage of decisions made in uncontrollable situations in at least two ways. First, marketers can use promotional methods to reinforce a specific selection of products when the consumer is confronted with a particular situation. For example, automotive services can be purchased that promise to service vehicles if the user runs into problems anywhere and at anytime. Second, marketers can use marketing methods that attempt to convince consumers that a situation is less likely to occur if the marketer's product is used. This can also be seen with auto products, where marketers explain that using their product will prevent unexpected damage to their vehicles.

CONSUMER RESEARCH METHODS

Market research is often needed to ensure that we produce what customers really want and not what we think they want. Primary vs. secondary research methods. There are two main approaches to marketing. Secondary research involves using information that others have already put together. For example, if you are thinking about starting a business making clothes for tall people. Primary research, in contrast, is research that you design and conduct yourself. For example, you may need to find out whether consumers would prefer that your soft drinks be sweater or tarter.

Research will often help us reduce risks associated with a new product, but it cannot take the risk away entirely. It is also important to ascertain whether the research has been complete. For example, Coca Cola did a great deal of research prior to releasing the New Coke, and consumers seemed to prefer the taste. However, consumers were *not* prepared to have this drink replace traditional Coke.

Sources of influence on the consumer. The consumer faces numerous sources of influence. Often, we take cultural influences for granted, but they are significant. An American will usually not bargain with a store owner. This, however, is a common practice in much of the World. Physical factors also influence our behaviour. We are more likely to buy a soft drink when we are thirsty, for example, and food manufacturers have found that it is more effective to advertise their products on the radio in the late afternoon when people are getting hungry. A person's self-image will also tend to influence what he or she will buy-an upwardly mobile manager may buy a flashy car to project an image of success. Social factors also influence what the consumers buy-often, consumers seek to imitate others whom they admire, and may buy the same brands. The social environment can include both the mainstream culture and a subculture. Thus, sneaker manufacturers are eager to have their products worn by admired athletes. Finally, consumer behaviour is influenced by learning-you try a hamburger and learn that it satisfies your hunger and tastes good, and the next time you are hungry, you may consider another hamburger.

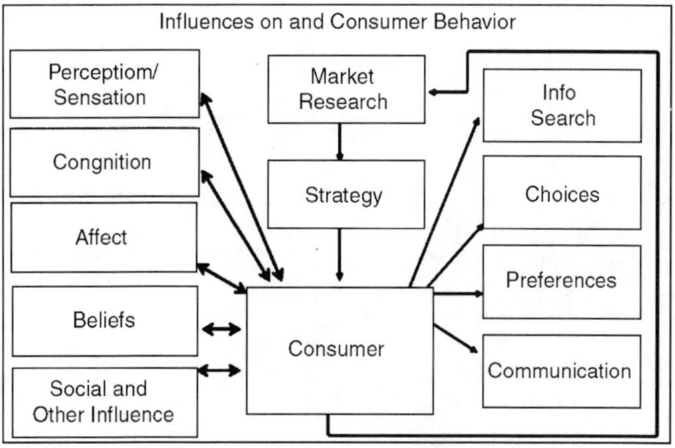

CONSUMER CHOICE AND DECISION-MAKING: PROBLEM

One model of consumer decision making involves several steps. The first one is problem recognition-you realise that something is not as it should be. Perhaps, for example, your car is getting more difficult to start and is not accelerating well. The second step is information search-what are some alternative ways of solving the problem? You might buy a new car, buy a used car, take your car in for repair, ride the bus, ride a taxi, or ride a skateboard to work. The third step involves evaluation of alternatives. A skateboard is inexpensive, but may be ill-suited for long distances and for rainy days. Finally, we have the purchase stage, and sometimes a post-purchase stage. In reality, people may go back and forth between the stages. For example, a person may resume alternative identification during while evaluating already known alternatives.

Consumer involvement will tend to vary dramatically depending on the type of product. In general, consumer involvement will be higher for products that are very expensive or are highly significant in the consumer's life in some other way.It is important to consider the consumer's motivation for buying products. To achieve this goal, we can use the Means-End chain, wherein we consider a logical progression of consequences of product use that eventually lead to desired end benefit. Thus, for example, a consumer may see that a car has a large engine, leading to fast acceleration, leading to a feeling of performance, leading to a feeling of power, which ultimately improves the consumer's self-esteem. A handgun may aim bullets with precision, which enables the user to kill an intruder, which means that the intruder will not be able to harm the consumer's family, which achieves the desired end-state of security. In advertising, it is important to portray the desired end-states. Focusing on the large motor will do less good than portraying a successful person driving the car.

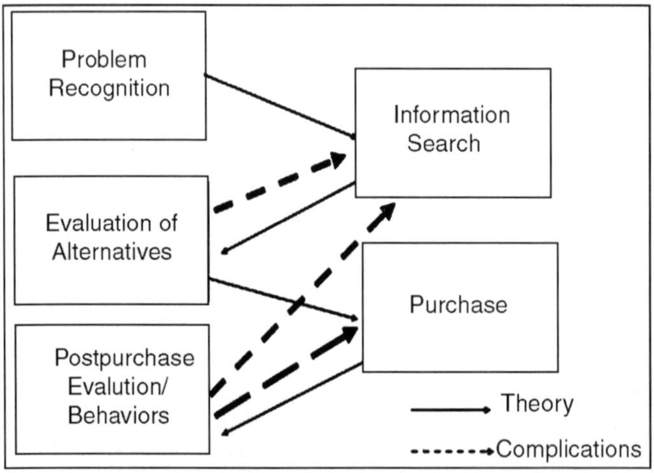

INFORMATION SEARCH AND DECISION-MAKING

Consumers engage in both internal and external information search. Internal search involves the consumer identifying alternatives from his or her memory. For certain low involvement products, it is very important that marketing prigrammes achieve"top of mind" awareness. For example, few people will search the Yellow Pages for fast food restaurants; thus, the consumer must be able to retrieve one's restaurant from memory before it will be considered.

For high involvement products, consumers are more likely to use an external search. Before buying a car, for example, the consumer may ask friends' opinions, read reviews in Consumer Reports, consult several web sites, and visit several dealerships. Thus, firms that make products that are selected predominantly through external search must invest in having information available to the consumer in need-*e.g.*, through brochures, web sites, or news coverage.

A compensatory decision involves the consumer"trading off" good and bad attributes of a product. For example, a car may have a low price and good gas mileage but slow acceleration. If the price is sufficiently inexpensive and gas efficient, the consumer may then select it over a car with better acceleration that costs more and uses more gas. Occasionally, a decision will involve a non-compensatory strategy. For example, a parent may reject all soft drinks that contain artificial sweeteners. Here, other good features such as taste and low calories cannot overcome this one"non-negotiable" attribute.

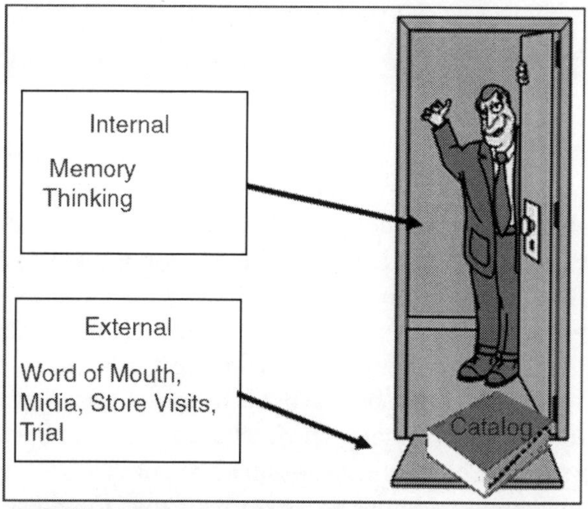

The amount of effort a consumer puts into searching depends on a number of factors such as the market, product characteristics, consumer characteristics, and situational characteristics.

Two interesting issues in decisions are:

- *Variety seeking* where consumers seek to try new brands not because these brands are expected to be "better" in any way, but rather because the consumer wants a "change of pace," and
- *"Impulse" purchases*—unplanned buys. This represents a somewhat "fuzzy" group. For example, a shopper may plan to buy vegetables but only decide in the store to actually buy broccoli and corn. Alternatively, a person may buy an item which is currently on sale, or one that he or she remembers that is needed only once inside the store.

A number of factors involve consumer choices. In some cases, consumers will be more *motivated*. For example, one may be more careful choosing a gift for an in-law than when buying the same thing for one self. Some consumers are also more motivated to *comparison shop* for the best prices, while others are more *convenience* oriented. *Personality* impacts decisions. Some like variety more than others, and some are more receptive to stimulation and excitement in trying new stores. *Perception* influences decisions.

Some people, for example, can taste the difference between generic and name brand foods while many cannot. *Selective* perception occurs when a person is paying attention only to information of interest. For example, when looking for a new car, the consumer may pay more attention to car ads than when this is not in the horizon. Some consumers are put off by perceived *risk*. Thus, many marketers offer a money back guarantee. Consumers will tend to change their behaviour through *learning—e.g.*, they will avoid restaurants they have found to be crowded and will settle on brands that best meet their tastes. Consumers differ in the *values* they hold. As suggested, consider the issue of lifestyle under segmentation.

ORGANIZATIONAL BUYERS

A large portion of the market for goods and services is attributable to *organizational*, as opposed to individual, buyers. In general, organizational buyers, who make buying decisions for their companies for a living, tend to be somewhat more sophisticated than ordinary consumers. However, these organizational buyers are also often more risk averse. There is a risk in going with a new, possibly better supplier whose product is unproven and may turn out to be problematic. Often the fear of running this risk is greater than the potential rewards for getting a better deal. In the old days, it used to be said that "You can't get fired for buying IBM." This attitude is beginning to soften a bit today as firms face increasing pressures to cut costs.

Organizational buyers come in several forms. *Resellers* involve either wholesalers or retailers that buy from one organization and resell to some other entity. For example, large grocery chains sometimes buy products directly from the manufacturer and resell them to end-consumers. Wholesalers may sell to retailers who in turn sell to consumers. *Producers* also buy products from sub-manufacturers to create a finished product. For example, rather than manufacturing the parts themselves, computer manufacturers often buy hard drives, motherboards, cases, monitors, keyboards, and other components from manufacturers and put them together to create a finished product. *Governments* buy a great deal of things. For example, the military needs an incredible amount of supplies to feed and equip troops. Finally, large *institutions* buy products in huge quantities. For example, UCR probably buys thousands of reams of paper every month.

Organizational buying usually involves more people than individual buying. *Often, many people are involved in making decisions as to*:

- Whether to buy,
- What to buy,
- At what quantity, and
- From whom.

An engineer may make a specification as to what is needed, which may be approved by a manager, with the final purchase being made by a purchase specialist who spends all his or her time finding the best deal on the goods that the organization needs. Often, such long purchase processes can cause long delays. In the government, rules are often especially stringent—*e.g.*, vendors of fruit cake have to meet fourteen pages of specifications put out by the General Services Administration. In many cases, government buyers are also heavily bound to go with the lowest price. Even if it is obvious that a higher priced vendor will offer a superior product, it may be difficult to accept that bid.

CUSTOMER VALUE AND SATISFACTION

CUSTOMER VALUE

As it is used in the business world, customer value is the amount of benefit that a customer will get from a service or product relative to its cost. Some businesspeople explain customer value as "realization" compared to "sacrifice." Realization is a formal term for what customers get out of their purchases. Sacrifice is what they pay for the product or service. Businesses of all sizes use customer value as part of a greater analysis to determine how well they are supplying their customer base. Detailed research might include what customers generally do with the products they receive, or how they use services to increase the value of assets like real estate. Businesses also look at the prices of their products in order to price them competitively.

Businesses that identify the value of their wares to customers might go a step further and consider other similar ideas. In order to generate more thought about customer value, and to reach out to a customer base, a business might promote a customer value proposition. The customer value proposition is basically a promise of benefits from a vendor to customers. We see examples of customer value propositions all the time in advertising. Companies pinpoint the benefits that they believe a customer will realise, and display them in advertising to attract more customers. The question is whether these propositions are made in good faith, or whether they may not be entirely true.

When business leaders and others are talking about customer value, it is important that everyone at the table understands that customer value does not relate to the value of customers, but to the value that customers receive from the business. Those who are talking about how valuable customers are to a business might use terms like customer retention, or refer to the customer base as "valued customers," or VIPs. Since customer service is also a critical element for many businesses, it's possible that these two ideas might sometimes get confused. Along with the basic idea of customer value, other terms help further define that value precisely. Relative performance identifies how the product or service gives customer value relative to what competitors offer. Access cost is something that business analysts add into the mix as an estimated cost of the effort involved in purchase. Value propositions often include these levels of detail to help leaders look at how well a business is serving its intended audience.

SATISFACTION

Customer satisfaction, a business term, is a measure of how products and services supplied by a company meet or surpass customer expectation. It is seen as a key performance indicator within business and is part of the four of a Balanced Scorecard. In a competitive marketplace where businesses compete for customers, customer satisfaction is seen as a key differentiator and increasingly has become a key element of business strategy. There is a substantial body of empirical literature that establishes the benefits of customer satisfaction for firms.

Measuring Customer Satisfaction

Organizations need to retain existing customers while targeting non-customers;. Measuring customer satisfaction provides an indication of how successful the organization is at providing products and/or services to the marketplace. Customer satisfaction is an abstract concept and the actual manifestation of the state of satisfaction will vary from person to person and product/service to product/service. The state of satisfaction depends on a number of both psychological and physical variables which correlate with satisfaction behaviours such as return and recommend rate. The level of satisfaction can also vary depending on other factors the customer, such as other products against which the customer can compare the organization's products.

Work done by Parasuraman, Zeithaml and Berry between 1985 and 1988 delivered SERVQUAL which provides the basis for the measurement of customer satisfaction with a service by using the gap between the customer's expectation of performance and their perceived experience of performance. This provides the researcher with a satisfaction "gap" which is semi-quantitative in nature. Cronin and Taylor extended the disconfirmation theory by combining the "gap" described by Parasuraman, Zeithaml and Berry as two different measures into a single measurement of performance relative to expectation. The usual measures of customer satisfaction involve a survey with a set of statements using a Likert Technique or scale. The customer is asked to evaluate each statement in terms of their perception and expectation of performance of the service being measured.

Improving Customer Satisfaction

Published standards exist to help organizations develop their current levels of customer satisfaction. The International Customer Service Institute has released The International Customer Service Standard. TICSS enables organizations to focus their attention on delivering excellence in the management of customer service, whilst at the same time providing recognition of success through a 3rd Party registration plan. TICSS focuses an organization's attention on delivering increased customer satisfaction by helping the organization through a Service Quality Model. TICSS Service Quality Model uses the 5 P's - Policy, Processes, People, Premises, Product/Services, as well as performance measurement. The implementation of a customer service standard should lead to higher levels of customer satisfaction, which in turn influences customer retention and customer loyalty.

CONSUMERISM

Consumerism is a social and economic order that is based on the systematic creation and fostering of a desire to purchase goods or services in ever greater amounts. The term is often associated with criticisms of consumption starting with Thorstein Veblen or, more recently by a movement called Enoughism. Veblen's subject of examination, the newly emergent middle class arising at the turn of the twentieth century, comes to full fruition by the end of the twentieth century through the process of globalization. In economics, consumerism refers to economic policies placing emphasis on consumption. In an abstract sense, it is the belief that the free choice of consumers should dictate the economic structure of a society.

FACTORS INFLUENCING CONSUMER BEHAVIOUR

Consumer purchases are influenced strongly by or there are four factors.

1.	Cultural Factor	2.	Social Factor
3.	Personal Factor	4.	Psychological Factor.

CULTURAL FACTOR

Cultural factor divided into three sub factors:

1. Culture
2. Sub Culture
3. Social Class

- *Culture*:
  - The set of basic values perceptions, wants, and behaviours learned by a member of society from family and other important institutions. Culture is the most basic cause of a person's wants and behaviour. Every group or society has a culture, and cultural influences on buying behaviour may vary greatly from country to country.
- *Sub Culture*:
  - A group of people with shared value systems based on common life experiences and situations.
  - Each culture contains smaller sub cultures a group of people with shared value system based on common life experiences and situations. Sub culture includes nationalities, religions, racial group and geographic regions. Many sub culture make up important market segments and marketers often design products.

- *Social Class*:
  - Almost every society has some form of social structure, social classes are society's relatively permanent and ordered divisions whose members share similar values, interests and behaviour.

SOCIAL FACTORS

A consumer's behaviour also is influenced by social factors, such as the:

a.Groups
b. Family
c. Roles and status

- *Groups*:
  - Two or more people who interact to accomplish individual or mutual goals.
  - A person's behavious is influenced by many small groups. Groups that have a direct influence and to which a person belongs are called membership groups.
  - Some are primary groups includes family, friends, neighbours and coworkers. Some are secondary groups, which are more formal and have less regular interaction. These includes organizations like religious groups, professional association and trade unions.
- *Family*:

– Family members can strongly influence buyer behaviour. The family is the most important consumer buying organization society and it has been researched extensively. Marketers are interested in the roles, and influence of the husband, wife and children on the purchase of different products and services.

- *Roles and Status*:
  - A person belongs to many groups, family, clubs, organizations.
  - The person's position in each group can be defined in terms of both role and status.
  - For example. M & "X" plays the role of father, in his family he plays the role of husband, in his company, he plays the role of manager, etc. A Role consists of the activities people are expected to perform just as to the persons around them.

PERSONAL FACTORS

- *It includes*:
- Age and life cycle stage
- Occupation
- Economic situation
- Life Style
- Personality and self concept.

- *Age and Life cycle Stage*:
- People changes the goods and services they buy over their lifetimes. Tastes in food, clothes, furniture, and recreation are often age related. Buying is also shaped by the stage of the family life cycle.
- *Occupation*:
- A person's occupation affects the goods and services bought. Blue collar workers tend to buy more rugged work clothes, whereas white-collar workers buy more business suits. A Co. can even specialize in making products needed by a given occupational group. Thus, computer software companies will design different products for brand managers, accountants, engineers, lawyers, and doctors.
- *Economic situation:*
- A person's economic situation will affect product choice
- *Life Style:*
- Life Style is a person's Pattern of living, understanding these forces involves measuring consumer's major AIO dimensions.
- *i.e.* activities interest and opinions
- *Personality and Self concept*:
- Each person's distinct personality influence his or her buying behaviour. Personality refers to the unique psychological characteri-stics that lead to relatively consistent and lasting responses to one's own environment.

PSYCHOLOGICAL FACTORS

- It includes these Factors.
- Motivation
- Perception
- Learning
- Beliefs and attitudes
- *Motivation*:
  - Motive a need that is sufficiently pressing to direct the person to seek satisfaction of the need
- *Perception*:
  - The process by which people select, Organize, and interpret information to form a meaningful picture of the world.
- *Learning*:
  - Changes in an individuals behaviour arising from experience.
- *Beliefs and attitudes:*
  - Belief is a descriptive thought that a person holds about something

– Attitude, a Person's consistently favourable or unfavourable evaluations, feelings, and tendencies towards an object or idea

MARKETING IMPLICATIONS

Marketers spend large sums of money in an attempt to get customers to have a positive impression of their products. But clearly the existence of a perceptual filter suggests that getting to this stage is not easy. Exposing consumers to a product can be very challenging considering the amount of competing product messages (ads) that are also trying to accomplish the same objective (*i.e.*, advertising clutter). So marketers must be creative and use various means to deliver their message.

Once the message reaches consumer it must be interesting enough to capture their attention (*e.g.,* talk about the product's benefits). But attending to the message is not enough. For marketers the most critical step is the one that occurs with awareness. Here marketers must continually monitor and respond if their message becomes distorted in ways that will negatively shape its meaning. This can often happen due in part to competitive activity (*e.g.,* comparison advertisements). Finally, getting the consumer to give positive meaning to the message they have retained requires the marketer make sure that consumers accurately interpret the facts about the product.

Knowledge

Knowledge is the sum of all information known by a person. It is the facts of the world as he/she knows it and the depth of knowledge is a function of the breadth of worldly experiences and the strength of an individual's long-term memory. Obviously what exists as knowledge to an individual depends on how an individual's perceptual filter makes sense of the information it is exposed to.

Marketing Implications

Marketers may conduct research that will gauge consumers' level of knowledge regarding their product. As we will see below, it is likely that other factors influencing consumer behaviour are in large part shaped by what is known about a product. Thus, developing methods (*e.g.,* incentives) to encourage consumers to accept more information (or correct information) may affect other influencing factors.

Attitude

In simple terms attitude refers to what a person feels or believes about something. Additionally, attitude may be reflected in how an individual acts based on his or her beliefs. Once formed, attitudes can be very difficult to change. Thus, if a consumer has a negative attitude towards a particular issue it will take considerable effort to change what they believe to be true.

Marketing Implications

Marketers facing consumers who have a negative attitude towards their product must work to identify the key issues shaping a consumer's attitude then adjust marketing decisions (*e.g.,* advertising) in an effort to change the attitude.

For companies competing against strong rivals to whom loyal consumers exhibit a positive attitude, an important strategy is to work to see why consumers feel positive towards the competitor and then try to meet or beat the competitor on these issues. Alternatively, a company can try to locate customers who feel negatively towards the competitor and then increase awareness among this group.

Personality

An individual's personality relates to perceived personal characteristics that are consistently exhibited, especially when one acts in the presence of others. In most, but not all, cases the behaviours one projects in a situation is similar to the behaviours a person exhibits in another situation. In this way personality is the sum of sensory experiences others get from experiencing a person (*i.e.*, how one talks, reacts). While one's personality is often interpreted by those we interact with, the person has their own vision of their personality, called Self Concept, which may or may not be the same has how others view us.

Marketing Implications

For marketers it is important to know that consumers make purchase decisions to support their self concept. Using research techniques to identify how customers view themselves may give marketers insight into products and promotion options that are not readily apparent. For example, when examining consumers a marketer may initially build marketing strategy around more obvious clues to consumption behaviour, such as consumer's demographic indicators (*e.g.,* age, occupation, income).

However, in-depth research may yield information that shows consumers are purchasing products to fulfil self-concept objectives that have little to do with the demographic category they fall into (*e.g.,* senior citizen may be making purchases that make them feel younger). Appealing to the consumer's self concept needs could expand the market to which the product is targeted.

Lifestyle

This influencing factor relates to the way we live through the activities we engage in and interests we express. In simple terms it is what we value out of life. Lifestyle is often determined by how we spend our time and money.

Marketing Implications

Products and services are purchased to support consumers' lifestyles. Marketers have worked hard researching how consumers in their target markets live their lives since this information is key to developing products, suggesting promotional strategies and even determining how best to distribute products. The fact that lifestyle is so directly tied to marketing activity will be further examined as we discuss developing target market strategies.

Roles

Roles represent the position we feel we hold or others feel we should hold when dealing in a group environment. These positions carry certain responsibilities yet it is important to understand that some of these responsibilities may, in fact, be perceived and not spelled out or even accepted by others. In support of their roles, consumers will make product choices that may vary depending on which role they are assuming. As illustration, a person who is responsible for selecting snack food for an office party his boss will attend may choose higher quality products than he would choose when selecting snacks for his family.

Marketing Implications

Advertisers often show how the benefits of their products aid consumers as they perform certain roles. Typically the underlying message of this promotional approach is to suggest that using the advertiser's product will help raise one's status in the eyes of others while using a competitor's product may have a negative effect on status.

Motivation

Motivation relates to our desire to achieve a certain outcome. Many internal factors we have already discussed can affect a customer's desire to achieve a certain outcome but there are others. For instance, when it comes to making purchase decisions customers' motivation could be affected by such issues as financial position (*e.g., Can I afford the purchase?*), time constraints (*e.g., Do I need to make the purchase quickly?*), overall value (*e.g., Am I getting my money's worth?*), and perceived risk (*e.g., What happens if I make a bad decision?*).

Marketing Implications

Motivation is also closely tied to the concept of Involvement, which relates to how much effort the consumer will exert in making a decision. Highly motivated consumers will want to get mentally and physically involved in the purchase process. Not all products have a high percentage of highly involved customers (*e.g.,* milk) but marketers who market products and services that may lead to high level of consumer involvement should prepare options that will be attractive to this group. For instance, marketers should make it easy for consumers to learn about their product (*e.g.,* information on web site, free video preview) and, for some products, allow customers to experience the product (*e.g.*, free trial) before committing to the purchase.

EXTERNAL INFLUENCES

Consumer purchasing decisions are often affected by factors that are outside of their control but have direct or indirect impact on how we live and what we consume.

Culture

Culture represents the behaviour, beliefs and, in many cases, the way we act learned by interacting or observing other members of society. In this way much of what we do is shared behaviour, passed along from one member of society to another. Yet culture is a broad concept that, while of interest to marketers, is not nearly as important as understanding what occurs within smaller groups or Sub-Cultures to which we may also belong. Sub-cultures also have shared values but this occurs within smaller groups. For instance, sub-cultures exist where groups share similar values in terms of ethnicity, religious beliefs, geographic location, special interests and many others.

Marketing Implications

As part of their efforts to convince customers to purchase their products, marketers often use cultural representations, especially in promotional appeals. The objective is to connect to consumers using cultural references that are easily understood and often embraced by the consumer. By doing so the marketer hopes the consumer feels more comfortable with or can relate better to the product since it corresponds with their cultural values. Additionally, smart marketers use strong research efforts in an attempt to identify differences in how sub-culture behaves. These efforts help pave the way for spotting trends within a sub-culture, which the marketer can capitalize on through new marketing tactics (*e.g.*, new products, new sales channels, added value, etc.).

Other Group Membership

In addition to cultural influences, consumers belong to many other groups with which they share certain characteristics and which may influence purchase decisions. Often these groups contain Opinion Leaders or others who have major influence on what the customer purchases. Some of the basic groups we may belong to include:

- *Social Class*: Represents the social standing one has within a society based on such factors as income level, education, occupation
- *Family*: One's family situation can have a strong effect on how purchase decisions are made

- *Reference groups*: Most consumers simultaneously belong to many other groups with which they associate or, in some cases, feel the need to disassociate

Marketing Implications

Identifying and understanding the groups consumers belong to is a key strategy for marketers. Doing so helps identify target markets, develop new products, and create appealing marketing promotions to which consumers can relate. In particular, marketers seek to locate group leaders and others to whom members of the group look for advice or direction. These opinion leaders, if well respected by the group, can be used to gain insight into group behaviour and if these opinion leaders accept promotional opportunities could act as effective spokespeople for the marketer's products.

Purchase Situation

A purchase decision can be strongly affected by the situation in which people find themselves. In general, a situation is the circumstances a person faces when making a purchase decision, such as the nature of their physical environment, their emotional state, or time constraints. Not all situations are controllable, in which case a consumer may not follow their normal process for making a purchase decision. For instance, if a person needs a product quickly and a store does not carry the brand they normally purchase, the customer may choose a competitor's product.

Marketing Implications

Marketers can take advantage of decisions made in uncontrollable situations in at least two ways. First, marketers can use promotional methods to reinforce a specific selection of products when the consumer is confronted with a particular situation. For example, automotive services can be purchased that promise to service vehicles if the user runs into problems anywhere and at anytime. Second, marketers can use marketing methods that attempt to convince consumers that a situation is less likely to occur if the marketer's product is used. This can also be seen with auto products, where marketers explain that using their product will prevent unexpected damage to their vehicles.

HOW CONSUMERS BUY

So now that we have discussed the factors influencing a consumer's decision to purchase, let's examine the process itself. This process is presented in a sequence of 5 steps as shown below. However, whether a consumer will actually carryout each step depends on the type of purchase decision that is faced. For instance, for minor re-purchases the consumer may be quite loyal to the same brand, thus the decision is a routine one (*i.e.*, buy the same product) and little effort is involved in making a purchase decision.

In cases of routine, brand loyal purchases consumers may skip several steps in the purchasing process since they know exactly what they want allowing the consumer to move quickly through the steps. But for more complex decisions, such as Major New Purchases, the purchasing process can extend for days, weeks, months or longer. So in presenting these steps marketers should realise that, depending on the circumstances surrounding the purchase, the importance of each step may vary.

Need/Want/Desire is Recognized

In the first step the consumer has determined that for some reason he/ she is not satisfied (*i.e.*, consumer's perceived actual condition) and wants to improve his/her situation (*i.e.*, consumer's perceived desired condition). For instance, internal triggers, such as hunger or thirst, may tell the consumer that food or drink is needed. External factors can also trigger consumer's needs. Marketers are particularly good at this through advertising, in-store displays and even the intentional use of scent (*e.g.*, perfume counters). At this stage the decision-making process may stall if the consumer is not motivated to continue. However, if the consumer does have the internal drive to satisfy the need they will continue to the next step.

Search for Information

Assuming consumers are motivated to satisfy his or her need, they will next undertake a search for information on possible solutions. The sources used to acquire this information may be as simple as remembering information from past experience (*i.e.*, memory) or the consumer may expend considerable effort to locate information from outside sources (*e.g.*, Internet search, talk with others, etc.). How much effort the consumer directs towards searching depends on such factors as: the importance of satisfying the need, familiarity with available solutions, and the amount of time available to search. To appeal to consumers who are at the search stage, marketers should make efforts to ensure consumers can locate information related to their product. For example, for marketers whose customers rely on the Internet for information gathering, attaining high rankings in search engines has become a critical marketing objective.

Evaluate Options

Consumers' search efforts may result in a set of options from which a choice can be made. It should be noted that there may be two levels to this stage. At level one the consumer may create a set of possible solutions to their needs (*i.e.*, product types) while at level two the consumer may be evaluating particular products (*i.e.*, brands) within each solution. For example, a consumer who needs to replace a television has multiple solutions to choose from such as plasma,

LCD and CRT televisions. Within each solution type will be multiple brands from which to choose. Marketers need to understand how consumers evaluate product options and why some products are included while others are not. Most importantly, marketers must determine which criteria consumers are using in their selection of possible options and how each criterion is evaluated.

Returning to the television example, marketing tactics will be most effective when the marketer can tailor their efforts by knowing what benefits are most important to consumers when selecting options (*e.g.*, picture quality, brand name, screen size, etc.) and then determine the order of importance of each benefit.

Purchase

In many cases the solution chosen by the consumer is the same as the product whose evaluation is the highest. However, this may change when it is actually time to make the purchase. The "intended" purchase may be altered at the time of purchase for many reasons such as: the product is out-of-stock, a competitor offers an incentive at the point-of-purchase (*e.g.*, store salesperson mentions a competitor's offer), the customer lacks the necessary funds (*e.g.*, credit card not working), or members of the consumer's reference group take a negative view of the purchase (*e.g.*, friend is critical of purchase). Marketers whose product is most desirable to the consumer must make sure that the transaction goes smoothly. For example, Internet retailers have worked hard to prevent consumers from abandoning online purchase (*i.e.*, online shopping carts) by streamlining the checkout process. For marketers whose product is not the consumer's selected product, last chance marketing efforts may be worth exploring, such as offering incentives to store personnel to "talk up" their product at the checkout line.

After-Purchase Evaluation

Once the consumer has made the purchase they are faced with an evaluation of the decision. If the product performs below the consumer's expectation then he/she will re-evaluate satisfaction with the decision, which at its extreme may result in the consumer returning the product while in less extreme situations the consumer will retain the purchased item but may take a negative view of the product. Such evaluations are more likely to occur in cases of expensive or highly important purchases. To help ease the concerns consumers have with their purchase evaluation, marketers need to be receptive and even encourage consumer contact. Customer service centers and follow-up market research are useful tools in helping to address purchasers' concerns.

CONSUMER MARKET

The consumer market is composed of individuals who buy a specific good or service. Rarely does one product interest the entire population. This statement applies even to staples, such as sugar, flour, and salt. A small percentage of households do not eat these products, so even if a company did target the entire population, not everyone would be a potential consumer. The same statistical truth applies to cultural products. However, because of the extremely fragmented nature of the cultural sector, some distinctions are in order. For example, looking at this sector as a whole, it can be said that nearly 100 per cent of the population consumes one type of cultural product or another. Indeed, in its broadest sense, the cultural sector encompasses everything from the performing arts to heritage, compact disks, movies, book and magazine publishing, and radio and television, with each of these disciplines appropriating a more or less important share of global demand.

In Canada, for example, statistics1 show that 37.0 per cent of families attend a performing arts event at least once a year: movies 62.2 per cent, museums and art galleries 32.9 per cent. In the United States the figures for cultural consumption are: classical music 15.6 per cent, opera 4.7 per cent, musicals 24.5 per cent, plays 15.8 per cent, ballet 5.8 per cent, art museums 34.5 per cent, and historical parks 46.9 per cent.2 In Australia3 the figures are: musical theatre 19.3 per cent, classical music 7.7 per cent, festivals 21.9 per cent, concerts 23 per cent, and museums 27.8 per cent. Of course, within each of these sectors, consumers cluster just as to specific poles of interest.

This leads to sharper market segmentation. The consumer makes a discriminating choice among various cultural products to acquire or consume the type of product desired. The distribution of consumers just as to various market segments differs in both time and space. Markets undergo and reflect the influence of opinion leaders, trends, tastes, and societal characteristics. Markets also vary from country to country just as to different social structures. Over the past 40 years, various surveys focusing on the sociodemographic profile of consumers of cultural products have been carried out in nearly every European country as well as in Canada, the United States, Australia, and Japan.4 It is fascinating to note that, regardless of whether the surveys were conducted in the 1970s, 1980s, or 1990s, they all obtained the same attendance rates and the same sociodemographic profiles.

Differences in the measuring tools used can sometimes make it difficult to compare countries; nonetheless, these studies have consistently and systematically revealed strong polarization of audiences between high art and popular culture across all countries over the past four decades. They show, for example, that cultural products catering to high art attract educated consumers, whereas those catering to popular culture draw on all segments of the population, in accordance with the relative weight of each.

The proportion of university graduates making up Canadian audiences, for example, ranges between 50 per cent and 70 per cent for high art, compared with 10 per cent to 25 per cent for popular culture. By way of comparison, the overall percentage of university graduates in Canada is 25 per cent. Similar results have been found in other countries, most notably in France5 but also in Russia, where university graduates make up 50 per cent of performing arts audiences but only 7 per cent of the general population. Other sociodemographic variables are also linked to attendance, including average income and type of occupation. It should be pointed out once again that this profile is based on averages. Less-educated individuals with lower income may be great consumers of culture, as is the case for students and those specialized or working in the cultural milieu.

Indeed, it is well known that, as a rule many people active in the arts are highly educated yet so ill paid that they struggle to stay above the poverty line. On the other hand, there are people with both very high salaries and very high educational levels who are not interested in the arts and gladly keep their distance. Four factors are known to influence an individual's penchant for complex cultural products: family values that encourage or discourage high art; the educational milieu and the value it places on high art; the fact of having attended performances or visited museums as a child; and amateur art practice.

A more detailed analysis of the typical cultural consumer's traits reveals other nuances based on the different disciplines. For example, dance audiences are relatively younger and even more female in composition than those of the other performing arts; similarly, more women than men read novels, although a larger proportion of men read daily newspapers. In the film sector, there are two very different segments of avid cinema-goers; one of these segments is dominated by a young clientele, while the other is made up of educated people. The majority of consumers in the film sector belong to one or the other of these two segments.

CONSUMER BOYCOTTS AND CERTIFICATION SCHEMES

Consumer markets also offer opportunities to punish and/or reward corporate behaviour. Product boycotts and product certification schemes represent contrasting mechanisms used by civil society groups, occasionally with governmental involvement or support, to influence MNE activities. Organized consumer boycotts usually target individual companies, either because the specific firm's actions are deemed particularly offensive or the company plays a prominent and influential role within an industry whose common practices generate opposition. Boycott mechanisms do not work equally well in all situations. Boycotts enjoy greatest success when directed against recognizable consumer goods whose market position relies on brand-name image and reputation and where substitute products of satisfactory quality and price are readily available. In addition, the issue motivating the boycott must be conveyed in an easily understandable fashion that will evoke broad sympathy in the general consuming public. By contrast, companies that engage in minimal advertising and produce intermediate products for sale to other businesses are less vulnerable to a consumer boycott mechanism.

The use of consumer boycotts to protest MNE actions developed from the same general time period and set of issues that produced the capital market mechanisms. Anti-apartheid campaigns included product boycotts, including the adoption by many US state and city governments of selective procurement regulations that restricted purchases from companies maintaining investments in South Africa. The loss of large sales contracts to state and municipal agencies may have provided more measurable effective leverage against MNEs than stock divestment actions by activist pension funds. Another high-profile campaign urged a boycott of Nestlé's numerous consumer products to protest the corporation's methods of promoting its infant formula in developing counties.

Similar to shareholder activism, the potential effects of consumer boycotts often surpass the actual financial loss in terms of immediate sales. In order to reach the broad consuming public, boycott organizers generally seek maximum publicity and may organize demonstrations, marches or even engage in acts of civil disobedience to draw media attention to their cause. The short-term demand on management response time and potential for longer-term damage to a company's reputation can add significantly to overall boycott costs. Opponents often assert that boycott campaigns unfairly single out one or a small number of companies to protest actions undertaken by many enterprises, including MNEs in countries where comparable consumer actions seldom occur. Sometimes boycott targets show only minimal or distant causal connections to wrong actions. Similar to secondary rather than primary boycotts, the targeted firm or product may simply be used as a means to exert leverage on a different offending actor.

For example, in 1990 a civil society group called Neighbour to Neighbour helped organize a boycott action against Folger's coffee, sold by Procter and Gamble. In this case, the boycott campaign stemmed from opposition to human rights violations by right-wing death squads in El Salvador, allegedly connected with that country's government. Although less than 2 per cent of the beans in Folger's coffee reportedly came from El Salvador, those purchases represented an important share of the country's coffee exports which in turn provided significant revenue to the government.

To help publicize their cause, the boycotting groups sponsored a dramatic television advertisement attacking Folger's and showing blood running from an overturned coffee cup. The advertisement was characterized by a P&G spokesperson as "inaccurate, grossly misleading and offensive." The company responded with its own type of boycott action, suspending advertising on some television stations that aired the anti-Folger's commercial. US government officials offered clear statements supporting P&G's coffee bean purchases, calling the actions "in the best interest of the peace process and the people of

El Salvador." The case illustrates how boycotts, even when motivated by laudable objectives, may become ethically problematic as causal and capability connections grow more distant between a targeted product or company and the offending actor and actions. Another case of a successful boycott describes a campaign organized by the Rainforest Action Network (RAN) against Scott Paper, aimed at stopping Scott's plans to use a rain forest concession on the Indonesian island of Irian Jaya to develop a eucalyptus plantation and sawmill to supply pulp for its various paper products.

An observer reports that, despite corporate efforts to work with local representatives to limit the project's environmental and social impact, "RAN convinced environmental groups from all over the world to boycott Scott products if the company did not withdraw from Irian Jaya. The campaign focused on a single thing: Scott's name, the company's most valuable, and most vulnerable, asset." The company announced its withdrawal from the project just before the boycott began, prompting RAN to take out newspaper advertisements "declaring victory" and "hailing the power of consumer boycotts." Without necessarily disputing the impact of the boycott mechanism, some critics subsequently questioned the substance of the victory as a state-owned forestry company replaced Scott in the project and, not subject to similar consumer pressures, reportedly engaged in broad deforestation actions. This case points up the challenge of projecting a boycott's effects which may depend on when outcomes are measured and whether or not potential impacts on other boycott actions are considered.

Product certification schemes also depend on consumer choice to provide leverage for influencing corporate behaviour. Contrasted with boycott mechanisms, certification schemes focus less on penalizing bad corporate conduct to induce change and more on rewarding good corporate operations by giving their products a market advantage over uncertified competitors. To be credible, groups using this mechanism must demonstrate that consumers are sufficiently aware and concerned about an issue to affect their purchasing decisions. In addition, consumers need enough knowledge and understanding about the certification process to recognize and favour certified products. These requirements place a premium on media coverage and the development of alliances and support networks among sympathetic civil society groups, particularly in major consumer market economies.

No clear consensus exists regarding either the breadth or the depth of probable consumer response to product certification schemes. Certainly participation will vary depending on the nature of the issue, the location of the consumer market and the effectiveness of a particular campaign. Other important variables include the cost, quality and convenience differential in choosing certified over uncertified products. Some polling data suggests that a core of committed individuals will act on certification criteria while a larger portion of the general public is open to considering corporate actions and reputation in their purchasing decisions. For example, a Mori survey in Great Britain defined 15 per cent of the population as corporate responsibility activists, reporting that ethical considerations led 17 per cent of adults to boycott a product and 14 per cent to purchase a company's product during 2003. The survey also reported that 38 per cent of the public stated corporate social responsibility was very important in making their purchases. The head of Mori's CSR research speculated that more individuals from this broader group might follow through with concrete actions if provided with more effective information.

The proliferation of product certification schemes touches many of the issues. A broad government-backed mechanism emerged to certify that international trade would be free of "conflict diamonds" associated with human rights violations in Africa. Exports of soccer balls and rugs from South Asia feature certification processes to assure the goods were not produced using child labour. "Green" labels tout the environment-friendly record of many products, from recycled paper or plastic products to energy-saving devices to "dolphin-safe" tuna. Remarkable variety exists in the types of issues addressed and certification measures employed. The constellation of certifying and supporting organizations can also mix public agencies, business organizations and civil society groups. Fair Trade initiatives represent a particular application of product certification schemes, usually but not exclusively applied to products based on agricultural commodities. The basic concept seeks to establish a dependable, long-term relationship with commodity growers in developing countries, offering them a higher price for their products by eliminating middlemen traders.

Many schemes also provide an additional premium to growers for using environmentally friendly methods and/or for community social development projects. The general approach reportedly stems from efforts begun in 1986 by the Max Havelaar Foundation in the Netherlands to respond to desires for development projects that emphasize trade rather than aid. Starting with coffee and expanding to honey, bananas, tea and orange juice, the Foundation supported Fair Trade products sold primarily in Europe.

During the 1990s fourteen other Fair Trade organizations were established, reaching over $200 million in sales by the end of the decade, still largely concentrated in European markets. Some approaches expect consumers to pay a somewhat higher price for certified Fair Trade products while other efforts try to remain price-competitive, using cost savings in the distribution chain to redistribute profits towards developing country growers. An important extension of the Fair Trade mechanism to the US market occurred in 2000 when Starbucks announced the introduction of a blend of Fair Trade coffee certified by the non-profit TransFair organization that encourages farmer co-operatives in developing countries to sell direct to coffee roasters or retailers.

The breakthrough with Starbucks came after some of its coffee houses were vandalized during anti-globalization protests at a World Trade Organization meeting hosted in the company's hometown of Seattle, Washington. This initiative complemented Starbucks' broader social responsibility programmes and helped expand Fair Trade coverage in the United States beyond craft shops and a few grocery stores.

Subsequent discussions between Starbucks and Oxfam also led to cooperation on a project to aid coffee growers in poverty-stricken areas of Ethiopia. The Rainforest Alliance, which promotes another certification scheme covering several products, has forged agreements with major coffee MNEs that could broaden the Fair Trade mechanism beyond the market for specialty coffees that represents only about 2 per cent of supply.

BUSINESS MARKETS COMPARE TO CONSUMER MARKETS

For marketers, the selling environment of business markets present uniquely different circumstances when compared to selling to consumers. At the beginning of this tutorial we saw two ways in which consumer and business markets differ: 1) business markets are more likely to be price driven than brand driven, and 2) demand in business markets tends to be more volatile than consumer markets. However, the two markets are dissimilar in other ways requiring marketers to take a different approach when selling to business customers than to consumers. These differences include:

- How Decisions Are Made
- Existence of Experienced Purchasers
- Time Needed to Make Buying Decision
- Size of Purchases
- Number of Buyers
- Type of Promotional Effort Needed to Reach Buyer

A further discussion of each of these differences is presented below:

How Decisions are Made

In the consumer market a very large percentage of purchase decisions are made by a single person. There are situations in which multiple people may be involved in a consumer purchase decision, such as a child influencing a parent to choose a certain brand of cereal or a husband and wife deciding together to buy a house, but most of the time purchases are individual decisions. The business market is significantly different. While single person purchasing is not unusual, especially within a small company, a significant percentage of business buying, especially within larger organizations, requires the input of many. In the marketing literature those associated with the purchase decision are known to be part of a Buying Centre, which consists of individuals within an organization that perform one or more of the following roles:

- *Buyer*: Responsible for dealing with suppliers and placing orders (*e.g.*, purchasing agent)
- *Decider*: Has the power to make the final purchase decision (*e.g.*, CEO)
- *Influencer*: Has the ability to affect what is ordered such as setting order specifications (*e.g.*, engineers, researchers, product managers)
- *User*: Those who will actually use the product when it is received (*e.g.*, office staff)
- *Initiator*: Any Buying Centre member who is the first to determine that a need exists
- *Gatekeeper*: Anyone who controls access to other Buying Centre members (*e.g.*, administrative assistant)

For marketers confronting a Buying Centre it is important to first identify who plays what role. Once identified the marketer must address the needs of each member, which may differ significantly. For instance, the Decider, who may be the company president wants to make sure the purchase will not negatively affect the company's bottom line while the Buyer wants to be assured the product will be delivered on time. Thus, the way each Buying Centre member is approached and marketed to requires careful planning in order to address the unique needs of each member.

Experienced Purchasers

As noted in the discussion of the Buying Centre, organizations often employ purchasing agents or professional buyers whose job is to negotiate the best deals for their company. Unlike consumers, who often lack information when making purchase decisions, professional buyers are generally as knowledgeable about the product and the industry as the marketer who is selling to them.

Decision Making Time

Depending on the product, business purchase decisions can drag on for an extensive period. Unlike consumer markets where impulse purchasing is rampant, the number of people involved in business purchase decisions results in decisions taking weeks, months or even years.

Larger Purchases

For products that are regularly used and frequently purchased, businesses will often buy a larger volume at one time compared to consumer purchases. Because of this business purchasers often demand price breaks (*e.g.*, discounts) for higher order levels.

Number of Buyers

While there are several million companies worldwide that operate in the overall business market, within a particular market the number is much smaller.

For example, while in the United States there are over 95 million households who may shop at a grocery store, there are only a few thousand grocery stores with many of these centrally controlled as part of a chain of stores. Additionally, within some industries buyers are highly concentrated in certain geographic areas. Consequently, compared to consumer products, marketing efforts are confined to a smaller targeted group.

Promotional Focus

Companies who primarily target consumers often use mass advertising methods to reach an often widely dispersed market. For business-to-business marketers the size of individual orders, along with a smaller number of buyers, makes person-to-person contact by sales representatives a more effective means of promotion.

TYPES OF BUSINESS PURCHASE DECISIONS

While it would appear business customers face the same four purchase situations faced by consumers (Minor New Purchase, Minor Re-Purchase, Major New Purchase, Major Re-Purchase), the nature of the business market noted above has led many marketing academics to group business purchase situations into only three categories. The reason is that the idea of a minor order may not hold as well in the business market, where buyers tend to place larger orders and where suppliers' marketing efforts are directed towards the most profitable buyers.

- *Straight Re-Purchase*: These purchase situations involve routine ordering. In most cases buyers simply reorder the same products or services that were previously purchased. In fact, many larger companies have programmed re-purchases into an automated ordering system that initiates electronic orders when inventory falls below a certain pre-determined level. For the supplier benefiting from the re-purchase this situation is ideal since the purchaser is not looking to evaluate other products. For competitors who are not getting the order it may require extensive marketing efforts to persuade the buyer to consider other product or service options.
- *Modified Re-Purchase*: These purchases occur when products or services previously considered a straight re-purchase are for some reason now under a re-evaluation process. There are many reasons why a product is moved to the status of a modified re-purchase. Some of these reasons include: end of purchase contract period, change in who is involved in making the purchase, supplier is removed from an approved suppliers list, mandate from top level of organization to re-evaluate all purchasing, or strong marketing effort by competitors. In this circumstance the incumbent supplier faces the same challenges they may have faced when they initially

convinced the buyer to make the purchase. For competitors the door is now open and they must work hard to make sure their message is heard by those in charge of the purchase decision.

- *New Task Purchase*: As the name suggests, these purchases are ones the buyer has never or rarely made before. In some ways new task purchases can be considered as either minor or major depending on the total cost or overall importance of the purchase. In either case the buyer will spend considerably more time evaluating alternatives. For example, if faced with a major new task purchase, which often involves complex items, such as computer systems, buildings, robotic assembly lines, etc., the purchase cycle from first recognizing the need to placement of the order may be months or even years. The business market we now look at how purchasing decisions are made. Business purchasing follows the same five-step buying process faced by consumers:
  - Need Recognition
  - Search:
  - Evaluate Options
  - Purchase
  - After-Purchase Evaluation.

While the steps are the same as consumer purchasing, the activities occurring within each step are quite different as we discuss below.

NEED RECOGNITION

In a business environment needs arise from just about anywhere within the organization. The Buying Centre concept shows that Initiators are the first organizational members to recognize a need. In most situations the Initiator is also the User or Buyer. Users are inclined to identify the need for new solutions (*i.e.*, new products) while Buyers are more likely to identify the need to re-purchase products. But marketers should also understand that more companies are replacing human involvement in re-purchase decisions with automated methods, thus making it more challenging for competitors to replace currently purchased products.

In straight re-purchase situations, whether there is human intervention or not, the purchasing process often jumps from Need Recognition to Purchase and little search activity is performed.

As part of this step, a specifications document may be generated that lays out the requirements of the product or service to be purchased. Several members of the Buying Centre may be involved in creation of the specifications. For the marketer, establishing close contact with those who draw up the specifications may help position the marketer's product for inclusion in the search phase.

SEARCH

The search for alternatives to consider as potential solutions to recognized needs is one of the most significant differences between consumer and business purchasing. Much of this has to do with an organization's motive to reduce costs. While a consumer will probably not search hard to save two cents a gallon on gas, a company that has a large fleet of cars or trucks certainly will. In fact, this step in the purchase process is where professional buyers make their mark.

The primary intention of their search efforts is to identify multiple suppliers who meet product specifications and then, through a screening process, offer a selected group the opportunity to present their products to members of the Buying Centre. Although in some industries, such as chemicals, online marketplaces and auction sites offer buyers another option for selecting suppliers that may not include supplier presentations. For suppliers, the key to this step of the purchase process is to make sure they are included within the search activities of the Buyer or others in the Buying Centre. In some instances this may require that a supplier work to be included within an approved suppliers list. In the case of online marketplaces and auction sites, suppliers should work to be included within relevant sites.

EVALUATE OPTION

Once the search has produced options, members of the Buying Centre may then choose among the alternatives. In more advanced purchase situations, members of the Buying Centre may evaluate each option using a checklist of features and benefits sought by the buyer. Each feature/benefit is assigned a weight that corresponds to its importance to the purchase decision. In many cases, especially when dealing with Government and Not-For-Profit markets, suppliers must submit bids with the lowest bidder often being awarded the order, assuming products or services meet specifications.

PURCHASE

To actually place the order may require the completion of paperwork (or electronic documents) such as a purchase order. Acquiring the necessary approvals can delay the order for an extended period of time. And for very large purchases, such as buildings or large equipment, financing options may need to be explored.

AFTER-PURCHASE EVALUATION

After the order is received the purchasing company may spend time reviewing the results of the purchase. This may involve the Buyer discussing product performance issues with Users. If the product is well received it may end up moving to a straight re-purchase status thus eliminating much of the evaluation process on future purchases.

3

Capital Marketing in Business Economics

CAPITAL MARKET: MEANING, FEATURES AND IMPORTANCE OF CAPITAL MARKET

MEANING AND FEATURES

The capital market is a market which deals in long-term loans. It supplies industry with fixed and working capital and finances medium-term and long-term borrowings of the central, state and local governments. The capital market deals in ordinary stock are shares and debentures of corporations, and bonds and securities of governments.

The funds which flow into the capital market come from individuals who have savings to invest, the merchant banks, the commercial banks and non-bank financial intermediaries, such as insurance companies, finance houses, unit trusts, investment trusts, venture capital, leasing finance, mutual funds, building societies, etc.

Further, there are the issuing houses which do not provide capital but underwrite the shares and debentures of companies and help in selling their new issues of shares and debentures. The demand for funds comes from joint stock companies for working and fixed capital assets and inventories and from local, state and central governments, improvement trusts, port trusts, etc. to finance a variety of expenditures and assets.

The capital market functions through the stock exchange market. A stock exchange is a market which facilitates buying and selling of shares, stocks, bonds, securities and debentures. It is not only a market for old securities and shares but also for new issues shares and securities. In fact, the capital market is related to the supply and demand for new capital, and the stock exchange facilitates such transactions.

Thus the capital market comprises the complex of institutions and mechanisms through which medium-term funds and long--term funds are pooled and made available to individuals, business and governments. It also encompasses the process by which securities already outstanding are transferred.

IMPORTANCE OR FUNCTIONS OF CAPITAL MARKET:

The capital market plays an important role immobilising saving and channel is in them into productive investments for the development of commerce and industry. As such, the capital market helps in capital formation and economic growth of the country. The capital market acts as an important link between savers and investors. The savers are lenders of funds while investors are borrowers of funds. The savers who do not spend all their income are called. "Surplus units" and the borrowers are known as "deficit units". The capital market is the transmission mechanism between surplus units and deficit units. It is a conduit through which surplus units lend their surplus funds to deficit units.

Funds flow into the capital market from individuals and financial intermediaries which are absorbed by commerce, industry and government. It thus facilitates the movement of stream of capital to be used more productively and profitability to increases the national income. Surplus units buy securities with their surplus funds and deficit units sells securities to raise the funds they need. Funds flow from lenders to borrowers either directly or indirectly through financial institutions such as banks, unit trusts, mutual funds, etc. The borrowers issue primary securities which are purchased by lenders either directly or indirectly through financial institutions.

The capital market prides incentives to savers in the form of interest or dividend and transfers funds to investors. Thus it leads to capital formation. In fact, the capital market provides a market mechanism for those who have savings and to those who need funds for productive investments. It diverts resources from wasteful and unproductive channels such as gold, jewellery, real estate, conspicuous consumption, etc. to productive investments.

A well-developed capital market comprising expert banking and non-banking intermediaries brings stability in the value of stocks and securities. It does so by providing capital to the needy at reasonable interest rates and helps in minimising speculative activities. The capital market encourages economic growth. The various institutions which operate in the capital market give quantities and qualitative direction to the flow of funds and bring rational allocation of resources. They do so by converting financial assets into productive physical assets. This leads to the development of commerce and industry through the private and public sector, thereby inducing economic growth.

In an underdeveloped country where capital is scarce, the absence of a developed capital market is a greater hindrance to capital formation and economic growth. Even though the people are poor, yet they do not have any inducements to save. Others who save, they invest their savings in wasteful and unproductive channels, such as gold, jewellery, real estate, conspicuous consumption, etc. Such countries can induce people to save more by establishing banking and non-banking financial institutions for the existence of a developed capital market. Such a market can go a long way in providing a link between savers and investors, thereby leading to capital formation and economic growth.

DEFINITION OF 'CAPITAL MARKETS'

Markets for buying and selling equity and debt instruments. Capital markets channel savings and investment between suppliers of capital such as retail investors and institutional investors, and users of capital like businesses, government and individuals. Capital markets are vital to the functioning of an economy, since capital is a critical component for generating economic output. Capital markets include primary markets, where new stock and bond issues are sold to investors, and secondary markets, which trade existing securities.

THE CAPITAL MARKETS

Selling securities to investors in the various capital markets provides the means for corporations, governments and government agencies to satisfy their need for capital, thus providing investors the opportunity to profit by trading capital for securities, which are transferable claims on the assets of the entity that originally sold the securities. More specifically, securities are financial assets that are transferable claims on the real assets of the issuer of the securities. The capital markets, a.k.a. securities markets, consist of the primary capital markets where securities are first sold to institutional investors and the various stock, bond and commodities exchanges where securities are subsequently traded.

There are two primary types of securities: debt and equity. Equities include common stock and preferred stock. Debt securities include bonds, convertible bonds, commercial paper, short-term government debt and certificates of deposit. A third type of security, derivatives, derive their value from some underlying asset that may be another security, a tangible asset, the option to buy or sell an asset at a predetermined price or a contract to buy or sell an asset at a predetermined price. However, derivatives are not used as a means for raising capital, rather, they are typically used as a means of hedging, financial engineering or speculating. Mutual funds are securities comprised of pools of other securities that may be debt, equities or derivatives. With the exception of commodities funds, mutual funds typically restrict their use of derivatives to hedging. Commodities funds use derivatives extensively to either model an index or to model a portfolio of their own design, thus eliminating the unnecessary expense and inconvenience of actually taking possession of the commodities in their portfolios.

Corporations, government agencies and municipal governments raise capital by selling their securities in the primary capital markets to institutional investors. After this initial sale the securities are traded in the secondary capital markets, which is where individual investors buy and sell securities. The U.S. Treasury sells its securities directly to institutional and individual investors.

After it's initial sale, Treasury debt also is sold in the secondary market. CDs also are sold directly to institutional and individual investors.

Nearly all U.S. equities are traded on one of the three U.S. stock exchanges: The New York Stock Exchange, the American Stock Exchange and the Nasdaq. These exchanges and the lesser-known exchanges make up the secondary market for equities, which serve both individual and institutional investors. The New York and American stock exchanges are physical auction-type exchanges where securities are traded at bid and asked prices and liquidity is provided by specialists who make up any imbalances between buy and sell orders. The specialists provide liquidity by keeping inventories of the stocks in which they specialize and by setting the bid price to maintain a balance between supply and demand (*i.e.*, sell orders and buy orders). When a balance can't be maintained, they absorb any excess sell orders and add to their inventories or sell from their inventories to cover excess buy orders. The bid-ask spread is the market specialists' profit, which compensates them for providing liquidity to these capital markets.

The Nasdaq, which stands for National Association of Securities Dealers Automated Quotation System, was formed in 1971 by the National Association of Securities Dealers (Nasd) then subsequently sold in 2000 and 2001, at which time it became The Nasdaq Stock Market. The Nasdaq also operates on a bid-ask basis but it is a fully automated electronic system. Liquidity is provided to this capital market by brokerages who act as dealers that fulfill the same function as the specialists on the physical exchanges. The dealers are said to make a market in the stocks in which they specialize and are thus known as market makers. They, too, are compensated for this service by the bid-ask spread.

Mutual fund shares are sold and redeemed by the fund companies and an exact balance is maintained between sales and redemptions by issuing or dissolving shares, thus there is no need for secondary capital markets for these securities. Individuals can deal directly with the mutual fund companies or through a discount or full-service broker. In the case of no load mutual funds, there will never be a charge for purchases or redemptions, but trades made through a discount brokerage may be subject to a transaction fee and trades made through a full-service brokerage will always be subject to a transaction fee. Individuals can buy and sell Treasury bonds through the U.S.

Treasury's Treasury Direct service, which is the Treasury's exclusive capital market. Individuals must trade corporate and municipal bonds through a brokerage in one of the secondary capital markets. Mutual funds and other institutional investors can purchase corporate and municipal bonds in the primary market and have more options than individuals for trading existing issues of all types of bonds. Whenever the need for capital arises, corporations, governments and government agencies will return to the capital markets to sell more debt and/or equity securities. Occasionally, corporations will use excess cash to buy back a portion of their outstanding common stock or callable bonds, or issue new debt when interest rates drop and use the proceeds to "call back" their older, higher interest callable bonds. When high-interest bonds are called and replaced with bonds that have a lower coupon, the companies' cost of capital is decreased assuming there is no concurrent change in the company's capital structure. There are a number of opinions as to what effect these actions could have on a company's stock under various scenarios. That issue is beyond the scope of this subsection.

The U.S. Federal Reserve Board of Governors' Federal Open Market Committee (FOMC) will from time to time buy Treasury debt in the capital markets as part of its monetary policy. By purchasing Treasury debt on the open market, the Fed increases the money supply. This is usually done to decrease interest rates and stimulate the economy. It also is done to ward off deflation, which is extremely rare. So rare, indeed, that it hasn't happened since the Great Depression, although we were close, by some accounts, in the early and late 2000s and looking at a distinct possibility in the early 2010s. Increasing the money supply for any reason other than to keep pace with ordinary economic expansion is inflationary, so there needs to be a good reason to do it, like reviving a faltering economy or countering deflation.

CAPITAL MARKET THEORY

Capital Market Theory tries to explain and predict the progression of capital (and sometimes financial) markets over time on the basis of the one or the other mathematical model. Capital market theory is a generic term for the analysis of securities. In terms of trade off between the returns sought by investors and the inherent risks involved, the capital market theory is a model that seeks to price assets, most commonly, shares.

In general, whenever someone tries to formulate a financial, investment, or retirement plan, he or she (consciously or unconsciously) employs a theory such as arbitrage pricing theory, capital asset pricing model, coherent market hypothesis, efficient market hypothesis, fractal market hypothesis, or modern portfolio theory. The most talked about model in Capital Market Theory is the Capital Asset Pricing Model. In studying the capital market theory we deal with issues like the role of the capital markets, the major capital markets in the US, the initial public offerings and the role of the venture capital in capital markets, financial innovation and markets in derivative instruments, the role of securities and the exchange commission, the role of the federal reserve system, role of the US Treasury and the regulatory requirements on the capital market.

The Capital Market Theory deals with the following issues:

- Importance of venture capital in the capital market
- Initial public offerings

- Role of capital market
- Major capital markets worldwide
- Markets and financial innovations in derivative instruments
- Role of Federal Reserve System
- Role of securities
- Capital market regulatory requirements
- Role of the government treasury.

Assumptions of Capital Market Theory

The capital market theory builds upon the Markowitz portfolio model. The main assumptions of the capital market theoryare as follows:

- *All Investors are Efficient Investors*: Investors follow Markowitz idea of the efficient frontier and choose to invest in portfolios along the frontier.
- *Investors Borrow/Lend Money at the Risk-Free Rate*: This rate remains static for any amount of money.
- *The Time Horizon is equal for All Investors*: When choosing investments, investors have equal time horizons for the chosen investments.
- *All Assets are Infinitely Divisible*: This indicates that fractional shares can be purchased and the stocks can be infinitely divisible.
- *No Taxes and Transaction Costs*: It is assumed that investors results are not affected by taxes and transaction costs.
- *All Investors Have the Same Probability for Outcomes*: When determining the expected return, assume that all investors have the same probability for outcomes.
- *No Inflation Exists*: Returns are not affected by the inflation rate in a capital market as none exists in capital market theory.
- *There is No Mispricing within the Capital Markets*: It is assumed that the markets are efficient and that no mispricings within the markets exist.

Mortgages, equities, bonds, and other investments are traded in the capital market. The financial instruments in this market have long maturity periods. Capital market theory states that federal funds, federal agency securities, treasury bills, commercial papers, negotiable certificates of deposits, repurchase agreements, Eurocurrency loans and deposits, options and futures are merchandised in the capital market.

When one has to put a price on a security, one has to determine the risk and return of the security both for single assets, as well as a portfolio of assets. The uncertainty and variability of returns on assets and the possibilities of losses can be defined as risks. The theory of capital market defines returns in the following manner:

$$K = Pt + Ct - Pt\text{-}1/\ Pt\text{-}1$$

Where the time of purchase of the asset of price Pt-1 is t-1. If this be the case, then the return (K) from the time period t-1 to t is the above mentioned formula. Ct is the cash gotten from assets between t-1 and t. Pt is the price of the asset at time t. For practitioners of the capital market theory, it has not lost its significance. It is still as important for retirement, financial, and investment plans.

CAPITAL MARKET TRANSACTIONS

A Government Raising Money on the Primary Markets

When a government wants to raise long term finance it will often sell bonds to the capital markets. In the 20th and early 21st century, many governments would use investment banks to organize the sale of their bonds. The leading bank would underwrite the bonds, and would often head up a syndicate of brokers, some of whom might be based in other investment banks. The syndicate would then sell to various investors. For developing countries, a multilateral development bank would sometimes provide an additional layer of underwriting, resulting in risk being shared between the investment bank(s), the multilateral organization, and the end investors. However, since 1997 it has been increasingly common for governments of the larger nations to bypass investment banks by making their bonds directly available for purchase over the Internet. Many governments now sell most of their bonds by computerized auction. Typically large volumes are put up for sale in one go; a government may only hold a small number of auctions each year. Some governments will also sell a continuous stream of bonds through other channels. The biggest single seller of debt is the US Government; there are usually several transactions for such sales every second, which corresponds to the continuous updating of the US real time debt clock.

A Company Raising Money on the Primary Markets

When a company wants to raise money for long-term investment, one of its first decisions is whether to do so by issuing bonds or shares. If it chooses shares, it avoids increasing its debt, and in some cases the new shareholders may also provide non- monetary help, such as expertise or useful contacts. On the other hand, a new issue of shares can dilute the ownership rights of the existing shareholders, and if they gain a controlling interest, the new shareholders may even replace senior managers. From an investor's point of view, shares offer the potential for higher returns and capital gains if the company does well. Conversely, bonds are safer if the company does poorly, as they are less prone to severe falls in price, and in the event of bankruptcy, bond owners are usually paid before shareholders.

When a company raises finance from the primary market, the process is more likely to involve face-to-face meetings than other capital market transactions. Whether they choose to issue bonds or shares, companies will typically enlist the services of an investment bank to mediate between themselves and the market. A team from the investment bank often meets with the company's senior managers to ensure their plans are sound. The bank then acts as an underwriter, and will arrange for a network ofbrokers to sell the bonds or shares to investors. This second stage is usually done mostly through computerized systems, though brokers will often phone up their favored clients to advise them of the opportunity. Companies can avoid paying fees to investment banks by using a direct public offering, though this is not a common practice as it incurs other legal costs and can take up considerable management time.

Trading on the Secondary Markets

Most capital market transactions take place on the secondary market. On the primary market, each security can be sold only once, and the process to create batches of new shares or bonds is often lengthy due to regulatory requirements. On the secondary markets, there is no limit on the number of times a security can be traded, and the process is usually very quick. With the rise of strategies such as high-frequency trading, a single security could in theory be traded thousands of times within a single hour. Transactions on the secondary market don't directly help raise finance, but they do make it easier for companies and governments to raise finance on the primary market, as investors know if they want to get their money back in a hurry, they will usually be easily able to re-sell their securities.

Sometimes however secondary capital market transactions can have a negative effect on the primary borrowers - for example, if a large proportion of investors try to sell their bonds, this can push up the yields for future issues from the same entity. An extreme example occurred shortly after Bill Clinton began his first term as President of the United States; Clinton was forced to abandon some of the spending increases he'd promised in his election campaign due to pressure from the bond markets. In the 21st century, several governments have tried to lock in as much as possible of their borrowing into long dated bonds, so they are less vulnerable to pressure from the markets. Following the financial crisis of 2007–08, the introduction of Quantitative easing further reduced the ability of private actors to push up the yields of government bonds, at least for countries with a Central bank able to engage in substantial Open market operations.

A variety of different players are active in the secondary markets. Regular individuals account for a small proportion of trading, though their share has slightly increased; in the 20th century it was mostly only a few wealthy individuals who could afford an account with a broker, but accounts are now much cheaper and accessible over the internet. There are now numerous small traders who can buy and sell on the secondary markets using platforms provided by brokers which are accessible via web browsers.

When such an individual trades on the capital markets, it will often involve a two-stage transaction. First they place an order with their broker, then the broker executes the trade. If the trade can be done on an exchange, the process will often be fully automated. If a dealer needs to manually intervene, this will often mean a larger fee.

Traders in investment banks will often make deals on their bank's behalf, as well as executing trades for their clients. Investment banks will often have a division (or department) called *capital markets*: staff in this division try to keep aware of the various opportunities in both the primary and secondary markets, and will advise major clients accordingly. Pension and sovereign wealth funds tend to have the largest holdings, though they tend to buy only the highest grade (safest) types of bonds and shares, and often don't trade all that frequently. According to a 2012 *Financial Times* article, hedge funds are increasingly making most of the short term trades in large sections of the capital market (like the UK and US stock exchanges), which is making it harder for them to maintain their historically high returns, as they are increasingly finding themselves trading with each other rather than with less sophisticated investors.

There are several ways to invest in the secondary market without directly buying shares or bonds. A common method is to invest in mutual funds or exchange-traded funds. It's also possible to buy and sell derivatives that are based on the secondary market; one of the most common being contract for difference - these can provide rapid profits, but can also cause buyers to lose more money than they originally invested.

SIZE OF THE GLOBAL CAPITAL MARKETS

All figures given are in Billions of US$ and are sourced to the IMF. There is no universally recognized standard for measuring all of these figures, so other estimates may vary. AGDP column is included as a comparison.

Year	Stocks	Bonds	Bank Assets	Total of Stocks, Bonds and Bank Assets.	World GDP
2013	62,552.00	99,788.80	120,421.60	282,762.40	74,699.30
2012	52,494.90	99,134.20	116,956.10	268,585.20	72,216.40
2011	47,089.23	98,388.10	110,378.24	255,855.57	69,899.22

CAPITAL CONTROLS

Capital controls are measures imposed by a state's government aimed at managing capital account transactions - in other words, capital market transactions where one of the counter-parties involved is in a foreign country.

Whereas domestic regulatory authorities try to ensure that capital market participants trade fairly with each other, and sometimes to ensure institutions like banks don't take excessive risks, capital controls aim to ensure that the macroeconomic effects of the capital markets don't have a net negative impact on the nation in question. Most advanced nations like to use capital controls sparingly if at all, as in theory allowing markets freedom is a win-win situation for all involved: investors are free to seek maximum returns, and countries can benefit from investments that will develop their industry and infrastructure.

However sometimes capital market transactions can have a net negative effect - for example, in a financial crisis, there can be a mass withdrawal of capital, leaving a nation without sufficient foreign currency to pay for needed imports. On the other hand, if too much capital is flowing into a country, it can push up inflation and the value of the nation's currency, making its exports uncompetitive. Some nations such as India have also used capital controls to ensure that their citizens' money is invested at home, rather than abroad.

MARKET VALUE OF INVESTED CAPITAL (MVIC)?

The Invested Capital (IC) of a company is one measure of total firm value. It represents the value of the core operations of the business. Alternatively, IC can also be defined as the combination of shareholder's equity and interest-bearing debt. Whereas invested capital typically refers to the book value of invested capital, market value of invested capital is the invested capital amount at market value.

In accounting we learn: All Assets = All Liabilities and Obligations, which consist of all debts and all equities.

$$CA + FA + IA = CL + LTD + SE$$

Where:

CA = Current Assets

FA = Tangible Fixed Assets

IA = Aggregate Intangible Assets

CL = Current Liabilities

LTD = Long-Term Interest Bearing Debt

SE = Shareholders Equity

Subtraction of CL from both sides of this equation yields:

$$(CA - CL) + FA + IA = (LTD + SE)$$

The company's MVIC can be thought of in two ways, each representing one side of the above equation. The first explanation for MVIC is that it represents the value of the core business, including net working capital and all fixed and intangible assets. It is the value of the assets that keep the company operating and is represented by the left side of the above equation. The right side of the above equation represents the value of the monetary amount of capital invested in the company. It is the total claim to assets that all asset holders have in the firm.

Therefore:

MVIC = NWC + FA + IA, which is also equal to, LTD + SE

Practically speaking, if we were to calculate the MVIC of a public company at its market value, we would add the fair market value of the interest-bearing debt and the fair market value of the equity. In the fair market value valuation of a private firm or a public company we would calculate the MVIC by utilizing the Income, Transaction and Guideline Company Approaches and adding excess and non-operating assets.

Excess Assets

Typical invested capital numbers *do not include* excess assets including cash. Excess cash is defined as any level of cash held on a company's balance sheet that is above what is necessary for core operations. This comes into importance when utilizing transaction multiples based on MVIC measures of firm value or comparing financial ratios using MVIC (such as ROIC) across firms in a given industry. The problem associated with MVIC calculations lie in the the definition of excess cash. Some analysts or transaction databases include *all cash* when calculating MVIC, and some deduct an excess amount. Neither action is right or wrong, but it is necessary for the analyst to determine what data they are utilizing in their analysis for apples to apples comparisons.

CAPITAL MARKET EFFICIENCY

An important debate among stock market investors is whether the market is efficient - that is, whether it reflects all the information made available to market participants at any given time. The efficient market hypothesis (EMH) maintains that all stocks are perfectly priced according to their inherent investment properties, the knowledge of which all market participants possess equally. At first glance, it may be easy to see a number of deficiencies in the efficient market theory, created in the 1970s by Eugene Fama. At the same time, however, it's important to explore its relevancy in the modern investing environment.

Financial theories are subjective. In other words, there are no proven laws in finance, but rather ideas that try to explain how the market works. Here we'll take a look at where the efficient market theory has fallen short in terms of explaining the stock market's behaviour.

EMH TENETS AND PROBLEMS WITH EMH

First, the efficient market hypothesis assumes that all investors perceive all available information in precisely the same manner. The numerous methods for analyzing and valuing stocks pose some problems for the validity of the

EMH. If one investor looks for undervalued market opportunities while another investor evaluates a stock on the basis of its growth potential, these two investors will already have arrived at a different assessment of the stock's fair market value. Therefore, one argument against the EMH points out that since investors value stocks differently, it is impossible to ascertain what a stock should be worth in an efficient market.

Secondly, under the efficient market hypothesis, no single investor is ever able to attain greater profitability than another with the same amount of invested funds: their equal possession of information means they can only achieve identical returns. But consider the wide range of investment returns attained by the entire universe of investors, investment funds and so forth. If no investor had any clear advantage over another, would there be a range of yearly returns in the mutual fund industry from significant losses to 50 per cent profits, or more? According to the EMH, if one investor is profitable, it means the entire universe of investors is profitable. In reality, this is not the case.

Thirdly (and closely related to the second point), under the efficient market hypothesis, no investor should ever be able to beat the market, or the average annual returns that all investors and funds are able to achieve using their best efforts. This idea would naturally imply, as many market experts often maintain, that the absolute best investment strategy is simply to place all of one's investment funds into an index fund, which would increase or decrease according to the overall level of corporate profitability or losses. There are, however, many examples of investors who have consistently beat the market - you need look no further than Warren Buffett to find an example of someone who's managed to beat the averages year after year.

Qualifying the EMH

Eugene Fama never imagined that his efficient market would be 100 per cent efficient all the time. Of course, it's impossible for the market to attain full efficiency all the time, as it takes time for stock prices to respond to new information released into the investment community. The efficient hypothesis, however, does not give a strict definition of how much time prices need to revert to fair value. Moreover, under an efficient market, random events are entirely acceptable but will always be ironed out as prices revert to the norm.

It is important to ask whether EMH undermines itself in its allowance for random occurrences or environmental eventualities. There is no doubt that such eventualities must be considered under market efficiency but, by definition, true efficiency accounts for those factors immediately. In other words, prices should respond nearly instantaneously with the release of new information that can be expected to affect a stock's investment characteristics. So, if the EMH allows for inefficiencies, it may have to admit that absolute market efficiency is impossible.

Increasing Market Efficiency?

Although it is relatively easy to pour cold water on the efficient market hypothesis, its relevance may actually be growing. With the rise of computerized systems to analyze stock investments, trades and corporations, investments are becoming increasingly automated on the basis of strict mathematical or fundamental analytical methods. Given the right power and speed, some computers can immediately process any and all available information, and even translate such analysis into an immediate trade execution.

Despite the increasing use of computers, most decision-making is still done by human beings and is therefore subject to human error. Even at an institutional level, the use of analytical machines is anything but universal. While the success of stock market investing is based mostly on the skill of individual or institutional investors, people will continually search for the surefire method of achieving greater returns than the market averages. If the EMH is accurate, however, it would have the following implications for investors.

EMH and Technical Analysis

Technical analysis bases decisions on past results. EMH, however, believes past results cannot be used to outperform the market. As a result, EMH negates the use of technical analysis as a means to generate investment returns. With respect to fundamental analysis, the EMH also states that all publicly available information is reflected in security prices and as such, abnormal returns are not achievable through the use of this information. This negates the use of fundamental analysis as a means to generate investment returns.

EMH and the Portfolio Management Process

As we have discussed, the portfolio management process begins with an investment policy statement, including an investor's objectives and constraints. Given EMH, the portfolio management process should not focus on achieving above-average returns for the investor. It should focus purely on risks given that above-average returns are not achievable. A portfolio manager's goal is to outperform a specific benchmark with specific investment ideas. The EMH implies that this goal is unachievable, and a portfolio manager should not be able to achieve above average returns.

Why Invest in Index Funds?

Given the discussion on the EMH, the overall assumption is that no investor is able to generate an abnormal return in the market. If that is the case, an investor can expect to make a return equal to the market return. An investor should thus focus on the minimizing his costs to invest. To achieve a market rate of return, diversification in a numerous amounts of stocks is required, which may not be an option for a smaller investor. As such, an index fund would be the most appropriate investment vehicle, allowing the investor to achieve the market rate of return in a cost effective manner.

Is The Market Truly Efficient?

It's safe to say the market is not going to achieve perfect efficiency anytime soon.

For greater efficiency to occur, the following criteria must be met:

- Universal access to high-speed and advanced systems of pricing analysis,
- A universally accepted analysis system of pricing stocks,
- An absolute absence of human emotion in investment decision-making,
- The willingness of all investors to accept that their returns or losses will be exactly identical to all other market participants. It is hard to imagine even one of these criteria of market efficiency ever being met.

CAPITAL MARKET INVESTMENT

A capital market is a market where both The capital market investment makes the investors to buy or sell securities in the capital markets. The stock market and bond market are types of capital markets where investors can trade in stocks and bonds. The investments in the capital market may be either in the bonds or stocks. Investments in the stocks or bonds may be either investing in the new issues or in the existing securities. The primary capital market handles the trading and investments in the new issues while the secondary capital market takes care of the trading of existing securities.

There are a number of financial regulators that monitor the capital market dealings in order to protect the investors from fraud. U.S. Securities and Exchange Commission is one such financial regulator that regulates the capital markets situated in their designated countries for the best interest of the investors.

STOCK INVESTMENT

The investment in stocks may in six different styles. Depending on the needs and reasons of the investors, the efficiency of the investment is estimated. There are some investors who depend on the advice of other people while purchasing or selling a particular stock.

There are technical investors who spend time in studying the stock patterns before trading any stock. The economist investors take their decision of stock trading depending on the economic forecasts. They are in the nature to take risks and get benefited in return following an efficient market hypotheses. There are some other types of investors who rely on the information given by the researchers, vendors and trade executives to make investment in the stocks. There are value investors who try to value the stock independently of its market price. Finally, there are conscious investors who depend on their own measurements and beliefs while making any stock investment.

Bond Investment

Bond investment is different from that of stock investment. Bond investment is investing in the debt instrument that is issued by a company or government. The bond investor is actually lending money to the company while in return is promised to be paid the full principal amount plus a fixed periodic payout. The yield on the bond is calculated by putting together the final principal and total payouts received. The yield is the effective interest rate for the tenure of the bond.

INVESTMENT CHOICES IN THE CAPITAL MARKET

Among all investment options available, securities are considered the most challenging as well as rewarding. But investment in securities requires considerable skill and expertise and carries the risk of loss if the choice of securities is not right or they are not bought/ sold at right time.

There are a large variety of instruments referred to as securities in common parlance. These include:

- Shares, scrips, stocks, bonds, debentures, debenture stock or other marketable securities of a like nature in or of any incorporated company or other body corporate;
- Derivative;
- Units or any other instrument issued by any collective investment scheme to the investors in such schemes;
- Security receipts;
- Units or any other such instrument issued to the investors under any mutual fund scheme;
- Any certificate or instrument issued to investor by any issuer being a special purpose distinct entity which possesses any debt or receivable including mortgaged debt assigned to such entity and acknowledging beneficial interest of such investor in such debt or receivable including mortgage debt as the case may be;
- Government securities;
- Such other instruments as may be declared by the central government to be securities;
- Rights or interest in securities.

Different securities carry different risk-return profiles. Generally, higher risks carry higher returns and vice-versa. The risk could be in the form of credit risk (counter party may default payment as it may not have integrity), return risk (the return from the investment may depend on several contingent factors) and liquidity risk (it may be difficult to convert security into cash). Investment decisions are based upon the investors' life cycle stages and other factors such as liquidity, safety, return on investments, tax savings, active involvement required to manage the investment, and minimum amount requirement for selecting the instruments. It is not always possible to meet all financial goals with available savings. If savings are limited but the needs are substantial, then the savings should be invested in avenues that would offer high returns. But usually, high return also means high risk. All investors are not in a position to take high risks. There are investment opportunities that are high on risk and there are investment opportunities that are low on risk. Each is called an asset class. An investor allocates his savings to one or more asset classes depending upon his circumstances.

This decision is called the asset allocation decision. Asset allocation decision is perhaps the most important decision in the investment process. The essence of asset allocation lies in the fact that, over time, it can determine up to 90 per cent of the portfolio's return. How much risk an investor can take depends on his financial circumstances and the mental make-up. Every investor must know his own unique risk profile and then make the investment decisions.

As such, the questions he should ask himself are:

- What kind of investor am I?
- Am I prepared to take high risks?
- Am I averse to taking risks?

There are scientific methods by which an investor can understand his risk profile. For example, answering the following set of questions could give him an idea about his risk profile:

Your age is

- Between 25-35
- Between 35-50
- Between 50-65
- Above 65

Your position is best described by

- You are self-dependent and do not support anybody
- You have dependent(s)
- Nearing retirement
- Retired

How much of the following needs have been taken care of? (Fully, partially, not at all)

- Insurance
- Retirement
- Children's education
- Housing

What proportion of your current expenses is funded from investments?

- Nil
- Up to 15 per cent
- Between 15 per cent and 30 per cent
- Between 30 per cent and 50 per cent
- More than 50 per cent

Your earnings in the future will

- far exceed inflation
- be marginally ahead of inflation
- keep pace with inflation
- not keep pace with inflation

When the price of the share you have purchased drops steeply you would

- Sell your investment
- Sell part of your investment
- Do nothing
- Buy more of the same investment

Each of the above questions would impact the risk profile of an investor. For example, lower the age, greater is the expected willingness to take risks. This is because younger people have a lifetime of earnings ahead of them and thus can afford to take higher risks with their present savings. Similarly, in case a person does not have any dependents, he can take more risk. At the very basic level, there are three asset classes from which to choose from based upon an investors' risk profile. They are equity, debt and cash. Equity is risky, debt has low risk and cash has even lower risk. Within each of the above asset classes, the investor has to select specific instruments for investment.

Financial circumstances and the investor profile dictate the investment avenues for an investor. Financial instruments vary in terms of the liquidity, safety, and returns they offer. The challenge in making the investment decision is to choose the right combination of instruments keeping in mind the financial situation and investor profile. Each investment option has some advantages and some limitations. For example, while bank savings account would be highly liquid (you can withdraw whenever you like), investment in Public Provident Fund would be difficult to withdraw.

Risks are generally positively correlated with probability of returns. For example, returns in equity shares can be high, but the associated risks are also relatively higher than other options. Risks can be classified into unsystematic and systematic. Unsystematic risks are those that can be minimized by diversifying one's portfolio. For example, instead of investing in the shares of steel companies alone, one could invest into other sectors like Pharmaceuticals and Software. In this situation, your portfolio may not be terribly affected even if the steel sector were to register a mediocre performance. On the other hand, systematic risks are those that cannot be minimized through portfolio diversification. For example, a Korean investor could not possibly have minimized or eliminated his loss due to the currency crisis in South East Asia, through a strategy of diversification of his portfolio. The character of the investor is also important. Some investors have the time and the knowledge to study their investment portfolios carefully- these could be called as 'active' investors. Others do not intend to watch their investments regularly, due to lack of time or knowledge or inclination, and are looking for essentially safer avenues for parking their funds.

INVESTMENT OPTIONS

Various options available are described in the following paragraphs and evaluated broadly on criteria such as

- Liquidity
- Safety
- Returns
- Tax savings
- Active involvement required to manage the investment
- Minimum amount that can be invested

Equity Shares

An equity share, commonly referred to as ordinary share represents a fractional ownership of the company in which a shareholder, as a fractional owner, undertakes the entrepreneurial risks and rewards associated with a business venture. The holders of such shares are members of the company and have voting rights. Equity Shares can be purchased in the Primary and Secondary Markets. Primary Market: Primary market refers to issue of securities by companies/entities to the public. Apart from shares, other instruments commonly issued in the primary market are debentures, convertible debentures, shares with attached options like warrants etc.

Secondary Market: Secondary market refers to the stock exchanges where an investor can buy (or sell) shares which are listed on them. As a result of significant changes in the recent past, particularly computerization, online trading, dematerialization and depository participation, investors are dealing with a much more transparent and efficient secondary market.

Equity Shares yield returns in two ways: one, dividends declared by companies usually at the end of a year (and sometimes during the course of the year) and, two, capital gains on selling. Liquidity of investments in equity shares depends upon the trading volumes of the share. If the share is actively traded, an investor can easily sell the shares and realize the sale proceeds. However, if the share is not traded (or is delisted), then liquidity is a constraint. Technically, it is possible to buy even one share in the dematerialized securities regime.

Equity is a volatile instrument. It is an appropriate investment avenue for an investor who is prepared to take risks in order to generate higher returns. Over the long term, returns from equity shares at aggregated levels have been historically higher than most other avenues. However, individual investors could gain or lose depending on the shares they invest in and when they buy and sell. An investor needs to be aware of the companies in which he invests and continuously monitor their performance. For this, he should have some basic knowledge of finance and of the market processes. The trends in equity market are reflected in the movement of the equity indices and the volume of the trading activity.

Preference Shares

- Preferred Stock/ Preference Shares: Owners of these kinds of shares are entitled to a fixed dividend or dividend calculated at a fixed rate to be paid regularly before a dividend can be paid in respect of equity share. These also enjoy priority over equity shareholders in payment of surplus. However, in the event of liquidation, their claims rank below the claims of the company's creditors, bondholders/ debenture holders.
- Cumulative Preference Shares: A type of preference share on which dividend accumulates if it remains unpaid. All arrears of preference dividend have to be paid out before paying dividend on equity shares.
- Cumulative Convertible Preference Shares: A type of preference shares where the dividend payable on the same accumulates, if not paid. After a specified date, these shares will be converted into equity capital of the company.
- Participating Preference Share: The right of certain preference shareholders to participate in profits after a specified fixed dividend contracted for, is paid. Participation right is linked with the quantum of dividend paid on the equity shares over and above a particular specified level.

Security Receipts

Security receipt means a receipt or other security, issued by a securitization company or reconstruction company to any qualified institutional buyer pursuant to a scheme, evidencing the purchase or acquisition by the holder thereof, of an undivided right, title or interest in the financial asset involved in securitization.

Debt Instruments

Debt instruments represent contracts where one party is the lender (investor) and the other party is the borrower (issuer). The debt contract specifies the rate of interest, time of interest payment, repayment of principal, etc. In India, the term “bond” is used to represent the debt instrument issued by the central and state governments and PSUs. The term “debenture” is used for debt issues from the private corporate sector.

The principal features of a debt instrument are:

- Maturity
- Coupon
- Principal

Maturity refers to the date on which the principal would be repaid. Coupon is the rate at which interest is calculated with reference to the face value. For example, a 10 per cent 2010 bond refers to face value of ₹ 100, coupon rate of 10 per cent p.a., and repayment of the face value in the year 2010.

The coupon rate may be fixed for the entire period or may be related to a benchmark rate. In the latter case, the coupon rate changes as the benchmark rate changes. This instrument is called a floating rate debt instrument. There are debt instruments that come with options to redeem the principal earlier than the maturity date. If the option rests with the issuer, it is a bond that is callable. If the option to redeem rests with the investor, it is puttable.

There are many different types of debt instruments in India. These are:

- Bonds (from PSUs and Financial Institutions)
- Government (Central or State) Securities
- Treasury Bills
- Company Debentures
- Commercial Paper
- Certificates of Deposit

The secondary market activity for debt instruments takes place in the debt segment of the exchange. The trends in the debt market are reflected in the debt indices and the turnover data. In India, the debt market activity is dominated by banks and institutions.

Bonds

A Bond is a loan given by the buyer to the issuer of the instrument. Bonds may be issued by companies, financial institutions or the government. Over and above the scheduled interest payments, the holder of a bond is entitled to receive the redemption value of the instrument at the specified maturity date. In simple terms, a bond investor lends money to the issuer and in exchange, the issuer promises to repay the loan amount on a specified maturity date and usually pay the periodic interest payments over the life of the loan. Few more popular types of Bonds are as follows:

- Zero Coupon Bonds: Bonds issued at a discount and repaid at a face value. No periodic interest is paid. The difference between the issue price and redemption price represents the return to the holder. The buyer of these bonds receives only one payment at the maturity of the bond. These are also sometimes referred to as deep-discount bonds.

- Convertible Bonds: Bonds giving the investor the option to convert the bond into equity at a fixed conversion price.
- Tax-Saving Bonds: Tax-Saving Bonds offer tax exemption up to a specified amount of investment.
- Regular Income Bonds: Regular-Income Bonds, as the name suggests, are meant to provide a stable source of income at regular, pre-determined intervals.

Similar instruments issued by companies are called debentures. Bonds are usually not suitable to achieve capital appreciation. Sometimes, an investor buys bonds at a lower price just before a decline in interest rates, and the subsequent drop in the interest rates leads to an increase in the price of the bond, thereby facilitating capital appreciation.

Bonds are suitable for regular income purposes. Depending on the type of bond, an investor may receive interest semi-annually or even monthly, as is the case with monthly-income bonds. Bond prices are dependent on the face value of these instruments. The most common face value is ₹ 100. Minimum amount of investment is generally around ₹ 5,000. An investor need not be actively involved in investment management.

Public Sector Undertakings and Financial Institutions Bonds:

Various bonds are floated from time to time by Public Sector Undertakings as well as Development Financial Institutions. Most such bonds offer attractive schemes like monthly interest, quarterly interest, various redemption options, deep discount bond options etc.

Government Securities (G-Secs)

These are sovereign (credit risk-free) coupon bearing instruments which are issued by the Reserve Bank of India on behalf of the Government of India, in lieu of the Central Government's market borrowing programme. These securities have a fixed coupon that is paid on specific dates on half-yearly basis. These securities are available in a wide range of maturity dates, from short dated (less than one year) to long dated (up to twenty years).

RBI Tax Free Bonds

RBI Tax Free Bonds are special bonds issued by the RBI offering tax-free facility. The rate of interest in such bonds is generally lower than regular bonds and hence these attract only high taxpayers. These bonds tend to be long-term instruments. RBI Tax free bonds are very safe as they come from the country's central bank. Returns from the bonds are steady and can be ascertained clearly in advance based on the YTM.

Treasury Bills

Short-term (up to 91 day) bearer discount securities issued by the Government as a means of financing its cash requirements.

Company Debentures

Instruments issued by a company bearing a fixed rate of interest usually payable half yearly on specific dates with the principal amount repayable on a particular date on redemption. Debentures are normally secured/ charged against the assets of the company in favour of the debenture holder. Companies borrow from debenture-holders and generally offer a fixed rate of interest to such investors. Most debentures are redeemed after a specified period. The period could be short (less than 18 months) or long depending on the terms of issue. In some cases, companies also pay a premium on maturity.

Investors can subscribe to public issue of debentures by companies or buy debentures from the secondary market. In view of the fixed returns from these securities, prices of debentures are generally much less volatile relative to shares. Investors earn interest and capital gains (difference between the purchase price and the sale price or if held till redemption, the difference between purchase price and the redemption price).

Yields on debentures could be higher or lower than the specified rate of interest depending on the correlation between face value and market value. For example, assume that a ₹ 100 debenture carrying 15 per cent interest is bought for ₹ 90. The price paid is ₹ 90 whereas the interest earned is ₹ 15. This would translate to a yield of 16.67 per cent. In the above example, the investor would get back ₹ 100 from the company (face value) if he holds the debentures up to maturity. Hence, apart from the interest yield of 16.67 per cent, he would also gain ₹ 10 by way of capital gain. When this capital gain is also considered for computing the yield, it is termed as Yield to Maturity (YTM).

Most debt issues are required to be rated by credit rating agencies. Rating indicates the quality of the instrument. An indication of credit rating is given below:

Table. Credit Rating Symbols and What They Mean

High Investment Grades	
AAA	Highest Safety
AA	High Safety
Investment Grades	
A	Adequate Safety
BBB	Moderate Safety
Speculative Grades	
BB	Inadequate Safety
B	High Risk
C	Substantial Risk
D	In Default

Different rating agencies might have different symbols than the ones given above. Returns from high quality debentures are steady and can be ascertained in advance based on the YTM. These returns would vary only if the company were to renege on its payment obligations. An investor need not be actively involved in investment management, except to the extent of keeping basic track of companies, which might be performing badly and could fail to fulfill their interest or repayment obligations.

Commercial Paper

A short term promise to repay a fixed amount that is placed on the market either directly or through a specialized intermediary. It is usually issued by companies with a high credit standing in the form of a promissory note redeemable at par to the holder on maturity and therefore, doesn't require any guarantee. Commercial paper is a money market instrument issued normally for a tenure of 90 days.

Certificate of Deposit

A time deposit with a bank. CDs are generally issued by commercial banks but they can be bought through brokerages. They bear a specific maturity date, a specified interest rate, and can be issued in any denomination, much like bonds. Like all time deposits, the funds may not be withdrawn on demand.

4

Production Analysis

DEFINITION OF PRODUCTION MANAGEMENT

It may be defined as:

- The performance of the management activities with regards to selecting, designing, operating, Controlling and updating production system.
- It is the processes of effectively planning, co-ordinating and controlling the production, that is the operations of that part of an enterprise, it means to say that production and operations Management is responsible for the actual transformation of raw materials into finished products.
- Production management is a function of Management, related to planning, coordinating and controlling the resources required for production to produce specified product by specified methods, by optimal utilization of resources.
- Production management is defined as management function which plans, organizes, coordinates, directs and controls the material supply and Processing activities of an enterprise, so that specified products are produced by specified methods to meet an approved sales programme. These activities are being carried out in such a manner that Labour, Plant and Capital available are used to the best advantage of the organization.

OBJECTIVE OF PRODUCTION MANAGEMENT

The objective of Production Management is to produce the desired product or specified product by specified methods so that the optimal utilization of available resources is met with. Hence the production management is responsible to produce the desired product, which has marketability at the cheapest price by proper planning, the manpower, material and processes. Production management must see that it will deliver right goods of right quantity at right place and at right price. When the objective is achieved, we say that we have effective Production Management system.

SCOPE OF PRODUCTION MANAGEMENT

In fact, we apply Principles of Management; and functions of Management in our day-to-day life. We all know, from morning till night, we plan our activities; we coordinate available resources and control our activities to achieve certain goals.

So also any organization must follow the Principles of Management for its survival and growth. The same is applicable to production Management also. Reading and learning Production Management will enable one to be capable of solving the problems of the organization, may be an Educational Institution, Production Shop, Hospital, Departmental shop or even a barber shop. The problems a manager face in various organizations are more or less similar to that of Production department but smaller in magnitude. Hence the knowledge of Production Management will help any professional Manager to tackle the problems of his business easily.

For example: The Production Management consists of Planning, selection of materials, planning of processes, Routing, Scheduling and controlling the activities etc., Take the example of an Educational Institution/University. Here also selection of raw students, Planning of the Course Work, Educating the students and conducting the examination. Therefore this knowledge will enable one to apply the principles of Production Management to any field of life without restriction. Here, we have to remember that this is also applicable to the management of a service organization and the management of a Project. Here it is better to distinguish between product, Service and Project, so as to help the reader to know on which particular aspect of Production Management to put much emphasis, in managing a service organization or a project.

- *Product*: Manufacturing system often produces standardized products in large volumes. The plant and machinery have a finite capacity. The facilities constitute fixed costs, which are allocated to the products produced. Variable costs, such as, labour cost and materials costs. While manufacturing the product use value and economic values are added to the product. Hence the product is a store of values added during manufacture. Because the input costs and output costs are measurable, the productivity can be measured with certain degree of accuracy. Product can be transported to the markets and stored physically until it is sold.
- *Service*: Service system present more uncertainty with respect to capacity and costs. Services are produced and consumed in the presence of the customer. We cannot store the service physically. Because of this the service organizations, such as Hotels, Hospitals, Transport Organizations and many other service organizations the capacity must be sufficiently or consciously managed to accommodate a highly variable demand. Sometimes services like legal practice and

medical practice involve Professional or intellectual judgements, which cannot be easily standardized. Because of this the calculation of cost and productivity is difficult.

- *Project*: Project system does not produce standardized products. The Plant, Machinery, Men and Materials are often brought to project site and the project is completed. The project is of big size and remains in the site itself after completion. As the costs can be calculated and allocated to the project with considerable accuracy, Productivity can be measured. Once the project is completed, all the resources are removed from site.

BENEFITS DERIVED FROM EFFICIENT PRODUCTION MANAGEMENT

The efficient Production Management will give benefits to the various parts of the society.

They are:

- Consumer benefits from improved industrial Productivity, increased use value in the product. Products are available to him at right place, at right price, at right time, in desired quantity and of desired quality.
- *Investors*: They get increased security for their investments, adequate market returns, and creditability and good image in the society.
- Employee gets adequate Wages, Job security, improved working conditions and increased Personal and Job satisfaction.
- *Suppliers*: Will get confidence in management and their bills can be realised with out any delay.
- *Community*: community enjoys Benefits from economic and social stability.
- The Nation will achieve prospects and security because of increased Productivity and healthy industrial atmosphere.

FUNCTIONS OF PRODUCTION MANAGEMENT DEPARTMENT

The functions of Production Management depend upon the size of the firm. In small firms the production Manager may have to look after production planning and control along with Personnel, Marketing, Finance and Purchase functions. In medium sized firms, there may be separate managers for Personnel, marketing and Finance functions. But the production planning and control and Purchase and stores may be under the control of Production management department. In large sized firms the activities of Production Management is confined to the management of production activities only. As such, there are no hard and fast rule or guidelines to specify the function of Production Management, but in the academic interest we can mention some of the functions, which are looked after by the Production Management department.

They are:

- *Materials*: The selection of materials for the product. Production manager must have sound Knowledge of materials and their properties, so that he can select appropriate materials for his product. Research on materials is necessary to find alternatives to satisfy the changing needs of the design in the product and availability of material resumes.
- *Methods*: Finding the best method for the process, to search for the methods to suit the available resources, identifying the sequence of process are some of the activities of Production Management.
- *Machines and Equipment*: Selection of suitable machinery for the process desired, designing the maintenance policy and design of layout of machines are taken care of by the Production Management department.
- *Estimating*: To fix up the Production targets and delivery dates and to keep the production costs at minimum, production management department does a thorough estimation of Production times and production costs. In competitive situation this will help the management to decide what should be done in arresting the costs at desired level.
- *Loading and Scheduling*: The Production Management department has to draw the time table for various production activities, specifying when to start and when to finish the process required. It also has to draw the timings of materials movement and plan the activities of manpower. The scheduling is to be done keeping in mind the loads on hand and capacities of facilities available.
- *Routing*: This is the most important function of Production Management department. The Routing consists of fixing the flow lines for various raw materials, components etc., from the stores to the packing of finished product, so that all concerned knows what exactly is happening on the shop floor.
- *Despatching*: The Production Management department has to prepare various documents such as Job Cards, Route sheets, Move Cards, Inspection Cards for each and every component of the product. These are prepared in a set of five copies. These documents are to be released from Production Management department to give green signal for starting the production. The activities of the shop floor will follow the instructions given in these documents. Activity of releasing the document is known as dispatching.

- *Expediting or Follow up*: Once the documents are dispatched, the management wants to know whether the activities are being carried out as per the plans or not. Expediting engineers go round the production floor along with the plans, compare the actual with the plan and feed back the progress of the work to the management. This will help the management to evaluate the plans.
- *Inspection*: Here inspection is generally concerned with the inspection activities during production, but a separate quality control department does the quality inspection, which is not under the control of Production Management. This is true because, if the quality inspection is given to production Management, then there is a chance of qualifying the defective products also. For example Teaching and examining of students is given to the same person, then there is a possibility of passing all the students in the first grade. To avoid this situation an external person does correction of answer scripts, so that the quality of answers are correctly judged.
- *Evaluation*: The Production department must evaluate itself and its contribution in fulfilling the corporate objectives and the departmental objectives. This is necessary for setting up the standards for future. What ever may be the size of the firm; Production management department alone must do Routing, Scheduling, Loading, Dispatching and expediting.

This is because this department knows very well regarding materials, Methods, and available resources etc. If the firms are small, all the functions (i to x) are to be carried out by Production Management Department. In medium sized firms in addition to Routing, Scheduling and Loading, Dispatching and expediting, some more functions like Methods, Machines may be under the control of Production Management Department. In large firms, there will be Separate departments for Methods, Machines, Materials and others but routing, loading and scheduling are the sole functions of Production Management. All the ten functions are categorized in three stage, that is Preplanning, Planning and control stages as shown in figure.

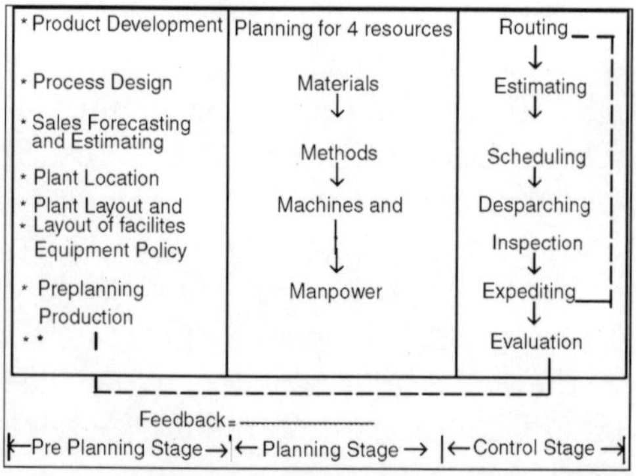

Fig. Production Function

PLACE OF PRODUCTION MANAGEMENT DEPARTMENT IN THE ORGANISATION

Production is the centre of all activities of an organization. This is to say all the activities of an organization, such as: Finance, Personnel, Marketing...etc., are exists in an organization because of production activity. Hence the position of Production Management in an organization is very important. Whether it should be a line function or Staff function, more or less depends upon the corporate management policy. In small organization, Production Management is whole and sole of it. In large industries, generally it is advisable to have Production as line function, because, the decision taken by the line manager and the advices given by the Staff personnel will be based on the Production activities.

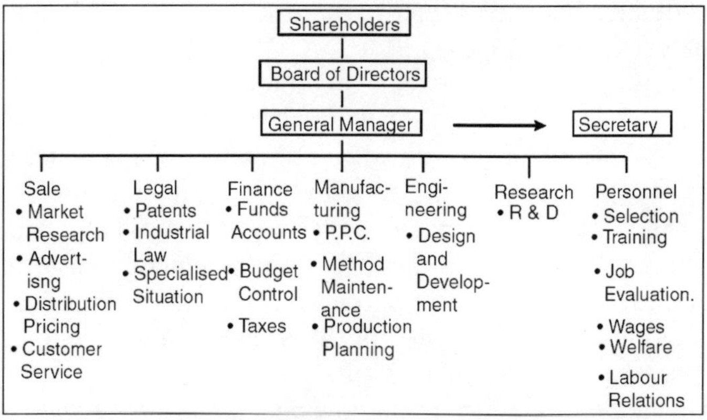

Fig. Typical Organisation Chat for an Organisation

The Production Manager, directly report to General Manager, who in turn report to the Board. The figure shows a typical organization structure showing the position of Production Management. Figure shows an organization chart for Production and Operations Management department.

ORGANISATION CHART FOR P.P.C. DEPARTMENT

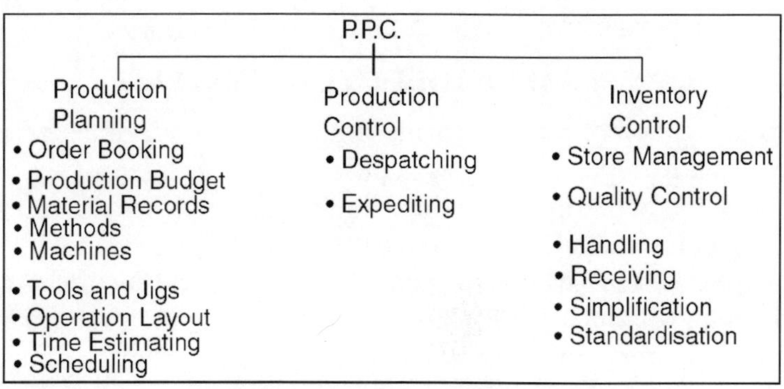

Fig. An Oeganization Chat for Production Management Department

PRODUCTION SYSTEM

Production system. any of the methods used in industry to create goods and services from various resources.

UNDERLYING PRINCIPLES

All production systems. when viewed at the most abstract level. might be said to be "transformation processes"—processes that transform resources into useful goods and services. The transformation process typically uses common resources such as labour. capital (for machinery and equipment. materials. etc.). and space (land. buildings. etc.) to effect a change. Economists call these resources the "factors of production" and usually refer to them as labour. capital. and land. Production managers refer to them as the "five M's": men. machines. methods. materials. and money.

When viewed as a process. a production system may be further characterized by flows (channels of movement) in the process: both the physical flow of materials. work in the intermediate stages of manufacture (work in process). and finished goods; and the flow of information and the inevitable paperwork that carry and accompany the physical flow. The physical flows are subject to the constraints of the capacity of the production system. which also limits the system's ability to meet output expectations. Similarly. the capacity of the information-handling channel of the production system may also be an important measure of a system's output.

The management of information flows. or the planning and control of the system to achieve acceptable outputs. is an important task of the production manager. While the capacity of the system is the major factor in determining whether output expectations can be met. the additional consideration of quality must also be seen as a limiting factor. The quality of a product. measured against some objective standard. includes appearance. performance characteristics. durability. serviceability. and other physical characteristics; timeliness of delivery; cost; appropriateness of documentation and supporting materials; and so on. It is an important part of the definition of a system.

TYPES OF PRODUCTION SYSTEMS

The organization of manufacturing systems, also planning and control of production greatly depends on type of product type of the product line. Basic principles that guide the formation of planning policy and its execution may be the same for all the manufacturing concerns.

But emphasis on a particular aspect of production management in fulfilling of specific requirement of the plant and the management approach to the problems of inventory, machine selection, machine setting, tooling, routing, scheduling, loading, follow up and general control will differ depending on the type of production system.

Three main factors generally determine this aspect are:

1. Type of production *i.e.*, quantities of finished products and regularity of manufacture. For example whether Job production or Batch Production or Continuous Production.
2. Size of the Plant *i.e.*, Small Industry, Medium sized Industry or Large Industry.
3. Type of Production: In general there are three classifications in types of Production system..
   - *Job Production*: In this system Products are manufactured to meet the requirements of a specific order. The quality involved is small and the manufacturing of the product will take place as per the specifications given by the customer. This system may be further classified as.
     a. *The Job produced only once*: Here the customer visit the firm and book his order. After the completion of the product, he takes delivery of the product and leaves the firm. He may not visit the firm to book the order for the same product. The firm has to plan for material, process and manpower only after receiving the order from the customer. The firms have no scope for pre-planning the production of the product.
     b. *The job produced at irregular intervals*: Here the customer visits the firm to place orders for the same type of the product at irregular intervals. The firm will not have any idea of customer's visit. Here also planning for materials, process and manpower will start only after taking the order from the Customer. In case the firm maintains the record of the Jobs Produced by it, it can refer to the previous plans, when the customer arrives at the firm to book the order.
     c. *The Jobs Produced periodically at regular intervals*: In this system, the customer arrives at the firm to place orders for the same type of product at regular intervals. Here firm knows very well that the customer visits at regular intervals, it can plan for materials, and process and manpower and have them in a master file. As soon as the customer visits and books the order, the firm can start production. If the volume of the order is considerably large and the number of regularly visiting customers are large in number, the Job Production system slowly transform into Batch Production system.
   - Batch Production: Batch Production is the manufacture of number of identical products either to meet the specific order or to satisfy

the demand. When the Production of plant and equipment is terminated, the plant and equipment can be used for producing similar products. This system also can be classified under three categories.

a. *A batch produced only once*: Here customer places order with the firm for the product of his specification. The size of the order is greater than that of job production order. The firm has to plan for the resources after taking the order from the customer.
b. *A Batch produced at irregular intervals as per Customer order or when the need arises*: As the frequency is irregular, the firm can maintain a file of its detailed plans and it can refer to its previous files and start production.
c. *A Batch Produced periodically at known Intervals*: Here the firm either receives order from the customer at regular intervals or it may produce the product to satisfy the demand. It can have well designed file of its plans, material requirement and instructions for the ready reference. It can also purchase materials required in bulk in advance. As the frequency of regular orders goes on increasing the Batch Production system becomes Mass Production System. Here also, incase the demand for a particular product ceases, the plant and machinery can be used for producing other products with slight modification in layout or in machinery and equipment.

– *Continuous Production*: Continuous Production system is the specialized manufacture of identical products on which the machinery and equipment is fully engaged. The continuous production is normally associated with large quantities and with high rate of demand. Hence the advantage of automatic production is taken. This system is classified as

a. *Mass Production*: Here same type of product is produced to meet the demand of an assembly line or the market. This system needs good planning for material, process, maintenance of machines and instruction to operators. Purchases of materials in bulk quantities is advisable.
b. *Flow Production*: The difference between Mass and Flow Production is the type of product and its relation to the plant. In Mass Production identical products are produced in large numbers. If the demand falls or ceases, the machinery and equipment, after slight modification be used for manufacturing products of similar nature. In flow

production, the plant and equipment is designed for a specified product. Hence if the demand falls for the product or ceases, the plant cannot be used for manufacturing other products. It is to be scraped. The examples for the production system are:

i. *Job Production Shop*: Tailors shop; cycle and vehicles repair shops, Job typing shops, small Workshops.

ii. *Batch Production Shop*: Tyre Production Shops, Readymade dress companies, Cosmetic manufacturing companies...etc.

iii. *Mass Production Shops*: Components of industrial products,

iv. *Flow Production*: Cement Factory, Sugar factory, Oil refineries...etc.,

Here will give the characteristics of intermittent and continuous Production system.

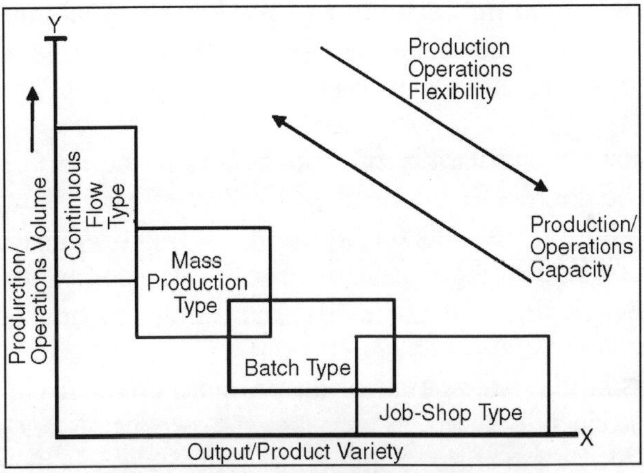

Fig. Production and Operations System

MANAGING PRODUCTS

Marketers are confronted with many issues when building the product component of their marketing strategy. While product decisions represent just one aspect of marketer's overall activities, these decisions are often the most important because they lead directly to the reasons (*i.e.*, benefits offered, solutions to problems) for why the customer decides to choose the organization's goods, services or ideas.The coverage of product decisions by exploring additional product issues facing the marketer. In particular, we examine four important areas. First, we categorize the roles played by those involved in product management and show how the scope of a manager's responsibilities changes as these roles take on greater importance.

Second, we return to a discussion of branding by focusing on overall branding strategies that may be adopted by the marketing organization. Third, we spend a large part of this tutorial covering the importance of ew product development including an analysis of the steps firms may follow to bring new products to market. Finally, we will see that once new products have been established in the market numerous factors force the marketer to continually adjust their product decisions.

PRODUCT MANAGEMENT RESPONSIBILITIES

While this tutorial touches on basic concepts and strategies applicable to a large percentage of marketing situations, the reader should understand that no two marketing situations are the same. Yet while some concepts and strategies important to one marketer may not hold the same weight with another, in general, the basic principles of marketing (*e.g.*, satisfying target markets, support decisions using research, etc.) hold no matter the type of industry, type of company or type of product being sold.

What is often different between two marketing situations is the level of complication and challenge that arises as a marketer's scope of responsibility increases. For our purposes a marketer's level of responsibility is measured in terms of:

- The number and variety of tasks that must be performed (*i.e.*, what has to be done)
- The value these tasks represent to the organization (*i.e.*, how important marketing is perceived within the company)
- The overall financial stake the marketing position holds (*i.e.*, total sales volume and profit generation).

As responsibilities change so to do the marketer's tasks. For instance, with regard to product decisions, as a marketer's responsibilities become greater her or his day-to-day job shifts from being involved in specific product issues (*e.g.*, finding a graphics design company to create a new label) to decisions concerning many products and focusing on setting the future marketing direction of the company (*e.g.*, developing marketing plans for numerous products). We can see this in greater detail by examining the responsibilities associated with four different marketing management levels:

- *Product Item Level:* At this level responsibilities are associated with marketing a single product or brand. By "single" we are limiting the marketer's responsibility to one item. For instance, a startup software development company may initially market just one product. In some organizations the person in charge has the title Product Manager, though in smaller companies this person may simply be the Marketing Manager.
- *Brand Product Line Level:* At this level responsibilities are associated with managing two or more similar product items. By "similar" we

are referring to products carrying the same brand name that fit within the same product category and offer similar solutions to customers' needs. Procter and Gamble, one of the largest consumer products companies in the world, markets Tide laundry detergent in several different packaging sizes (*e.g.*, 50oz., 100oz., 200oz.), in different forms (*e.g.*, powder, liquid) and with different added features (*e.g.*, softener, bleach). Tide's product line consists of over 100 different versions of the product. Differences in the product offerings indicate these are targeted to different segments within the larger market (*e.g.*, those preferring liquid vs. those preferring powder), however, it may also represent a choice for the same target market who may seek variety. A product line is often measured by its depth, relative to competitors, with deep product lines offering extensive product items. Brand product lines are often managed by a Brand or Product Line Manager.

- *Category Product Line Level*: At this level responsibilities are associated with managing two or more brand product lines within the same product category. In this situation the marketer may manage products that offer similar basic benefits (*e.g.*, clean clothes) but target their offerings to slightly different needs (*e.g.*, product for tough to clean clothing vs. product to clean delicate clothing). Multiple brand product lines allow the marketer to cover the needs of more segments and, consequently, increase their chance to generate sales. Often in larger companies category product lines are the responsibility of the Product Category or Divisional Marketing Manager who may have Brand Product Managers reporting to him/her.
- *Product Mix Level:* At this level responsibilities include two or more category product lines that are directed to different product categories. In some cases the category product lines may yield similar general solutions (*e.g.*, cleaning) but are aimed at entirely different target markets (*e.g.*, cleaning dishes vs. cleaning automobiles). In large companies, the product lines are very diverse and offer different solutions. For example, BIC sells writing instruments, shaving products, and lighters. This diversification strategy cushions against an "all-eggs-in-one-basket" risk that may come if a company directs all resources to one product category. A product mix can be classified based on its width (how many different category product lines) and its depth (how many different brand product lines within a category product line). Generally responsibility for this level belongs to a company's Vice President for Marketing.

BRANDING STRATEGY

Branding is an important decision designed to enhance the identity of the product through the use of unique brand names, symbols and other distinctive measures. With competition growing more intense in almost all industries, establishing a strong brand allows an organization's products to stand out and avoid potential pitfalls, such as price wars, that have befallen many products. Therefore, a clear understanding of branding strategy is essential in order to build solid products and product lines. In particular, marketers should be aware of various branding approaches that can be pursued.

By branding approach we are referring to different product identification strategies that can be deployed to establish a product within the market. As we will see, the purpose of these approaches is to build a brand that will exist for the long term. Making smart decisions up front is crucial since a company may have to live with the decision for a long time.

Branding approaches include the following:

- *Individual Product Branding*: Under this branding approach new products are assigned new names with no obvious connection to existing brands offered by the company. Under individual product branding the marketing organization must work hard to establish the brand in the market since it cannot ride the coattails of previously introduced brands. The chief advantage of this approach is it allows brands to stand on their own thus lessening threats that may occur to other brands marketed by the company. For instance, if another company brand receives negative publicity this news is less likely to rub off on the company's other brands that carry their own unique names. Brands can create financial gains through the concept known as brand equity. Under an individual branding approach, each brand builds its own separate equity which allows the company, if they choose, to sell off individual brands without impacting other brands owned by the company. The most famous marketing organization to follow this strategy is Procter and Gamble, which has historically introduced new brands without any link to other brands or even to the company name.
- *Family Branding:* Under this branding approach new products are placed under the umbrella of an existing brand. The principle advantage of this approach is that it enables the organization to rapidly build market awareness and acceptance since the brand is already established and known to the market. But the potential disadvantage is that the market has already established certain perceptions of the brand. For instance, a company that sells low-end, lower priced products may have a brand that is viewed as an economy brand. This brand image may create customer confusion and hinder the company

if they attempt to introduce higher-end, higher priced products using the same brand name. Additionally, with family branding any negative publicity that may occur for one product within a brand could spread to all other products that share the same name.

- *Co-Branding:* This approach takes the idea of individual and family branding a step further. With co-branding a marketer seeks to partner with another firm, which has an established brand, in hopes synergy of two brands on a product is even more powerful than a single brand. The partnership often has both firms sharing costs but also sharing the gains. For instance, major credit card companies, such as Visa and MasterCard, offer co-branding options to companies and organizations. The cards carry the name of a co-branded organization (*e.g.*, University name) along with the name of the issuing bank (*e.g.*, Citibank) and the name of the credit card company. Besides tapping into awareness for multiple brands, the co-branding strategy is also designed to appeal to a larger target market, especially if each brand, when viewed separately, does not have extensive overlapping target markets with the other brand. Thus, co-branding allows both firms to tap into market segments where they did not previously have a strong position.
- *Private or Store Branding:* Some suppliers are in the business of producing products for other companies including placing another company's brand name on the product. This is most often seen in the retail industry where stores or online sellers contract with suppliers to manufacture the retailer's own branded products. In some cases the supplier not only produces product for the retailer's brand but also markets their own brand so that store shelves will contain both brands.
- *No-Name or Generic Branding:* Certain suppliers supply products that are intentionally "brandless." These products are mostly basic commodity-type products that consumer or business customers purchase as low price alternatives to branded products. Basic household products such as paper products, over-the-counter medicines such as ibuprofen, and even dog food are available in a generic form.
- *Brand Licensing:* Under brand licensing a contractual arrangement is created in which a company owning a brand name allows others to produce and supply products carrying the brand name. This is often seen when a brand is not directly connected with a product category. For instance, several famous children's characters, such as Sesame Street's Elmo, have been licensed to toy and food manufacturers who market products using the branded character's name and image.

PRODUCTION STRATEGY

Perhaps in no other functional area is the task of reflecting business-level strategic choices in functional strategy as demanding as it is in the production area. During the press of current operational snags, it is easy for production managers to exchange strategic relevance in operational decisions for tactical convenience. An industrial equipment manufacturer, for example, having developed a strategy stressing high quality and rapid delivery at premium prices, may suddenly cut inventory levels or the number of workers, or both to meet period-end cash flow needs. The restaurant chain store manager stressing product quality will precook food for the noon rush hour to hasten service when customers arrive.

These short-term departures from higher-level strategy not only have the effect of shocking the production system, but they also can produce results that are in conflict with that strategy— in these examples, the creation of a reputation for high-quality products. To guide manufacturing managers in the operation of the production function in a way consistent with other strategy levels, production strategy should at the minimum address capacity, facilities, product quality, process, technology, and control.

Production Capacity

When business-level goals and strategy involve manufacturing, production capacity required to meet sales and inventory requirements should be specified. Thus to begin to set production goals and formulate strategy, the strategist must first forecast sales.

Capacity is the amount of labour and equipment that will be required within specific time periods to meet expected demand. The strategist can express capacity in either total or incremental terms, whichever is consistent with the scope of strategy. As for units of analysis, capacity is usually specified as units of output per time period for labour, machines, and plant space required to meet expected demand. More specifically, production system capacity can be expressed as system efficiency (SE), the measure used to describe a firm's actual output as a function of production capacity:

$$\text{SE} = \text{System capacity}$$

in which system capacity and actual output are expressed as numbers of units per time period. The system efficiency ratio is also called utilization rate. It may range from 85 to 95 per cent, or even higher, depending on industry, investment levels, and economic conditions. Of course, the precise maximum output capability of a firm varies somewhat with conditions. But management usually recognizes a certain capacity utilization rate as the level above which the firm cannot produce without adding facilities. This capacity limit is the one against which a new business-level strategy's production expectations are compared to determine whether or not new facilities are needed.

The seven basic ways in which a firm can be managed in order to respond to an increase in capacity requirements are shown. These management approaches actually constitute the fundamental thrusts of production strategy choices available to the strategist. Only one—vary physical capacity—involves a permanent increase in facilities.

They are goals or directions, not precisely implementable actions. In reality production strategy will tend towards one, or some combination, of them and selection is a function of business-level strategy. Each approach carries distinct costs, as indicated, which can interfere with achievement of goals in other functional areas and in higher levels. Thus the approaches must be carefully evaluated in terms of potential adverse effects in addition to their immediate advantages.

Production Processes

Production strategy should also specify the type of manufacturing processes to be used to produce the products called for by business-level strategy. There are three basic types of production—repetitive (continuous), intermittent (job order), and project systems—and two hybrids, job lot and limited-quantity large-scale systems.Explanations and examples of each are presented.

Quality

Also as part of production goals and strategy, the strategist can guide the production department in reaching the appropriate product quality level by specifying values for inspection costs and defective unit costs. It may not be necessary to specify quantities for both, since they are highly negatively correlated. That is, when inspection costs are low, the proportion of defective units of output is high; when inspection costs are high, defects are low.

For new products and new production processes, it is difficult to know a priori what values to assign for desired inspection or defective unit costs. Standards for quality, which arise from strategic analysis and parts of marketing strategy, usually cannot be interpreted directly in terms of inspection costs or defective units.

For example, with no experience in producing a new product item, the strategist would have no basis for setting inspection cost levels or defective cost proportions even though a desired quality goal in a general sense is clearly understood.

Thus a period of experimentation by acceptance sampling would be necessary to establish reliably what cost control guidelines are appropriate to produce the desired and affordable level of defective units.

"A general guideline is to inspect when the cost of inspection at a given stage is less than the probable loss from not inspecting." In the absence of quality guidelines set by management, individual employees will set their own quality guidelines at the stage of production in which they are involved. This inconsistency can lead to chaos in production processes as product move between stages or activities, and ultimately can result in an unacceptably low level of product quality.

For new entries or existing products in extant markets, either through market research or information gathered from customers by salespeople, data can be developed on competitors' proportions of defective units.

Then relative quality goals can be generally determined and inspection costs can be set by acceptance sampling techniques. Of course, responsibility for seeing that a desired product quality level is maintained rests with everyone who is in a position to affect quality.

One of the key reasons for the success of Japanese manufacturers in acquiring reputations for quality products has been their ability to develop this sense of quality responsibility among all employees. To do so strategic quality or service goals (or intentions) must be manifested in all activities, from the very top to the bottom of the organization, through production quality strategy.

Facilities

When more capacity is required to carry out a business-level strategy, whether it involves new construction or the upgrading of old facilities, guidelines are needed to evaluate facility proposals.

In service businesses owned or leased buildings have to be evaluated. Evaluating proposals properly requires cost data. Industrial engineering may supply labour and productivity estimates; accounting may furnish labour rates, overhead rates, tax rates, and cost-of-capital rates.

The proposal should also be supported by a demand forecast so that expected revenues or savings can be compared with costs. At least two stages of analysis are usually undertaken.

Preliminary analysis is used to screen out unacceptable proposals by break-even analysis, payback period, simple rate of return, or average annual cost methods. Those projects that survive preliminary screening are then analyzed in more detail.

This detailed analysis involves consideration of the time value of money and results in a rank ordering of proposals. It normally follows the other capital budgeting techniques identified in the financial strategy section (net present value, discounted rate of return, etc.).

There may also be a final analysis stage, which requires selection from among rank-ordered proposals. The firm's cost of capital, historical rate of return, or industry averages can be used as cutoff points for selection of the best proposal. Replacement of existing facilities is guided by calculations based on costs. Although replacement decisions are usually operational in nature and ongoing, a new strategy can involve replacement of facilities as opposed to new acquisitions.

Facilities' replacements, a capital expenditure problem requiring large amounts of capital, are different from the more common component replacement decisions associated with maintenance management.

Component replacement often involves expense items, charged to the current period, or relatively small capitalized expenditures. Facility replacement expenditures tend to have longer-term effects on the firm than do those for component replacement.

A more comprehensive model of the categories of decisions which make up production strategy is proposed by Wheelwright. It consists of the following eight elements: Capacity, facilities, technology, vertical integration, workforce, quality, production planning/materials control, and organization.

Although we agree with this proposal, the parts of this list not addressed in our elements of production strategy can be addressed in the other functional strategy areas.

For example, the question of organization of the production effort would be confronted in organization strategy; desired level of technology in production would be a matter of reflecting technological preferences delineated in business level strategy; workforce issues would comprise personnel strategy, and so on.

PRODUCTION CYCLE AND DESIGN

The production cycle starts from Market Research. Market research reveals consumer preferences and needs. The marketing department will transfer this information to the design department.

The design department basing on the information received from marketing department designs the product to fulfill consumer needs and supplies design specifications and drawings to production department.

The production department verifies whether the product can be manufactured with the technology and skill available in the firm. If yes it will give the acceptance. Otherwise the Production Manager, Design engineer and Marketing Manager, discuss together and make alterations in the product without sacrificing the customer needs.

Once this is done the design department conduct the market survey and analyse the demand and submits its sales programme to the top management. The top management after going through the proposals sanctions the budget and gives green signal for production.

Production department produces a trial run and sales department release the product in the test markets to get consumer acceptance sells the products. Meanwhile, the production department prepares the detailed production plans and production scheduling. After getting the acceptance from the marketing department, actual production of product starts to meet the marketing programme.

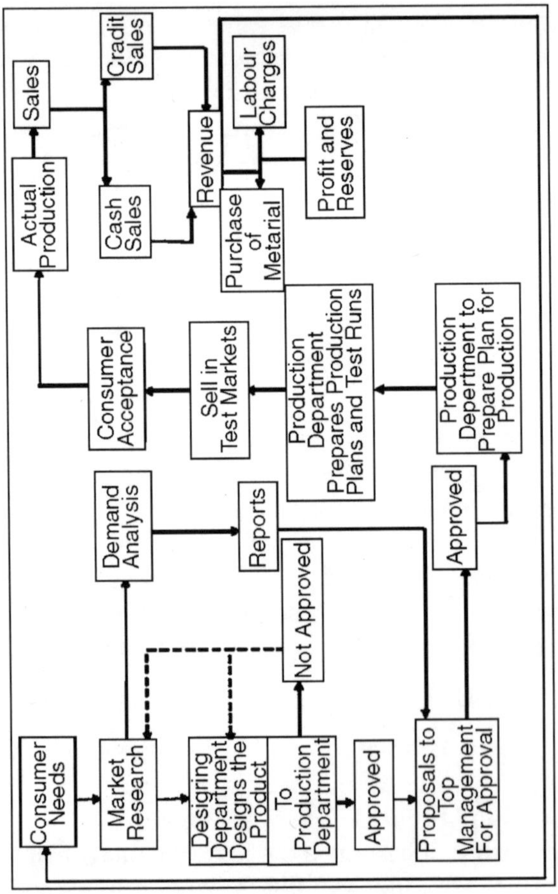

Fig. Production cycle.

PRODUCTION DESIGN

Production design is the creation and organization of the physical world surrounding a film story. The term was coined by producer David O. Selznick to describe the greater-than-normal contribution of designer William Cameron Menzies to Gone with the Wind, but the exact responsibilities of a production designer inevitably vary from film to film. In some cases, the production designer is almost completely responsible for the overall look of a film; in others, particularly when working with directors with strong visual styles, a designer's contribution tends to be much more limited. Art direction and production design often overlap, although credit for production design is seen as more inclusive. During the studio era, production designers, as opposed to art directors, were the exception.

The production designer's primary, though by no means exclusive, responsibility is the design of the sets. Exact responsibility varies from one film industry to another. In the United States, for example, production design and costume design are usually two separate professions. In other major film industries, the two responsibilities are often held by a single person.

Before designing anything, the designer develops a "design concept," an overarching metaphor for the film's appearance that governs individual choices. This "concept" may or may not be established in conjunction with the director. Once settled upon, however, it structures all decisions made, helping the art staff to give an individual film visual distinction.

PRODUCT DESIGN PROCESS

There are various product design processes and many focus on different aspects. The process shown below. for example. is "The Seven Universal Stages of Creative Problem-Solving." outlined by Don Koberg and Jim Bagnell. It helps designers formulate their product from ideas. This process is usually completed by a group of people. *i.e.* industrial designers. field experts (*e.g.* prospective users). engineers. etc. depending upon the products involved. The process focuses on figuring out what is required. brainstorming possible ideas. creating mock prototypes. and then generating the product. However. that is not the end of the process.

At this point. product designers would still need to execute the idea. making it into an actual product and then evaluate its success by seeing if any improvements are necessary.The product design process has experienced huge leaps in evolution over the last few years with the rise and adoption of 3D printing. New consumer-friendly 3D printers can produce dimensional objects and print upwards with a plastic like substance opposed to traditional printers that spread ink across a page.

The design process follows a guideline involving three main sections:

- Analysis
- Concept
- Synthesis

The latter two sections are often revisited. depending on how often the design needs touch-ups. to improve or to better fit the criteria. This is a continuous loop. where feedback is the main component. To break it down even more. the seven stages specify how the process works. Analysis consists of two stages. concept is only one stage. and synthesis encompasses the other four.

Analysis

- Accept Situation: Here. the designers decide on committing to the project and finding a solution to the problem. They pool their resources into figuring out how to solve the task most efficiently.
- Analyze: In this stage. everyone in the team begins research. They gather general and specific materials which will help to figure out

how their problem might be solved. This can range from statistics. questionnaires. and articles. among many other sources.

Concept

- Define: This is where the key issue of the matter is defined. The conditions of the problem become objectives. and restraints on the situation become the parameters within which the new design must be constructed.

Synthesis

- Ideate: The designers here brainstorm different ideas. solutions for their design problem. The ideal brainstorming session does not involve any bias or Judgement. but instead builds on original ideas.
- Select: By now. the designers have narrowed down their ideas to a select few. which can be guaranteed successes and from there they can outline their plan to make the product.
- Implement: This is where the prototypes are built. the plan outlined in the previous step is realized and the product starts to become an actual object.
- Evaluate: In the last stage. the product is tested. and from there. improvements are made. Although this is the last stage. it does not mean that the process is over. The finished prototype may not work as well as hoped so new ideas need to be brainstormed.

DEMAND-PULL INNOVATION AND INVENTION-PUSH INNOVATION

Most product designs fall under one of two categories: demand-pull innovation or invention-push innovation.Demand-pull happens when there is an opportunity in the market to be explored by the design of a product. This product design attempts to solve a design problem. The design solution may be the development of a new product or developing a product that's already on the market. such as developing an existing invention for another purpose.Invention-push innovation happens when there is an advancement in intelligence. This can occur through research or it can occur when the product designer comes up with a new product design idea.

PRODUCT DESIGN EXPRESSION

Design expression comes from the combined effect of all elements in a product. Colour tone. shape and size should direct a person's thoughts towards buying the product.Therefore it is in the product designer's best interest to consider the audiences who are most likely to be the product's end consumers. Keeping in mind how consumers will perceive the product during the design process will direct towards the product's success in the market. However. even within a specific audience. it is challenging to cater to each possible personality within that group.

The solution to that is to create a product that. in its designed appearance and function. expresses a personality or tells a story. Products that carry such attributes are more likely to give off a stronger expression that will attract more consumers. On that note it is important to keep in mind that design expression does not only concern the appearance of a product. But also its function.

For example. as humans our appearance as well as our actions are subject to people's Judgement when they are making a first impression of us. People usually do not appreciate a rude person even if they are good looking. Similarly. a product can have an attractive appearance but if its function does not follow through it will most likely drop in regards to consumer interest. In this sense. designers are like communicators. they use the language of different elements in the product to express something.

PRODUCT DESIGN CONSIDERATIONS

Product design is not an easy task. The stakeholders involved all demand something different from the product designer and from the design process.

- The manufacturer is concerned with production cost; in the end. the manufacturer wants an economically produced product.
- The purchaser looks at price. appearance. and prestige value.
- The end user is concerned with usability and functionality of the final product.
- The maintenance and repair department focuses on how well the final product can be maintained: is the product easily reassembled. disassembled. diagnosed. and serviced?

Stakeholders' needs vary from one another and it is the product designer's job to incorporate those needs into their design.

TRENDS IN PRODUCT DESIGN

Product designers need to consider all of the details: the ways people use and abuse objects. faulty products. errors made in the design process. and the desirable ways in which people wish they could use objects. Many new designs will fail and many won't even make it to market. Some designs eventually become obsolete. The design process itself can be quite frustrating usually taking 5 or 6 tries to get the product design right. A product that fails in the marketplace the first time may be re-introduced to the market 2 more times. If it continues to fail. the product is then considered to be dead because the market believes it to be a failure. Most new products fail. even if it's a great idea. All types of product design are clearly linked to the economic health of manufacturing sectors.

Innovation provides much of the competitive impetus for the development of new products. with new technology often requiring a new design interpretation.

PRODUCT PRESENTATION

Non-store retailers have a real challenge when it comes to product presentation. If a product is largely standardised and its tangible features wholly understood, for example a CD or a book, then the presentation of the product is less problematic. If the benefits of a product are mainly functional rather than aesthetic, then again a photographic image and a wealth of product performance detail is likely to be sufficient.

However, for goods where the aesthetics and the sensory elements of the product are important, for example, fresh food, clothing and cosmetics, then a two-dimensional image may not adequately represent its benefits. Representing the product in use may help, for example showing clothing modelled or home furnishings in room settings, but problems concerning the match between customers' own self-image and that of the photographic image can arise. Some mail order companies are adopting magazine type layouts, to offer a more lifestyle approach to product presentation and to transfer media familiarity to shopping formats.

Internet sites are considered by Din (2000) to be visually lacking in stimulation, with too much written text and essentially offering the customer little more than the pages of a catalogue. The product offer is often presented on web sites in a list type of format, and can be organised according to retail categorisation rather than being consumer orientated.

For example, Tesco have used the term 'dry goods' on their Web site, which is a trade term for packaged goods like sugar and flour and not a term that would necessarily be understood by customers. However, unlike static pages, the internet does allow some moving imagery to be lodged in the Web site, such as a fashion show or a live product demonstration. In addition, the opportunity to deal directly with internet customers offers the possibility of tailoring the Web site image to individual customers. Home shopping retailer Land's End, for example, has experimented with displaying merchandise in a variety of ways, according to the demographics of the on-line customer.

Internet shopping via the mobile phone clearly offers market opportunities, given the popularity of the handset as a communication medium with its convenience, easy access and low cost. However, product presentation on a mobile handset is challenging: transmission bandwidth can make screen information slow to receive and limited in scope. Mobile shopping requires a handset that incorporates a mini-web browser (the Wireless Application Protocol or WAP), which is accessed via the phone keypad, and in itself presents difficulties with site navigation.

The web pages written for a PC (in hypertext mark-up language, HTML) may continue to be too complex for mobiles, which have to be written in wireless mark-up language (WML), and so compatibility and consistency between the two media becomes an issue.

However, in the spring of 2000, mobile phone retailer Carphone Warehouse was preparing to pre-install a shopping and information portal in every WAP phone sold, confident in the viability of the mobile as a means of trading information-based service products, such as travel and entertainment tickets. An indication of the potential for this method of shopping is the willingness of grocery retailer Waitrose to become involved in WapWorld, the mobile phone portal company founded by Sir Bob Geldof.

Interactive TV offers much more flexibility in product presentation, in particular through links from TV programming and interactive advertisements to web sites. The first interactive TV advertisement in the UK aired by Open, for example, was for 'Chicken Tonight' cooking sauces, which linked the advertisement to recipes, related product and vouchers. Although this is an interesting development, it raises a complex issue concerning the blurring of the distinction between programming and advertising and the freedom of viewers to 'surf away' from other advertisements and programming, which is an issue of concern for the Independent Television Commission.

THE SELLING ENVIRONMENT

Creating an atmosphere within the brick walls that represent the store is not easy, but creating an atmosphere on the flat and static page of a catalogue or on a Web site is even more difficult. The principles behind a store design and a non-store format design are, however, essentially the same. The layout must be logical and easy to browse around, products should be easy to locate within the sub-sections of the format, there should be links between complementary merchandise, and there should be consistency between the merchandise and the retailer's brand image.

For example, internet retailer BagsOfTime.com offers a wide range of impulse and emergency products, with a one-hour delivery promise within London. The Web site is easy to navigate, and despite a wide range of goods on offer, which includes shirts, sandwiches, toiletry items and a large selection of gifts, there is a consistent image across the site. When the on-line customer reaches the pay point, they are presented with a list of further impulse items, in a way completely comparable to the impulse items presented at a retail store checkout.

PRICING

Home shopping retailers have the potential to offer goods at competitive prices because they do not have the expense of running a portfolio of stores.

However, in traditional mail order retailing, much of this saving is offset by the need to finance the high stock holding level that is necessary to guarantee good service, as well as the funding of long customer credit terms.

In theory, an internet retailer can reduce these two costs: payment is usually taken at the point of product dispatch (if not earlier) and arrangements could be made for direct delivery from a supplier. However, skimping on infrastructure seems to be one of the commonest reasons for internet retailing failure, and so virtual retailing at very pared down prices becomes a risky business.

Nevertheless, price comparison is very easy to make between alternative internet offers, with shopping portals such as Yahoo Shopping and Shopsmart offering to undertake this process in an extremely convenient manner for the shopper, free of charge. It is difficult to justify a premium pricing policy without the benefit of the store environment as an arena for adding value to the shopping process. One further issue with home shopping media is pricing flexibility. Catalogues have a comparatively long lead-time, and price changes have to be communicated separately once the catalogue has been issued. Store retailing offers much more immediacy in terms of price changes, and discounted items can be visibly promoted in a much more effective way, for example by moving the goods to the front of the store.

Internet retailing, again in theory, offers price flexibility, as an immediate medium, but promoting offers is more complex, requiring flexibility in the web page design. One of the most complex issues regarding pricing is consistency when a retailer is using more than one shopping channel. Next, the UK clothing specialist, for example, does not discount products in its stores outside the strictly controlled end of season sales periods in order to protect the integrity of its catalogue, which offers a high proportion of products that are identical to the range found in the stores.

SERVICE

Both customer service and stock service are important when carrying out a retail transaction. Dealing with live people in real time is one aspect of store shopping that eventually may be its salvation. Information about the product, its applications and uses, demonstrations and trials are available on demand within a shop. Also the stock position is immediately apparent and if a product variant is not in stock, the position can be established immediately and/or alternatives offered.Therefore the store arena offers the opportunity as a stage for delivering an excellent standard of customer service. In addition, the quality of the service is relatively easy to measure in this environment. Poor quality service can be detected through visible signs of customer disatisfaction or via customer complaints. It is much more difficult and in many cases impossible to evaluate levels and frequencies of poor customer service with an impersonal medium. Customer service through non-store channels is not only different, but provides more opportunities for service implementation. A customer has to make a contact, for example by telephone or e-mail, in order to find out any information about the product that is not immediately apparent. The stock position may be communicated, but this information has to be accurate and therefore continually to be updated.

If the communication is via e-mail the customer has to wait for a response. Following transactions the customer waits for the product to be delivered whereas in store retailing the customer (usually) departs with the product. Again the delivery promise must be rigidly adhered to in order to prevent customer dissatisfaction. The infrastructure that supports the product communication is absolutely vital to the success of any non-store retailer.

One of the most frequent causes of internet shopping dissatisfaction ('cyber-shopping rage') is poor response times to enquiries and poor order fulfilment, and in such cases all the convenience advantage of the shopping format for the customer is lost. Some internet retailers who have become aware of these problems have taken steps to prevent customer loss by incorporating service orientation in the Web site design, for example by including e-mails contact points and 'phone-me' options.

Some sites also allow customers to access real-time stock availability and delivery information, so there is no need for them to wait for an order acknowledgement or delivery arrangement.

One feature of home shopping that is attractive to consumers is the ease with which goods can be returned. Catalogue retailers accept that around one-third of customer purchases will be returned, and in some departments, such as clothing and footwear, this proportion can be considerably higher, as the customer will order two or more sizes to try, only ever intending to purchase one. Reducing the amount of returns is a way of improving retail productivity, whether store or non-store based, but internet retailers have to accept that returns are a necessary evil of home shopping, and make adequate provision for this service, clearly setting out the returns policy for the customer.

One of many problems cited in the demise of on-line clothing retailer Boo.com was an indiscriminate returns policy and an inadequate infrastructure to deal with returned goods. Again, multi-channel retailers have to consider how flexible their various outlets will be in terms of offering a multi-channel service, as well as a multi-channel selling strategy. Nordstrom, the highly service orientated US department store, allows catalogue returns to be taken back to the store, but many retailers are not able to offer this flexibility.

CONVENIENCE

One of the most oft-quoted sayings in the retail industry is the following: 'There are three factors for success in retailing; these are location, location and location' (anon.). Perhaps the most pleasant and convenient location for a consumer is at home. Traffic jams, weather and crowds can be avoided, prices can quickly be compared between outlets, and heavy and bulky shopping is delivered rather than having to be carried and loaded.

In addition the consumer gains privacy and personal efficiency as they browse through non-store outlets that are geared to their individual needs. In a convenience orientated society, home shopping clearly purports to offer a set of tangible benefits. However, home shopping is only convenient if it delivers its promised service; if it does not, then it is highly inconvenient and risks high levels of customer frustration. The infrastructure behind the non-store outlet must therefore not only support the product offer but also the stated or assumed service offer.

PRODUCT DEVELOPMENT

Product development is the process of designing, creating, and marketing an idea or product. The product can either be one that is new to the marketplace or one that is new to your particular company, or, an existing product that has been improved. In many instances a product will be labelled new and improved when substantial changes have been made.

PRODUCT DEVELOPMENT PROCESS

All product development goes through a similar planning process. Although the process is a continuous one, it is crucial that companies stand back after each step and evaluate whether the new product is worth the investment to continue.

That evaluation should be based on a specific set of objective criteria, not someone's gut feeling. Even if the product is wonderful, if no one buys it the company will not make a profit. Brainstorming and developing a concept is the first step in product development. Once an idea is generated, it is important to determine whether there is a market for the product, what the target market is, and whether the idea will be profitable, as well as whether it is feasible from an engineering and financial standpoint.

Once the product is determined to be feasible, the idea or concept is tested on a small sample of customers within the target market to see what their reactions are.

DOCUMENTATION

Simply having an "idea"is worthless--you need to have proof of when you came up with the idea for your invention. Write down everything you can think of that relates to your invention, from what it is and how it works to how you'll make and market it. This is the first step to patenting your idea and keeping it from being stolen.

You've probably heard about the "poor man's patent"--writing your idea down and mailing it to yourself in a sealed envelope so you have dated proof of your invention's conception. This is unreliable and unlikely to hold up in court. Write your idea down in an inventor's journal and have it signed by a witness. This journal will become your bible throughout the patent process. An inventor's journal can by any bound notebook whose pages are numbered consecutively and can't be removed or reinserted.

You can find specially designed inventor's journals at bookstores or you can save money and purchase a generic notebook anywhere they're sold, such as the grocery store, office supply store, stationary store, etc.

RESEARCH

You will need to research your idea from a legal and business standpoint.

Before you file a patent, you should:

- *Complete an initial patent search*: Just because you haven't seen your invention doesn't mean it doesn't already exist. Before you hire a patent attorney or agent. You should also complete a non-patent "prior art"search. If you find any sort of artwork or design related to your idea, you cannot patent it-regardless of whether a prior patent has been filed.
- *Research your market*: Sure, your brother thinks your idea for a new lawn sprinkler is a great idea, but that doesn't mean your neighbour would buy one. More than 95 per cent of all patents never make money for the inventor. Before you invest too much time and money into patenting your invention, do some preliminary research of your target market. Is this something people will actually buy? Once you know there's a market, make sure your product can be manufactured and distributed at a low enough cost so that your retail price is reasonable. You can determine these costs by comparing those of similar products currently on the market. This will also help you size up your competition--which you will have, no matter how unique you think your invention is.

MAKING A PROTOTYPE

A prototype is a model of your invention that puts into practice all of the things you have written in your inventor's journal. This will demonstrate the design of your invention when you present it to potential lenders and licensees. Do not file a patent before you have made a prototype.

You will almost always discover a flaw in your original design or think of a new feature you would like to add. If you patent your idea before you work out these kinks, it will be too late to include them in the patent and you will risk losing the patent rights of the new design to someone else.

Here are some general rules of thumb when prototyping your invention:

- *Begin with a drawing*: Before you begin the prototyping phase, sketch out all of your ideas into your inventor's journal.
- Create a concept mockup out of any material that will allow you to create a 3-D model of your design.
- Once you're satisfied with the mockup, create a full-working model of your idea. There are many books and kits that can help you create prototypes. If your invention is something that will cost a lot of money or is unreasonable to prototype, consider using a computer-animated virtual prototype.

FILING A PATENT

Now that you have all of the kinks worked out of your design, it's finally time to file a patent. There are two main patents you will have to choose from: a utility patent or a design patent. You can write the patent and fill out the application yourself, but do not file it yourself until you have had a skilled patent professional look it over first.

If the invention is really valuable, someone will infringe on it. If you do not have a strong patent written by a patent attorney or agent, you will be pulling your hair out later when a competitor finds a loophole that allows them to copy your idea. It's best to get the legal help now to avoid any legal problems in the future. When searching for a patent attorney or agent, remember one thing: If you see them advertised on TV, run away!

Once you are far, far away, follow these steps to choosing the best patent professional:

- *Do your homework*: Have your inventor's journal, prototype and notes with you. This will save them time, and you money. This will also help persuade them to work with you.
- *Make sure they are registered with the U.S*: Patent and Trademark Office.
- *Ask them what their technical background is*: If your invention is electronic, find a patent professional who is also an electrical engineer.
- *Discuss fees*: Keep your focus on smaller patent firms. They are less expensive and will work more closely with you. Agree to the estimated total cost before hiring your patent professional.

MARKETING YOUR INVENTION

Now it's time to figure out how you're going to bring your product to market. Create a business plan: How will you get money? Where will you manufacture the product? How will you sell it? Now is a good time to decide if you will manufacture and sell the product yourself, or license it for sale through another company. When you license your product you will probably only receive two per cent to five per cent in royalty fees. This often scares away inventors who feel they deserve more. But consider the upside: You will not have the financial burden associated with maintaining a business. This could end up making you more money in the long run.

Following these five steps will ensure an easy road to patenting your invention. Just remember that an easy road doesn't necessarily mean a short one. From the time you conceive your idea to the time you see your product on the shelf is a very long process. Most inventions take years to come to fruition. Have patience and follow due diligence in your steps to patenting your invention and your years of hard work will finally pay off.

NEW PRODUCT DEVELOPMENT

The dynamics of markets, technology, and competition have brought changes to virtually every market sector and have made new product development one of the most powerful business activities. The monumental changes that constantly impact commerce have forced companies to innovate with increasing speed, efficiency, and quality. In turn, this has made new product development one of the most complex and difficult business functions. However, firms must innovate in order to survive. The power of innovation is revealed in numerous studies, which show that companies leading their industries attribute about half of their revenues to products developed in the most recent five years. By comparison, companies at the bottom of their industries achieve approximately one-tenth of their sales from new products.

A firm's new product development efforts are shaped by its size, as well as the nature of the industry in which it operates. New products may be defined as any product, service, or idea not currently made or marketed by a company, or which the consumer may perceive as new.

Many types of new products exist, from never-seen-before products like Apple's personal communicator, to repositioned standards like Sears' shift to Sears Brand Central. Various studies suggest that between 50 and 80 per cent of new products fail—the greater the rate of new product development, the higher the failure rate.

New Product News predicts that more than 36,000 new products will be brought to market in 2005. Although there are numerous reasons why new products fail, faulty management and planning are at the core of most failures. Therefore, managing the new product development process is a key to a healthy organization.

HISTORY

The history of product innovation can be divided into three stages, beginning with the product-oriented or technology-pushed stage. In the post-World War II era Americans were coming off wartime shortages and were in the mood to buy the many goods that manufacturers produced.

Engineers, who were more product-oriented than consumer oriented, designed new products that might or might not find places in consumers' hearts and minds.

This was a product-oriented process in which the market was considered the receptacle for products that emerged from the firm's research and development efforts. However, competition escalated and consumers became more skeptical and selective about the types of products they purchased. Marketers found it increasingly difficult to rely on persuasive sales techniques to move products. Retailers grew restless when these products did not move off shelves as quickly as planned. Companies had to know more about their target markets. What were the wants and needs of the people who were buying their products? How could their firm satisfy these wants and needs?

The second stage was marked by the emergence of the market as the driver of innovation. Instead of being technology-driven, new product development evolved into a market-led process in which new products emerged from well-researched customer needs. The new product development process was placed in the hands of marketers who knew consumers' wants and needs. Customer demand "pulled" the product through the development process. Modern new product development is a blending of these two orientations into a "dual-drive" approach to innovation. Companies recognize that innovation is a complex process that requires sound investment in research and development, as well as significant marketing expertise that focuses on satisfying consumers' wants and needs.

The rapid pace of change that engulfed businesses towards the end of the twentieth century put an even greater burden on companies to build adaptive capabilities into their organizations. Global competition means there are more competitors capable of world-class performance. This has made competition more intense, rigorous, and aggressive than ever before. Fragmenting and more sophisticated markets mean that consumers demand more from products in terms of quality, differentiation, and "meaningfulness."

New technologies have had two important outcomes in regards to innovation. First, new technologies are responsible for this new market sophistication in which consumers have more choices and are thus more demanding. Secondly, new technology has increased manufacturers' capabilities for rapid response to shifting market needs.

Finally, product life cycles have become more compressed as the skills required for developing new products increase in complexity. For example, consider the development of a new type of computer software. The expertise needed to develop the software from conception to commercialization might take years. The product's life cycle in such a competitive and turbulent environment might last only a few months. Therefore, companies have embraced the view that new products are transient, whereas the skills and expertise needed to develop these products are a much more persistent requirement for success. Instead of the mono-approach, in which technology or markets drive innovation, new product development now requires a convergence of technology, marketing, product design, engineering, and manufacturing capabilities. Speed, efficiency, and quality in product development are the challenges that new product development faces in today's intense competitive environment.

TYPES AND SOURCES OF NEW PRODUCTS

There are five categories of new products. New-to-the-world products or services are new inventions like in-line skates and health maintenance organizations. New category entries, such as sport utility vehicles, are products or services that are new to a firm. Additions to product lines add products or services to a firm's current markets. For example, when a powder laundry detergent offers a liquid version it is considered a line extension. Product improvements are another type of new product and are common to every product category. Repositionings target products to new markets or for new uses. Firms can obtain new products internally or externally. External sourcing means the company acquires the product or service, or obtains the rights to market the product or service, from another organization. Internal development means the firm develops the new product itself. This is riskier than external development because the company bears all of the costs associated with new product development and implementation. Collaborations, which include strategic partnerships, strategic alliances, joint ventures, and licensing agreements, occur when two or more firms work together on developing new products.

NEW PRODUCT DEVELOPMENT PROCESS

Historically, the new product development process has been conceived in discreet terms with a beginning and an end. Different companies and different industries may alter this seven-step process for different products, or the steps themselves may become blurred as companies become engaged in several stages at the same time. The process begins with idea generation. For every successful new product, many new product ideas are conceived and discarded. Therefore, companies usually generate a large number of ideas from which successful new products emerge.

Idea screening, the second step, considers all new product ideas in the idea pool and eliminates ones that are perceived to be the least likely to succeed. Not only should the firm's manufacturing, technology, and marketing capabilities be evaluated at this stage, but also how the new idea fits with the company's vision and strategic objectives. The third stage, concept development and testing, requires formal evaluations of the product concept by consumers, usually through some form of marketing research. New product ideas with low concept test scores are discarded or revised. While the Internet is making it easier to gather consumer data, there are limitations. As people get deluged with an increasing number of surveys and solicitations, it is possible that they will grow tired of helping marketers.

The business analysis stage is next. At this point the new product idea is analysed for its marketability and costs. After passing the first three stages an idea may be discarded once marketing and manufacturing costs are analysed, due to limited potential for profitability or commercial success. Throughout these four stages, the new idea has remained on document with a relatively small investment required.

The fifth stage, prototype development, is the first stage where new product costs begin to escalate. Because of this, many companies have placed greater emphasis on the first four stages and reduced the proportion of new products that reach the prototype stage from about 50 per cent to around 20 per cent. At this stage the concept is converted into an actual product. A customer value perspective during this phase means the product is designed to satisfy the needs expressed by consumers. Firms may use quality function deployment as they develop the prototype. QFD links specific consumer requirements such as versatility, durability, and low maintenance with specific product characteristics. The customer value perspective requires the new product to satisfy customer needs and meet desired quality levels at specified production costs.Test marketing tests the prototype and marketing strategy in simulated or actual market situations. Because of the expense and risks associated with actual test markets, marketers use them with caution. Products that test poorly are pulled back and reconceptualized or discarded.

Commercialization, the final stage, is when the product is introduced full scale. The level of investment and risk are highest at this stage. Consumer adoption rates, timing decisions for introduction, and coordinating efforts with production, distribution, and marketing should be considered.

FACTORS INFLUENCING NEW PRODUCT DEVELOPMENT

The seven-step process assumes a definite beginning and end. However, studies suggest that what goes on before and after new products are introduced is as important as the process itself. Organizational structure, leadership, and team building influence the speed and efficiency with which new products are introduced. Structure influences efficiency, autonomy, and coordination. New product innovation requires structure that optimizes direction and guidance. Structure that facilitates internal information exchange, decision making, and materials flow is essential. A "fast-cycle" structure allows more time for planning and implementing activities to gain competitive advantage. This type of structure also cuts costs because production materials and information collect less overhead and do not accumulate as work-in-process inventory. Autonomy refers to the amount of decision making allowed at lower levels of management. The coordination of the engineering, product design, manufacturing, and marketing functions in the new product development process is vital.

Leadership influences strategy, culture, and the firm's overall ability to undertake new product development. Top management can demonstrate involvement in the development process by providing career advancement for entrepreneurial skills and encouraging broad employee participation. Clarity and vision are crucial to ensuring that new product ideas are good strategic fits for the company. The degree to which leadership allows trial and error and promotes individual initiative positively influences the development of new products. This acceptance of risk and support for an entrepreneurial spirit within the organization are crucial in order for innovation to flourish. New products emerge in a variety of ways and their development does not always proceed in rational and consistent manners.

It is necessary for leadership to view the process as iterative and dynamic, and to foster adaptation and flexibility. Management flexibility and responsiveness to change also are needed. This type of leadership is particularly important to the project manager who must coordinate and integrate the various parts of the new product development process so that a coherent system emerges that produces a product with compelling value. Initiative encourages creativity and problem-solving skills. Teams provide mechanisms for breaking down functional biases created by a strict adherence to structure. The amount of interdepartmental conflict in the organization, the social cohesion among team members, and the frequency and directionality of interdepartmental communication influence team building. Through shared understanding of the objectives and purposes of the project, as well as the tasks required in the development process, teams can shape the project and influence how work gets done in the organization.

IMPROVING SPEED, EFFICIENCY, AND QUALITY

New products often fail because of unanticipated market shifts that result in missed opportunities and misused channels of distribution. Failures also occur because companies miscalculate their own technological strengths or the product's technological challenges. These potential problems often crop up in the latter stages and result in delays, redesigns, or poor quality products.

Companies are constantly seeking ways to avoid these pitfalls. One solution is new product development maps that chart the evolution of a company's product lines. This historical perspective helps the firm to identify and analyse functional capabilities in a systematic, repetitive fashion that allows for the development of linkages and the identification of resources for new endeavours. These maps can direct the firm to new market opportunities and point out technological challenges.

Aggregate plans for projects offer another solution. Rather than viewing each new product development project individually, they consider all of the new product development projects under consideration by the firm. This is particularly important in firms with hundreds of new product development projects going on at the same time. Projects are categorized according to resources required and contribution to the firm's bottom line.

Aggregate project plans enable management to improve the management of new product development by providing greater control over resource allocation and utilization. These plans help to point out where capabilities need to be improved, how sequencing projects may help, and how projects fit with the firm's development strategies. Return maps graphically represent the contributions of all team members to product success in terms of time and money. Their focus is on the point at which product sales generate sufficient profit so that the firm's initial investment in development is returned. Return maps show team members the time and money needed to complete their tasks in the development process so that they may estimate and re-estimate their investment in the process. In doing this return maps show the impact of their actions on the project's overall success.

Another way to improve the speed and efficiency with which new products are introduced is to involve purchasing in the development process. When purchasing expertise is introduced into the development project team, quality may increase, time to market entry may decrease, investment in inventory may diminish, and costs may significantly decrease.

Technology continues to change and create new opportunities and threats. Customer requirements and expectations continue to shift and create new demands. Old channels of distribution are becoming obsolete and new channels are opening new opportunities. Some competitors are falling by the wayside while others are surging to the forefront by making new and unexpected moves to gain advantage. The very structure of industry is changing. A key to success in this tumultuous environment will continue to be the ability to sustain a competitive advantage through innovation. However, speed, efficiency, and quality in product development will be paramount. Building capabilities in all aspects of product creation and implementation, overcoming uncertainty and facilitating decision-making, ensuring these innovations are strategically linked to the firm's vision, and doing this on a continuous basis is the challenge of new product development in the next century.

PRODUCT AND MARKETING MIX DEVELOPMENT

Ideas passing through business analysis are given serious consideration for development. Companies direct their research and development teams to construct an initial design or prototype of the idea. Marketers also begin to construct a marketing plan for the product. Once the prototype is ready the marketer seeks customer input. However, unlike the concept testing stage where customers were only exposed to the idea, in this step the customer gets to experience the real product as well as other aspects of the marketing mix, such as advertising, pricing, and distribution options (*e.g.*, retail store, direct from company, etc.). Favorable customer reaction helps solidify the marketer's decision to introduce the product and also provides other valuable information such as estimated purchase rates and understanding how the product will be used by the customer. Reaction that is less favorable may suggest the need for adjustments to elements of the marketing mix. Once these are made the marketer may again have the customer test the product. In addition to gaining customer feedback, this step is used to gauge the feasibility of large-scale, cost effective production for manufactured products.

Market Testing

Products surviving to Step 6 are ready to be tested as real products. In some cases the marketer accepts what was learned from concept testing and skips over market testing to launch the idea as a fully marketed product. But other companies may seek more input from a larger group before moving to commercialization. The most common type of market testing makes the product available to a selective small segment of the target market (*e.g.*, one city), which is exposed to the full marketing effort as they would be to any product they could purchase. In some cases, especially with consumer products sold at retail stores, the marketer must work hard to get the product into the test market by convincing distributors to agree to purchase and place the product on their store shelves. In more controlled test markets distributors may be paid a fee if they agree to place the product on their shelves to allow for testing.

Another form of market testing found with consumer products is even more controlled with customers recruited to a "laboratory" store where they are given shopping instructions. Product interest can then be measured based on customer's shopping response.

Finally, there are several high-tech approaches to market testing including virtual reality and computer simulations. With virtual reality testing customers are exposed to a computer-projected environment, such as a store, and are asked to locate and select products. With computer simulations customers may not be directly involved at all. Instead certain variables are entered into a sophisticated computer programme and estimates of a target market's response are calculated.

Commercialization

If market testing displays promising results the product is ready to be introduced to a wider market. Some firms introduce or roll-out the product in waves with parts of the market receiving the product on different schedules.

This allows the company to ramp up production in a more controlled way and to fine tune the marketing mix as the product is distributed to new areas.

MANAGING EXISTING PRODUCTS

Marketing strategies developed for initial product introduction almost certainly need to be revised as the product settles into the market. While commercialization may be the last step in the new product development process it is just the beginning of managing the product. Adjusting the product's marketing strategy is required for many reasons including:

- Changing customer tastes
- Domestic and foreign competitors
- Economic conditions
- Technological advances

To stay on top of all possible threats the marketer must monitor all aspects of the marketing mix and make changes as needed. Such efforts require the marketer to develop and refine the product's marketing plan on a regular basis. The marketing strategies change as a product moves through time leading to the concept called the Product Life Cycle (PLC). We will see that marketers make numerous revisions to their strategy as product move through different stage of the PLC.

DEVELOPING NEW PRODUCTS

By its nature marketing requires new ideas. Unlike some organizational functions, where basic processes follow a fairly consistent routine (*e.g.*, accounting), successful marketers are constantly making adjustments to their marketing efforts. New ideas are essential for responding to changing demand by the target market and by pressure exerted by competitors. These changes are manifested in decisions in all marketing areas including the development of new products.

In addition to being responsive to changing customer tastes and competitive forces, there are many other reasons why new product development is vital. These include:

- Many new products earn higher profits than older products. This is often the case for products considered innovative or unique which, for a period of time, may enjoy success and initially face little or no competition.
- New products can help reposition the company in customer's minds. For instance, a company that traditionally sold low priced products with few features may shift customers' perceptions about the company by introducing products with more features and slightly higher pricing.
- Fierce global competition and technological developments make it much easier for competitors to learn about products and replicate

them. To stay ahead of competitors marketers must innovate and often create and introduce new products on a consistent schedule.

- Companies with limited depth in a product line may miss out on more sales unless they can add new products to fill out the line.
- Some firms market seasonal products that garner their highest sales during a certain time of the year or sell cyclical products whose sales fluctuate depending on economic or market factors. Expanding the firm's product mix into new areas may help offset these fluctuations. For manufacturing firms an additional benefit is realized as new products utilize existing production capacity that is under-used when seasonal or cyclical products are not being produced.

CATEGORIES OF NEW PRODUCTS

New products can fall into one of several categories. These categories are defined by the type of market the product is entering (*i.e.*, newly created, existing but not previously targeted, existing and targeted) and the level of product innovation (*i.e.*, radically new, new, upgrade).

- *Creates New Market with Radically New Product or Product Line:* This category is represented by new breakthrough products that are so revolutionary they create an entirely new market. Recent examples include digital music players, such as Apple's iPod, that have spawned new delivery methods (downloadable music) and new media (podcasting). Highly innovative products are rare so very few new products fall into this category.
- *Enters Existing But Not Previously Targeted Market with New-Product or Product Line*: In this category a marketer introduces a new product item or product line to an existing market which they did not previously target. Often these products are similar to competitors' products already available in the market but with some level of difference (*e.g.*, different features, lower price, etc.). Microsoft's entry into the video gaming system market with their Xbox is an example.
- *Stays in Existing and Previously Targeted Market by Enhancing Existing Product or Product Line*: Under this development category the marketer attempts to improve its current position in the market by either improving or upgrading existing products or by extending a product line by adding new products. This type of new product is seen in our earlier example of Procter and Gamble's Tide product line which contains many product variations of the basic Tide product.

HOW NEW PRODUCTS ARE OBTAINED

Marketers have several options for obtaining new products. First, products can be developed within an organization's own research operations. For some companies, such as service firms, this may simply mean the marketer designs new service options to sell to target markets. For instance, a marketer for a mortgage company may design new mortgage packages that offer borrowers different rates or payment options. At the other extreme companies may support an extensive research and development effort where engineers, scientists or others are engaged in new product discovery. A second way to obtain products is to acquire them from external sources. This can occur in several ways including:

- Purchase the Product - With this option a marketer purchases the product outright from another firm that currently owns the product. The advantage is that the product is already developed, which reduces the purchasing company's time and cost of trying to develop it themselves. On the negative side the purchase cost may be high.
- License the Product – Under this option the marketer negotiates with the owner of the product for the rights to market the product. This may be a particularly attractive option for companies who have to fill a product need quickly (*e.g.*, give a product line more depth) or it may be used as a temporary source of products while the marketer's company is developing its own product. On the negative side the arrangement may have a limited time frame at which point the licensor may decide to end the relationship leaving the marketer without a source for the product.
- Purchase Another Firm - Instead of purchasing another company's products marketers may find it easier to just purchase the whole company selling the products. One key advantage to this is that the acquisition often includes the people and resources that developed the product which may be a key consideration if the acquiring company wants to continue to develop the acquired products.

NEW PRODUCT DEVELOPMENT PROCESS

Because introducing new products on a consistent basis is important to the future success of many organizations, marketers in charge of product decisions often follow set procedures for bringing products to market. In the scientific area that may mean the establishment of ongoing laboratory research Programmes for discovering new products (*e.g.*, medicines) while less scientific companies may pull together resources for product development on a less structured timetable.

We present a 7-step process comprising the key elements of new product development. While some companies may not follow a deliberate step-by-step approach, the steps are useful in showing the information input and decision making that must be done in order to successfully develop new products. The process also shows the importance market research plays in developing products. We should note that while the 7-step process works for most industries, it is less effective in developing radically new products. The main reason lies in the inability of the target market to provide sufficient feedback on advanced product concepts since they often find it difficult to understand radically different ideas. So while many of these steps are used to research breakthrough ideas, the marketer should exercise caution when interpreting the results.

Idea Generation

The first step of new product development requires gathering ideas to be evaluated as potential product options. For many companies idea generation is an ongoing process with contributions from inside and outside the organization. Many market research techniques are used to encourage ideas including: running focus groups with consumers, channel members, and the company's sales force; encouraging customer comments and suggestions via toll-free telephone numbers and Web site forms; and gaining insight on competitive product developments through secondary data sources.

One important research technique used to generate ideas is brainstorming where open-minded, creative thinkers from inside and outside the company gather and share ideas. The dynamic nature of group members floating ideas, where one idea often sparks another idea, can yield a wide range of possible products that can be further pursued.

Screening

In Step 2 the ideas generated in Step 1 are critically evaluated by company personnel to isolate the most attractive options. Depending on the number of ideas, screening may be done in rounds with the first round involving company executives judging the feasibility of ideas while successive rounds may utilize more advanced research techniques. As the ideas are whittled down to a few attractive options, rough estimates are made of an idea's potential in terms of sales, production costs, profit potential, and competitors' response if the product is introduced. Acceptable ideas move on to the next step.

Concept Development and Testing

With a few ideas in hand the marketer now attempts to obtain initial feedback from customers, distributors and its own employees. Generally, focus groups are convened where the ideas are presented to a group, often in the form of concept board presentations (*i.e.*, storyboards) and not in actual working form. For instance, customers may be shown a concept board displaying drawings of a product idea or even an advertisement featuring the product. In some cases focus groups are exposed to a mock-up of the ideas, which is a physical but generally non-functional version of product idea. During focus groups with customers the marketer seeks information that may include: likes and dislike of the concept; level of interest in purchasing the product; frequency of purchase (used to help forecast demand); and price points to determine how much customers are willing to spend to acquire the product.

Business Analysis

At this point in the new product development process the marketer has reduced a potentially large number of ideas down to one or two options. Now in Step 4 the process becomes very dependent on market research as efforts are made to analyse the viability of the product ideas. (Note, in many cases the product has not been produced and still remains only an idea.) The key objective at this stage is to obtain useful forecasts of market size (*e.g.*, overall demand), operational costs (*e.g.*, production costs) and financial projections (*e.g.*, sales and profits).

Additionally, the organization must determine if the product will fit within the company's overall mission and strategy. Much effort is directed at both internal research, such as discussions with production and purchasing personnel, and external marketing research, such as customer and distributor surveys, secondary research, and competitor analysis.

PRODUCTION PLANNING AND EXECUTION AND QUALITY CONTROL

Since knowledge is considered to be the basis of a dynamically managed factory, it behooves manufacturing management to have a knowledge management system that not only assists in production planning and execution on the production floor but also aids in effective quality control (*i.e.*, TQM). A manufacturing knowledge base generally consists of various elements, such as rules, heuristics, principles, strategies, standards, facts, and procedures as well as fuzzy knowledge and modeling knowledge. Within a KMS environment, a well-designed manufacturing knowledge base assists managers and their staffs in knowledge acquisition, knowledge inference, and knowledge explanation.

In addition, the design should utilize a user-friently interface for knowledge retrieval, knowledge validation, and knowledge updating. Such is the approach taken in this section on production planning and execution and quality control. Since information is the backbone of manufacturing knowledge, the focus will be on information that is supplemented by knowledge where deemed necessary.

The production planning and execution department for a typical manufacturing oriented company is responsible for all physical movements between manufacturing departments and within their respective work centers at the plant level. This important department coordinates all activities concerning a production order from its initial recording, through inventory layup and manufacturing, to getting the finished goods ready for shipment to customers (*i.e.*, direct shipments) or to company warehouses for shipment subsequently to customers. Production planning and execution relies heavily on the plant's database and its communications with all manufacturing work centers. Although daily manufacturing activities are the responsibility of the production planning and execution department, they need to be analyzed periodically by manufacturing managers for efficiency and effectiveness using OLAP analysis. Similarly, there may be a need to discover and track manufacturing problems. In this manner, manufacturing managers and their staffs can be assured that short-range manufacturing plans are being implemented on a current basis as mandated.

Before looking at planned and actual manufacturing activities, manufacturing partnerships and their relationship with production planning and execution are examined. Determining the appropriate production planning and execution technique for current operations on a daily as well as monthly basis is also discussed. Information furnished to manufacturing management and their staffs over time can provide knowledge to discover and track quality problems.

MANUFACTURING PARTNERSHIPS AND THEIR TIE-IN WITH PRODUCTION PLANNING

Not too long ago, many large manufacturers, especially in Japan, formed *keiretsu*, or company partnerships, by grouping the subcontractors who supply them with parts. The result is a production system, distributed among many companies, that has helped manufacturers strengthen their global competitiveness. More recently, however, the subcontracting system has started changing to reflect the structural sophistication in Japanese industries.

Automakers, electric machinery manufacturers, and other large Japanese firms that are suffering from sagging demand and decreasing earnings are increasingly pressuring subcontractors to cut production costs. If they do not comply, they will be excluded from the *keiretsu*. In this new and realistic business environment, many subcontractors are looking for business partners outside their company groups.

This presents a good opportunity for subcontractors to become independent. The *keiretsu* system is evolving from the existing pyramid-type coalition to horizontal or network-type coalitions. In the process, an increasing number of subcontractors are seeking to improve their technology and production to satisfy key manufacturers.

Some are pursuing new business partners outside their company groups while others aim to become independent specialists in processing or manufacturing. In the United States, car manufacturers (as noted previously) are heavily involved in sophisticated supply chain management systems. These systems currently include a focus on various cost-cutting programmes, including reduction of work hours and model lines, extension of model-change cycles, and increased use of common parts.

Determine the Appropriate Production Planning and Execution Technique

Once appropriate manufacturing partnerships have been established, there is a need to determine the appropriate planning and execution technique for manufacturing operations. Currently, the focus is on client/server manufacturing systems. Also noted previously, a comprehensive approach to manufacturing that utilizes this system is *enterprise resource planning* (ERP).

ERP is real-time manufacturing software that incorporates the entire supply chain from sales and order processing to production, inventory, and distribution. Related to the ERP approach is a *manufacturing execution system* (MES) that utilizes software to manage shop-floor activities.

Essentially, a manufacturing execution system represents the CIM concept at the lower levels of the manufacturing process. It is a set of software applications that can easily integrate into everyday legacy systems and reside on any platform, though the current trend is for PC-based client/server networks. It allows a manufacturer to produce products more effectively on the factory floor by making production visible and information accessible to factory-floor personnel. It is used by operators, setup and tool-room personnel, and supervisors. An MES can provide the following information:

- Resource scheduling/allocation and status
- Operations/detailed scheduling
- Dispatch production units
- Document control
- Data collection/acquisition
- Labour management
- Quality management
- Performance analysis
- Process management
- Product tracking
- Maintenance management

Together these systems allow improved production beyond what is possible with a typical manufacturing system, like MRP-II. MRP-II systems tend to focus on accounting transactions, at best keeping score for the factory floor, but not helping to dispatch production, allocate resources, pace, and otherwise manage production.

In contrast, an MES is the data collection and dissemination of production/process information that makes it truly the new E-mail of the factory floor. It includes such functionalities as resource use, scheduling, quality management, and engineering-change notices. Typically, an MES requires a lot of data collection points that give users a real-time view of manufacturing. A recent survey of manufacturers who have used MES over the past five years confirms that the technology can be applied successfully to a broad range of shop-floor functions. Respondents cited reduced manufacturing cycle time as a very important MES benefit. The average reduction in production cycle time of surveyed respondents was 45 per cent.

Typically, an integral part of the production planning and execution technique is *just-in-time* (JIT) *inventory*, which is based on the elimination of wasteful or non-value-added activity within a company. Its primary goal is to reduce inventory as close to zero as possible and to reduce lead time via reduced setup and reduced lot sizes. While inventory has always been considered an asset in the past, today inventory is a liability. The more excess inventory a company has, the more the root problems that have caused a company to hold excess inventory lie hidden. Manufacturing flexibility is a key aspect of JIT, where quick response to a customer's needs means producing lot sizes when needed. Another issue addresses the reduction in the number of suppliers with which a company has to deal. Rather than having multiple product sources, one or two are now sufficient.

Daily and Periodic Production Planning and Execution

Typically, a manufacturing company's products can be produced upon receipt of customers' orders, in anticipation of demand, or in some combination of the two. If goods are being produced to order, the usual arrangement is to have the production planning and execution department initiate action on the order via its data communications network, which is then distributed on-line to stock control, shipping, and accounting departments.

However, for many companies, products are produced in anticipation of demand. Then the focus is on planning manufacturing activities on a monthly basis at the corporate level, then controlling on a daily basis using one of the current MES software packages at the manufacturing plant(s).

The procedure for determining next-period's sales forecasts (one month hence) after adjusting for finished goods on order and on hand is the starting point, as shown in Figure 8-3, for on-line production planning and execution. Because finished goods production requirements for the *next month* provide the necessary input for the manufacturing function, linear programming is utilized to determine the quantity of each product that will be produced in each of the manufacturing plants. After next-period production schedules have been computed by plant, the next phase is "exploding" bills of materials.

The materials planning-by-periods programme multiplies the quantity needed of each component times the number of final products that must be manufactured. Also, it places the component requirements in the appropriate planning period, because some parts will be needed before others. In this manner, purchased parts and raw materials are placed on a just-in-time basis for production needs.

The output for the materials requirements by future-planning periods in Figure 8-3 can take two paths. The *first* one is the purchasing of raw materials and parts from outside vendors, and the *second* one is the manufacturing of parts within the plants. The outside raw materials provide the basic inputs for manufacturing specific parts used in the assembly of the finished product. Likewise, outside purchased parts are used in the assembly of the final product.

Before materials are manufactured or purchased, it is necessary to determine on line if present inventories and materials on order are capable of meeting the company's needs for future planning periods. At this point, it is important to note that perpetual inventories stored on line have been adjusted to reflect physical counts in order to produce accurate output for the materials availability and EOQ (economic ordering quantity) programme. In this manner, the planned requirements for purchased and manufacturing parts can reflect actual conditions.

The integrated and continuous operating mode does not stop here. Based upon established monthly production quotas that have been translated into planned daily requirements, the MES software provides the means for scheduling (*i.e.*, executing) production orders on line through the manufacturing work centers on a *daily* basis. Additionally, other operational programmes are available to record and execute daily activities (including attendance, payroll, work-in-process, etc.).

The output of these programmes provides operations evaluation reports on manufacturing activities. In addition, the output can be analyzed in more detail on a daily basis using OLAP analysis. In turn, these types of analyses can be extended over a longer period of time to develop knowledge about what is actually going on in the company's manufacturing operations—good, bad, or indifferent.

In order to smooth production for each working day, a daily computerized scheduler is employed at each plant. Before the start of each working day (the programme is actually run at the end of the prior day shift and reviewed by the plant's management), the scheduler considers where jobs are backed up or behind schedule and where production bottlenecks are currently occurring. Based on these basic inputs, the scheduler simulates the activities of the plant for the coming day and determines what will happen as the day begins, thereby alerting the plant manager and supervisors to critical areas that need attention. Because all data affecting manufacturing activities are entered as they occur, the scheduler feeds back information in sufficient time to execute upcoming manufacturing operations. This daily computerized scheduler also allows the production planning and execution department to make adjustments, if deemed necessary, to accommodate last-minute changes that may not have been entered as yet on the plant database.

In summary, periodic (*i.e.*, monthly) programmes do not operate individually but are integrated with daily on-line operations, as shown in Figure 8-3. Sales forecasts (as discussed in the previous chapter) serve as input for finished goods product requirements which, in turn, constitute input for the next month's production schedule for each plant. In a similar manner, this monthly output is input for "exploding" bills of materials, forming the basis for materials requirements by future planning periods.

This monthly information is then employed for manufacturing orders within the company's plants and for placing orders with outside suppliers on a just-in-time basis. This input-output approach using the appropriate software at the corporate level and the plant level provides a basis for day-to-day scheduling and dispatching of various manufacturing operations.

The manufacturing execution system software, which is assisted by the daily scheduler, provides the means for managing the ongoing shop-floor activities of the plants on a continuous basis. Using Knowledge to Discover and Track Quality Problems

Although the MES software and the daily scheduler are quite capable of keeping a typical company's operations under control on a daily basis, there is a need to go a step further to discover and track quality problems and resolve them. For example, knowledge sharing is one of the major keys to an effective quality partnership between General Motors and its main union, the United Automobile Workers (UAW). This jointly developed GM-UAW Quality Network has been a vital tool in transferring knowledge throughout the giant automaker's far-flung operations.

Communication has been an essential tool of the network both in terms of transferring best practices from one plant to another and in building an atmosphere of trust in which collaboration and knowledge sharing can happen. For example, at the Delphi Energy and Engine Management Systems (a division of GM's Delphi Automotive Systems unit), the plant manager spends every Friday discussing quality concerns with members of the plant's 80-plus self-empowered work teams. The outcome of these meetings is that there is an invaluable avenue for learning and knowledge transfer across the enterprise.

A typical situation centers around quality problems for such a manufacturer. The goal of the analysis is to look through a database of assembly-line products in order to discover and track quality problems. Basically, quality problems are isolated and can be classified on the basis of two critical factors. The classification tree is then grown to a depth of three levels in order to illustrate that while a factor may not be relevant in predicting quality problems at the "general" (first level) of the tree, it becomes important when considered in the context of other factors.

The example below uses a KnowledgeSEEKER analysis of engineering quality control data. In this analysis, the "exception code" field was examined. All database records were examined and edited, producing a "clean" data set of 2,001 records. Installation date and removal date were recorded and duration of service was computed.

The specific goal of the analysis was to explain an "overheating" exception code. Thus, the question was: "What characteristics in the data set tend to predict that the unit will be removed because of overheating?" If the factors that affect overheating can be identified, then potentially the production process can be improved to lower the incidence of overheating problems. Alternatively, if the circumstances that lead to overheating can be isolated, then increased quality control can be applied to the areas that characterize these circumstances. Because time is of essence in industrial processes, the sooner a problem can be fixed the less expensive the remedy. And since it is expensive to apply high levels of vigilance across all processes, any information that points to problem areas sooner, rather than later, can lead to major cost savings (for both vigilance and repair).

The data set exception code was mapped into two values: "Overheat" and "Other." This will allow the focus to be on overheating as a particular problem (separate from all the particular exception codes that are recorded by the manufacturing process). The first level of the decision tree shows that, overall, there were 1,037 "Overheat" exception codes in the data set.

Although a number of factors turned out to be significant predictors of overheating, the field "Install duration" produced the most dramatic effect. The likelihood of an "overheat" failure increases dramatically when the length of service is more than two days. At two days only 35.6 per cent of the units produce an "overheat" exception condition. For units that have been in service longer than 12 days, the "overheat" exceptions constitute 80.9 per cent of the cases.

When the second level of the classification tree is grown as shown in Figure, "Series number" is introduced as an important classifier.

This is true for both the extreme left (short install duration) node and the extreme right (long duration) node. Although different series numbers are susceptible to an overheating exception in these two short and long duration extremes, it is useful to look at the "2A" and "2B" series.

In the long duration installations, these two series numbers have the highest incidence of overheating exceptions, 92.3 per cent. It should be noted that these two series numbers are also members of the node that characterize high numbers of overheating exceptions in the low duration node as well. Here codes "2A" and "2B" are grouped in with codes that produce an overheating exception rate of 53.6 per cent.

The analysis in Figure 8-4(c) can continue to a third-level depth. As can be seen in the lower left-hand side of the classification tree, other factors in addition to service duration and series can be used to explain the presence of overheating exceptions in the data—sometimes (as shown here) in unusual ways. "Installation date" affects the presence of overheating exceptions for the lowest service duration group (less than two days) as follows: If the unit was installed in the first 19 days of the month, then the chances of it being an overheating exception increase from 35.6 per cent to 58.7 per cent (first-level node results compared to the third-level node results).

This applies to units with a series number of 1A, 1B, 2A, or 2B. This represents an increase of almost 25 per cent and places these units in the same group as units that have been in service for two to five days (the second node at the first level of the tree shown above). It raises the question of why overheating exceptions should be higher in the first 19 days of the month, the exception rate for the installation dates 20th to 31st was less: 44.6 per cent.

A further examination of the procedures involved in short-duration series 1B, 2A, 2B, and 1A units would generally shed light on this question. Thus, the company has the capability to discover important causes of overheating exceptions. In turn, this knowledge is of paramount importance for suggesting appropriate remedial action.

5

Analysis Cost

Cost management is the process by which companies control and plan the costs of doing business. Individual projects should have customised cost management plans, and companies as a whole also integrate cost management into their overall business model. There is no single accepted definition for this term, because it has such broad applications and possible strategies.

When properly implemented, cost management will translate into reduced costs of production for products and services, as well as increased value being delivered to the customer. For a company's management to be effective overall, cost management must be an integral feature of it. It is easiest to understand this concept if it is explained in the context of a single project.

For instance, before a project is started, the anticipated costs should be identified and measured. These expenses should then be approved before any purchasing occurs. During the process of completing a project, all incurred costs should be noted and kept in a record of some kind, to help ensure that the costs are controlled and kept in line with initial expectations, to the extent that this is possible.

Taking this approach to cost management will help a company determine whether they accurately estimated expenses at first, and will help them more closely predict expenses in the future. Any overspending can also be monitored in this way, and either eliminated in future projects or specifically approved if the expense was necessary. Cost management cannot be used in isolation; projects must be organised and tailored with this strategy in mind. Starting a project with cost management in mind will help to avoid certain pitfalls that may be present otherwise.

If the objectives of the project are not clearly defined at first, or are changed during the course of the project, cost over-runs will be more likely. If costs are not fully researched before the project, they may be underestimated, thereby inflating the expectation of the project's success unrealistically. Construction projects are subject to their own particular challenges; these can include constraints in the form of laws and regulations that must be planned around. If the project is completely and clearly defined, this will facilitate effective management of the costs it will incur. Effective cost management strategies will help a team deliver a finished project within the allocated budget, while also making it as valuable as possible to the company. There is always the possibility of unexpected costs, but preparation in the form of cost management will likely make them much easier to deal with when they occur.

COST FUNCTION

The econometrical model which is used to analyse costs is a model in which explanatory variable represents total costs and endogenous variables represent factors that influence their level. Production quantity is the most important factor which determines the level of total costs.

TOTAL COST

In economics, and cost accounting, total cost describes the total economic cost of production and is made up of variable costs, which vary according to the quantity of a good produced and include inputs such as labour and raw materials, plus fixed costs, which are independent of the quantity of a good produced and include inputs that cannot be varied in the short term, such as buildings and machinery. Total cost in economics includes the total opportunity cost of each factor of production in addition to fixed and variable costs.

The rate at which total cost changes as the amount produced changes is called marginal cost. This is also known as the marginal unit variable cost. If one assumes that the unit variable cost is constant, as in cost-volume-profit analysis developed and used in cost accounting by the accountants, then total cost is linear in volume, and given by: total cost = fixed costs + unit variable cost * amount.

FIXED COST

In economics, fixed costs are business expenses that are not dependent on the activities of the business They tend to be time-related, such as salaries or rents being paid per month. This is in contrast to variable costs, which are volume-related. In management accounting, fixed costs are defined as expenses that do not change in proportion to the activity of a business, within the relevant period. For example, a retailer must pay rent and utility bills irrespective of sales. Along with variable costs, fixed costs make up one of the two components of total cost. In the most simple production function, total cost is equal to fixed costs plus variable costs.

AREAS OF CONFUSION

Fixed costs should not be confused with sunk costs. From a pure economics perspective, fixed costs may not be fixed in the sense of invariate; they may change but are fixed in relation to the quantity of production for the relevant period. For example, a company may have unexpected and unpredictable expenses unrelated to production. On the other hand, production output may vary sharply without changing the fixed costs.

Strictly speaking, there is not absolute fixed cost in long-run if the relevant range is long enough. Investments in facilities, equipment, and the basic organisation that can't be significantly reduced even for short periods of time without making fundamental changes are referred to as committed fixed costs. Discretionary fixed costs usually arise from annual decisions by management to spend on certain fixed cost items. In business planning and management accounting, usage of the terms fixed costs, variable costs and others will often differ from usage in economics, and may depend on the intended use.

Some cost accounting practices such as activity-based costing will allocate fixed costs to business activities, in effect treating them as variable costs. This can simplify decision-making, but can be confusing and controversial. In accounting terminology, fixed costs will broadly include almost all costs which are not included in cost of goods sold, and variable costs are those captured in costs of goods sold.

The implicit assumption required to make the equivalence between the accounting and economics terminology is that the accounting period is equal to the period in which fixed costs do not vary in relation to production. In practice, this equivalenceies does not always hold, and depending on the period under consideration by management, some overhead expenses can be adjusted by management, and the specific allocation of each expense to each category will be decided under cost accounting.

TOTAL VARIABLE COST

Total variable cost is the opportunity cost incurred in the short-run production that depends on the quantity of output. As the name clearly implies, total variable cost is variable, it changes. If a firm produces a little output, then total variable cost is less. If a firm produces a lot of output, then total variable cost is more. A firm can avoid variable cost in the short run by reducing production to zero. This bit of information often comes in handy when the price received by a firm is so low that it falls short off covering variable cost at any positive quantity of production. As such, the firm might find it most "profitable" to cut losses by shutting down production and avoiding variable cost, until the price increases.

VARIABLE INPUTS

Total variable cost is usually, not always but usually, associated with inputs that are variable in the short run. For example, The Wacky Willy Company operates in the short run with labour as a variable input and capital as a fixed input. The cost associated with labour is a prime candidate to be a variable cost. This includes hourly wage payments to the workers and any hourly fringe benefits paid on behalf of the workers. While labour is usually isolated as the variable input in the short run, most short-run production has other variable inputs, too. The Wacky Willy Company uses an assortment of other variable inputs, all of which are part of variable cost—including cuddly cloth, squeezeably soft stuffing, and thread that make up the Stuffed Amigos; electricity needed to run the machinery; and boxes, plastic wrapping, and other packing materials used to ship the Stuffed Amigos to customers. When The Wacky Willy Company makes more Stuffed Amigos, they incur a greater cost for these variable inputs.

COST OF STUFFED AMIGOS

The table to the right summarises the total variable cost of producing Wacky Willy Stuffed Amigos. The left-hand column is the quantity of Stuffed Amigos coming off the assembly line each minute, ranging from 0 to 10. For reference, the right-hand column is the total cost of producing Stuffed Amigos, the combination of total variable and total fixed cost. The centre column is the total variable cost of producing each quantity, which is exactly $0 if no Stuffed Amigos are produced and rises to $43 if 10 Stuffed Amigos are produced. This is the essence of variable cost. Greater production entails greater total variable cost.

- The most obvious point is that total variable cost increases with increased production. Producing more Stuffed Amigos means higher total variable cost. This makes sense. To produce more Stuffed Amigos, The Wacky Willy Company needs to hire more labour and buy more materials. Because these inputs incur a cost, total variable cost rises with extra production.
- Moreover, total variable cost is zero when no Stuffed Amigos are produced. The Wacky Willy Company incurs no variable cost when they employ no workers and buy no materials—their variable inputs.
- A last note is that the incremental increase in total variable cost is NOT the same for each quantity. In other words, total variable cost does not rise at a constant rate. This incremental change in total variable cost reflects marginal cost, a key concept in the short-run production and supply decision of a firm.

TOTAL VARIABLE COST CURVE

The total variable cost curve graphically represents the relation between total variable cost incurred by a firm in the short-run product of a good or service and the quantity produced. The total variable cost curve for Wacky Willy Stuffed Amigos production is emphasised in the graph to the right. Because total variable cost increases with the quantity produced, the total variable cost curve has a positive slope.

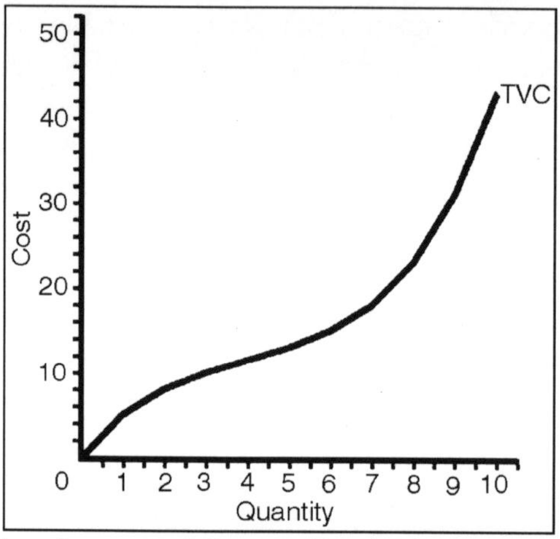

The most striking feature of the total variable cost curve is its shape. The total variable cost curve emerges from the origin, then twists and turns its way to $43. This curve begins relatively steep, then flattens, before turning increasingly steep once again. The slope of the total variable cost curve flattens as the first four Stuffed Amigos are produced due to increasing marginal returns found in Stage I of production.

The slope of the total variable cost curve becomes increasingly steeper after the fourth Stuffed Amigo is produced. This range of output corresponds with decreasing marginal returns, and the extremely important law of diminishing marginal returns, found in Stage II of production.

AVERAGE VARIABLE COST

Total variable cost can be used to derive a related variable cost concept–average variable cost. Average variable cost is simply variable cost per unit of output, which can be found by dividing total variable cost by the quantity of output. If, for example, total variable cost is $43 and the quantity of output produced is 10 Stuffed Amigos, then average variable cost, that is the variable cost per unit produced, is $4.30 (= $43/10). The connection between total variable cost and average variable cost is mathematically represented by this equation:

$$\text{Average Variable Cost} = \frac{\text{Total variable cost}}{\text{Quantity of output}}$$

A FIXED ALTERNATIVE

Total variable cost is one of two components of total cost. The other is total fixed cost. Total fixed cost is the opportunity cost incurred in the short-run production by a firm that does NOT depend on the quantity of output.

A firm can produce a little output or a lot, increase or decrease production, or even stop producing altogether, but fixed cost remains unchanged. Total fixed cost is closely connected to the use of fixed inputs.

This means that total fixed cost is unaffected by the law of diminishing marginal returns. The connection between total cost, total variable cost, and total fixed cost is often summarised in this handy equation:

Total cost = Total fixed cost + Total variable cost

DETERMINANTS OF COST

The determinants of cost varies so much from firm to firm and from problem to problem that no general set is applicable to all. Nevertheless, there are a few determinants which are important enough in modern manufacturing enterprises so as to deserve special mention.

They are:

- Rate of output (*i.e.*, utilisation of fixed plant).
- Size of plant.
- Prices of input factors (materials and labour).
- Technology.
- Size of lot.
- Stability of output.
- Efficiency (of management as well as labour).

The word "cost" that we are using has different meanings in different settings. The kind of cost concepts to be used in a particular situation depends upon the business decision to be made. Hence an understanding of the meaning of various concepts is essential for clear business thinking.

One way of getting clear-cut distinctions among different notions of cost is to set up several alternative bases of classifying costs and show the relevance of each for different kinds of problems. Although there are difficulties, workable approximations can be made if these concepts of cost can be developed by having (1) a clear understanding of the management problem and of the concept of cost that is relevant for it; (2) familiarity with the business and its records (2) familiarity with the business and its records an (2=3) ingenuity and boldness.

These special cost-estimates are based mainly on the accounting and statistical records of the company, though sometimes they need to be supplemented by collection of special data.

FIXED, VARIABLE, TOTAL, AVERAGE AND MARGINAL COSTS

Economists try to use language precisely. The words cost and prices are often confused. When we discuss costs we mean, how much did something cost to produce. This might be expressed as an opportunity cost, or in a currency such as dollars. When price is mentioned, economists mean the amount the consumer pays. Economists also try to explain the nature of costs. Why does one thing cost more to produce than another? Why does making an airplane cost so much less in a big factory than in a small factory. To help explain, total costs are broken down into several parts and looked at in different ways. Before we start we make one basic assumption that the firm is operating in the short-run time period.

FIXED COSTS

If aircraft are to be made then a factory is required. The land, the factory building, the machinery and office equipment must be bought or rented. These costs are called *fixed costs* and must be paid even when the factory has not produced anything. Fixed costs are costs that do not change, whatever the level of output is. Assuming an airplane factoryís fixed costs is a $60 million. Table below A graph of the fixed costs (FC) would look like this;

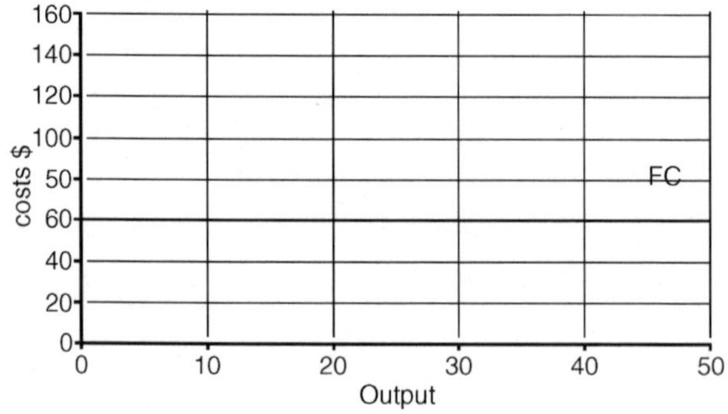

VARIABLE COSTS AND TOTAL VARIABLE COSTS

Variable costs do change as the level of output changes. These costs are costs such as raw materials in production. In our example this would be the steel, components and labour needed to make each airplane. If nothing were made the variable costs would of course be nothing. But as production rises the *total variable costs* (TVC) would rise. The variable cost is the cost per unit. The total variable cost is found by multiplying the variable cost (VC) by the level of output (Q), so TVC = VC x Q. Assuming that variable costs are constant at $1 million per airplane, a graph of TVC would look like this;

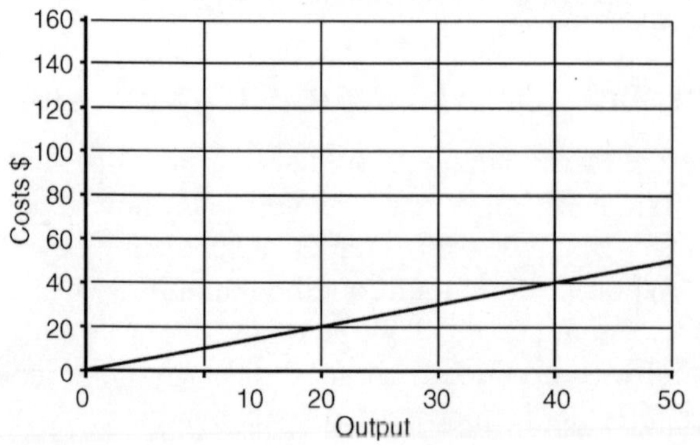

TOTAL COSTS

Total costs are simply the sum of the total variable costs and the fixed costs. Note that the TC and TVC lines are parallel. The distance between the two lines is the amount of the fixed costs.

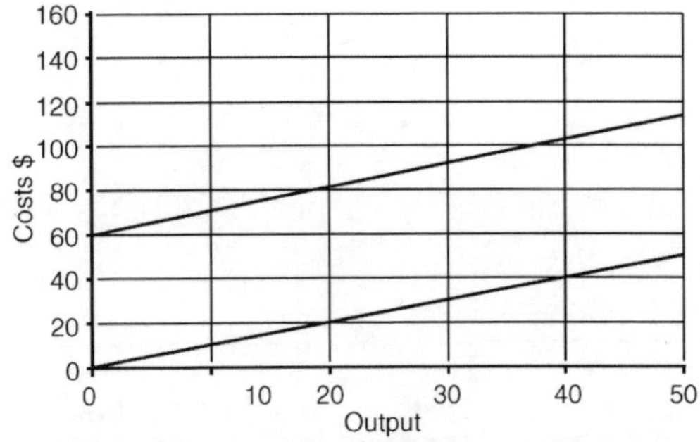

Output	Fixed cost	Total cost variable	Total cost
0	60	0	60
10	60	10	70
20	60	20	80
30	60	30	90
40	60	40	100
50	60	50	110

MARGINAL COST

Marginal cost is the cost of producing one extra unit. marginal cost = the change in total costs the change in output Using mathematical notation where the Greek letter delta is used to signify - change in.

$$MC = \frac{\Delta TC}{\Delta Q}$$

Notice that this equation is the same as the formula for the gradients of the variable cost and the total cost lines. When output rises from 0 to 10 the change in output is 10. The corresponding change in total cost is 70 – 60 = 10. The cost of producing 10 extra units has been $10 million. Therefore the cost of producing one extra unit is $1 million.

$$MC = \frac{\Delta TC}{\Delta Q} = \frac{10}{10} = 1$$

Output	Total cost	Marginal cost
0	60	
10	70	1
20	80	1
30	90	1
40	110	1
50	120	

Notice that the marginal cost in this example is the same as the variable cost. This is because we assumed that variable costs are not always the same.

In the later unit on the law of diminishing returns we will see that calculating and graphing marginal cost is a little more complicated than in this example.

AVERAGE COSTS

Average fixed costs (AFC) are the fixed costs divided by the level of output (FC/Q). So when output is 10 the AFC is 60/10 = 6. Average total costs (ATC) are the total costs divided by the level of output (TC/Q). So when output is 10 the average fixed cost is 70/10 = 7.

So using the costs in table above

Output	Fixed cost	Total cost	Average fixed cost	Average total cost
0	60	60	-	-
10	60	70	6	7
20	60	80	3	4
30	60	90	2	3
40	60	110	1.5	2.5
50	60	120	1.2	2.2

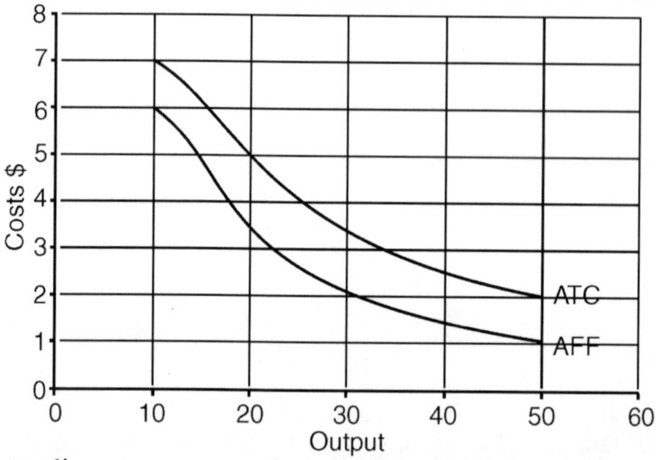

Understanding cost curves is best done by calculating and graphing examples yourself.

THE LAW OF DIMINISHING (MARGINAL) RETURNS

Although this is not needed for standard level when studying unit 2, the law of diminishing returns is important for unit 5 on development as a barrier to development.

When one of the factors of production is held fixed in supply, successive additions of the other factors will lead to an increase in returns up to a point, but beyond this point returns will diminish.

This famous law was first written about by a Frenchman, Anne Robert Jacques Turgot and then alluded to by Thomas Malthus in his *Essay on the Principle of Population* (1798). The law was discussed in England during debates on free trade and the Corn Laws. Sometimes textbooks call it the law of decreasing (marginal) returns or the law of variable proportions.

Imagine a farm growing wheat. There are a number of jobs that need doing at harvest time and these must be done quickly before weather ruins the crop. First the wheat must be cut and gathered, the wheat and chaff must then be separated.

The wheat has then to be carted to a barn, weighed, dried out in some instances, and then stored. All the farm machinery needs maintained, the paperwork completed and last but not least breakfast, lunch and dinner prepared. One man working alone will have difficulty doing all these tasks. By dividing the labour there will be gains in productivity.

If a second worker is employed the tasks can be shared. This means that productivity increases. They each become more skilled in the tasks that they specialise in and save time previously wasted by switching between tasks. However both have to stop when a piece of machinery breaks down or one of them stops for lunch.

Employing yet another person may once again improve their productivity. The harvest may continue as they take their lunch in rotation for example. But employing a fourth worker might mean productivity begins to fall (diminish). The gains made by employing the 4th are not as great as employing the 3rd worker.

Eventually adding more employees might even lead to an overall decrease in production as they become bored with nothing to do and begin to interfere with production. The table below shows what happens as each extra worker is employed.

Marginal means the next unit. So the marginal physical product (MPP) is the amount by which production rises when one extra worker is employed. MPP is calculated by measuring the change in total physical production per worker.

The average physical product (APP) is simply the total physical product (TPP) divided by the number of workers

Number of Physical (TPP)	**Total Physical Product (MPP)**	**Marginal Physical Product (APP)**	**Average workers**	**Product**
1	10	10	10	
2	30	30 – 10 = 20	15	
3	90	90 – 30 = 60	30	
4	120	120 – 90= 30	30	
5	130	130 – 120 = 10	26	
6	120	120 – 130 = –10	20	

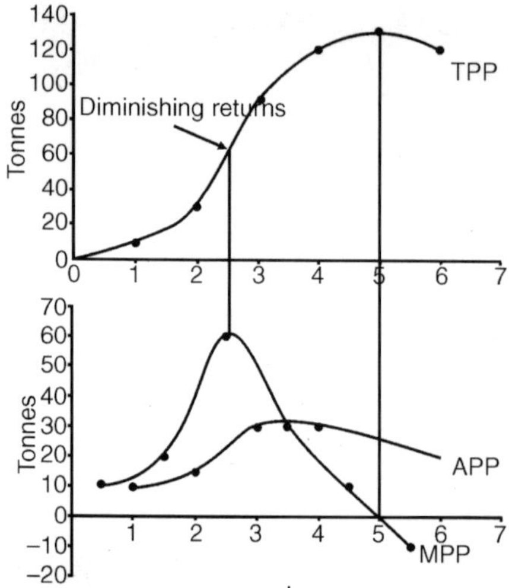

In the example the factors of production land and capital are constant but the amount of labour is being varied. The marginal physical product, (MPP) increases to start. When the 4th worker is employed the total still increases from 90 to 120 tonnes, but the increase of 30 tonnes is not as great as the previous increase of 60. It as this point that we say the marginal return diminishes.

The diagram and table shows that when the marginal physical product curve reaches its peak and then changes direction downwards that this is the point of diminishing marginal returns. On the total physical product curve diminishing returns do not occur at the peak of the curve (a common mistake), but where the gradient of the curve instead of becoming steeper changes and becomes less steep (known in maths as the point of inflection). When MPP becomes negative this means that additional workers are causing a reduction in the total production and the TPP curve changes direction downwards.

The relationship between the marginal and average curves is important to understand. Notice that MPP intersects the APP when APP is at its maximum point. The reason is merely a simple mathematical relationship between marginal and averages. Think of a class of students. The average age in the class is 17. If another student comes in the room and they are 18, what will happen to the average? – It will of course increase. On the other hand if the student were 16 the average age in the class would fall. So in the graph, as long as the marginal is higher than the average the average curve goes up and when the marginal is below the average. The average falls.

The demonstration of the law above rests on a couple of assumptions. First we assume that each unit of labour is homogenous. That is that each worker has the same skills and works equally hard. Second, all the other factors of production are held fixed in quantity. The law of diminishing marginal returns has two main applications for IB students.

- The shape of the short run cost curve is determined by the principles above and,
- Diminishing marginal returns in agriculture act as a barrier to economic development

CLASSIFICATION OF COSTS

Classification of cost means, the grouping of costs according to their common characteristics. The important ways of classification of costs are:

- By nature or element: materials, labour, expenses
- By functions: production, selling, distribution, administration, R&D, development,
- By Traceability: Direct and Indirect
- By variability: fixed, variable, semi-variable
- By controllability: controllable, uncontrollable
- By normality: normal, abnormal.

STANDARD COST ACCOUNTING

In modern cost accounting, the concept of recording historical costs was taken further, by allocating the company's fixed costs over a given period of time to the items produced during that period, and recording the result as the total cost of production. This allowed the *full cost* of products that were not sold in the period they were produced to be recorded in inventory using a variety of complex accounting methods, which was consistent with the principles of GAAP (Generally Accepted Accounting Principles). It also essentially enabled managers to ignore the fixed costs, and look at the results of each period in relation to the "standard cost" for any given product.

For example: if the railway coach company normally produced 40 coaches per month, and the fixed costs were still $1000/month, then each coach could be said to incur an overhead of $25 ($1000/40). Adding this to the variable costs of $300 per coach produced a full cost of $325 per coach. This method tended to slightly distort the resulting unit cost, but in mass-production industries that made one product line, and where the fixed costs were relatively low, the distortion was very minor.

For example: if the railway coach company made 100 coaches one month, then the unit cost would become $310 per coach ($300 + ($1000/100)). If the next month the company made 50 coaches, then the unit cost = $320 per coach ($300 + ($1000/50)), a relatively minor difference. An important part of standard cost accounting is a variance analysis, which breaks down the variation between actual cost and standard costs into various components (volume variation, material cost variation, labour cost variation, etc.) so managers can understand *why costs were different from what was planned* and take appropriate action to correct the situation.

THE DEVELOPMENT OF THROUGHPUT ACCOUNTING

As business became more complex and began producing a greater variety of products, the use of cost accounting to make decisions to maximize profitability came under question. Management circles became increasingly aware of the Theory of Constraints in the 1980s, and began to understand that "every production process has a limiting factor" somewhere in the chain of production. As business management learned to identify the constraints, they increasingly adopted throughput accounting to manage them and "maximize the *throughput dollars*" (or other currency) from each unit of constrained resource.

For example: The railway coach company was offered a contract to make 15 open-topped streetcars each month, using a design that included ornate brass foundry work, but very little of the metalwork needed to produce a covered rail coach. The buyer offered to pay $280 per streetcar. The company had a firm order for 40 rail coaches each month for $350 per unit.

LEAN ACCOUNTING

Lean accounting has developed in recent years to provide the accounting, control, and measurement methods supporting lean manufacturing and other applications of lean thinking such as health care, construction, insurance, banking, education, government, and other industries. There are two main thrusts for Lean Accounting. The first is the application of lean methods to the company's accounting, control, and measurement processes. This is not different from applying lean methods to any other processes. The objective is to eliminate waste, free up capacity, speed up the process, eliminate errors and defects, and make the process clear and understandable.

The second (and more important) thrust of Lean Accounting is to fundamentally change the accounting, control, and measurement processes so they motivate lean change and improvement, provide information that is suitable for control and decision-making, provide an understanding of customer value, correctly assess the financial impact of lean improvement, and are themselves simple, visual, and low-waste.

Lean Accounting does not require the traditional management accounting methods like standard costing, activity-based costing, variance reporting, cost-plus pricing, complex transactional control systems, and untimely and confusing financial reports.

These are replaced by:

- Lean-focused performance measurements
- Simple summary direct costing of the value streams
- Decision-making and reporting using a *box score*
- Financial reports that are timely and presented in "plain English" that everyone can understand

- Radical simplification and elimination of transactional control systems by eliminating the need for them
- Driving lean changes from a deep understanding of the value created for the customers
- Eliminating traditional budgeting through monthly sales, operations, and financial planning processes (SOFP)
- Value-based pricing
- Correct understanding of the financial impact of lean change.

As an organization becomes more mature with lean thinking and methods, they recognize that the combined methods of lean accounting in fact creates a lean management system (LMS) designed to provide the planning, the operational and financial reporting, and the motivation for change required to prosper the company's on-going lean transformation.

MARGINAL COSTING

This method is used particularly for short-term decision-making. Its principal tenets are:

- Revenue (per product) " variable costs (per product) = contribution (per product)
- Total contribution " total fixed costs = (total profit or total loss).

Thus, it does not attempt to allocate fixed costs in an arbitrary manner to different products. The short-term objective is to maximize contribution per unit. If constraints exist on resources, then Managerial Accounting dictates that marginal cost analysis be employed to maximize contribution per unit of the constrained resource.

COST STRUCTURE OF THE FIRM

We can look at the business firm from at least two points of view: productivity, inputs and outputs (as we have just done) or outputs and costs. In advanced microeconomics, these two points of view are called "duals."

They are equally valid, but they point up different things. They are also opposites from a certain point of view—the higher the productivity, the lower the costs.

By looking at the firm from the point of view of costs, we shift our perspective somewhat and gain a much more direct understanding of supply.

We also look more directly at the difference between the long and short run. In the short run, we have two major categories of costs:

- Fixed costs and
- Variable costs

In the long run, however, all costs are variable. Thus, we must study costs under two quite different headings. Costs will vary quite differently in the long run and in the short.

FIXED AND VARIABLE COSTS

Variable costs are costs that can be varied flexibly as conditions change. In the John Bates Clark model of the firm that we are studying, labour costs are the variable costs. Fixed costs are the costs of the investment goods used by the firm, on the idea that these reflect a long-term commitment that can be recovered only by wearing them out in the production of goods and services for sale.

The idea here is that labour is a much more flexible resource than capital investment. People can change from one task to another flexibly (whether within the same firm or in a new job at another firm), while machinery tends to be designed for a very specific use. If it isn't used for that purpose, it can't produce anything at all. Thus, capital investment is much more of a commitment than hiring is. In the eighteen-hundreds, when John Bates Clark was writing, this was pretty clearly true. Over the past century, a) education and experience have become more important for labour and have made labour more specialized and b) increasing automatic control has made some machinery more flexible.

So the differences between capital and labour are less than they once were, but all the same, it seems labour is still relatively more flexible than capital. It is this (relative) difference in flexibility that is expressed by the simplified distinction of long and short run. Of course, productivity and costs are inversely related, so the variable costs will change as the productivity of labour changes. Here is a picture of the fixed costs (FC), variable costs (VC) and the total of both kinds of costs (TC) for the productivity example in the last unit:

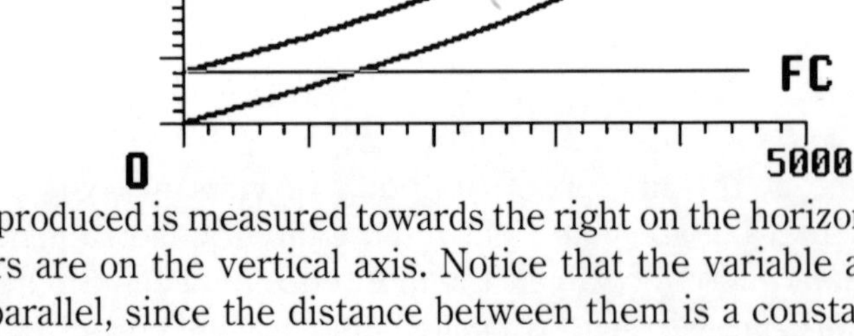

Output produced is measured towards the right on the horizontal axis. The cost numbers are on the vertical axis. Notice that the variable and total cost curves are parallel, since the distance between them is a constant number—the fixed cost.

OPPORTUNITY COST

What is the connection between the distinction we have just made—fixed vs variable costs—and opportunity cost, the key concept in some earlier units? In economics, all costs are included—whether or not they correspond to money payments. If we have opportunity costs with no corresponding money payments, they are called implicit costs. The implicit costs (as well as the money costs) are included in the cost analysis we have just given. There is some correlation between implicit costs and fixed or variable costs, but this correlation will be different in such different kinds of firms as:

A factory owned by an absentee investor: This is the easiest case to underst and. All of the labour costs to the absentee investor are money costs, including the manager's salary. If the investor has borrowed some of the money he invested in the factory, then there are some money costs of the capital invested—interest on the loan. However, we must consider the opportunity cost of invested capital as well.

The investor's own money that he has used to buy the factory is money that she could have invested in some other business. The return she could have gotten on another investment is the opportunity cost of her own funds invested in the business. This is an implicit cost and in this case the implicit cost is part of the cost of capital and probably a fixed cost.

A "mom- and-pop" store: A "mom- and-pop" store (family proprietorship or partnership) is a store in which family members are self-employed and supply most of the labour. Typically, "Mom" and "Pop" don't pay themselves a salary—they just take money from the till when they need it, since it is their property anyway. As a result, there are no money costs for their labour. But their labour has an opportunity cost—the salary or wages they could make working similar hours in some other business—and so, in this case, the implicit costs include a large component of variable labour costs.

A large modern corporation: The corporation has relatively few implicit costs, but generally will have some. All labour costs will be expressed in money terms (though benefits and bonuses have to be included), since the shareholders don't supply labour to the corporation as "Mom and Pop" do in a family proprietorship.

It will pay interest to bondholders and dividends to shareholders. But the dividends aren't really a cost item—they include profits distributed to the shareholders. Moreover, the typical corporation will retain some profits and invest them within the business, a "plowback" investment. Conversely, shareholders may take a large part of their payout in appreciation of the stock value—and plowback investment is one reason for the appreciation.

Thus we would say that the corporation has a net equity value, that is, that the corporation "owns" a certain amount of capital that it invests in its own business (very much like the absentee owner in the first example). This capital has an opportunity cost and that opportunity cost is an implicit cost. The stockholders, who own the corporation, ultimately receive (as dividends or appreciation) both the opportunity cost of the equity capital and any profit left over after it is taken out.

UNIT COST

Here are the average, average variable and average fixed costs for our example firm.

Q	AC	AFC	AVC
945	138	85	53
1780	101	45	56
2505	92	32	60
3120	90	26	64
3625	91	22	69
4020	95	20	75
4305	100	19	81
4480	107	18	89
4545	117	18	99

Here are the average cost (AC), average variable cost (AVC) and average fixed cost (AFC) in a diagram. This is a good representative of the way that economists believe firm costs vary in the short run.

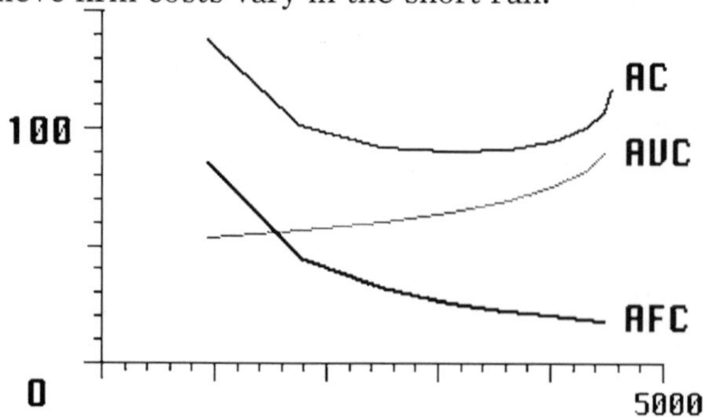

Notice how the average fixed costs decline as the fixed costs are "spread over more units of output." For large outputs, however, average variable costs rise pretty steeply. The idea is that with a limited capital plant and thus limited productive capacity—in the short run—costs would rise much more than proportionately to output as output goes beyond "capacity." The average total cost, dominated by fixed costs for small output, declines at first, but as output increases, fixed costs become less important for the total cost and variable costs become more important and so, after reaching a minimum, average total cost begins to rise more and more steeply.

MARGINAL COST

As before, we want to focus particularly on the marginal variation. In this case, of course, it is marginal cost. Marginal cost is defined as,

$$MC = \frac{\Delta C}{\Delta Q}$$

As usual, Q st ands for (quantity of) output and C for cost, so Q st ands for the change in output, while C st ands for the change in cost. As usual, marginal cost can be interpreted as the additional cost of producing just one more ("marginal") unit of output. Let's have a numerical example of the Marginal Cost definition to help make it clear. In the John Bates Clark style example we have been using, total cost is 280000 for an output of 3120 and it is 33000 for an output of 3625. So we have $\Delta C = 330000 - 280000 = 50000$ and $\Delta Q = 3600 - 3120 = 505$ so that,

$$\frac{\Delta C}{\Delta Q} = \frac{50000}{505} = 99.01$$

for a marginal cost of $99.01 for the next unit produced. As usual, this is an approximation and the smaller the change in output we use, the better the approximation is. Here is the marginal cost for our example firm, along with output and average cost.

Output	Average Cost	Marginal Cost
0	0	9.45
945	137.57	52.91
1780	101.12	59.88
2505	91.82	68.97
3120	89.74	81.30
3625	91.03	99.01
4020	94.53	126.58
4305	99.88	175.44
4480	107.14	285.71
4545	116.61	769.23

Here is a picture of marginal cost for our example firm, together with average cost as output varies. As before, the output produced is measured by the distance to the right on the horizontal axis. The average and marginal cost are on the vertical axis. Average cost is shown by the curve in yellow and marginal cost in red. Notice how the marginal cost rises to cross average cost at its lowest point.

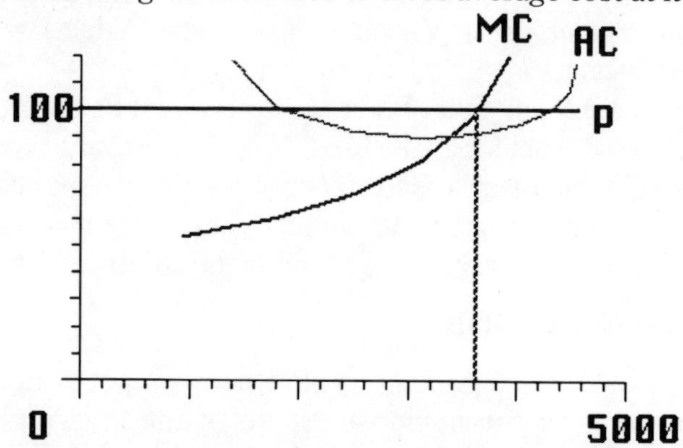

MAXIMIZATION OF PROFITS

We can now give another rule for the maximization of profits. The new rule is really just the same rule as we saw before, only now we state it in terms of price and costs. It is the equimarginal principle in yet another form. The question is: "I want to maximize profits. How much output should I sell, at the given price?"

The answer is: increase output until,

$$p=MC$$

The point is illustrated by the following table, which extends the marginal cost table in an earlier page to show the price and the profits for the example firm.

Output	Average Cost	Marginal Cost	price	profit
0	0	100	0	9.45
945	137.57	100	-35503.65	52.91
1780	101.12	100	-1993.60	59.88
2505	91.82	100	20490.90	68.97
3120	89.74	100	32011.20	81.30
3625	91.03	100	32516.25	99.01
4020	94.53	100	21989.40	126.58
4305	99.88	100	516.60	175.44
4480	107.14	100	-31987.20	285.71
4545	116.61	100	-75492.45	769.23

Notice how profits are greatest (at 32516.25) when the marginal cost is almost exactly equal to the price of $100. This occurs at an output of 3625, with marginal cost at 99.01. The profit-maximizing output would be very slightly more than 3625.

MARGINAL COSTING

This method is used particularly for short-term decision-making. Its principal tenets are:

- *Revenue (per product):* Variable Costs (per product) = Contribution (per product)
- *Total Contribution:* Total Fixed Costs = Total Profit or (Total Loss)

Thus it does not attempt to allocate fixed costs in an arbitrary manner to different products. The short-term objective is to maximise contribution per unit. If constraints exist on resources, then Managerial Accounting dictates that marginal cost analysis be employed to maximise contribution per unit of the constrained resource.

OTHER COSTING METHODS

More varieties of costing methods have been proposed in order to tailor for different aspects of the business. Some of the uprising ones include inventory costing method, process costing method, average costing method, target costing method. Still, the standard methods and normal costing methods are the most established methods in the world of public accounting. For management accountants in private industry, throughput accounting is rapidly becoming the standard for use in decision making in a fast-paced business environment.

CLASSIFICATION OF COSTS

An important business objective is to break-even *i.e.* to exactly cover your total costs by sales revenue. It is even more desirable to make a profit. The diagram below illustrates a firm's costs and revenues and illustrates three possible situations:

- Loss making (outputs to the left of the break-even point)
- Break-even
- Profit-making (outputs to the right of the break-even point.)

In order to understand break-even, we first need to define key terms:

- *Fixed costs*: Costs that do not vary with output or sales *e.g.* managers salaries, rent and rates on business premises.
- *Variable costs*: Costs that vary with the quantity produced or sold *e.g.* costs of raw materials, sales staff commissions, etc.
- *Total cost*: Fixed costs variable costs at each possible level of output.

Sales revenue:

- *Profit*: The difference between total revenue and total cost (where revenues are higher than costs).
- *Loss*: The difference between total revenue and total cost (where costs are higher than revenues).

There are two simple ways of calculating the break-even point of a business:

- Draw a chart showing:
- Sales revenue at different levels of output
- Fixed costs at different levels of output
- Total costs at different levels of output
- The break-even point where total cost = total sales revenue.
- Calculating the contribution of each unit sold or made. The contribution is the difference between the sales revenue and the variable cost of each unit sold or made.

The number of units needed to be sold (or made) to break-even is then calculated by: An importer buys bottles of a particular type of French wine for £2 a bottle, stores them in a warehouse in this country and then advertises them for sale over the Internet at £4 each. The fixed costs of running the business are £10,000 a month. We can calculate the break-even point by using the two methods, described above:

- *Drawing a chart:* Costs and revenues
- *Calculating contribution per bottle:* Fixed costs = £10,000 Variable cost = £2 per bottle

Sales revenue = £4 per bottle
Contribution = £2 (£4 – £2 = £2).

Now work out these two examples on your own:

- Calculate the break-even point for a newspaper vendor. He buys in newspapers at 20p each and sells them for 50p each. His fixed costs are £60 a day including the rate he pays to the local council. How many newspapers must he sell each day to break-even?
- A large business has fixed costs of £250,000 per week. Its average sales revenue per item is £2, and its variable costs are on average 50p per item. How many items does it need to sell to break-even?

COST-OF-PRODUCTION THEORY OF VALUE

In economics, the cost-of-production theory of value is the theory that the price of an object is determined by the sum of the cost of the resources that went into making it. The cost can be composed of the cost of any of the factors of production including labour, capital, land, or technology. The theory makes the most sense under assumptions of constant returns to scale and the existence of just one non-produced factor of production. These are the assumptions of the so-called non-substitution theorem. Under these assumptions, the long run price of a commodity is equal to the sum of the cost of the inputs into that commodity, including interest charges.

RETURNS TO SCALE

In economics, returns to scale and economies of scale are related terms that describe what happens as the scale of production increases. They are different terms and are not to be used interchangeably. Returns to scale refers to a technical property of production that examines changes in output subsequent a proportional change in all inputs. Where all inputs increase by a constant. If output increases by that same proportional change then there are constant returns to scale (CRTS), sometimes referred to simply as returns to scale. If output increases by less than that proportional change, there are decreasing returns to scale (DRS). If output increases by more than that proportion, there are increasing returns to scale (IRS).

Short example: Where all inputs increase by a factor of 2, new value for output should be:

- Two times previous output given constant returns to scale (CRTS)
- Less than twice previous output given decreasing returns to scale (DRS)
- More than two times previous output given increasing returns to scale (IRS)

ECONOMIES OF SCALE

Production may be subject to economies of scale (or diseconomies of scale). Increasing returns to scale are said to exist if additional units can be produced for less than the previous unit, that is, average cost is falling. This can only occur if average cost at any given level of production is higher than the marginal cost. Conversely, there may be levels of production where marginal cost is higher than average cost, and average cost will rise for each unit of production after that point.

This type of production function is generically known as diminishing marginal productivity: at low levels of production, productivity gains are easy and marginal costs falling, but productivity gains become smaller as production increases; eventually, marginal costs rise because increasing output (with existing capital, labour or organization) becomes more expensive. For this generic case, minimum average cost occurs at the point where minimum average cost and marginal cost are equal (when plotted, the two curves intersect); this point will *not* be at the minimum for marginal cost if fixed costs are greater than zero.

Economies of scale and diseconomies of scale refer to an economic property of production that affects cost if quantity of all input factors are increased by some amount. If costs increase proportionately, there are no economies of scale; if costs increase by a greater amount, there are diseconomies of scale; if costs increase by a lesser amount, there are positive economies of scale. When combined, economies of scale and diseconomies of scale lead to ideal firm size theory, which states that per-unit costs decrease until they reach a certain minimum, then increase as the firm size increases further. Economies of scale refers to the decreased per unit cost as output increases. More clearly, the initial investment of capital is diffused (spread) over an increasing number of units of output, and therefore, the marginal cost of producing a good or service decreases as production increases (note that this is only in an industry that is experiencing economies of scale)

An example will clarify.

AFC is average fixed cost

If a company is currently in a situation with economies of scale... let's say electricity, then as their initial investment of $1000 is spread over 100 customers, their AFC is $\left(\frac{1000}{100}\right) = \$10$.

If that same utility now has 200 customers, their AFC becomes $\left(\frac{1000}{200}\right) =$ $5... their fixed cost is now spread over 200 units of output. In economies of scale this results in a lower average total cost.

The advantage is that "buying bulk is cheaper on a per-unit basis." Hence, there is *economy* (in the sense of "efficiency") to be gained on a larger *scale.* Economies of scale tend to occur in industries with high capital costs in which those costs can be distributed across a large number of units of production (both in absolute terms, and, especially, relative to the size of the market). A common example is a factory. An investment in machinery is made, and one worker, or unit of production, begins to work on the machine and produces a certain number of goods. If another worker is added to the machine he or she is able to produce an additional amount of goods without adding significantly to the factory's cost of operation. The amount of goods produced grows significantly faster than the plant's cost of operation. Hence, the cost of producing an additional good is less than the good before it, and an economy of scale emerges. Economies of scale are also derived partially from learning by doing. The exploitation of economies of scale helps explain why companies grow large in some industries.

It is also a justification for free trade policies, since some economies of scale may require a larger market than is possible within a particular country — for example, it would not be efficient for Liechtenstein to have its own car maker, if they would only sell to their local market. A lone car maker may be profitable, however, if they export cars to global markets in addition to selling to the local market. Economies of scale also play a role in a "natural monopoly." Typically, because there are fixed costs of production, economies of scale are initially *increasing,* and as volume of production increases, eventually *diminishing,* which produces the standard U-shaped cost curve of economic theory. In some economic theory (*e.g.,* "perfect competition") there is an assumption of *constant* returns to scale.

NETWORK EFFECT

Network externalities resemble economies of scale, but they are not considered such because they are a function of the number of users of a good or service in an industry, not of the production efficiency within a business. Economies of scale external to the firm (or industry wide scale economies) are only considered examples of network externalities if they are driven by demand side economies.

FORMAL DEFINITIONS

Formally, a production function $F(K, L)$ is defined to have: constant returns to scale if (for any constant a greater than 1)

$$F(aK, aL) = aF(K,L)$$

increasing returns to scale if $F(aK, aK) > aF(K,L)$: decreasing returns to scale if $F(aK, aL) < aF(K,L)$ where K and L are factors of production, capital and labour, respectively.

As an example, the Cobb-Douglas functional form has constant returns to scale. The function is:

$$F(K,L) = AK^{b}L^{1-b}$$

where $A > 0$ and $0 < b < 1$. Thus,

$$F(aK, aL) = A(aK)^{b}(aL)^{1-b} = Aa^{b}a^{1-b}K$$

Historically, the most well known proponent of such theories is probably Adam Smith. Piero Sraffa, in his introduction to the first volume of the "Collected Works of David Ricardo", referred to Adam Smith's adding up theory. Smith contrasted natural prices with market prices. Smith theorized that market prices would tend towards natural prices, where outputs would be at what he characterized as the "level of effectual demand". At this level, Smith's natural prices of commodities are the sum of the natural rates of wages, profits, and rent that must be paid for inputs into production.

David Ricardo mixed such cost of production theory of prices with the Labour theory of value, as that latter theory was understood by Eugen von Bohm-Bawerk and others. This is the theory that prices tend towards proportionality to the socially necessary Labour embodied in a commodity. Ricardo also refutes the Labour theory of value in later sections of that chapter. This refutation leads to what later became known as the transformation problem. Karl Marx later takes up that theory in the first volume of "Capital", while indicating that he is quite aware that the theory is untrue at lower levels of abstraction. This has led to all sorts of arguments over what both David Ricardo and Karl Marx "really meant".

Nevertheless, it seems undeniable that all the major classical economics and Marx explicitly rejected the Labour theory of price. The Polish economist Micha Kalecki distinguished between sectors with "cost-determined prices" (such as manufacturing and services) and those with "demand-determined prices" (such as agriculture and raw material extraction). One might think of this theory as equivalent to modern theories of markup-pricing, full-cost pricing, or administrative pricing. Every since Hall and Hitch, economists have found that the evidence gathered in surveys of businessmen support such theories. Most contemporary economists probably accept neo-classical economics or mainstream economics. The non-substitution theorem is presented in graduate level microeconomics textbooks as a theorem of mainstream economics. Also many mainstream economists think they can justify theories of full-cost pricing within their theory. The majority of mainstream economists would probably then accept this theory as an element in their theory which does not give adequate attention to issues of consumer demand and marginal utility.

BREAK-EVEN ANALYSIS

Break-even analysis is a technique widely used by production management and management accountants. It is based on categorising production costs between those which are "variable" and those that are "fixed". Total variable and fixed costs are compared with sales revenue in order to determine the level of sales volume, sales value or production at which the business makes neither a profit nor a loss.

THE BREAK-EVEN CHART

In its simplest form, the break-even chart is a graphical representation of costs at various levels of activity shown on the same chart as the variation of income with the same variation in activity. The point at which neither profit nor loss is made is known as the "break-even point" and is represented on the chart by the intersection of the two lines:

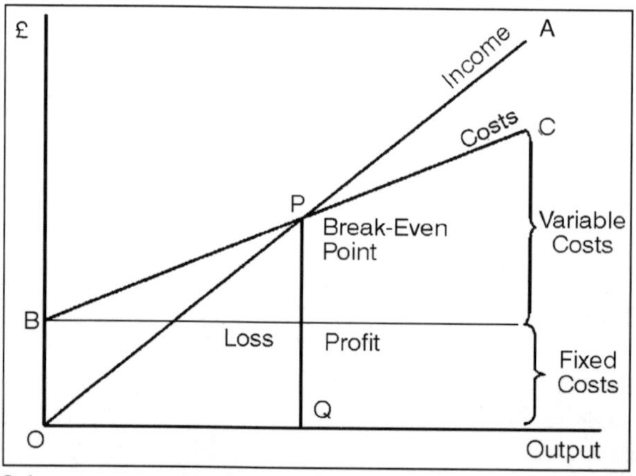

The line OA represents the variation of income at varying levels of production activity. OB represents the total fixed costs in the business. As output increases, variable costs are incurred, meaning that total costs also increase. At low levels of output, Costs are greater than Income. At the point of intersection, P, costs are exactly equal to income, and hence neither profit nor loss is made.

FIXED COSTS

Fixed costs are those business costs that are not directly related to the level of production or output. In other words, even if the business has a zero output or high output, the level of fixed costs will remain broadly the same. In the long term fixed costs can alter–perhaps as a result of investment in production capacity or through the growth in overheads required to support a larger, more complex business.

Examples of fixed costs:

- Rent and rates.
- Depreciation
- Research and development.
- Marketing costs.
- Administration costs.

VARIABLE COSTS

Variable costs are those costs which vary directly with the level of output. They represent payment output-related inputs such as raw materials, direct labour, fuel and revenue-related costs such as commission. A distinction is often made between "Direct" variable costs and "Indirect" variable costs. Direct variable costs are those which can be directly attributable to the production of a particular product or service and allocated to a particular cost centre.

Raw materials and the wages those working on the production line are good examples. Indirect variable costs cannot be directly attributable to production but they do vary with output. These include depreciation, maintenance and certain labour costs.

SEMI-VARIABLE COSTS

Whilst the distinction between fixed and variable costs is a convenient way of categorising business costs, in reality there are some costs which are fixed in nature but which increase when output reaches certain levels. These are largely related to the overall "scale" and/or complexity of the business. For example, when a business has relatively low levels of output or sales, it may not require costs associated with functions such as human resource management or a fully-resourced finance department. However, as the scale of the business grows then more resources are required. If production rises suddenly then some short-term increase in warehousing and/or transport may be required. In these circumstances, we say that part of the cost is variable and part fixed.

6

Demand Analysis

AN OVERVIEW

A market exists when buyers and sellers interact to exchange products. You might think that the easiest market to explore would be the interaction between one buyer and one seller. For example, suppose Crusoe has coconuts and would really like some fish, and Friday has fish and would really like some coconuts. There is the possibility for a mutually beneficial trade here, but we cannot predict what the price or quantity will be even if we know their preferences because the outcome depends on their relative bargaining skills.

Hence, economic theory has little to tell us about this most simple of markets. It is easier to analyse a market in which there are many buyers and sellers, each small relative to the overall market. It helps also if both buyers and sellers are well informed, and buyers and sellers form distinct and separate groups.

To explain a market with these qualities, economists use supply and demand analysis. You should be aware that supply and demand analysis does not work in all markets, but only in those with the characteristics. If buyers are a group distinct from the sellers, we can analyse how they act separately from how sellers act. Only after we have looked at these two groups separately will we combine them and see how they interact.

As suggested, begin by looking at the buyers. What determines the amount of a product that people are willing and ready to buy during some period of time? For example, what determines the amount of hamburger purchased in Chicago during a week? Economists answer such questions by examining the costs and benefits of buying the product.

When any of the costs or benefits changes, the amount of the product that people will buy should also change. The benefits a person gets from a product depend on his goals. These goals are referred to in many ways in discussions of demand. The words "tastes," "wants," "needs," "preferences," and "usefulness" all refer to goals. When people's goals change, the amount of benefit they get from the good changes, and this will cause them to change the amount of the good they want to buy. Goals depend on many factors, such as the age of people and the amount of education they have. Social custom is an important determinant of preferences and can account for many differences in demand among groups. One can explain the large differences in squid sales in Japan and the United States, or the large differences in consumption of horse meat in Europe and the United States, almost entirely in terms of differences in preferences caused by differences in social custom.

The most obvious cost a person bears in buying a product is the price of the product. Price reflects cost because people have a limited amount of funds that they can spend, and if they spend their money on one thing, they cannot spend it on another. When the price of a product goes up, the amount of other things that a person must give up in order to buy the product rises.

As a result, we expect people to buy more hamburger if the price is $1.00 per pound than if it is $2.00 per pound. The amount of income a person receives affects the cost of buying an item because it determines which options a person must give up when buying a product. If a person with a low income spends $5000 for a trip around the world, he will have to cut back on food, clothing, or shelter.

The same trip will cause a person with a high income to cut back on a very different set of options. Increases in people's incomes raise consumption of most products. These products are called normal goods. There are some products, however, that people use less of as their income increases; these products are called inferior goods.

Public transportation is an example—as people's incomes rise, they stop riding the bus and drive their own cars. Blue jeans were once another example--people with higher incomes bought them less frequently than people with lower incomes. It was because they were a symbol of "working-class" clothes that they were adopted by the radical left in the 1960s, and from there they moved into high fashion.

Prices of related goods also influence how much of a product people buy. Goods that are substitutes satisfy the same set of goals or preferences. An example of a substitute for hamburger is pork. If pork prices are high, people are tempted to shift away from pork to hamburger, and if pork prices are low, people are tempted to shift from hamburger to pork.

The opposite of a substitute is a complement, a good that helps complete another in some way. Catsup and hamburger buns are complements to hamburger, and if they are priced low enough, consumption of hamburger may rise.

Sometimes goods are such good complements that they are sold together and we think of them as a single item. Left shoes and right shoes are an example. There are other factors that influence the amount of a particular product that people are willing to buy, such as the number of consumers in the market and their expectations about future prices, incomes, and quality changes. To get a complete list for any product might be time consuming and difficult, but it is not necessary because we want to focus on the relationship between price and the quantity of a product that people are willing to buy during some interval of time. To do this, as suggested, assume that all other factors are held constant.

TRANSPORTATION OF DEMAND ANALYSIS

Transportation demand, simply stated, is the demand for trips that exist in any area. All of this demand, however, may or may not materialise into physical trips—and some of it generally remains latent and is referred to as hidden demand. The importance of analysing the transportation demand in order to be able to predict the expected number of trips in a given network cannot be overstated.

The demand for transportation forms the primary input in any decision related to creation and management of transportation and traffic facilities, such as roads, intersections, parking lots, transit system, and so on.

The lecture is divided into three parts. The first part describes the nature of transportation demand and how it can be analysed. Then it presents the sequential demand analysis technique—the most frequently used method of determining transportation demand. Finally, it briefly describes some of the data collection mechanisms employed in travel demand analysis.

Transportation demand, unlike demand for other commodities, such as wheat, coffee, housing, clothing, etc., is a derived demand. That is, one demands to be transported not because he/she just wants to move but because he/she wants to achieve some other purpose such as reaching school, or office or a movie theatre.

In other words, the need for achieving some goal creates the need to travel. Hence, travel demand is primarily generated by the population's need to work, entertain, socialise, study, etc. Therefore, it is not surprising that two of the major aspects in travel demand analysis are land use and trip purpose. Land use refers to the pattern of land usage in an area. Land use affects transportation demand through generation and distribution of trips.

The effect of land use on transportation demand is not necessarily a one-way effect but rather a part of cycle in which land use changes transportation needs which in turn change land use. Figure shows a simple schematic of how land use and transportation demand are related.

Trip purpose refers to the purpose for which the trip is being undertaken. Travel demand behaviour changes with the trip purpose.

For example, a person hardly exercises any choice for work trips; *i.e.*, does not necessarily decide every time whether to go to work or not. A person obviously does not decide where to go to work, even the choice of route and mode are not daily decisions.

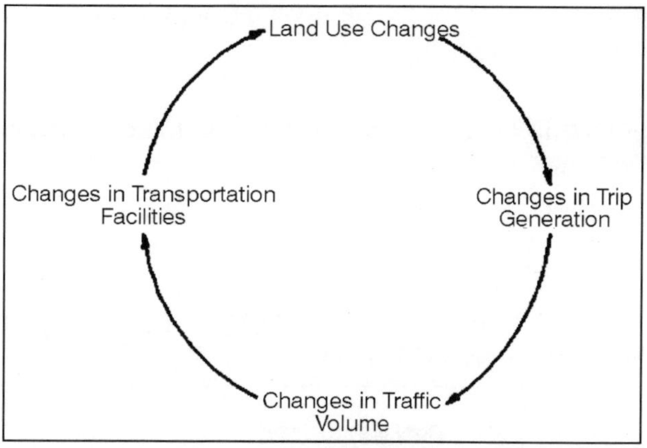

Fig. Relationship between Land use and Transportation Demand.

On the other hand, for recreational trips, an individual makes a large number of decisions, such as whether to go or not, where to go, how to go. Consequently, the travel demand behaviour for work trips varies considerably from that of recreational trips.

This example, can obviously be extended to other types of trips such as shopping trips, etc. Given the effect of trip purpose on travel demand behaviour, the analysis of travel demand is done separately for different trip-purposes. Although, the discussion throws light on some of the factors which affect travel demand, some more understanding of travel demand is necessary before one can analyse the demand and can, with some degree of confidence, predict the volume on various links of a network. Generally, a trip materialises after the trip-maker makes certain decisions.

These decisions can be broadly classified as follows:

- *The Decision to Travel*: The trip-maker, given his/her requirements, makes a conscious decision to travel so that the requirements can be met.
- *The Decision on the Choice of Destination*: The tripmaker also makes a decision as to where he/she wants to go; for certain kinds of trip purpose, such as work trips, this decision may not exist; yet for other kinds of trips, such as shopping trips, there may be certain alternative locations to choose from.
- *The Decision on the Choice of Mode*: The trip-maker also takes a decision as to what mode of transport to use for a given trip. This decision, however, is only available to those who have access to different modes and are not captive users of any particular mode.
- *The Decision on the Choice of Route*. The trip-maker on any given trip takes a definite decision on which route to take so as to reach the destination. Again, this decision is available to only those tripmakers who have access to modes which can use different routes as per the

wishes of the tripmaker. Such modes would generally include personal automobiles or two wheelers.

Although, there is unanimity on the fact that the decisions can aptly capture the entire trip-making behaviour of an individual and hence can be used to analyse travel demand pattern of an area, it is difficult to ascertain whether there exists any definite sequence in which these decisions are made. Generally it is assumed, primarily for the ease of analysis rather than anything else, that the decisions are made in a strict sequence as shown in Figure. Analysis techniques which assume that such a sequence exists are referred to as sequential demand analysis techniques.

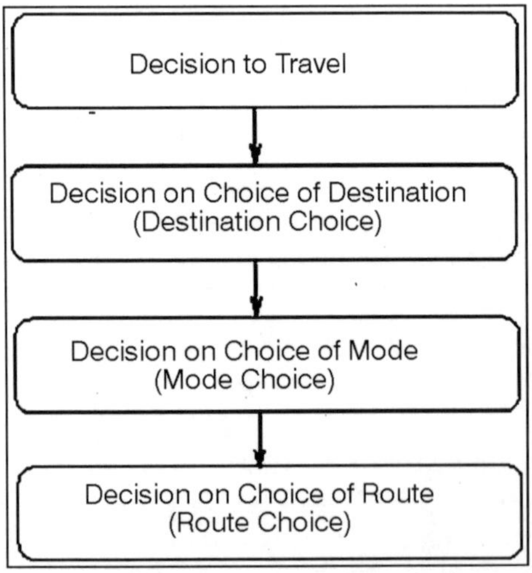

Fig. Schematic Representation of the Assumption of Sequential Decision-making.

Although, even today transportation demand is analysed sequentially, the assumption that the four major decisions of a trip-maker follow a strict sequence is possibly not the most appealing. Quite often, the *decision to travel* is changed because an appropriate destination does not exist; or an *initial choice of destination* is changed because it cannot be reached by the desirable mode of transport. It is possibly a truer picture of reality if the decision-making framework is assumed to have feedback loops. One such possible structure is shown in Figure. In this structure, there are feedback loops indicating that decisions taken earlier can be changed based on a latter decision. For example, the decision to travel may be aborted because at the *mode choice* stage if it is realised that none of the available modes suit the requirements. As stated earlier, even though the assumption of the existence of a strict sequence in the decision-making process of a potential trip-maker may be debatable, generally sequential demand analysis is used to determine the travel demand. As will be seen throughout this lecture, even with this simplifying assumption of sequential decision making, the analysis of transportation demand remains sufficiently complex. Figure shows a schematic of the sequential demand analysis procedure.

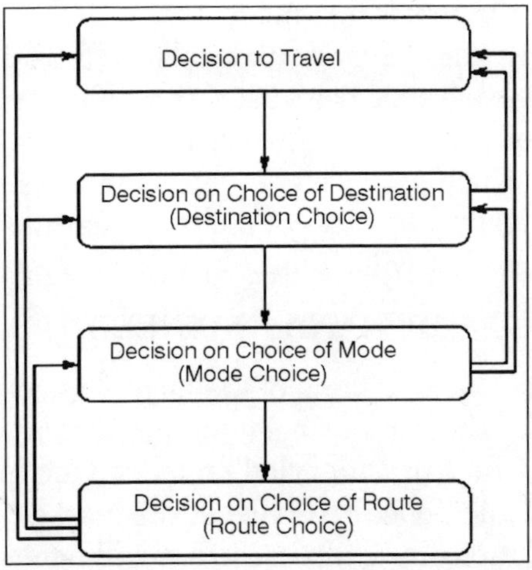

Fig. An Example of the Assumption of Non-sequential Decision-making

The figure attempts to not only emphasise the logic of the analysis procedure but also gives the names of the different classes of models used to mathematically describe each decision-making phase of the analysis procedure. Before presenting the models, a general overview of the entire process is provided. In this analysis procedure, first the entire study area is divided into various zones.

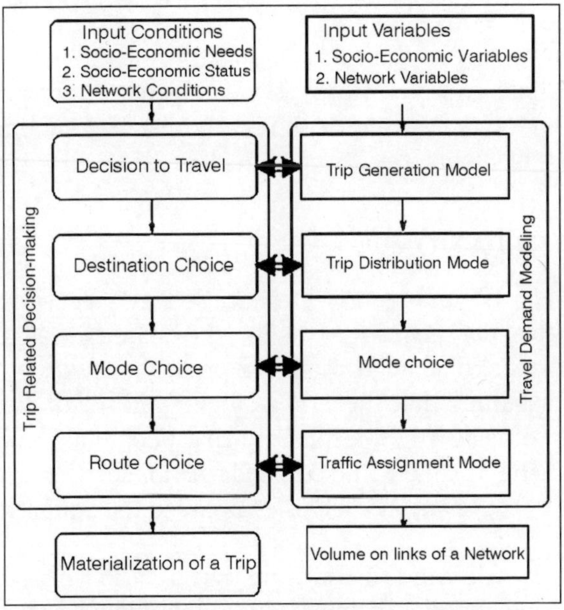

Fig. Sequential Demand Analysis Procedure.

These zones are generally obtained from the land-use pattern of the area. Next, for each zone the total number of trips generated in that zone are estimated using the trip-generation models.

The outputs of the trip-generation models are then used to determine the number of trips between all zone pairs using the trip-distribution models. Given the trip-distribution pattern, the relative shares of these trips for the different modes are estimated using the mode-choice models. Finally, the traffic-assignment models estimate the volume on each link of the network by determining the routes that will be used by the trips.

DEMAND AND NEED

To keep it simple, we may think of the buyers as consumers. Clearly, the buyers are the people who want or need the product or service—but there is more to it than that. The word "demand" refers to the willingness and ability of people to purchase the good or service in the market.

The demand relationship expresses that willingness and ability for the whole range of prices. To say that a person has a demand for a particular product is to say that the person has money with which to buy and is willing to exchange the money for the good. People will not demand what they do not want or need, but a want or a need unbacked by purchasing power is not a demand.

Similarly, it is not enough that the suppliers possess the good or (the capacity to perform) the service. Supply also means willingness to sell. Most of us have experience living in the market economic system and that makes economics seem like a common-sense field—but sometimes that common-sense feel can be deceptive.

People sometimes use the term "demand" ambiguously—as if "demand" were the same thing as need. But it is not. Need without purchasing power will not create effective demand in the marketplace. Economists sometimes stress this point by using the term "effective demand" in place of simple "demand."

THE DEMAND RELATION

"Demand" can be ambiguous in another way. We should not think of "demand" as a particular quantity—because the quantity that people are willing and able to purchase will change when the price changes.

Economics assumes that there is a systematic relationship between the price in the marketplace and the quantity that people are willing and able to buy. This relationship is called "the demand relationship" or, simply "demand." The quantity that people buy at each price is called the "quantity demanded" at that price.

We think of the "demand relationship" as a relationship between the price and the quantity demanded. It is important to distinguish between the demand relationship and the quantity demanded. This may seem like "splitting hairs," but not making the distinction between them causes a lot of confusion. The convention in economics is to use the word "demand" to mean the demand relationship and "quantity demanded" for the specific quantity that people are willing to purchase, when there could be confusion.

EXAMPLE OF THE DEMAND RELATION

As we have seen, economists think of the demand for a good or service as a relationship between the price of the good or service and the quantity demanded of that good or service.

Common sense says that the relationship is an inverse one; that is, that an increase in price will result in a decrease in the quantity demanded. In this, common sense is absolutely right. The higher the price, the less quantity demanded and conversely, the lower the price, the more quantity demanded.

Many economics textbooks use examples based on hypothetical (made-up) numbers. There is nothing wrong with that and we shall use some of them later on. But why not use a real example? Several years ago, the author estimated the demand relationship for beer. Here is an example based on that estimate. The prices quoted are wholesale prices, in cents of 1972 purchasing power. Quantity demanded is measured in millions of gallons, for the United States as a whole.

Table. Demand Schedule Beer, 1960

Price, cents/gal.	Quantity demanded, millions of gals.
50	4899.27
60	4355.67
70	3812.07
80	3268.47
90	2724.87
100	2181.27
110	1637.67
120	1094.07

DEMAND DIAGRAM FOR BEER

The demand relationship can also be expressed as a diagram, with the price on one axis and the quantity demanded on the other axis.

Conventionally, in economics, we put the price on the vertical axis and the quantity demanded on the vertical axis. This diagram will usually take the form of a line or curve. We usually call it "the demand curve" (even when it is a straight line).

Here is a "demand curve" of the demand for beer in 1960, based on the estimated numbers.

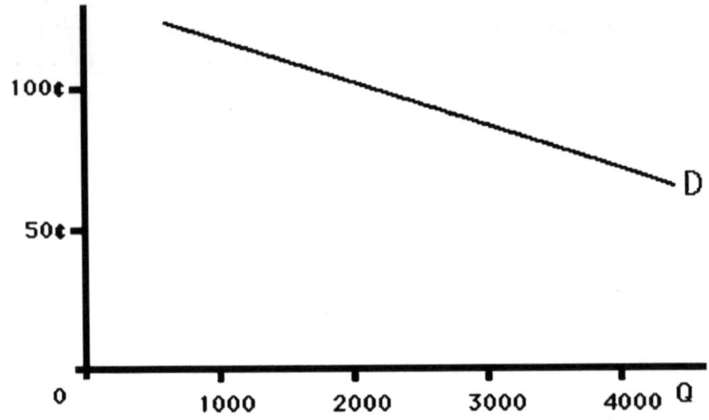

Fig. Demand for Beer

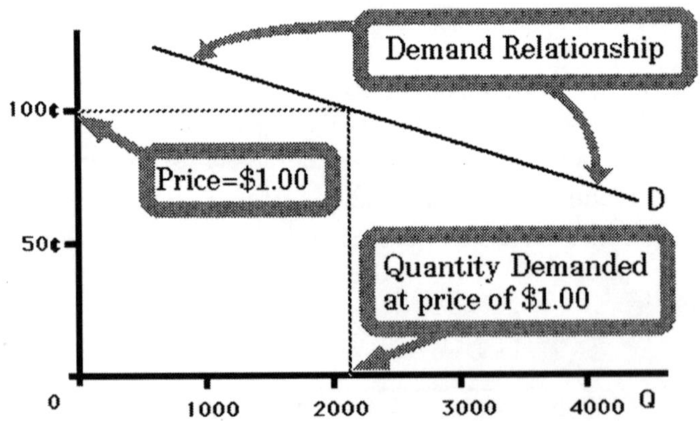

Fig. Demand Terminology

THE DEMAND RELATIONSHIP, AGAIN

Remember: when we speak of "demand" we usually mean the *entire demand relationship,* that is, the entire demand curve or table.

By contrast, the "quantity demanded" is the *particular point* on the demand curve, or the quantity in a particular line of the table.

THE CURVE DEMAND

The relationship between price and the amount of a product people want to buy is what economists call the demand curve. This relationship is inverse or indirect because as price gets higher, people want less of a particular product. This inverse relationship is almost always found in studies of particular products, and its very widespread occurrence has given it a special name: the law of demand.

The word "law" in this case does not refer to a bill that the government has passed but to an observed regularity. There are various ways to express the relationship between price and the quantity that people will buy. Mathematically, one can say that quantity demanded is a function of price, with other factors held constant, or:

$$Qd = f$$

A more elementary way to capture the relationship is in the form of a table. The numbers in the table are what one expects in a demand curve: as price goes up, the amount people are willing to buy decreases.

Table. A Demand Curve

Price of Widgets Want to Buy	Number of Widgets People
$1.00	100
$2.00	90
$3.00	70
$4.00	40

The same information can also be plotted on a graph, where it will look like the graph.

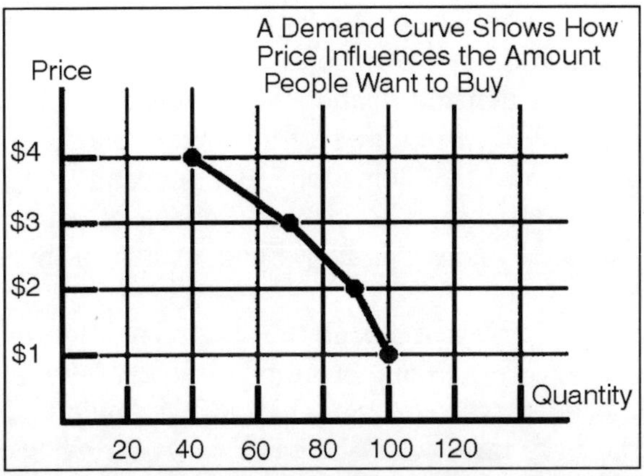

If one of the factors being held constant becomes unstuck, changes, and then is held constant again, the relationship between price and quantity will change. For example, suppose the price of getwids, a substitute for widgets, falls.

Then, people who previously were buying widgets will reconsider their choices, and some may decide to switch to getwids.

This would be true at all possible prices for widgets. These changes in the way people will behave at each price will change the demand curve to look like the table.These are the same changes shown in a graph.

Table. A Demand Curve can Shift

Price of Widgets	Number of Widgets People	Want to Buy
$1.00	[100] becomes	80
$2.00	[90] becomes	70
$3.00	[70] becomes	50
$4.00	[40] becomes	10

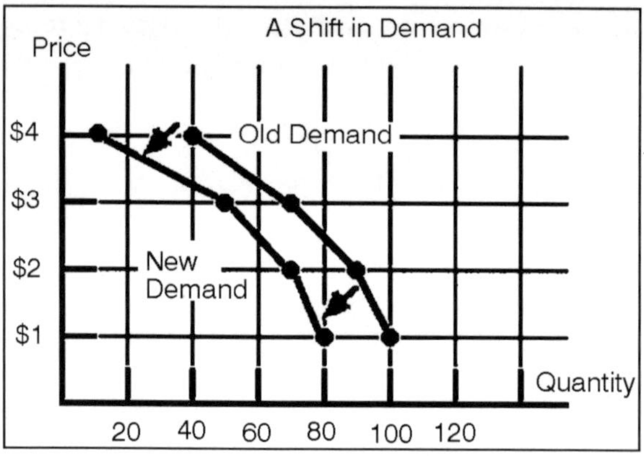

DEMAND TERMINOLOGY

If the price of widgets is originally $1.00 and people are buying 100, they may change to 90 for two reasons. One reason is that the price may rise to $2.00. The other reason is that one of the factors that is assumed to be constant may change, so that even though the price has not changed, quantity will. Economists distinguish these two cases.

In the first case the demand relationship or schedule has not changed, but there has been movement within the relationship. Economists call a change of this sort a change in quantity demanded. The second sort of change is an alteration of the relationship. The original pairing of price and quantity is destroyed and replaced by a new pairing. Economists call this sort of change a change in demand.

It is important to realise that though the demand relationship looks concrete when it is emphasised with a table or graph, in everyday life demand curves are hidden. A demand curve refers to what people would do if various prices were charged, and very rarely are enough prices charged so a clear demand curve can be seen.

This is not to say that the concept is of no importance to people who sell. They may not be interested in the demand curve as a relationship, but they do find it a boundary or constraint on their behaviour.

If there were an actual widget seller facing the demand curve in our demand table, he would find that he could not sell more than 90 widgets if he wanted to charge $2.00. He could of course sell fewer if he wanted to. He could sell only 70 at $2.00, but if he did this, he would earn far less than he could. If he wanted to sell more than 90, he would have to lower his price.

Thus, to an actual businessman the demand curve is important as a limitation on what he can do. A businessman may not know exactly where the demand curve is, and he may not think of it as fixed.

Advertising—either informing or persuading people—can move the boundary. As we proceed further, as suggested, see that there are still other ways to view the demand curve in addition to seeing it as a mathematical relationship and as a boundary that limits sellers.

DETERMINANTS OF DEMAND ANALYSIS

Economic analysis has recognised the role of key variables in determining demand and consumption. In practice, the distinction between demand and consumption as an equilibrium quantity at a given price, is frequently ignored. The development of "gap" type models emphasise the common approach of projecting 'demand' as a fixed quantity independent of price. Demand, as the relationship between price and quantity, is subject to change over time due to changes in the underlying factors held constant by the static notion of demand. Changes in demand "shifters" are often included in economic estimation of demand representing anticipated dynamics in these determinants.

LEVELS OF INCOME

A key determinant of demand is the level of income evident in the appropriate country or region under analysis. As a generality, the higher the level of aggregate and/or personal income the higher the demand for a typical commodity, including forest products. More of a good or service will be chosen at a given price where income is higher. Thus determinants of demand normally utilise some form of income measure, including Gross Domestic Product.

POPULATION

Population is of course a key determinant of demand. Although all forest products do not necessarily enter final consumer markets, the actual markets are largely presumed to be functionally related to population. Growing populations are positively correlated to timber demands in the aggregate, as well as specifically to individual forest products. Frequently, population and income estimators are combined, as in the case of the use of Gross Domestic Product per capita.

END MARKET INDICATORS

The use of end market indicators as determinants of demand is frequently incorporated into demand analysis. For example, much of the final use of forest products is linked to construction. Indicators and trends related to construction activities, or which are determinants of construction, provide indirect estimates of the influence of these activities as the source of derived demand for wood. Housing starts, public investments, interest rates, etc., can be highly correlated to timber demand.

AVAILABILITY AND PRICE OF SUBSTITUTE GOODS

Consumption choices related to timber are also influenced by the alternative options facing users in the relevant marketplace. The availability of potential substitute products, and their prices, weigh heavily in determining the elasticity of demand, both in the short run sense and over time. Fuelwood, as a dominant use of timber in the Asia Pacific Region, reflects conditions of very limited options for energy sources at 'reasonable' prices. Rural low income or subsistence populations simply do not have 'options' regarding energy - they use wood or go without. Demand, at this basic level, in almost perfectly inelastic. The cost does not materially affect consumption quantity.

Suitability of alternative goods and services is, in part, a question of knowledge as well as availability. Market information regarding alternative products, quality, convenience, and dependability all influence choices.

Under conditions of increased scarcity and rising prices for tropical hardwood panels, for example, users have a positive incentive to search for and investigate the suitability of alternatives that were previously overlooked or ignored.

TASTES AND PREFERENCES

All markets are shaped by collective and individual tastes and preferences. These patterns are partly shaped by culture and partly implanted by information and knowledge of products and services.

Different societies use forest products differently because of these differences in taste and preferences. For example, markets for wood products in Japan are commonly recognised as requiring very high product quality standards, the importance of visual attributes of wood, and other preferences not commonly found in many other markets.

THE LONG AND SHORT RUN

Here's a complication: The supply relationship will depend on how long the suppliers have to adjust to a change in the price. With respect to supply, time plays a role that it does not (in most cases) play in the case of demand. If there is plenty of time for the suppliers to adjust to a change in the price, we have a long run analysis.

This means the sellers can invest and exp and productive capacity, in response to a high price, or can gradually reduce the productive capacity by under-replacing worn-out equipment in the case of a low price. However, if the sellers are not sure the high or low price will continue for a long time, a short run analysis may be more appropriate.

In a short run analysis, we treat the plant and equipment of the industry as inflexibly given. In that case, output can be increased only by using that fixed plant and equipment more intensively. Thus, we would expect the adjustment of supply to a change in price to be more complete in the long run than in the short run.

We do not ordinarily apply the long run versus short run distinction to demand, but there are some special cases where it might be important.

For example, for durable goods such as cars, buyers might adjust less completely in the short run than in the long, since they can postpone replacement of their durable goods until the price comes down. In the long run, the goods wear out and so the consumers cannot postpone replacement long enough.

In summary:

- In the *short run* the plant and equipment (productive capacity) of the industry are fixed
- In the *long run* sellers can change the productive capacity, in response to the price

EQUILIBRIUM OF SUPPLY AND DEMAND

Now that we have introduced the concepts of supply and demand separately—with illustrative examples of the demand for and supply of, beer—it is time to move on from analysis to synthesis and put the two concepts together. In economic theory, the interaction of supply and demand is understood as *equilibrium*.

We may think of demand as a force tending to increase the price of a good and of supply as a force tending to reduce the price.

When the two forces balance one another, the price would neither rise nor fall, but would be stable. This analogy leads us to think of the stable or natural price in a particular market as the "equilibrium" price.

This sort of "equilibrium" exists when the price is just high enough so that the quantity supplied just equals the quantity demanded. If we superimpose the demand curve and the supply curve in the same diagram, we can easily visualize this "equilibrium" price. It is the price at which the two curves cross. The corresponding quantity is the quantity that would be traded in a market equilibrium.

Let's see what that looks like in the market for beer.

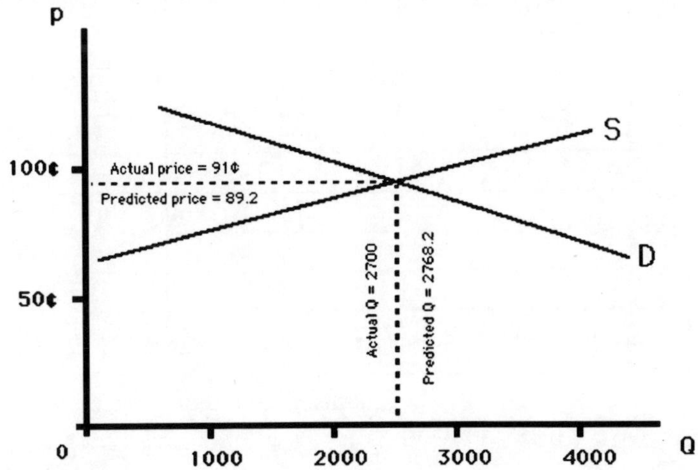

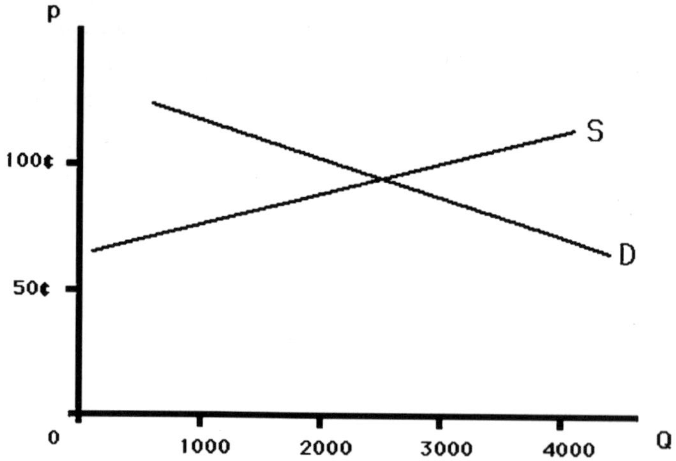

EQUILIBRIUM OF ESTIMATED SUPPLY AND DEMAND FOR BEER

As usual, we illustrate the concept with the estimated supply and demand for beer in 1960. Approximates the equilibrium of supply and demand for beer in 1960, on the basis of the estimates given before.

THE SUPPLY AND DEMAND DIAGRAM

Here is the supply and demand diagram you just saw, with some of the detail removed. This is a very common kind of diagram in economics, so it might be a good idea to pause and review the principles it expresses.

EXCESS DEMAND

Why do we call this an "equilibrium?" Let's see what happens when price is not high enough to make quantity supplied equal to quantity demanded:

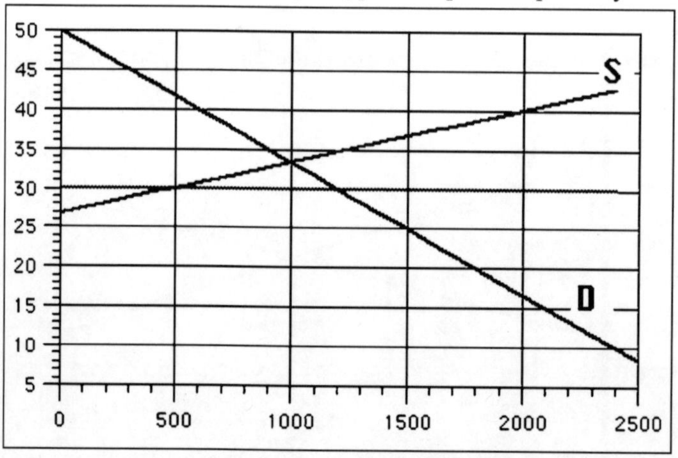

What we see here is that the quantity demanded exceeds the quantity supplied—we have excess demand.

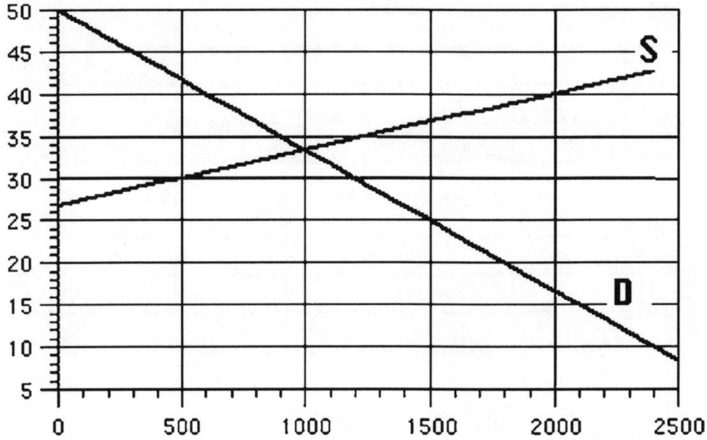

Fig. Price Rises to Equilibrium

With a price of $30, quantity supplied is 500, while quantity demanded is about 1200.

Thus, demanders will compete against one another, offering higher prices for the limited supply and the price will rise. Here's an animated diagram that shows about what we think will happen in these circumstances:

EXCESS SUPPLY

What if the price is too high?

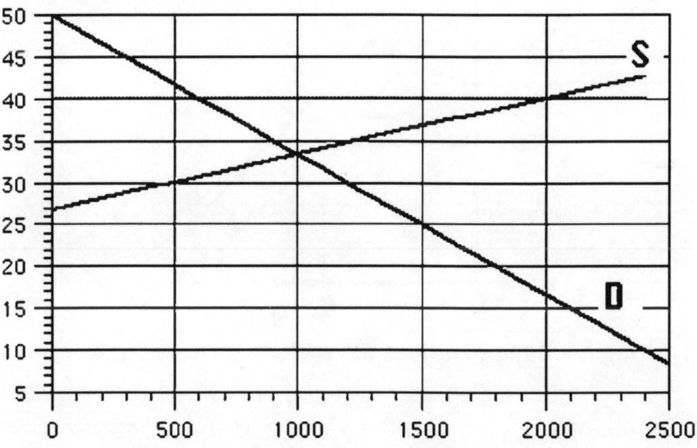

Fig. Excess Supply

Here we have excess supply—the quantity supplied exceeds the quantity demanded.

Quantity supplied is 2000 at a price of 40, while quantity demanded is only 600.

Thus, suppliers will compete to sell what they can by cutting the price. Here's another animated diagram that shows about what we think will happen in these circumstances:

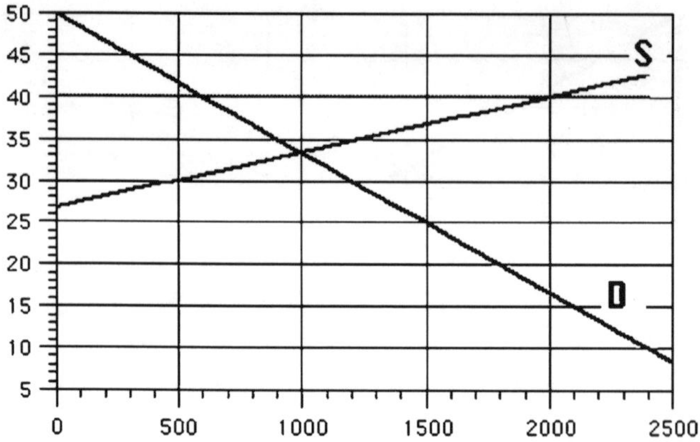

Fig. Price Drops to Equilibrium

A CHANGE IN DEMAND

Now let's put these concepts to work with some applications. First, a pretty simple one. In the early stages of industrialization, in Britain, new jobs in industry made people better off—for the first time, they had enough money income to buy food and improve their nutrition. That was the good news. The bad news was that the supply of food did not increase.

This means there was an increase in the demand for food, as shown in Figure:

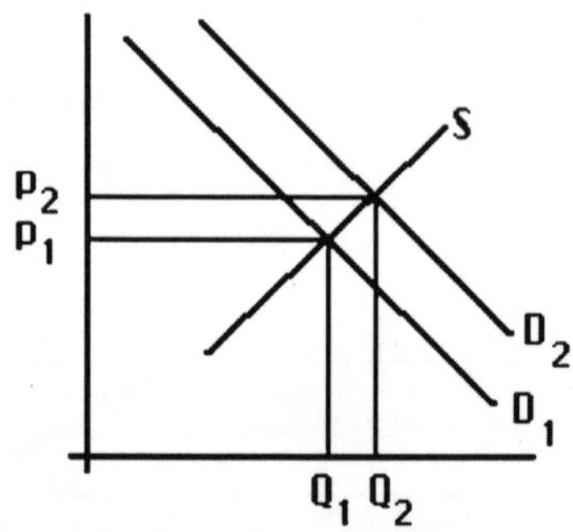

Fig. Changing Equilibrium with an Increase in Dem.

Before the increase in income, demand was D_1 and supply was S, so that the equilibrium quantity of food sold was Q_1 and the price per unit of food sold was p_1. However, the increase in income resulted in a shift of the demand curve rightward, as shown by D_2 and a new equilibrium quantity at Q_2 and a price of p_2.

Historically, this increase in the price of food led to agitation for the government to repeal the tariff on food (the "corn laws, " as they were called) and move towards free trade. This controversy on the "corn laws" played a great role in the early evolution of economic thinking, as economists joined the argument on both sides.

A CHANGE IN SUPPLY

Shows a decrease in the supply of food.

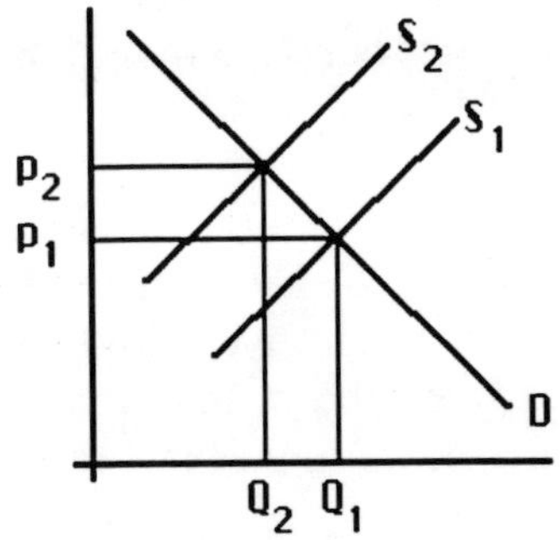

Fig. Changing Equilibrium with a Reduction in Supply

We will continue with another example of the supply and demand for food. Agriculture is very sensitive to the weather and bad weather can cause a reduction in the supply of food from normal levels. With normal weather, supply would be S_1 and demand is D, so that the equilibrium quantity of food sold was Q_1 and the price per unit of food sold was p_1. However, bad weather shifts the supply curve leftward, as shown by S_2 and a new equilibrium quantity at Q_2 and a price of p_2. Fluctuations in weather conditions from year to year result in changes in prices and production of food and agricultural commodities of all kinds. Since the weather is different in different parts of the world, there will usually be some crop in some part of the world that is in less supply because of weather conditions. Follow the business news for a while and you are sure to see some examples. Now, let's go on to a more complicated—but classical and practically important—example of application of supply and demand theory.

EXCISE TAX

Here's an application: There is an "excise tax" on beer. What happens to price and sales when such a tax is imposed? (The term "excise tax" is a bit redundant, since "excise" is an old word for "tax." Conventionally, though, an excise tax means a tax per physical unit; for example, per gallon).

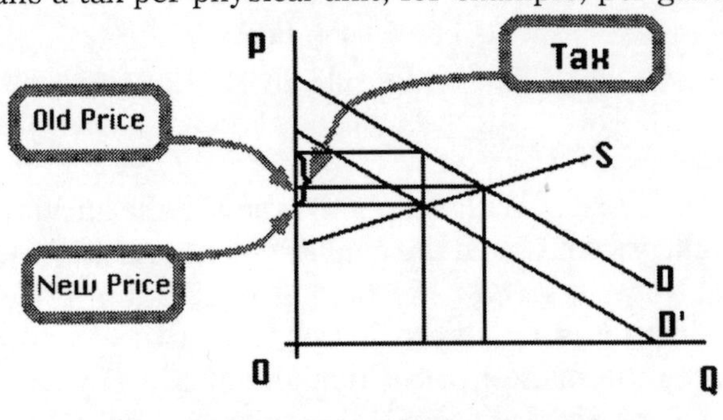

Fig. Who Pays an Excise Tax?

The figure shows the impact of an excise tax. From the point of view of sellers, the tax decreases demand from D to D'; the vertical distance between the two curves is the tax. The price paid to the seller falls, but not as much as the tax, because the cutback in production moves downward along the supply curve.

SUBSIDY

Let's use the same approach to analyse the effect of a subsidy.

Subsidy: A subsidy is a payment from the government to a firm or individual in the private sector, usually on the condition that the person or firm that receives the subsidy produce or do something, or to increase the income of a poor person.

For our example, we will think of a subsidy for the production of corn. (Some countries have paid subsidies for the production of grain in order to make food cheaper for poor people). Let us suppose the government pays corn farmers a dollar per bushel of corn, in addition to whatever price they get in the marketplace. Figure shows the supply and demand for corn. A subsidy per unit of production works pretty much like an excise tax, except in reverse. In particular, we can look at the change from the point of view either of buyers or sellers. In this example, we will look at the subsidy from the point of view of the buyers. From their point of view, the subsidy is an increase in supply.

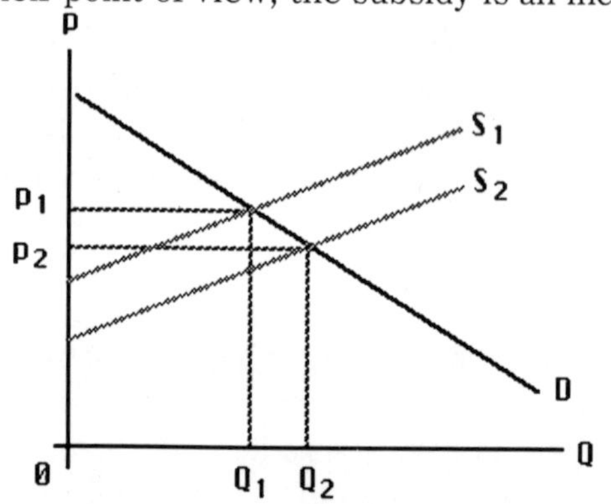

Fig. A Subsidy

Accordingly, the figure shows the subsidy shifting the supply curve to the right, from S_1 to S_2. The vertical distance is the amount of the subsidy: one dollar per bushel.

Demand is D, as usual. With supply S_1—before the subsidy is given—the market equilibrium price is p_1 and the equilibrium production is Q_1. With supply S_2—when the subsidy is given—the market equilibrium price is p_2 and the equilibrium production is Q_2. We may conclude that a subsidy per unit of production reduces the market price (though not quite by the full amount of the subsidy) and increases the production of the item subsidized.

DEMAND FORECASTING

A demand forecast is the prediction of what will happen to your company's existing product sales. It would be best to determine the demand forecast using a multi-functional approach. The inputs from sales and marketing, finance, and production should be considered.

The final demand forecast is the consensus of all participating managers. You may also want to put up a Sales and Operations Planning group composed of representatives from the different departments that will be tasked to prepare the demand forecast.

Determination of the demand forecasts is done through the following steps:

- Determine the use of the forecast
- Select the items to be forecast
- Determine the time horizon of the forecast
- Select the forecasting model(s)
- Gather the data
- Make the forecast
- Validate and implement results

The time horizon of the forecast is classified as follows:

Description	Forecast Horizon		
	Short-range	**Medium-range**	**Long-range**
Duration	Usually less than 3 months, maximum of 1 year	3 months to 3 years	More than 3 years
Applicability	Job scheduling, worker assignments	Sales and production planning, budgeting	New product development, facilities planning

HOW IS DEMAND FORECAST DETERMINED?

There are two approaches to determine demand forecast:

- The qualitative approach, and
- The quantitative approach.

The comparison of these two approaches is shown:

Description	Qualitative Approach	Quantitative Approach
Applicability	Used when situation is vague and little data exist	Used when situation is stable and historical data exist
Considerations	Involves intuition and experience	Involves mathematical techniques
Techniques	Jury of executive opinion Sales force composite Delphi method Consumer market survey	Time series models Causal models

QUALITATIVE FORECASTING METHODS

Your company may wish to try any of the qualitative forecasting methods if you do not have historical data on your products' sales.

Qualitative Method	Description
Jury of executive opinion	The opinions of a small group of high-level managers are pooled and together they estimate demand. The group uses their managerial experience, and in some cases, combines the results of statistical models.
Sales force composite	Each salesperson is asked to project their sales. Since the salesperson is the one closest to the marketplace, he has the capacity to know what the customer wants. These projections are then combined at the municipal, provincial and regional levels.
Delphi method	A panel of experts is identified where an expert could be a decision maker, an ordinary employee, or an industry expert. Each of them will be asked individually for their estimate of the demand. An iterative process is conducted until the experts have reached a consensus.
Consumer market survey	The customers are asked about their purchasing plans and their projected buying behaviour. A large number of respondents is needed here to be able to generalise certain results.

QUANTITATIVE FORECASTING METHODS

There are two forecasting models here:

- The time series model; and
- The causal model.

A time series is a set of evenly spaced numerical data and is obtained by observing responses at regular time periods. In the time series model, the forecast is based only on past values and assumes that factors that influence the past, the present and the future sales of your products will continue. On the other hand, the causal model uses a mathematical technique known as the regression analysis that relates a dependent variable to an independent variable in the form of a linear equation. The time series forecasting methods are:

Time Series Forecasting Method	Description
Naïve Approach	Assumes that demand in the next period is the same as demand in most recent period; demand pattern may not always be that stable. *For example*: If July sales were 50, then August sales will also be 50.

Time Series Forecasting Method	Description
Moving Averages	MA is a series of arithmetic means and is used if little or no trend is present in the data; provides an overall impression of data over time. A simple moving average uses average demand for a fixed sequence of periods and is good for stable demand with no pronounced behavioural patterns. *Equation*: F 4 = [D 1 + D2 + D3] / 4 F – forecast, D – Demand, No. – Period. A weighted moving average adjusts the moving average method to reflect fluctuations more closely by assigning weights to the most recent data, meaning, that the older data is usually less important. The weights are based on intuition and lie between 0 and 1 for a total of 1.0. *Equation*: WMA 4 = (W) (D3) + (W) (D2) + (W) (D1) WMA – Weighted moving average, W – Weight, D – Demand, No. – Period.
Exponential Smoothing	The exponential smoothing is an averaging method that reacts more strongly to recent changes in demand by assigning a smoothing constant to the most recent data more strongly; useful if recent changes in data are the results of actual change instead of just random fluctuations. F t + 1 = a D t + (1 - a) F t Where, F t + 1 = the forecast for the next period D t = actual demand in the present period F t = the previously determined forecast for the present period o = a weighting factor referred as smoothing constant
Time Series Decomposition	The time series decomposition adjusts the seasonality by multiplying the normal forecast by a seasonal factor

COMPETITION AND EQUILIBRIUM

What we have seen is that the price will be in constant motion, up or down, except when quantity demanded is equal to quantity supplied. That is the position of rest. Put another way, it is the price towards which competition pushes the price.

At equilibrium, there is no competition either to buy or to sell, because everyone can buy or sell however much they may wish, *at the going price.* But whenever the market is away from equilibrium, competition will arise and tend to force it back.

Competition eliminates itself, by forcing the market into an equilibrium in which there is no need to compete. (This is a very different concept of competition than the biological "struggle for survival!)

FORCES OPPOSING COMPETITION

We have seen that competition forces the market into equilibrium. However, this might fail if:

- There is only one seller or buyer, hence no competition
- Sellers or buyers agree ("conspire") not to compete in this way
- It is illegal to compete by offering a higher or lower price
- People are unable to compete by price offer—for example, they do not know who else buys or sells the item, or are unsure of the quality of the good or dervice offered by other traders.

CHANGING DEMAND AND SUPPLY

We have seen how demand and supply interact, giving rise to an equilibrium price and quantity traded. In order to use these concepts for practical purposes, we need to think about the ways in which demand and supply can change and what happens when they do change.

Remember that economists think of "a change in demand" as a shift of an entire demand curve. Thus, a change in any one of the non-price determinants—a change in income, population, or expectations, for example—would shift the demand curve to the right or to the left. Likewise supply. By the way, always think of a shift in supply as "leftward" or "rightward, " not "up" or "down." Thinking in terms of "up" and "down" will cause confusion!

INCREASE IN DEMAND

Here is a figure to illustrate an increase in demand. The demand curve shifts from D_1 to D_2. With the new demand curve, there is a greater quantity demanded at every price. That is what we mean by an increase in demand.

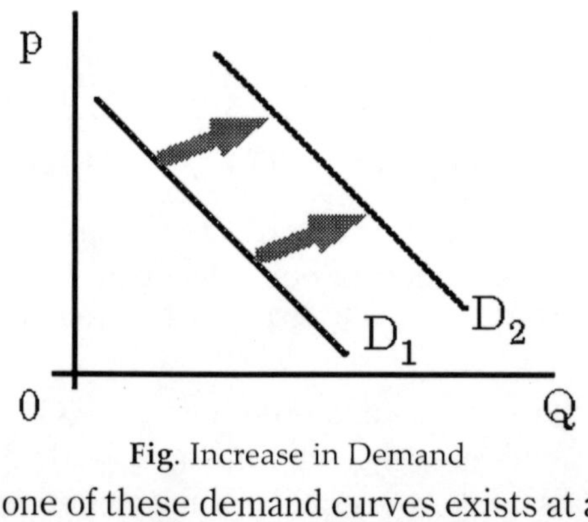

Fig. Increase in Demand

Of course, only one of these demand curves exists at any one time. Here's an animation that gives a more dynamic idea of what economists have in mind by "a change in demand."

We see the demand curve moving fairly smoothly to the right, then stabilizing at its new position.

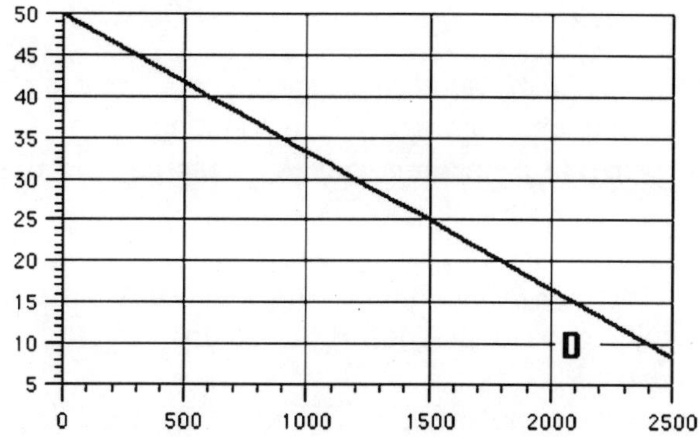

Fig. Animation 3a: Increase in Demand

DECREASE IN DEMAND

Here is a figure to illustrate a decrease in demand. The demand curve shifts from D_1 to D_2. With the new demand curve, there is a smaller quantity demanded at every price. That is what we mean by a decrease in demand.

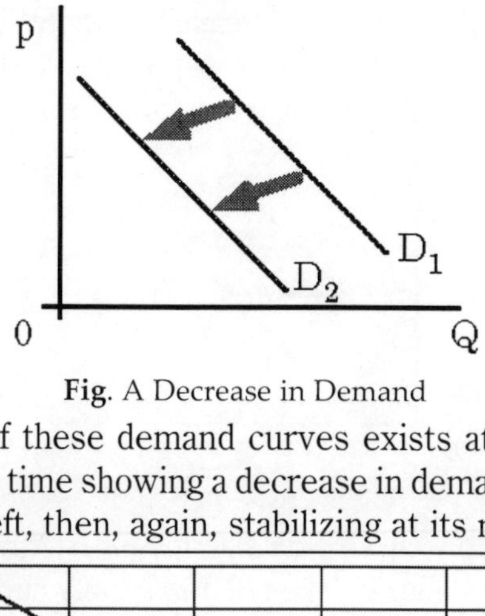

Fig. A Decrease in Demand

Again, only one of these demand curves exists at any one time. Here's another animation, this time showing a decrease in demand. We see the demand curve moving to the left, then, again, stabilizing at its new position.

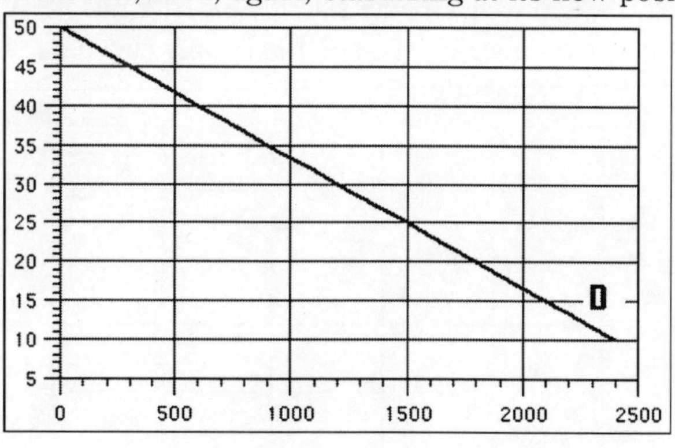

Fig. Animation: Decrease in Demand

Again: hit the reload button on your browser window to see it again.

SHIFTING DEMAND

Here are some things that would cause the demand curve to shift:

- A change in income for the average consumeR;
  - If an increase in income causes an increase in the demand for a particular good, that good is called a "normal" good. Example: steak.
  - If an increase in income causes a decrease in the demand for a particular good, that good is called an "inferior" good. Example: red beans.
- A change in the population.
- Changes in the prices of other goods.
  - Complements.
  - Substitutes.
- Changes in consumer tastes.

INCREASE IN SUPPLY

Here is a figure to illustrate an increase in supply. The supply curve shifts to the right, from S_1 to S_2, so that the new supply curve shows a greater quantity supplied at every price. That is what we mean by an increase in supply.

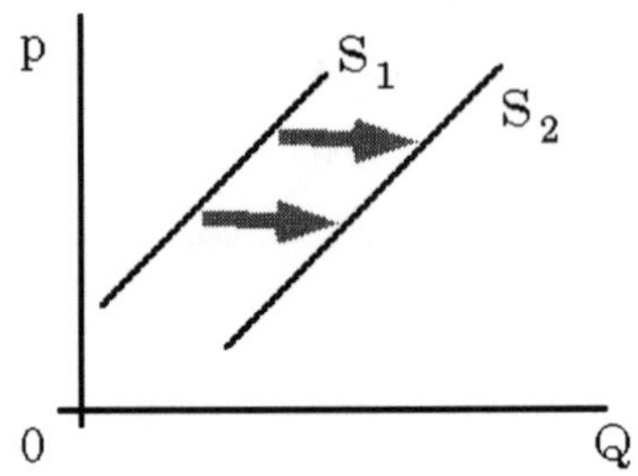

Fig. Increase in Supply

Again, only one supply curve exists at any given time. Here is an animation to illustrate the idea dynamically. We see the supply curve moving to the right, then stabilizing at its new position.

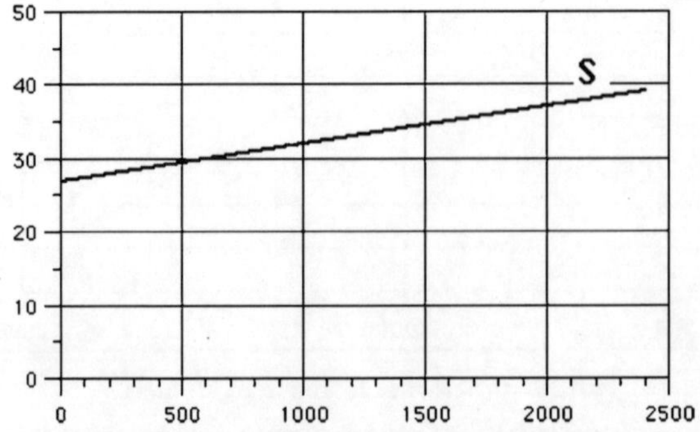

Fig. Animation 4a: Increase in Supply

DECREASE IN SUPPLY

This figure illustrates a decrease in supply. The supply curve shifts to the left, from S_1 to S_2. The new supply curve shows a smaller quantity supplied at every price and that is what we mean by a decrease in supply.

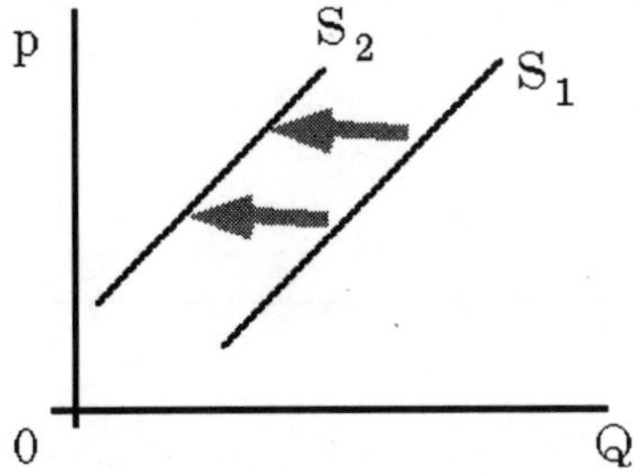

Fig. A Decrease in Supply

We see the supply curve moving to the left, then stabilizing at its new position.

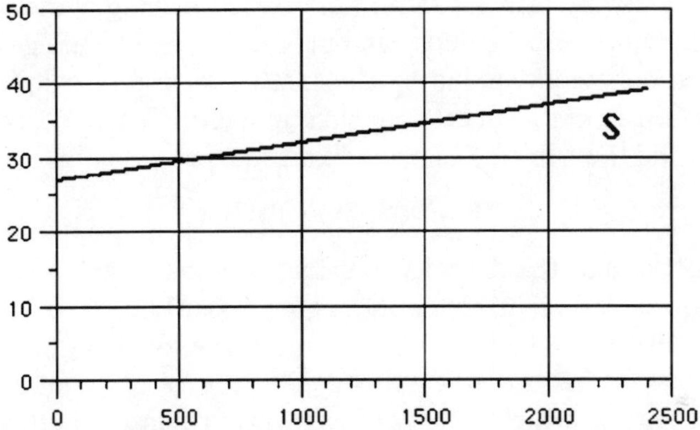

Fig. Animation 4b: Decrease in Supply

SHIFTING SUPPLY

Here are some things that would cause the supply curve to shift:

- Changes in the prices of input goods.
  - Labour
  - Raw materials
- A change in technology.
- Changes in natural conditions.
  - Rainfall
  - Environmental Conditions

7

Market Situations and Pricing

Prices and the price-making process are subjects that have occupied the serious attention of economists and economic analysts as well as businessmen for many generations. Numerous treatises have been written on their various phases as well as on the general subject, especially from a theoretical approach. It is intended to devote principal attention to the meaning of the term price, to the price-making process in theory and in practice, and to the general pattern of actual price behaviour, ncluding the matter of price flexibility and price rigidity. Certain specific price and discount policies used by marketing organizations and the subjects of price-fixing and price control are considered.

MEANING OF PRICE

Any good that has the capacity to satisfy a human want is said to possess *utility*. The power of such utility or of the good possessing it to command other goods in normal and regular exchange is its *value*. Such value, expressed in monetary terms, is the *price* of the good. Thus, price is the money value of a commodity or service which emerges in a market transaction. In a competitive economy, prices are the grist that markets grind.

Economists generally distinguish between two types of prices — the *actual or market price* and the *normal price*. The actual or *market* price is the price that exists in the market at any given place or time or in different places and at different times. It is the price which the seller actually receives for his product and which the buyer actually pays for it.

Some leading economists consider market price as the price during a period within which the supply of the commodity is fixed. In the case of farm crops, for example, the supply may be known and fixed for a given season. In such a case, the seller must accept the market price which then prevails at his point of supply. His only alternatives are to ship to another market or to hold off from the market until some future time when better prices are anticipated.

The *normal* price is altogether a theoretical concept and is presumed to be the price towards which the market price tends, although the two may at no time coincide.

The normal price, in turn, may be of two species: short run and long run. The former emerges when the seller has a definitely fixed size of plant, and the industry has a fixed number of firms; while the long-run normal price is that ruling over a period long enough to permit entrepreneurs to build plants of any size or to divest themselves of plants entirely. Generally, the economist's concern with price is what may be labeled "the long-run normal price" and not so much with everyday market prices.

This is not difficult to understand, for, *theoretically*, it is the long-run normal price which will tend to bring upon the market just that supply for which buyers will be willing to pay enough to cover the costs of providing and marketing that commodity and yield a reasonable net profit. A firm cannot continue permanently to sell its product below cost.

It would certainly have to cease operations, due to exhaustion of financial resources caused by continuous losses. This would-curtail the supply, which would gradually cause prices to advance sufficiently to yield a profit to the firms remaining in business.

Consequently, the lower limit of price for any commodity would, in the long run, be fixed by the costs of the marginal units. The upper limit of the normal price tends to be determined, in the long run, by what buyers are willing to pay for an existing supply.

Both upper and lower limits supposedly operate over a period of time. Market prices, on the other hand, are the prices that prevail from day to day and may, at least temporarily, greatly deviate from the *normal* price limits. When quantities of highly perishable fruits and vegetables much in excess of local requirements are received in a given market, prices are depressed much below cost. When a manufacturer or retailer accumulates an excessive inventory, it may become necessary for him to dispose of the surplus at reduced prices which may not cover actual costs.

Conversely, under other conditions the price may be substantially higher than cost. When new styles of garments prove to be popular, the price at which the garments are sold is considerably above cost, for under these circumstances producers and distributors charge all that the traffic will bear. A similar situation obtains when certain brands have become well established and the demand for them is widespread and constant, for this condition virtually marks the product as a semi monopoly. In business practice, price generally has the same meaning as in economic theory, namely the money received by the seller of a product or money paid by the buyer for it. In particular situations, it is often necessary, however, to be much more specific. From the standpoint of the buyer, price is cost and may be viewed differently than the seller thinks of it.

It may be necessary to indicate very precisely, in some cases, whether transportation is or is not included, and whether certain kinds of discounts are price adjustments or are compensation granted for other reasons as, for example, cash discounts for prepayment of invoices. In interpreting certain legislation, price may have to be defined as specified for purposes of enforcement.

To illustrate, in delivered pricing systems, prices have been judged as the "mill net," meaning the delivered price received by the seller minus transportation costs which he paid on shipments of sales. Distinctions must also be made in many situations between quoted prices and prices actually paid, which may vary considerably when negotiation is common.

PRICES AND MARKETING

The subject of prices has many facets. Marketing administrators and informed students of marketing should have knowledge pertaining to a number of price and pricing questions which, for convenience, are outlined as follows:

- Meaning of price
- Importance of prices
- Price determination in theory and in practice
- Pricing as a part of the marketing mix
- Price and discount policies
- Price behaviour and price patterns at different distributive levels and in different commodity or industrial groups
- Nature and implications of price flexibility and price rigidity
- Price trends of a long-term nature and current movements as reflected by appropriate price indexes
- Price change
- Price regulation
- Price control in time of emergency and in time of peace

IMPORTANCE OF PRICES IN THE ECONOMY

Prices paid for goods and services play a dominant part in our economic life. In actual practice, they help to determine the *money* wages paid for labour and the *real* wages received by labour, *i.e.*, the amounts of goods and services which the money wages will buy. For consumers generally, prices have a significant bearing on their standard of living. For the seller of goods they are of utmost importance. A major aim of all marketing and merchandising is to sell goods at a price that will cover all product costs including operating expenses, and leave a reasonable net profit to the entrepreneur.

Thus prices are directly related to net profit, and net profit—the principal motivating force of business—depends largely upon the price policies adopted and upon the price-making process. Without net profits, our competitive system could not continue to function. Thus reasonable net profits are essential for industrial and social progress within the framework of a democracy. In the long run, prices serve to regulate economic activity. When prices become relatively low in a given industry because of increased supply in that industry or decreased demand for its products, profits tend to decline, vanish, or to be replaced by losses. Under such circumstances, capital, land, labour, and enterprise are shifted from that industry to others that are more remunerative. This process, in actuality, is often slow, painful, and involves significant social costs related to the relocation of economic resources, including labour.

It is necessary, however, if the goal of marketing effort is to be the satisfaction of the wants of customers which find expression in free markets. On the other hand, when prices are relatively high in a given field of economic activity, capital, land, labour, and enterprise are attracted to it and the supply of its products is thereby enhanced. In this manner, in a competitive economy, prices tend to determine the allocation of economic resources to the most effective uses.

PRICE DETERMINATION IN THEORY

Price determination as analyzed and explained in economic theory provides a desirable point of departure for subsequent discussion of price determination in practice and its relationship to the total marketing process. In order to understand the economist's explanation of the price making process, to which he often refers as the market-type analysis, one must be familiar with the hypotheses used and the general framework of discussion.

Commonly, he starts with an analysis of pure or perfect competition and the prices that emerge under such conditions; then he considers the several forms of monopoly, and their role in price determination; and finally, he deals with what he generally terms the forms of imperfect or monopolistic competition (which in reality represent what should probably be termed normal or workable competition) and the functioning of the price-making process in that environment.

NATURE OF PURE OR PERFECT COMPETITION

Probably one of the best generic definitions of this kind of competition, from the sellers' Viewpoint, is the following: "Competition is rivalry in selling goods, in which each selling unit normally seeks maximum net revenue, under conditions such that the price or prices each seller can charge are effectively limited by the free option of the buyer to buy from a rival seller or sellers of what we think of as 'the same' product, necessitating an effort of each seller to equal or exceed the attractiveness of the others' offerings to a sufficient number of buyers to accomplish the end in view."

In order to have pure or perfect competition, the following conditions or prerequisites are essential:

- A *large number of small sellers,* so that no one seller's action will have any appreciable effect on the *supply* of the product and consequently its price.

- A *large number of small buyers,* so that the action of any one buyer will have no appreciable effect on the *demand* for the product and on the resultant price.
- The *product must be completely identical, standardized, or thoroughly homogeneous,* so that it would make no difference whether it is obtained from one seller or another.
- There must be *complete and accurate knowledge of conditions of supply and demand,* and all buyers and sellers must be in possession of such knowledge.
- All buyers must buy and all sellers must offer to sell *under exactly the same conditions* with regard to credit terms, delivery, guaranties, etc.
- *Every buyer and every seller must act in a rational or sensible way* and must in no way be affected by any consideration other than price. In a system of this kind there must be no room for complicated motives or for human frailties; there is room only for the economic man."

There must be a perfectly elastic supply of the factors of production. In order to make for such elasticity of supply, there must be free and easy entry into the business of new sellers or of an expansion in plant on the part of existing sellers. This, of course, also implies free and easy exit from business if a curtailment in supply is warranted.

MARKET PRICE UNDER PURE OR PERFECT COMPETITION

If it were possible to achieve these conditions, *market prices would be established at a point where the existing demand for a given commodity would clear the market of the available supply.*

Demand may be defined as want coupled with ability to buy. Generally, more units of a given commodity will be purchased at a lower price and fewer units at a higher price. By supply is meant a schedule of the amounts which will be offered by sellers as the price varies. Sellers will make available larger supplies whenever price is greater than cost of production, and conversely, they will shift their efforts to other activities when the price is not sufficient to cover costs.

Because no individual seller has any effect upon total supply and no single buyer has any effect upon total demand, prices are beyond the control of individual buyers or sellers. If the market price is currently below the cost of production for a given seller, he must take a loss; and if this continues he must ultimately go out of business. If the same situation confronts a number of sellers, the number dropping out of the industry may have some effect upon the total supply that will be made available at a given price. If supply decreases relative to demand, buyers are forced to bid up the price, and in this way upward revisions of price are accomplished. Such upward revisions may again encourage greater production.

Similarly, if the price of a commodity is too high for a given buyer, he must pay the high price or go without the article. When he decides to go without it, demand is decreased only by a negligible amount; but if the same situation confronts a number of buyers, total demand is measurably affected.

When demand declines relative to supply, under conditions of pure competition, prices will drop in order to clear the market. As prices decline, more buyers enter the market and their activity prevents the price of the commodity from going lower than necessary to balance supply and demand.

Thus, market price is the price at which the amount of the commodity that buyers are willing to take and the amount that sellers offer are in *equilibrium.* It would result in perfect balance, as no one who is willing to buy at the going price would fail to find a seller, and no one who is willing to sell would fail to find a buyer. Price would move in one direction or another and so adjust itself through the play of demand and supply forces to bring about this equilibrium. This is known as the *free price system.*

Since it is impossible for any buyer or seller to affect his total revenue by a change in price (over which he has no control), the only manner in which a firm's total revenue may be increased is by selling more units of a product. Furthermore, under such competition, no individual seller or buyer would advertise, for advertising would merely add to his cost. No benefit would be derived by the advertiser because the product he buys or sells would be no different from that bought or sold by his competitors.

PURE OR PERFECT COMPETITION IS MYTHICAL

From the very listing of the conditions and prerequisites for pure or perfect competition it would appear extremely doubtful whether such conditions could ever be met collectively in any important part of our economy.

It is, therefore, equally doubtful whether such competition ever existed. Even in farm products like wheat where the conditions most closely approximate those of pure or perfect competition, there are certain "imperfections," such as marketing cooperatives which control a large part of the supply in some areas, a limited number of large buyers in some local markets, and government price support programmes.

A leading student of the subject admits the impracticability of the assumptions made by the analytical economist who tries to explain price in such an economy in actual, precise terms. Such an economist must either "include in his list assumptions which bring the problem close to the real problems, but which make it insoluble by the technique at his command, or to confine the problems within the limits which make it soluble but to hide the assumptions which bound it (if he is too honest to omit them altogether) in a dusty corner of the footnotes where he hopes that no one will notice them." That is why a leading contemporary economist stated: "With this had come the realization that 'perfect competition' does not and cannot exist and has presumably never existed.... What we have left is an unreal or ideal standard which may serve as *a starting point of analysis and a norm with which to compare actual competitive conditions.*"

MARKET PRICE UNDER MONOPOLY

Monopoly obtains when a single seller has complete control over the entire output of a given product or service, but no complete monopoly is really possible except in the absence of reasonably close substitutes. The nearest approach to such complete monopolies is to be found in the field of public utilities, and at one time probably one or two industrial concerns may have qualified for such classification. So-called monopoly does, however, exist in several other forms. There are *oligopoly* situations where the supply is controlled by a very small number of firms selling at quoted prices and anticipating one another's reactions.

Forms of monopoly may also be found on the buying side of the market and are in that case of the *monopsonistic* type. A single buyer of a given product in a certain area may exploit his advantage by paying a lower price than otherwise justified. A *monopsony* condition may take the form of price discrimination, so that one buyer may negotiate a better price than another buyer of the identical commodity. Frequently a monopsonistic situation arises not so much from the action of the buyer as from the preference accorded him by the seller or sellers.

All cases of monopoly or monopsony are characterized by *non-price competition.* In case of monopoly, the seller exercises full control over the price of his product. This does not necessarily mean that the price he will set will be the highest or even a high price, for he will attempt to set the price at a point which will maximize his profits. Obviously, then, if he sets the price so high as to discourage all or most of the potential customers, he will defeat his own end.

On the other hand, if he sets the price extremely low, there may be no net profit at all, or the net profit per unit of product may be so small that the total amount of such revenue will be much less than if he sold fewer units at a higher price. His task, therefore, is to discover that price which, multiplied by the number of units he expects to sell at that price, *will yield the maximum total net profit.* The consequence of a search for maximum total profits is that the monopolist will control both output and price entirely to his advantage, if he acts merely as an economic man.

The first major problem is the determination of demand, that is, a schedule of the quantities that may be sold at each of various alternative prices. Second, probable costs of production at each different level of output must be estimated. Profits are maximized by producing at the level at which there is the greatest difference between total production costs and total expected revenue.

Thus if the demand for the product is inelastic, the greatest total revenue is obtained by selling a smaller number of units, each at a relatively high price. If, however, the demand for his product is elastic, more units will be sold at a relatively low price. Theoretically, in either case, *the monopolist will market additional units until his marginal cost equals his marginal net revenue,* that is, until the last unit added to his supply costs as much as the net which that product is yielding when selling at a given price. Furthermore, advertising and other sales promotional effort may be very profitable for the monopolist, especially if the demand for his product is elastic.

NORMAL OR WORKABLE COMPETITION

By and large, however, our economic world today and for many generations past has been characterized by significant deviations from the assumptions underlying perfect or pure competition, nor has it been dominated, except in public utilities subject to government regulation and in a few rare examples in industry and business, by strict monopoly. That is why our competitive system has been labeled by various economic analysts as one of imperfect, monopolistic, modified, intermediate, workable, or hybrid competition. In this connection the term "imperfect competition" has been used most commonly.

To such characterization of our competitive system, there are serious objections. In the first place, it implies that perfection in competition is possible, which is contrary to any reasonable expectation. Second, it connotes an ethical appraisal of our system, surrounded by an undesirable odour, for which there is little basis in fact. Third, it implies that price competition is the only kind of competition that matters.Inasmuch as this kind of competition pervades our entire economic system and the instances of perfect competition on the one hand and real monopoly on the other are totally lacking or relatively rare, and in view of the objections just stated to the label "imperfect" competition, it would seem best to designate the so-called "imperfect" competition as *normal* or *workable* competition. It is the kind of competition that is prevalent and workable in everyday economic life. It is the kind of competition that is normal and is universally so regarded by the public. The major reasons for the prevalence of this normal or workable competition are obvious from its principal characteristics which are as follows:

- Most products are physically differentiated in varying degrees. A relatively small number of them are completely homogeneous and thoroughly standardized. There may be many grades of the same commodity, and even in the same grade the quality of the commodity may vary, depending upon whether it is in the upper, lower, or middle part of that grade. Leaf tobacco is a good illustration.
- There is much brand differentiation. Similar products may be and are sold under different brand names each of which has its own image or

personality. Even though the physical difference may be ever so slight or entirely non-existent, if the buyer *thinks* that the product bearing a certain label is different, it is different as far as that buyer is concerned, and he may derive from that fact enormous "psychic" value.

- There are differences in the conditions under which a commodity may be bought or sold. A buyer may be willing to pay a higher price for a given grade of product to one source of supply that is in closer proximity than to another more distant source. The preferred source of supply may also be deemed to be more reliable, more pleasant to deal with, may extend more liberal credit accommodations, may have a more pleasant environment in which to shop, and may make adjustments more satisfactorily, thus developing a unique or preferred enterprise image or personality.
- In the case of many products the style element differentiates one product from all the others.
- Advertising may influence buyers to patronize one source of supply in preference to others.
- Installation, maintenance, and repair services may differ considerably and thus prove to be a strong factor in attracting patronage.

MARKET PRICE UNDER WORKABLE COMPETITION

In a competitive economy, that is, one in which a substantial degree of, or normal, competition exists, market price is, by and large, a resultant of the interplay of supply and demand factors in a relatively free market, particularly the demand factors.

There is no question but that costs play a significant part in price determination. This is particularly true of commodities that are standardized and the units of which are interchangeable, as in the case of grain, steel, and many other raw materials and semi manufactures. Under these circumstances, cost affects the selling price profoundly through its influence upon the quantity marketed. When brand and style differentiation become important elements, a different situation results.

Each manufacturer and distributor of such goods may exert control over current and future demand. Not only may existing *expressed* demand be directed along a given channel, but demand in general may be influenced by the efforts of vendors to arouse, through aggressive merchandising methods, *latent* buying motives and to intensify desires of potential purchasers.

In all cases, whether or not the product is highly differentiated, the elasticity of demand, shifts in demand, and the action of competitors have an important bearing in determining the individual prices of commodities. At best, the relation between selling price and cost is elastic, varying with the business cycle, with the efficiency of the seller, and with the character and maturity or market saturation of the product. This must not be confused with the economist's cost-price analysis in which he concerns himself chiefly with the long-run normal price previously discussed, and invariably refers to alternative or opportunity cost which has to do with the next most profitable use or combination of uses of the factors of production.

ACTUAL PRICE DETERMINATION

Price determination in practice is indeed a complex matter. An entire volume could easily be filled with examples illustrating different methods used in determining actual selling prices. For purposes of this book, it will be sufficient to examine the role of pricing in the marketing mix and then to consider various specific approaches to price determination.

PRICE LEVELS AND THE MARKETING MIX

It is common to hear a businessman say that prices are one of his most important problems.

This may have either of two meanings, as follows:

- That the prices which he can get under prevailing competitive circumstances are such that his profit opportunities are quite limited; or
- That decisions about what prices to establish constitute one of his most difficult managerial tasks. The question as to which meaning to impute to a statement about the importance of prices in a particular firm may often be answered by examining the role of pricing in the marketing mix.

The term marketing mix is used to denote the amount of *relative* emphasis placed upon different components of a firm's marketing programme. In the business world, it is not ordinarily possible to consider price as a single variable to be manipulated under conditions where all other factors are held constant, as is often done in economic analysis. Price is one element of marketing strategy which must be decided within the firm on the basis of its role relative to other ingredients. A low initial price for a new product, or a reduced price for: an established product, is, for example, a possible alternative to greater expenditures for advertising, or for more intensive personal selling effort, or for expanded customer service activities.

A progressively managed company utilizing concepts of customer oriented marketing management is likely to approach major pricing decisions in a series of stages or successive steeps, each one of which is dependent upon a previous and more basic decision, thus minimizing the probability of making a strategical or tactical blunder. First, the firm would identify its market target, that is, the segment of the total potential market to which it wishes to make its strongest appeal. Second, it must consider its enterprise or brand image, or analyse the extent to which such an image may be modified if it is practical to do so. The type of image has some significance with respect to the segment of the market to be cultivated, but it also is a major determinant of the role to be assigned to pricing.

Third, the desirable composition of a marketing mix would be decided upon the basis of the market target, the firm's brand image, and the activities and brand images of competing organizations. Fourth, within the framework of a conception of an ideal marketing mix, a basic policy with respect to the level of the firm's prices would be established. Finally, prices are determined for specific products, in conformance with basic decisions about price levels.

There may be all kinds of variations with respect to decisions about a firm's price level but these may be grouped for purposes of discussion into three choices, as follows:

- Selling below prevailing market prices;
- Selling at market price levels; and
- Selling at relatively high prices.

LOW-PRICE POLICIES

Some vendors follow a policy of underselling competitors. A notable historical example is the famous R. H. Macy, and Company department store in New York. Over a number of generations, its policy has been to sell at less than the shopped price for comparable items. More recently, this policy has been used by various discount houses, especially Masters, Inc., and E. J. Korvette, Inc., both of which operate a number of establishments in eastern markets, and Polk Bros. of Chicago. This price policy is by no means confined to the field of retailing. In the wholesaling of goods, arrangements are frequently made whereby the vendor agrees to supply his customers with merchandise at or below the lowest price quoted by competitors, thus following the policy of "meet or beat" competitor's prices.

There are some manufacturers who believe in and follow a low or lowest price policy. In some cases a low-price policy may be a relatively temporary expedient to meet conditions in an unsettled market. For example, the St. Joseph Lead Co. attracted considerable attention in 1960 with a policy announcement that it would discount any competitive posted price for zinc by one-half cent per pound. This policy was adopted when prices for the commodity were very unsettled, and all suppliers were making special concessions of one form or another to customers.

Buyers were uncertain about alternative costs available to them. Hence the policy announcement of this major supplier was a means of communicating to the trade that a customer could not likely do better by buying elsewhere. When market conditions became more settled in early 1961, and discounting of base selling prices diminished, St. Joseph rescinded its lowest price policy and reverted to its previous policy of selling at the market level. A low-price policy, pursued on a continuing basis, is likely to succeed in markets in which there are considerable latent demands at lower prices, and the manufacturers most likely to do so are those with a relatively high physical efficiency. Such a policy tends to widen the market and to give the seller the opportunity of utilizing his facilities to best advantage.

A bold and imaginative policy of low or greatly reduced prices can sometimes reach such broader bases of potential demand involving new applications that the low price becomes in itself a product innovation. This has been aptly illustrated as follows: A new synthetic fibre, for example, may be so costly and high priced that it is used only for surgical and other very limited purposes. By dropping the price in anticipation of reduced costs, the hosiery and fine apparel markets may be reached; still further down the price scale, the rug, carpet, and industrial markets may be tapped.

There are definite limits, however, to what may be deemed desirably low prices for any period of time. Unless the reduction is a matter of competitive necessity, no businessman can be expected to reduce his prices materially in the face of a belief that he would not be compensated by sufficient increases in sales volume and satisfactory profitability on the basis of cost and revenue factors applying to the larger volume marketed. Assuming a homogeneous product, the price of the product may be constant at a given time and no firm may be able to sell above the ruling price. No lower price, therefore, need be quoted in order to get the business. In fact, a further lowering of price may bring retaliatory action from competitors or at best may result in a permanent lowering of prices by all of them. In any event, when the basic policy is to sell at relatively low prices this is assigning to pricing a major and an offensive role in the marketing mix.

SELLING AT MARKET LEVELS

The great majority of business firms do not have much trouble in deciding just what selling prices to establish for individual items. Most retail stores and wholesale establishments are in competition with others selling identical or similar products and quickly make whatever adjustments are necessary when competitors change their prices. Among manufacturers of commonplace articles, such as gasoline, food products, and household appliances, selling at or near to what is regarded as a competitive level is the general rule. When a firm's basic policy is to market at prevailing competitive prices, the role assigned to price in the marketing mix is essentially a neutral one. There is no intention to win customers by underselling major competitors and, on the other hand, no intention to lose significant amounts of business to others who may have lower prices. In such situations, promotional activities other than pricing become relatively more important than is the case with firms adopting a low-price policy.

TAXATION IMPACT ON TRANSFER PRICING

Companies operating in the United States are guided by Section 482 of the Internal Revenue Code when setting transfer prices. Specifically, the IRS, through the Secretary of the Treasury, has the right to "distribute, apportion, or allocate gross income, deductions, credits, or allowances... between or among... businesses, if he determines that such distribution, apportionment, or allocation is necessary in order to prevent evasion of taxes. The IRS has been granted wide latitude to do whatever it wants if the IRS deems that dealings between a U.S. parent and its affiliates do not meet its standards.

For instance, the IRS can reallocate income and deductions if loans have been made between a parent corporation and an affiliate at an unrealistic interest rate. Unrealistic interest rates are those that would not occur for similar transactions between unrelated third parties. This also applies to charging for services and use of property, and transfers of tangible and intangible property including lease payments and royalties.

A reference to IRS guidelines has already been made in discussing R&D and intangible costs in setting transfer prices by the production cost approach. Basing transfer pricing on published data rather than corporate derived prices is another example of the close working relationship, voluntary or not, between tax authorities and managers responsible for transfer prices.

In general, the IRS standard for determining transfer pricing, and other dealings between a parent and its affiliates, is whether it is an "arm's-length" transaction—one that would occur between a company and a third party having no affiliation other than the commercial transaction under consideration. This is independent of whether the transfer price is based on the cost of production or on market prices. If the transfer price between affiliates is seemingly out of line with a price that would have been charged to an unrelated party, then the IRS has the right to reallocate income or deductions according to what it feels to be the appropriate transfer price.

The IRS specifies various methods for establishing an appropriate transfer price. The preferred one is the comparable uncontrolled price method where prices are the same for goods sold to affiliated and to non-affiliated companies. The price for goods sold to an unrelated third party establishes the transfer price for goods transferred to an affiliate.

This method does not work when goods are not sold to third parties, but are totally transferred between affiliates. Under these circumstances, the second method for setting the transfer price is the resale price method. This is the price for which the company would sell the item to an unspecified third party. The third party would add the same comparable value as the affiliate and sell the completed product with an appropriate markup.

By netting the market price of the appropriate markup and the value added to the product by an affiliate, one can "back into" an appropriate transfer price from the point of view of the tax authority. The third method is the "cost plus" method, where the IRS permits three different ways of allocating costs (full absorption, direct cost, and incremental cost). All these methods leave some margin of discretion as to what is the appropriate transfer price.

If all these fail, as they frequently do for high-technology products, customised components, or subassemblies, then so-called fourth methods are permitted, such as determining transfer pricing on the basis of a predetermined profit for the foreign firm's operations and, through a netting process of accounting for applicable costs, establishing an appropriate transfer price.

Regardless of the methodology, the burden of proof in supporting a transfer price is with the taxpayer, not the IRS. To confuse matters more, there have been occasions when the tax courts have rejected the notion of arm's-length transfer pricing in settling tax disputes between corporations and the IRS.

OTHER NATIONS' POLICIES CONCERNING TRANSFER PRICING

The tax authority in Canada views transfer pricing of goods similar to the way the United States does. Transfer pricing for services differs in that it is based on a pro rata sharing of actual incurred costs between the parent corporation and its affiliate, and not necessarily at an arm's-length price.

Tax authorities in Japan follow a system comparable to that of the United States. German tax code provisions permit the reallocation of domestic source income if revenue or income has been shifted to another nation through a transaction that is different from those that would have been entered into by unrelated parties. In other words,

transfer pricing should be arm's-length, although the code is not specific in defining arm's-length pricing. The United Kingdom is similar to Germany in not specifically defining arm's-length pricing. The Inland Revenue may adjust taxable income based on fairness and arm's-length criteria. Disputes between corporations and Inland Revenue agents are frequently settled by negotiation, resulting in some sort of compromise between the two parties. This is unlike in Germany, where the adjustments made by the tax authorities are considered final, and unlike in the United States, where adjustments are litigated in tax courts.

Tax authorities in many nations are currently taking a much closer look at transfer pricing practices. Recently, the U.K. Inland Revenue recast the accounts of one non-British company operating in the United Kingdom and assessed back taxes of nearly 2 billion pounds. In the United States, there is growing political pressure for the IRS to take more vigourous action against foreign-owned companies operating through U.S. based affiliates. This pressure stems from the realization that the aggregate expenses for foreign-owned businesses operating in the United States exceed aggregate revenues. This means that, in the aggregate, foreign-owned subsidiaries are claiming to operate at a loss, although individual foreign-owned subsidiaries may be paying taxes on profits. Some foreign-owned affiliates operating in the United States have a twenty-year string of consecutive losses. This is not considered a realistic appraisal of performance because there are few profit-motivated foreign-based parent companies that would support twenty years of successive losses were they real. Poor or non-existent profits for foreign-based affiliates operating in the United States are blamed on transfer pricing. Transfer price manipulation is felt to have resulted in tax underpayments of between $12 and $50 billion.

Legislation was passed in 1989 to require foreign-owned businesses in the United States to keep records, in English, of transactions with foreign related parties. Much of this legislation has to do with substantiating transfer pricing on either a cost or arm'slength transaction with an unrelated third party. A growing risk associated with manipulating transfer prices for the purpose of tax minimization.

The risk is that the tax authorities will recast the company's statements with their own version of the proper transfer price, thus exposing a company to the risk of double taxation. Most nations have entered into tax treaties with various other nations with regard to taxing of affiliates of parent organizations domiciled in the treaty nations. These treaties determine withholding taxes on dividends, interest, and royalties; relief from double taxation; and the types of taxes and organizations covered by the treaty. Overall exposure to taxation can be reduced by judicious structuring of the legal corporate entities of a parent company and its affiliates in accordance with the provisions of these treaties.

Some of these treaties contain formal agreements for the mutual examination of the tax returns of affiliates of a parent company. The tax returns of affiliates and parent organizations are exchanged and examined by the tax authorities to determine correct tax liabilities, detect tax avoidance manoeuvres, scrutinize transfer pricing practices, and exchange information useful to the tax authorities. These treaties also provide a forum for one tax authority to complain about the actions taken by another, when these actions are deemed detrimental to its interests.

Recent developments in international cooperation of tax authorities include the establishment of a formal agreement on transfer prices. The mutual agreement of various nations to reference a published source for tanker rates in determining oil company tax liabilities is an example of this. Australia and the United States are attempting to grant "advance determinations" of the proper transfer price for Australian companies dealings with their U.S. affiliates. A recent survey has shown that about half of IRS tax examinations of multinational companies involve transfer prices. If a mutually agreeable methodology could be arranged between a company and the IRS, many of these tax examinations could be eliminated. The IRS is attempting to develop a procedure whereby a company and the IRS would mutually agree to a transfer-pricing agreement covering the distribution of finished goods, sales of raw materials and components, general and administrative expenses, and managerial and technical services. If the taxpayer develops an acceptable transfer-pricing methodology, then the taxpayer and the IRS would enter into an advance-pricing agreement. The IRS would limit its examinations to an audit to ensure that the taxpayer has complied with the agreement.

However, the taxpayer is obliged to submit pricing data of independent transactions, or an adequate substitute, to show that the transfer price possesses the necessary attributes of an arm's-length transaction. The taxpayer is also responsible to show that the agreed transfer-pricing methodology is generating acceptable transfer prices from an arm's-length perspective.

The preference of tax authorities in many nations for arm's-length transfer pricing may act as an inducement to switch from the cost-of-production to the market price approach in setting transfer prices because, presumably, they are one and the same. The financial and taxation departments of multinational, or global, companies must deal daily with what are considered to be the most pressing issues in international accounting today. Those involved with transfer pricing must measure the consequences of their transfer-pricing decisions both on corporate profits and on current and potential tax liabilities. Potential tax liabilities, stemming from tax authorities rejecting management's transfer price decisions, and substituting their own, are enormous. This must weigh heavily on the shoulders of those responsible for setting transfer prices.

TRANSFER PRICING AND JOINT VENTURES

A joint venture partner, a local partner owning a portion of an affiliate, and a minority shareholder are going to be as interested in transfer pricing as the local tax authority. Less often, a partnership is structured on the basis of a claim, or royalty, on revenue. More often, it is a claim on profits. If one party to a venture or partnership can influence revenue, costs, and profitability through transfer pricing, then the other party or partner, or a minority shareholder, will be deservedly concerned. One way to manage transfer pricing with regard to having partners or minority shareholders is to formalize the setting of transfer prices in some verifiable manner such as a set markup above costs, another is to reference transfer prices to an observable market transaction.

Either way minimizes the opportunity for one party to a partnership or joint venture to manipulate transfer prices to its advantage. If the partners, participants, and minority shareholders feel that their interests are vulnerable by virtue of the other party to a business venture controlling transfer prices, then they may not contribute to the venture that which was expected of them.

Avoiding these problems can be more easily said than done. Some years ago, Ford Motor Company purchased the minority shares of its partially owned subsidiaries because the company felt that it could not administer transfer pricing in a way that was fair to all concerned.

Some managements have made the strategic decision not to enter into joint ventures, or have local partners or minority shareholdings in corporate affiliates, where they can manage the profitability of the venture through transfer prices. Sometimes, the solution for a problem is to avoid the problem.

TRANSFER PRICING AND MANAGERIAL PERFORMANCE EVALUATION

It may be in the interest of the corporation as a whole to transfer in components that are more highly priced than those an affiliate can purchase from other sources. It may be in the interest of the corporation as a whole to transfer goods made in one affiliate to another affiliate for less than what the affiliate can sell them for to third parties.

Although the corporation may gain by such a set of transfer prices for goods moving among affiliates, it does not serve the interests of the affiliate managers if they are subsequently judged on profitability. This dichotomy of purpose in establishing a transfer-pricing policy for the good of the whole company, yet holding managers of affiliates accountable for profits that are contaminated, so to speak, by transfer prices has not been successfully addressed when transfer prices are different from market prices.

In fact, this is one potent argument in favour of companies having transfer pricing policies based on the market price for comparable goods. If transfer prices are set at the price for goods exchanged between unrelated parties, then there is no dichotomy of purpose in setting transfer prices and measuring performance. Managers of affiliates can be judged in an unbiased fashion on the profitability of their operations because they are buying and selling at market prices—the same prices that would prevail if they were independent companies.

The disadvantage of letting the market set transfer prices is that the parent corporation can no longer utilize transfer pricing as a means to pursue the overall optimization of the financial performance of the corporation. One possible approach to the dysfunctional aspects of setting transfer prices at other than market prices and measuring management performance of affiliates is to isolate and separately state the amount of inter company "profit" or "loss" that each affiliate is experiencing in its transactions with other affiliates. This approach provides the parent organization with information on whether an affiliate is suffering from unwarranted decreased profitability or enjoying unwarranted increased profitability because of transfer pricing.

SETTING TRANSFER PRICES BY COST OF PRODUCTION

There are two general approaches for setting transfer prices: the cost of production and market prices associated with third party, or unrelated, transactions. The cost-of-production approach bases the price of goods to be transferred between affiliates on the variable cost of production, an allowance for fixed costs that are general in nature and are apportioned over the entire product line, and an allowance for fixed costs that can be apportioned among the individual products.

This latter category usually includes research and development costs and selling and administrative costs. The remaining components may include financial fees and royalties associated with tangible and intangible assets to be apportioned to individual products and the selection of an appropriate profit margin.

The variable cost of production includes labour, material, and other direct costs that are consumed in the production of an item. If the policy of the company is to hire and fire (lay off) factory workers as production rises and falls, then labour is a variable cost. If a company is reluctant to let go of their workers when sales decline, then factory labour should be considered part of fixed costs. Factory labour costs are usually part variable and part fixed. Other variable costs can be the unit financing and utility costs associated with machinery and processes used in the manufacture of a particular product and unit shipping costs. These costs can also be treated as fixed costs depending on how the company's cost accounting system is set up.

Fixed costs are all costs not included in variable costs. Fixed costs are the financing or depreciation costs of the factory; the overhead costs of marketing, accounting, and supervision; the cost of inventories, warehouses, insurance, utilities, communication, property taxes, and other non-variable cost items.

Fixed costs may not be entirely fixed in that there is some variation as production levels change. For instance, bonuses, which would be considered part of the fixed costs of having an executive suite, rise and fall with profits, which are related to production levels. The number of staff personnel in marketing, accounting, engineering, and other overhead functions can vary with the production level.

Some elements of fixed costs are allocated in the transfer price setting mechanism in a way that fairly apportions the fixed cost burden among the various products. Other elements of fixed costs can be apportioned more on the basis of the benefit derived by an individual product. One of these is research and development, where the allocation can be made over a product line in proportion to the degree of R&D expenditures associated with the development of an individual product.

Although there is general agreement that this is a fair way to apportion R&D expenses of successful undertakings, there is lack of agreement on how to apportion R&D expenses for failed projects. Some maintain that the allocation of expenses associated with failed R&D projects should be apportioned to all products on the basis that every product should bear the risk of failed R&D efforts. Others object on the grounds that had the R&D effort succeeded, a particular product might not have benefited. Therefore, it makes no sense for the transfer price to contain the cost of a failed R&D effort, which, had it succeeded, would not be part of the transfer price of the product.

The question as to the proper treatment of failed R&D projects is not an internal accounting matter. Tax authorities are interested in who takes the write off of a failed R&D project. In the United States, the Internal Revenue Service (IRS) is concerned whether a transfer price contains a provision for failed R&D expenditures. If a transfer price contains only that portion of R&D expenditures that were successful with regard to a particular product, then failed R&D projects of a U.S. corporation are being written off solely against U.S. income. A portion of the tax loss write-off is passed on to the tax authority of another nation by including an element of failed R&D expenditures in the transfer price.

Another fixed cost element that can be separated and apportioned in a different manner than general fixed costs are services provided to an individual product. These may be coordination and control expenses associated with a product; costs for enhancing the efficiency of operations for manufacturing the product or expanding the scope of its market; and the costs of recruiting and training of management and operations personnel associated with manufacturing, marketing, and repairing or servicing the product. The allocation of these service costs to individual products provides another element in deriving their transfer prices.

The derivation of the transfer price also includes elements for tangibles and intangibles associated with a product. Tangibles are the plant, equipment, and other physical assets dedicated to the manufacture of the product. Part of the transfer price provides a financial return for tangibles based on their value. Intangibles represent the technical knowledge and expertise and applicable patents that can be allocated to a particular product. The transfer price also contains an element that provides a company with a return on intangibles.

Intangible costs within a transfer price cannot be capriciously determined by management because intangible costs affect taxable profits. For this reason, the IRS has established guidelines for determining the intangible cost element in a transfer price. An intangible cost element must be present if there are intangible costs associated with the manufacture or marketing of a product and must be so identified. Intangible costs can be proportioned in relation to the income attributable to the intangibles by units of production, sales, net or gross profits, or other reasonable methods. The fee for intangible property incorporated in a transfer price must be similar to what would have been arranged with an independent third party.

The last part of the cost approach in setting transfer prices is determining the proper profit margin on the goods made by one affiliate and shipped to another. This may be the average profit margin for the company as a whole or a profit margin associated with a specific product line. Regardless, the stipulated profit margin must be reconciled in some manner with the profitability of the company or a product line to satisfy the tax authorities.

The need for reconciliation of the profit and the various cost elements of the transfer price with the tax authorities sometimes results in the tax group within the finance department of a company being responsible for administering transfer prices. However, this choice may hinder general management from using transfer prices as a means to achieve corporate objectives. The chief advantage of the cost of production approach for setting transfer prices is that the costs are available and are subject to quantification. For this reason, the production cost approach has been more common in the past than the market price approach. The chief disadvantage is that there is no real incentive for an affiliate to improve its manufacturing process, to enhance its efficiency, or to take steps to lower costs. Mistakes, errors, inefficiencies in manning or machinery, management inattention to detail, worker carelessness, and excessive remuneration of white and blue collar workers alike may all be incorporated in the determination of costs and passed on to the affiliates in the transfer price. Another disadvantage is that both the tax authority and the affiliates may object to the nature of the apportionment of R&D, S&A, tangibles, and intangibles among the various products and the assigned profit margin.

SETTING TRANSFER PRICES BY MARKET PRICES

The disadvantages associated with the cost-of-production method of setting transfer prices can be mostly avoided by referencing transfer prices to third party transactions for identical, or nearly identical, products. If an affiliate can obtain the item being purchased from a third party for a certain price, then that price can be the basis for setting the transfer price. The proponents of market-oriented transfer prices maintain that letting the market set the transfer price is inherently more fair than a production-cost-based system because one affiliate is not supporting the inefficiencies of another.

If an affiliate receives only the global competitive price for its products, then there is an incentive for it to take whatever actions are needed to correct the inefficiencies in its operations that are resulting in higher costs. In a truly decentralized operation, managers are expected to make their decisions on an independent basis, and unrelated companies are permitted to compete for the business of an affiliate, along with other affiliates.

The parent organization does not set transfer prices and has little or no influence over the decisions made by the managers of the affiliates. No favour or special consideration is shown to fellow affiliates in the competitive process of selecting suppliers for components and goods. The hope, of course, is that everyone is kept on his or her competitive toes to produce salable goods at the lowest possible cost. This managerial philosophy, where each affiliate is treated as an independent company, is sometimes referred to as the small business unit (SBU) management philosophy. The disadvantage is that, although each affiliate is focused on optimizing its operations, the end result may be suboptimal performance of the corporation as a whole. Suppose that affiliate X produces all of a component (part X) for a number of widget manufacturing affiliates. Total demand for part X is 2 million per year. Affiliate X has $10 million in fixed annual costs, which include a profit margin on the investment in manufacturing facilities plus a return on the R&D investment for the development of part X. The variable costs for manufacturing part X is $5. The transfer price based on the fixed and variable costs of affiliate X supplying all other affiliates with part X is $10.

Table. Volume Of Sales: 2,000,000

Fixed Costs	$10,000,000
Variable Costs at $5 per Unit	10,000,000
Total Costs	$20,000,000
Transfer Price Based on Cost of Making 2,000,000	$10.00

Affiliate A is free to cut its best deal and obtains a quote of $9.50 from another company. Affiliate A does what is best for maximizing its profits and purchases 200,000 part X's from a third party for $9.50 rather than pay $10 to affiliate X. Affiliate X has lost a contract for 200,000 part X's and now operates on a basis of a sales volume of 1,800,000 per year.

Table. Volume Of Sales: 1,800,000

Fixed Costs	$10,000,000
Variable Costs at $5 per Unit	9,000,000
Total Costs	$19,000,000
Transfer Price Based on Cost of Making 1,800,000	$10.56

The remaining affiliates must pay a higher price because there is less sales volume to cover the fixed costs of affiliate X. The increase in transfer price to cover the fixed and variable costs is essentially equivalent to treating fixed costs as a component of variable costs, which it is not. Nevertheless, affiliate X must cover all its costs. When affiliate X announces the increase in price, affiliate B concludes a deal with a third party at $9.75 causing another loss of 200,000 for affiliate X.

Table. Volume Of Sales: 1,600.000

Fixed Costs	$10,000,000
Variable Costs at $5 per Unit	8,000,000
Total Costs	$18,000,000
Transfer Price Based on cost of Making 1,600,000	$11.25

Now it's time for affiliate C to say goodbye to affiliate X, as it maximizes its profit by reducing the cost of part X by paying $10.50 to another outside source. This is higher than the $10 price that applied when all the affiliates received part X from affiliate X. It is clear from the continuation of this exercise that, as each affiliate maximizes its profits by cutting costs, the corporation as a whole is being sub optimized. Even if the various affiliates do not pay more than an average price of $10 per unit for part X in purchasing all part X's from outside sources, the global company is stuck with an affiliate with no sales and a fixed annual cost of $10 million that represents, in large measure, financing costs on plant and equipment.

It is highly likely that the fixed costs in affiliate X contain an allowance for R&D expenses and product development that have to be recouped in the operation of a company, but do not have to be recouped by another company if it is essentially manufacturing a copy of part X. Copying is fairly common in global commerce because patent protection is limited to the nation issuing the patent. Global companies often obtain patents in a number of nations, but this may not be possible for all nations.

A company may manufacture a copy of a product in one of these nations. Although it is true that affiliate X is free to pursue patent infringement action against sales in a particular nation where it has patent protection, the time involved in enforcement proceedings and the legal expenses may make such protection prohibitively expensive. Furthermore, there is no internationally recognized legal structure to handle patent infringements.

In addition to R&D expenses, the fixed costs of affiliate X may also contain a service element for the benefit of the affiliates purchasing its output that may not be provided by third parties. By each affiliate "doing its own thing," the R&D and service costs cannot be covered. One principal problem associated with using market reference points for transfer pricing is that the affiliates may be shipping components and parts that are not readily available from other firms.

Most components and parts are specifically designed for a company's product line and are not available from third parties unless contracted for by an affiliate. Market prices for similarly designed components that cannot be actually used in the company's product line may not be relevant. Moreover, the quality inherent in third-party quotes for similar parts may not be up to the standards imposed on products made within a global corporate family.

There is no easy answer as to which approach for determining transfer prices should be followed. Both have their adherents and detractors. Either approach restricts transfer prices to something related to third-party, or market, transactions or to the cost of manufacture. Surveys have shown that nations seem to exhibit cultural preferences as to which approach to follow and as to what motivates companies in setting transfer prices. Companies in some countries favour costbased transfer prices, whereas companies in other nations favour market-based transfer prices. U.S. based corporations have historically preferred setting transfer prices by the cost approach because the necessary data is available, whereas the necessary data for setting transfer prices on the basis of market transactions may not be available. Oftentimes, market quotes for uniquely designed parts and components may have to be derived rather than observed because there are no market transactions for the precise item.

Should General Motors set its transfer price on carburetors being shipped to Europe based on its cost of production or on what Toyota charges its U.S. transplants? The two carburetors are not the same and do not have the same cost of production. Furthermore, there may not be a data base available for prices for carburetors sold between related and unrelated parties from which to derive a market price.

Preferences change with time. Surveys done in the 1970s indicated that the preponderance of U.S. companies were motivated by tax minimization in setting transfer prices. More recent surveys indicate that companies are more interested in setting transfer prices on the basis of measuring the performance of affiliate managers and of providing reliable and unbiased information for the making of decisions.

This change in attitude in U.S. companies may be the result of the United States becoming a relative tax haven compared to other nations. Its corporate tax rate of 34 per cent, plus state taxes, is less than in many other industrialized nations, where tax rates range between 40 per cent and 55 per cent. A U.S. company's total tax bill may, in fact, be reduced by allocating more profits to the United States. Regardless of changes in attitudes as to what is important in setting transfer prices, the essential point is that there is no unanimity on which approach to use and on what motivates companies in setting transfer prices.

Up to this point, an important assumption has been that the parent company has real control over transfer prices to manage corporate cash flows and the profits reported by affiliates and to overcome artificial barriers to trade in the form of custom duties, currency exchange, and price controls. Some recent surveys suggest that competitive forces and market conditions within a nation seem to be more important in setting transfer prices than decisions made by a parent organization. If transfer prices are being set by exogenous commercial forces, then the presumption that a parent organization is able to achieve optimal financial performance of a global family of affiliates through the careful orchestration of transfer pricing is being challenged.

SELLING AT RELATIVELY HIGH PRICES

Some firms find it possible to market products at a relatively high price. This is not ordinarily practical on a sustained basis unless there is a strong degree of market control. Such control may be achieved by significant differentiation in the physical attributes or the functioning of products which are protected by patents or which are manufactured according to complex or secret processes that are difficult to duplicate.

In some cases significant differentiation may exist as a result of unusually successful promotional effort which has created an exceptional favorable enterprise or brand image. If the product is a complicated durable good, either consumer or business equipment, differentiation may exist in the form of an outstanding reputation for installation or maintenance service, which may be more important to the user than initial cost. Selling at a relatively high price level may also be a temporary expedient under certain conditions. For example, a firm brings out a product which is entirely new in its class in some distinctive way, but feels that competitors will follow with similar product modifications after some period of time. The decision may be to price at a relatively high level initially, to recover product research, developmental, and promotional costs as quickly as possible, before it becomes necessary to meet intensive competition.

As another example, relatively high price levels are sometimes established on new products or substantial product modifications in order "to try the market." The firm may be totally lacking in information about the nature of elasticity of demand. If it must actually experiment, it is much easier to start with a price that is too high and lower it later, if necessary, than to do the opposite. When a firm decides to sell at relatively high prices, the assumption is that price is not a very important factor in getting or retaining business. The role of price in the marketing mix is nearly a negative one, having been subordinated almost completely to product development, advertising, or other ingredients. There remains, nevertheless, the major management problem about deciding just what specific price to establish.

BASIC APPROACHES TO PRICE DETERMINATION

The numerous methods of determining specific selling prices may be classified into two main groups or approaches. One of these is to establish prices primarily on the basis of cost considerations. The other is to determine prices largely with reference to the market or to competitive circumstances.

THE COST-PLUS APPROACH

One general method is for a seller of a product to establish his prices *on the basis of costs* of manufacturing or of purchasing for resale, plus whatever markup or margins are deemed necessary to cover relevant overhead or marketing expenses and to provide for some net profit realization which may have been predetermined as a specific objective. This approach is commonly used under three types of circumstances:

- When a firm finds it desirable, for reasons explained above, to adopt a basic policy of selling above prevailing competitive levels; or

- When most competitors have similar costs and follow similar pricing practices; or
- When the cost structure will likely be greatly changed by appealing to a broader demand at lower levels of pricing. The application of the costplus approach varies somewhat depending upon whether it is being used by a manufacturer or by a middleman and whether total costs or only variable costs are being covered by a specific pricing process.

APPLICATION BY MANUFACTURERS

Various important studies of business practice in this country and abroad have indicated that cost-plus pricing is the most common method used by manufacturing firms. By cost is usually meant the cost of manufacturing a unit of product, including not only variable costs, such as raw materials and direct labour, but also fixed expense such as depreciation on equipment and plant and supervisory expenses. Just what figure is used for manufacturing cost varies from one situation to another.

Some manufacturers use their actual costs for the most recent accounting period, including direct wages, material, and whatever loading charge for overhead was necessary at the current rate of output. In industries where the volume of output may vary considerably from one period to another, standard or so-called "normal" costs may be determined on the basis of average annual rates of output.

In certain instances, the cost may be a forecasted figure, based on the volume of output expected in a future period. If the product is new, the cost may be altogether conjectural, being derived from engineering estimates and historical experience with costs of similar or related items.

The amount of markup to be added to cost also varies widely, but is likely to be rather definitized within a given firm and sometimes within a group of firms constituting a particular industry classification. In general, the markup is a factor deemed adequate to cover the expense of general corporate administration and marketing and to allow for a reasonable net profit realization.

If the product is to be sold through middlemen to final industrial users or to ultimate consumers, the manufacturer must allow also for the margins of middlemen in arriving at final or list prices. The case of a manufacturer of a new home furnishings product who has estimated that total manufac-turing costs will amount to $94 per unit at an anticipated output of 200,000 units annually. General administrative costs and marketing costs, including freight prepaid to distributors, amount to about 25 per cent of sales on somewhat similar items. It is desired to realise a net profit of 10 per cent of sales.

A margin of 35 per cent of sales is therefore necessary. Manufacturing costs must not exceed 65 per cent of the manufacturer's selling price, which is calculated to be $144.62. Wholesale distributors handling this: product are to be granted a discount of 20 per cent from their selling prices to compensate them for the cost of performing their marketing services and to provide them with a net profit. A distributor's cost is therefore 80 per cent of his selling price which would amount to $180.78. Retailers handling the product are to be allowed a discount of 35 per cent from the final selling price, so their cost must not exceed about65 per cent of the list price. The retail or list price would then be $278.12. This might be modified slightly upward or downward, to arrive at an odd price, which is presumed to have more psychological appeal to the consumer.

APPLICATION BY MIDDLEMEN

Selling prices of wholesalers and retailers are determined in part by the resale price maintenance policies of their suppliers, in part by competitive circumstances, and in part by managerial judgement within the organization. When the middleman determines his own selling prices without being influenced by heavy competitive pressure, this is often done by applying an average markup per cent. Such markups consist of three ingredients: the normal cost of rendering the marketing services provided by the middleman; the anticipated markdowns or stock shortages on the merchandise handled; and the net profit goal of the organization.

In an empirical study of the pricing practices of wholesalers in the hardware/ dry goods and drug trades, it was found that a markup of 33 per cent of the invoice cost of goods purchased was encountered much more frequently than any other markup percentage. Markups of 33 per cent of selling price have been traditional on the less competitive items in the retail hardware and retail drug trade.

In the merchandising of women's ready-to-wear apparel in department and specialty stores, typical initial markups have been 40 per cent of retail and in the retail furniture trade they have been 50 per cent of initial retail prices. Such *average markup percentages*, whether applied by retailers or by wholesalers, are usually considerably higher than the average *realized gross margin*. This happens because many items, especially those selling in largest volume, are priced much below the average markup figure as dictated by competitive pressures; and many others are sold after deducting or experiencing markdowns, losses on trade-in allowances, and special discounts or other price concessions from initial selling prices.

STRATEGIC PRICING

One of the four major elements of the marketing mix is price. Pricing is an important strategic issue because it is related to product positioning. Furthermore, pricing affects other marketing mix elements such as product features, channel decisions, and promotion. While there is no single recipe to determine pricing, the following is a general sequence of steps that might be followed for developing the pricing of a new product:

- *Develop marketing strategy*: Perform marketing analysis, segmentation, targeting, and positioning.
- *Make marketing mix decisions*: Define the product, distribution, and promotional tactics.
- *Estimate the demand curve*: Understand how quantity demanded varies with price.
- *Calculate cost*: Include fixed and variable costs associated with the product.
- *Understand environmental factors*: Evaluate likely competitor actions, understand legal constraints, etc.
- *Set pricing objectives*: For example, profit maximization, revenue maximization, or price stabilization.
- *Determine pricing*: Using information collected in the steps, select a pricing method, develop the pricing structure, and define discounts.

These steps are interrelated and are not necessarily performed in the order. Nonetheless, the list serves to present a starting framework.

MARKETING STRATEGY AND THE MARKETING MIX

Before the product is developed, the marketing strategy is formulated, including target market selection and product positioning. There usually is a tradeoff between product quality and price, so price is an important variable in positioning.

Because of inherent tradeoffs between marketing mix elements, pricing will depend on other product, distribution, and promotion decisions.

ESTIMATE THE DEMAND CURVE

Because there is a relationship between price and quantity demanded, it is important to understand the impact of pricing on sales by estimating the demand curve for the product. For existing products, experiments can be performed at prices above and below the current price in order to determine the price elasticity of demand. Inelastic demand indicates that price increases might be feasible.

CALCULATE COSTS

If the firm has decided to launch the product, there likely is at least a basic understanding of the costs involved, otherwise, there might be no profit to be made. The unit cost of the product sets the lower limit of what the firm might charge, and determines the profit margin at higher prices. The total unit cost of a producing a product is composed of the variable cost of producing each additional unit and fixed costs that are incurred regardless of the quantity produced. The pricing policy should consider both types of costs.

ENVIRONMENTAL FACTORS

Pricing must take into account the competitive and legal environment in which the company operates. From a competitive standpoint, the firm must consider the implications of its pricing on the pricing decisions of competitors.

For example, setting the price too low may risk a price war that may not be in the best interest of either side. Setting the price too high may attract a large number of competitors who want to share in the profits.

From a legal standpoint, a firm is not free to price its products at any level it chooses. For example, there may be price controls that prohibit pricing a product too high. Pricing it too low may be considered predatory pricing or "dumping" in the case of international trade.

Offering a different price for different consumers may violate laws against price discrimination. Finally, collusion with competitors to fix prices at an agreed level is illegal in many countries.

PRICE DISCOUNTS

The normally quoted price to end users is known as the list price. This price usually is discounted for distribution channel members and some end users.

There are several types of discounts:

- *Quantity discount*: Offered to customers who purchase in large quantities.
- *Cumulative quantity discount*: A discount that increases as the cumulative quantity increases. Cumulative discounts may be offered to resellers who purchase large quantities over time but who do not wish to place large individual orders.
- *Seasonal discount*: Based on the time that the purchase is made and designed to reduce seasonal variation in sales. For example, the travel industry offers much lower off-season rates. Such discounts do not have to be based on time of the year; they also can be based on day of the week or time of the day, such as pricing offered by long distance and wireless service providers.
- *Cash discount*: Extended to customers who pay their bill before a specified date.
- *Trade discount*: A functional discount offered to channel members for performing their roles. For example, a trade discount may be offered to a small retailer who may not purchase in quantity but nonetheless performs the important retail function.
- *Promotional discount*: A short-term discounted price offered to stimulate sales.

PRICING OBJECTIVES

Pricing objectives or goals give direction to the whole pricing process. Determining what your objectives are is the first step in pricing.

When deciding on pricing objectives you must consider:

- The overall financial, marketing, and strategic objectives of the company;
- The objectives of your product or brand;
- Consumer price elasticity and price points; and
- The resources you have available.

Some of the more common pricing objectives are:

- Maximize long-run profit
- Maximize short-run profit
- Increase sales volume
- Increase monetary sales
- Increase market share
- Obtain a target rate of return on investment
- Obtain a target rate of return on sales
- *Stabilize market or stabilize market price*: an objective to stabilize price means that the marketing manager attempts to keep prices stable in the marketplace and to compete on non-price considerations. Stabilization of margin is basically a cost-plus approach in which the manager attempts to maintain the same margin regardless of changes in cost.
- Company growth
- Maintain price leadership
- Desensitize customers to price
- Discourage new entrants into the industry
- Match competitors prices
- Encourage the exit of marginal firms from the industry
- Survival
- Avoid government investigation or intervention
- Obtain or maintain the loyalty and enthusiasm of distributors and other sales personnel
- Enhance the image of the firm, brand, or product
- Be perceived as "fair" by customers and potential customers
- Create interest and excitement about a product
- Discourage competitors from cutting prices
- Use price to make the product "visible"

- Build store traffic
- Help prepare for the sale of the business
- Social, ethical, or ideological objectives
- Get competitive advantage

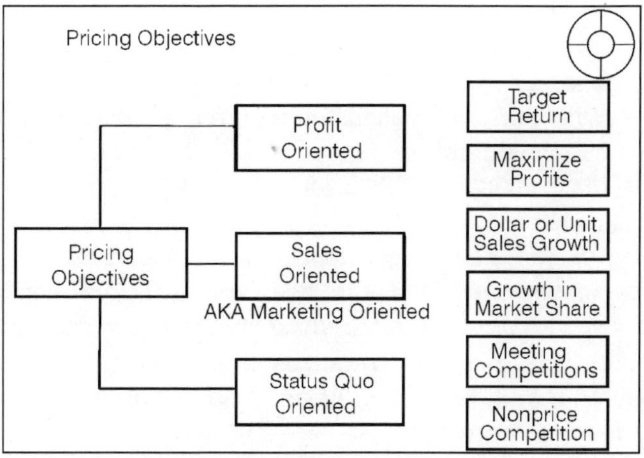

PRICE DETERMINATION

Determination of the prices depends internal and external factors. Pricing goals represents internal policy. Also, price policy should be aligned on several other factors.

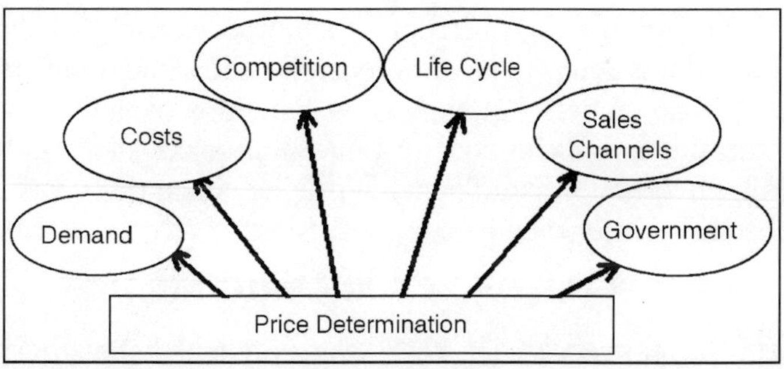

Demand is the key determinant for market oriented company. Demand is the starting point for all activities. Simply, the average customer will be demanding different product quantities, depending on price. Law of the market says that demand and price are counter proportional. Competition has a significant influence to price determination of market oriented companies. Prices need to be adjusted in order to address the competition. Every company should research market and competition, prior to launch of the new product. Survey should include direct competitors but also the substitutes. Based on market survey and the strength of the company the prices can be the same, lower or higher. Costs–While demand and competition are external factor, the costs are internal. The costs must be embedded in every stage of price determination process.

There are several methods of cost embedding into price:

- *Costs Plus*: Company calculates the costs and increase price for the specific profit.
- *Markup*: Price based on cost increased for amount of specific markup percentage.
- *Target Return Method*: Calculated required markup, in order to achieve return on investment.
- Profit Maximizing is the price where the marginal profit equals marginal cost.
- *Breakeven Analysis*: Is the number of units sold that generates profit that can cover cost. This point does not have profit nor lost.

Life Cycle pricing approach analysis the current phase of product life in market:

- Entering phase usually requires higher sales prices in order to payback initial development costs. Also customers are willing to pay more for a new product.
- Growth phase is bringing the market stabilization. Prices are more or less stabile.
- Saturation phase leads to price decline, due to competition entrance and loss of consumer's interest
- Declining phase is the last part of product life cycle. Prices are still going down.

Sales Channels have the different shopping occasion. Consequently the pricing is adjusted to sales channel. For example, the same products is cheaper in hypermarket than on petrol station. Government is usually do not interfere into price determination. Exceptionally it may limit maximal prices for a certain products. Still, government is influencing pricing, since the taxes and custom duties are the part of the price.

RATE-OF-RETURN PRICING

A concept that has received increasing attention is that of pricing to realise some predetermined rate of return on capital investment. The application of this specific approach to cost plus pricing in an automobile manufacturing company was widely publicized as early as 1924. In the distributive trades, this approach has been popularized in the 1950's especially in connection with the operation of large volume, high turnover, discount-house types of stores.

The general principle of rate-of-return pricing may be stated as follows: *the greater the number of times that the total capital investment is turned over in sales volume, the smaller is the net profit per cent to sales volume that is required to realise a given per cent of return on capital investment.*

Many manufacturing and merchandising organizations have attempted to realise a satisfactory profit return on capital investment by an approach to pricing which results in relatively low prices, in comparison with historical or competitive standards, and in an unusually large volume of sales with high turnover.

When high turnover is actually achieved, it permits relatively low expenses of operation resulting from the optimum utilization of fixed facilities. In 1956 the General Electric Company used this approach in making substantial revisions of its price structure for small appliances. For example, prices of its vacuum cleaner were modified as follows:

	Prior Price or Margin	**New Price or Margin**	**Per Cent Reduction**
Factory selling price to wholesale distributor	$33.93	$27.23	20.0
Distributor's margin	10.49	6.49	38.1
Distributor's selling price to retailer	44.42	33.72	24.1
Retailer's margin	25.53	16.23	36.5
Retailer's price to consumer	69.95	49.95	28.6

These drastic revisions were established after careful consideration was given to the effect of presumed larger sales volume at lower prices upon costs of manufacturing and costs of performing marketing services within the manufacturing company and throughout its channels of distribution. The expectation was that the manufacturer and its distributors and dealers could realise greater dollar profits and a better profit return on investment by selling in larger volume at a lower markup.

This approach is most likely to be acceptable to businessmen when there is very good reason to believe that such a change in pricing can produce a *much larger* volume of sales without proportional increases in costs. It can be done most readily when there presently exists considerable unused or surplus capacity in terms of physical facilities or administrative overhead expense items.

INCREMENTAL COST APPROACH TO PRICING

In the foregoing paragraphs, attention has been devoted to pricing on the basis of costs, but with regard to full costs or, more specifically, to the sum of the variable and the fixed costs involved in the manufacture and marketing of a unit of product. In some instances, products are priced on the basis of the variable costs involved rather than full costs. This approach is used most widely under special circumstances as when a business is depressed, is selling outside of its normal market, or has considerable unused capacity.

For example, in what would otherwise be an idle season, a shoe manufacturing company may gladly accept a large order from a chain of price appeal stores on a basis which barely covers the cost of materials and direct factory labour. Such an order may help to keep the plant's labour force intact, avoid costly shutdowns, and also make a small contribution to overhead expense which would be incurred, even if the order were not accepted.

A similar approach is followed by retailers who occasionally negotiate prices with consumers. A furniture retailer, for example, may decide to take a sudden markdown before letting a customer who wishes to make a large purchase walk out of the store.

If the price, after granting the concession, more than covers the cost of the merchandise plus an adequate markup to cover also the direct costs of sales compensation, warehousing handling, and delivery, the merchant is better off to realise some contribution to store overhead expense than to miss the sale.

Such reasoning assumes, of course, that the merchant has some assured source of so-called "regular price" business adequate in volume to cover the total of his expenses of operation and that the practice of negotiating prices on some sales to some customers does not lead all customers to expect to buy on the basis of prices which merely cover variable costs. In other words, this reasoning is based on the assumption that the sales so obtained are what may be called "plus business" and will not affect unfavorably the seller's regular volume.

MARKET OR COMPETITIVE APPROACH

When a firm's basic policy is to sell at or near to the prevailing competitive price level, the problem of price determination is largely one of adjusting to market changes. Marketing effort is devoted to adapting selling effort, marketing services, product features, and costs to selling prices which are more or less given. As in the case of the cost-plus approach, this method has a number of specific variations.

ADAPTATION OF THE PRODUCT TO ESTABLISHED PRICES

Many manufacturers design products to be offered on the market at a prevailing competitive price or at some established retail price line. A manufacturer may decide that in view of the existing conditions he can market a given number of units of his product at a certain final selling price. Starting with that price, he deducts from it the various margins required by the retailers and wholesalers through whom the product is distributed, transportation expenses, and his own cost of marketing and advertising the product. The remainder represents what he can afford to spend for the manufacture of the article. He then puts his engineers and others to work to draw up the specifications that will produce the desired product at the predetermined cost figure.

This method of price determination is most feasible when manufacturing costs can be definitely controlled and hazards minimized. For example, a toy manufacturer may wish to produce a child's kitchen tool set for Christmas business to retail at the popular price of $1.98. If the product is to be sold through department stores, variety chains, and automotive accessory chains, a markup of about 40 per cent must be allowed for retailers.

The manufacturer's selling price could not be more than about 60 per cent of retail or $1.19 per unit. If the manufacturer's administrative costs, marketing expense, and net profit requirement aggregate about 30 per cent, then the allowable cost of manufacturing would be about 83 cents ($1.19 X.70). Product design personnel are expected to come up with an attractively packaged item with sales appeal that can be manufactured within this limit.

COMPETITIVE CIRCUMSTANCES

An important specific price-determining factor in almost all cases is the nature and extent of competition. Sometimes it may be of paramount importance. In the case of actual or alleged monopolies, competition is of least significance; but even here it enters as a factor, for there usually is a possibility of substituting other products.

Cellophane, for example, must compete in end uses with a wide variety of other transparent and non-transparent packaging materials. Brand development has modified the competitive situation in many cases. The establishment of a reputation for a certain brand sometimes removes the product from the purely competitive realm and gives it a semimonopolistic quality.

A higher price may then be charged for the commodity because of its brand than otherwise would have been possible. Aggressive brand-name advertising is very common, however, in industries in which price competition is extremely important among all agencies on each level in the distribution channel. In the field of household detergents and soap products, for example, the consumer is price conscious because of the frequency of purchase and the large relative importance of such expenditures in total annual household spending. Each manufacturer must be competitive with every maker of a similar product. All wholesalers must meet the prices charged for each brand by other wholesalers who provide similar services for customers. All supermarkets in a given trading area are likely to have identical competitive prices on such products on any given day.

The effect of varying competitive pressures upon different lines of merchandise handled by a single marketing institution may be illustrated by an example from the supermarket industry. In an extensive study of the gross margins of profit realized by such institutions, it was found that the total gross margin for the grocery department during the period of the study amounted to 18.2 per cent of sales. Marked variations by product groups within this department were found, however, and margins were especially low on items that were highly advertised and purchased most frequently.

Even on these items the variation was quite substantial as indicated by the following: cigarettes, 6.0 per cent; sugar, 8.0 per cent; soaps, 10.5 per cent; shortening, 9.7 per cent; canned and powdered milk, 13.5 per cent; baby foods, 14.1 per cent; beverages, 12.1 per cent; and soups, 15.0 per cent. In all these categories competition has forced retail selling prices markedly below the average cost of doing business in supermarkets. Obviously, such stores can operate profitably only because of their ability to realise considerably higher margins on products which are not so intensely competitive.

PRICE LEADERSHIP OR "FOLLOWERSHIP."

A single firm sometimes takes the initiative in instituting price changes and others follow, selling at, above, or below the competitor's prices, depending upon the policy in operation. Usually the smaller firms, whether retailers, wholesalers, or manufacturers, follow such a leader rather closely in adopting a similar price or one which enables them to compete successfully. Each store, for example, watches its competitors with great care, many of them employing shoppers to visit competing concerns and make comparisons as to prices, qualities, and services. In the manufacturing field, also, recognized leaders are followed.

A few examples are afforded by the Standard Oil Company of New Jersey, the American Sugar Refining Company, and the United States Steel Corporation, whose prices are closely watched by the less powerful competitors. In practically every market there are one or more firms which are recognized as leaders in the trade and whose prices are used as a basis for the determination of the prices to be charged for competing goods. Prices announced in catalogs by a leader in an industry are usually watched closely by the other members of the industry who then determine their prices accordingly.

WHAT TRAFFIC WILL BEAR

Prices frequently are a direct reflection of the amount which it is believed purchasers will pay. Through past experience and a thorough knowledge of his clientele, it should not be difficult for a retailer, wholesaler, or manufacturer to determine the price range at which certain goods can best be sold.

This method, sometimes referred to as the "eye-value" or "estimating" method of price determination, applies principally to style goods and is based on previous experience, knowledge of own clientele and their reactions, prices charged by competitors, advice from sellers, and the judgement of competent sales clerks, department managers, and shoppers employed by the firm under consideration. It is not uncommon for a millinery store, for example, to sell at widely different prices, a group of hats purchased at the same figure, merely because of some slight variations of individuals hats of the group in colour, pattern, style, shape, or design.

Men's clothing and women's ready-to-wear in particular fall in this category. A policy of this sort appears to be justifiable, for in the handling of certain goods it is the only means of securing ample reward for merchandising ability, initiative, and ingenuity.

Moreover, extra profits on the popular styles tend to offset losses on merchandise that may prove relatively unpopular or on sales made towards the end of the season. A modification of this method of pricing is that of "price lining," that is, producing goods to fit into certain price lines. For example, a dress manufacturer may wish to appeal to retailers who offer dresses at $19.95. The price on his merchandise is automatically determined by that desire, and his price to such retailers must then be $19.95 less the margin required by them. Similarly, the retailer who operates within a certain price line has his prices automatically determined by such a policy.

CUSTOMARY OR CONVENIENT PRICES

Prices and markups on specific items are often varied from the normal or average in order to sell at customary or convenient prices. When a price has prevailed for some time, it is often taken for granted both by buyer and seller alike. Various brands of chewing gum, candy bars, certain cosmetics and toilet articles, and numerous other products have been selling at the same prices for a considerable period of time regardless of business cycles and tremendous fluctuations in the prices of raw materials, labour, and capital entering into their production.

These prices are both customary and convenient from the standpoint of payment and making change. Once prices have become established as customary, it may be extremely hazardous to undertake upward changes. If wholesale prices rise high enough to threaten the retailer's margin, the latter in some cases prefers to discontinue the line rather than raise the price to a new level. Sometimes the price unit remains the same, but an adjustment is made in quality or quantity. Prices of candy bars, for example, have been maintained at customary levels over periods of fluctuating cost conditions by varying the weight of the product.

OVERLAPPING OF BASIC APPROACHES

When a firm uses some form of either one of the two basic approaches to price determination (*i.e.*, cost-plus or market and competitive conditions), it does not exclude consideration of the other.

Differences are largely a matter of emphasis. A manufacturer who prices primarily on the basis of costs must give some attention to competitive conditions and, indeed, the prices of his rivals may cause him to modify the price arrived at on the basis of cost factors. Similarly, as indicated in several of the preceding examples, one who prices competitively does not disregard costs. His starting point may be a competitive market price, but he studies costs carefully, attempting to adjust them to prevailing conditions.

GENERAL PATTERN OF PRICE BEHAVIOUR

Despite numerous attempts at careful analysis, relatively little is known of the behaviour of prices of the thousands of individual commodities that enter into everyday commerce. Some idea can be had, however, from such studies of the *general* pattern of these prices.

In general, retail prices are fixed ultimately by the reaction of consumers and their wherewithal. Ultimate consumers are final judges in the matter, and they necessarily establish upper limits to prices at all preceding points in the chain of distribution. In other words, prices quoted by wholesalers to the retail merchants depend largely upon the prices at which those goods can be resold to the consumer. Manufacturers, in turn, in selling to wholesalers, must make quotations so that the latter may resell to the trade at a profit. This does not mean that all prices fluctuate in exactly the same way at all times or that the prices of all commodities are affected in the same manner.

PRICE INDEXES

Most of our knowledge about price behaviour comes from studies of data included in published price indexes, particularly the Wholesale Price Index and the Consumer Price Index of the U.S. Bureau of Labour Statistics. Such indexes are not without limitations. All commodities are not covered. Prices included are generally published prices, price quotations, or regular selling prices and, hence, do not always accurately reflect prices actually paid by many purchasers, as in the case of competitive bidding, price negotiation, and special sales events.

There is, moreover, a serious problem with respect to quality changes. A 1962 model of refrigerator is a different thing, for example, than a 1952 model, but there is no satisfactory method of accounting for a long series of product modifications in a price index for such items.

In spite of such reservations, data from such indexes are the best available means of making comparisons between different classes of commodities and on different levels of distribution channels.

WHOLESALE PRICES

The term wholesale prices applies to prices in all wholesale transactions, whether the seller be a farmer, manufacturer, wholesaler, broker, or other person or firm selling for business use or for resale. The Wholesale Price Index does not include all such prices but is restricted to those involved at the first or at an early commercial transaction in the domestic market—that is, prices at point of manufacture or point of import and, in the case of agricultural commodities, prices in primary concentration markets, as reflected by organized commodity exchange quotations.

Even though prices of wholesalers are not included, the index undoubtedly provides a reasonable indication of price behaviour in all of wholesaling, particularly for purposes of making comparisons with retail price behaviour. Numerous fluctuations in price are quite common in commodities that are free from monopolistic control and the prices of which are not stabilized or administered by producer, combination, or association.

These fluctuations are generally caused by changes in supply and demand conditions. They are usually more frequent but less violent in major wholesale markets, than at points of original production or in retail stores, for such markets are sensitive and highly organized. Operators in the major wholesale markets are the first recipients of market information relating to conditions of supply and demand affecting the products in which they are interested.

Furthermore, all wholesale dealers in a given market are likely to receive such information simultaneously. Dealing in large quantities and operating on a relatively small margin of profit, a slight change in price may sometimes spell success or failure and certainly may make the difference between profit and loss; hence, it is essential that they receive all relevant market news as promptly as possible, and that they develop skill in interpreting it.

Over a period of time, particularly when reckoned in terms of cyclical fluctuations, some wholesale prices undergo a more radical change than others. Prices of many manufactured industrial commodities are administered. Consequently, they change relatively little during slumps in general business or on the upward grade of the business cycle. Prices of agricultural products, on the other hand, drop precipitously in periods of depression, except as limited by government price support programmes, and make an upward adjustment when conditions improve. Even in the field of manufactured products, prices of consumer goods follow cyclical movements more closely than do the prices of capital goods.

RETAIL PRICES

Retail prices fluctuate less frequently than wholesale prices, whether taken in major wholesale market centers or at points of original production. For this several reasons may be cited. In the first place, as customary or convenient prices may prevail in certain lines, variations can be made only from one customary or convenient price to another, and these variations are often so great that minor fluctuations in the wholesale price must be disregarded.

Second, retail prices cannot be varied with every change in wholesale prices. Fluctuations in the latter are so numerous that practical difficulties would be encountered by a retailer in re-marking goods and keeping track of all such changes from day to day.

Chaos and confusion would invariably result, for it would be impossible for retailers to remember the current prices of the numerous items carried. Furthermore, consumers are likely to resent such practice. They much prefer a reasonable degree of price stability to frequent changes which they may find embarrassing and annoying. Consumers do not follow the market closely and are consequently unfamiliar with slight changes in the wholesale price. Retailers' margins are usually wide enough to absorb minor unfavorable price fluctuations.

Favorable changes, on the other hand, cannot conveniently be passed along unless they are substantial, for changes in retail prices are seldom made in fractional amounts. On a rising market, the retailer often hesitates to raise prices for fear of creating an undesirable impression on his trade. On a falling market, he likewise hesitates to sell his high-cost inventory at lower prices. This has often proved a grave error, for it is usually better, if the market is definitely declining, to continue moving merchandise and take the loss at once. This makes possible the purchase of lower priced goods on which a profit is more probable. Eggs afford an excellent illustration of the relationship between retail prices and wholesale prices at different market levels in the channel.

In the major organized wholesale markets, prices are quoted on the basis of carload quantities of 14,400 dozen, with minimum price variations of 1/20 of a cent per dozen or $7.20 per car. As may be observed from published wholesale market quotations, prices change daily and, in some seasons of the year, much more frequently than that.

Prices paid to producers at country points fluctuate less often but more violently, in conformity with the general trend of the wholesale market. Prices to consumers, however, may not change for a week or more at a time, but whenever such changes are effected, they usually amount to from 1 to 5 cents per dozen.

PRICE FLEXIBILITY AND PRICE STABILITY

These are two terms which are in common use among economists and statisticians and simply refer to different ways in which prices respond to changes in market conditions. This is especially noticeable during periods of violent economic change, as in times of business recession or in times of relative scarcity of commodities culminating in a period of high prosperity.

During such periods prices of some commodities move freely and widely, while other prices change infrequently and very narrowly. Prices of the first type are designated as *flexible* or *sensitive,* while those of the second type are known as *rigid, stable,* or *insensitive.* In between the two extremes, there are many gradations of price flexibility or stability. Those that are relatively, though not completely, rigid are often called rigid prices, especially where the price adjustments are not only slow to respond to changing conditions of supply and demand but are also made periodically and infrequently.

The importance of this distinction stems from the fact that prices are said to be most flexible when sellers enjoy very little discretion in their determination, for they are governed entirely by competitive conditions and by the law of supply and demand. On the other hand, prices are deemed most rigid where the seller has the highest latitude in their determination, either as a result of a monopolistic situation or through collusive restraints of trade. It is on this assumption that price stability has been regarded by government and certain other economists with suspicion and as a sure sign of price control by monopolistic devices.

By the same token, price flexibility has been regarded favorably, for ups and downs are presumed to retard or quicken demand, to accelerate or arrest supply, and to maintain harmony between the flow of goods and effective demand for them. That is why it has been accepted by many as the unfailing sign of competition at work.

The position just outlined with regard to price stability or rigidity on the one hand and price flexibility on the other must be criticized on several scores. First, flexible price as a regulator of demand does not have a perfect medium in which to work. It is subject to the check of custom, and it does not measure off the supply of goods to the effective wants of consumers. Second, price stability or steadiness is more common than constant fluctuations when commodities are sold openly on a market price basis. This is true of agricultural products as well as of manufactured goods.

Examination of the peacetime Wholesale Prices published by the Bureau of Labour Statistics reveals that such products as cotton, hay, fluid milk, seeds, and wool sell at the same wholesale prices in a given market for months at a time and frequently for an entire season. Such is also the case with many manufactured products that are known to be highly competitive in the sense of normal or workable competition previously discussed, as illustrated by condensed milk, bread, rice, baked beans, sugar, cornstarch, many textiles, paper, and bar iron. Third, it depends to a large extent at what level the price rigidity is being maintained.

If a rigid or stable price is maintained at a very low level, it may be the result of extremely keen and almost cut-throat competition rather than a result of a monopolistic device. It would thus seem that a mere "jitterbugging" of prices per se has little meaning, and the same is true of price rigidity in itself and without reference to the level and to the effect upon the public. The matter of price rigidity or flexibility must, therefore, be considered merely as a starting point in any investigation of the existence or absence of competition.

MATHEMATICAL MODELS AND PRICE ANALYSIS

To an increasing extent, elaborate mathematical models are being used for purposes of analyzing price behaviour. Such models involve the construction of a framework for organizing a vast array of quantitative data in a manner that will assure internally consistent final results.

By means of high-speed computing devices, many more variable factors can be analyzed than can be handled practically by any other means. The technique of model building is beyond the scope of this text. Indeed, to go into the subject in connection with this discussion of pricing would have a number of disadvantages. First, it would tend to focus attention upon model images, statistical techniques, and the specialized language or symbolism of the mathematical analyst, rather than upon the factors being analyzed. Second, it would unduly complicate the objective of obtaining a basic understanding of the marketing process.

Another factor is that the nature of the contributions eventually to be made by computer approaches to such analysis is not yet clear. At the present, models contain many items of assumed data which, if not properly appreciated, can easily give the impression of empirical reality, owing to the elaborate manner in which the data may be processed and findings presented. In short, the study of mathematical models of pricing or other marketing topics is not for the novice.

One should have a good background in mathematical analysis plus a sophisticated understanding of the field of activity being analyzed in order properly to appraise such techniques and their contribution to knowledge in general or to the solutions of particular problems. It is expected, however, that as experience is gained with such techniques, as their use becomes more widespread, and as increasingly greater amounts of empirical information can be substituted for assumed or hypothetical information, our knowledge of pricing and price behaviour will be enlarged.

8

Evolution of Strategic Business Management

INTRODUCTION

Strategic thinking evolved from the different approaches that companies utilize to plan their business activities. Prior to the 1920s, few firms did any of what today might be called "long-term planning." Most businesses were run more or less entrepreneurially, and business decisions were relatively short term in focus. Manufacturing produced products, sales sold them, and accounting counted the money. Many businesses were driven by a focus on survival.

With the advent of the modern corporation, such as General Motors and DuPont in the 1920s, larger and more far-flung enterprises needed mechanisms to plan and allocate resources. Financial planning provided senior managers with a sophisticated set of tools with which to plan annual production, expenses, and capital investments.

The methods typically involved translating sales forecasts into production schedules, estimating the costs associated with the planned volume, and deriving profit forecasts. Once capital appropriations, research, development, advertising, and administrative overhead were taken into account, projecting cash flows available for dividends was a simple and straightforward matter.

This approach, however, was based on a fundamental assumption that sales projections could be made. In a stable world, this assumption held. Sales forecasters had only to extrapolate from the past.

But when times changed—the economy slowed, markets got saturated, or other events affected demand—the limitations of this method became obvious. Also, this approach tended to treat departments within the business as separate functions (sales forecast ? manufacturing costs ? financial results) and tended to have a one-year horizon.

As a consequence, changes occurring over several years, such as shifting consumer preferences or market saturation, would go unnoticed. Finally, the driver of business behaviour under financial planning systems tended to have short-term goals, which were often oriented towards meeting the budget for the year.

To deal with longer-horizon changes, forecast-based planning was developed in the 1950s and 1960s. Here, the rigour of analyses jumped dramatically, as planners began using such tools and concepts as product life cycles, discounted cash flows and net present value analyses, and statistically valid market research of consumer preferences and buying behaviour.

Because the level of sophistication and time required by these tools was significantly greater than called for previously, managers needed assistance from a new breed of technical experts—strategic planners, business school graduates, and consulting firms. Business schools grew at unprecedented rates in the 1960s and 1970s, and the consulting profession boomed as new strategic planning firms, such as the Boston Consulting Group and Bain & Company, were founded and flourished. The behaviour driver under forecast-based planning was to predict the future and to plan strategies that would adapt the firm to that future.

In other words, it was reactive. At the same time, staff planners and consultants found that many of their strategic recommendations were not getting implemented. This occurred for two reasons. One reason was that often the analyses and recommendations were performed by people who were not responsible for executing the strategy. Without the ownership that comes with participation, many line executives either rejected plans or, at best, were lukewarm in their compliance.

The second reason was that plans that were based on analyzing consumer trends and product acceptance often failed to take *competitor* behaviour into account. The strategic management approach was developed in response to these limitations. Strategic *management,* in contrast to strategic *planning,* is the function of line executives—the people on the firing line who deal with the real world of customers, machines, products, and people.

The philosophy is simple: the people closest to the action are in the best position to know what is going on in the business, what works, what trends are developing, and what competitors are doing. In other words, those who must execute must be involved in developing strategy. A second part of the philosophy is also simple: it is not sufficient to look for-ward (at potential consumer demand for a new product, for example). Managers must also look to the right and to the left—at what competitors are doing. In other words, competitive analysis becomes a key feature in strategic thinking.

The dilemma, however, is twofold:

- Usually, line managers do not have the time to do strategic analyses. As you will see in the Astral Records case, a general manager's life is cluttered with a multitude of conflicting demands on his or her time. So, managers must either take time out—such as at a planning retreat, for example—or they must learn so much about strategy and competition that they are thinking strategically on the job.

- Even if managers create the time for strategic planning, they often lack the tools. Their training may have been thorough in the *functional* areas of marketing, accounting, engineering, or human resources, but it may have been insufficient in *strategic* concepts, frameworks, and tools. As stated earlier, the purpose of this book is to provide these tools.

In a firm equipped with strategic management tools and strategic thinking managers and executives, the behaviour driver shifts from a mentality of survival, meeting the budget, or merely forecasting the future, to one of *creating* the future by shaping one's industry and markets rather than reacting to them.

A firm that is truly thinking strategically can be identified in a number of ways. First, its executives know and understand what the firm's mission and strategy are. Second, they know their core competencies and capabilities as an organization. Third, they can identify their competitors and predict their reactions to the firm's strategic moves. Fourth, they have developed a culture that supports their strategy. Finally, they are constantly developing new capabilities for renewing their strategies and for competing successfully in the future.

BECOMING A STRATEGIC THINKER

So, how do managers and their companies develop strategic thinking? Must they go through the stages listed above, one at a time? Fortunately, no. It is essential that managers know how to do financial planning, market research, and other fundamental business analyses. But they need not wait to master these before progressing to strategic management and thinking.

ELEMENTS OF STRATEGIC THINKING

Strategic *planning* has a fairly well-established history. The first book on strategy was written in 1965 by Igor Ansoff, an executive at Lockheed Aerospace. Titled *Corporate Strategy,* it presented an extraordinarily logical, step-by-step set of concepts and approaches to making diversification decisions. When presented with this model as a how-to-do-strategy template, most practicing managers run for cover. The thoroughness of the model forces the analyst to think through the logic and economics of the business. But this thoroughness comes at the price of appearing overwhelming to busy line executives.

All strategic planning approaches attempt to find an optimal match between the resources and capabilities available within the firm (Strengths and Weaknesses) and the external market conditions and environmental trends (Opportunities and Threats). This match or coalignment (often called a SWOT analysis) results in a strategy, whose efficacy translates into some level of corporate performance.

A key feature in the basic strategy model is the reciprocal influence of all of the variables. For example, in the late 1960s a major science-based consulting firm, Sigma Consultants, observed that:

- The level of expenditures on health care in the United States was accelerating, a trend likely to continue,
- The firm had several competent professionals on its staff who had carried out health care related assignments such as designing hospitals and evaluating medical group acquisitions.

By responding to the market opportunity and articulating a health care strategy or consulting practice, Sigma would define a new domain.

Having chosen the new domain, the firm would now have to respond to the dictates of the marketplace (arrow from environment to strategy) by, for example, designing products and services that were in demand or adapting to whatever governmental regulation might be relevant. To implement the new strategy, Sigma might reorganize its staff so that all professionals working on health care related assignments were grouped together.

Over time, this group might increase its proficiency by sharing experience, knowledge, and the like. The degree of success would be manifested in some level of performance (arrow from strategy to performance), and, in turn, the performance level would serve as feedback, indicating that further adaptations of strategy might be in order.

In essence, then, the model represents a system of interacting parts. But the picture painted thus far is not complete. A "perfect" strategy may be found that violates managers' predispositions. Conversely, management's values may suggest strategies that are not optimal in an economic sense. For example, President Jay Monroe of the Tensor Corporation refused to change his very "functional" high-intensity Tensor lamps when new competitors started introducing style variations.

As a result, his company lost 60 per cent of the market, which it probably could have retained had Monroe's values been more economic than aesthetic. In our Sigma Consultants example, there was strong support for the health care venture among senior management and some of the professional staff. That is, the venture fit the values of top management. However, Sigma was originally organized on the model of a research lab, in which professionals were unimpeded by bureaucratic hierarchy and were free to choose their projects.

Assignment to projects was by invitation, and, assuming the invited person was billing sufficient time to avoid the pressure to join projects indiscriminately, he or she could turn these projects down. The health care strategy, in contrast, suggested an organizational unit in which consultants would be expected to dedicate themselves to one major type of activity. This ran smack against the prevailing culture. The strategy was abandoned. Although it is a very "rational" model of strategy, needs to be amplified to consider thc imple-mentabilityof strategy. Management needs to include the "soft" sides of strategy, political feasibility, and organizational acceptability.

THE SELECTED STRATEGY OF BUSINESS

Several structures have been proposed for testing the acceptability of a chosen strategy. They consist of lists of criteria that the goals and action plans should meet. They can be used as the elements on one axis of a matrix that has the strategy set choices arranged on the other. Then each strategy can be scored on each criterion. The sum of criteria scores for each strategy can then be used to select the best one(s). In this way the criteria can be used in place of other measures of strategy acceptability in a modified rational model. The following strategy choice criteria have been synthesized from similar lists prepared by other authors.

- The selected strategy should be consistent with the
  - Organization's environment,
  - Internal capabilities and characteristics,
  - Available resources, and
  - Risk preferences
- The action plan choices should be aimed at clearly identified goals (objectives and targets) and should have a high chance of successfully reaching or guiding behaviour towards them.
- The selected strategy should have appropriate timing.
- The strategy choice should allow sufficient flexibility for adjustment to deal with competitors' responses and environmental changes.
- The organization's leadership should be committed to support of the chosen strategy.

Consistency Tests

Four consistency tests should be performed on the selected strategy.

Environmental Factors: The selected strategy should be consistent with the environmental factors identified during the environmental analysis. The selected strategy should address the major threats and opportunities, both present and future. After all, one of the major purposes of the strategy is to integrate the organization and the environment. By taking advantage of opportunities and either avoiding or overcoming threats, that integration can take place.

Internal Characteristics: The chosen strategy should be consistent with major internal characteristics of the organization, whose competencies and skills should be incorporated into the strategy so that they become emphasized; weaknesses should be addressed so that they can be corrected within an appropriate amount of time. Another internal characteristic is management capability.

Selected strategy must be implementable by either present management or new management people. Also, the ways in which the new strategy relates to past strategy should be clear. There is a strong relationship between past strategy and new strategy in most firms.The ways in which the new one is expected to improve on the old should be understood.

Resource Availability. New strategy should be consistent with physical facilities and financial resource availability in the present and future. Future resource needs should be within the organization's capability and understood in detail. Pro forma financial statements constructed to show the financial impact on the organization of the new strategy will help to demonstrate the ability of the firm to produce the necessary resources.

Risk/Return Preference: The final consistency test involves making sure that the selected strategy meshes well with the risk/return preference of management and owners. Risk-takers will be inclined towards strategies that involve relatively high levels of risk with commensurate high possible payoffs. They tend to stress organizational strengths and environmental opportunities, operate with confidence and aggressiveness, and tackle challenges head on; innovation is typically preferred over imitation.

Alternatively risk-averters prefer more defensive, conservative strategies. They will try to stay within present capabilities without entering into projects requiring new strengths or skills, will balk at uncertainty, and will tend to be followers rather than leaders in their markets. When Friendly Ice Cream Corporation, a family-style restaurant chain with several hundred retail outlets in the Northeast, went public in 1969, the Wall Street Journal described Curtis and Preston Blake, the company's cofounders, as using both belts and suspenders to hold up their pants. Their risk-averting orientation included such features as the discounting of every payable since the company's inception, refusal to use long-term debt, and reliance on extensive test marketing of minor product additions.

Clarity of Goals

The selected action plans should be linked with clearly understood objectives and targets, especially those related to profit performance. It will be difficult to monitor performance when action plans are not tied to goals that are widely adopted and understood. In addition to relating clearly to goals, the selected action plans should have a high chance of reaching them by minimizing the effectiveness of competitors' counterattacks. There are two considerations here. First, strategy should avoid direct confrontation with rivals in areas where they are strongest. Rivals will often respond with less conviction when they do not perceive a direct attack on one of their strengths.

The large amount of investment necessary to mount a successful challenge to competitors' strengths may actually prohibit such a move. If it is done with too little investment, it can carry a higher chance of failure than would typically be true if the competitor were weaker on this attribute. Second, attacking a competitor's weaknesses, a less risky alternative, may carry insufficient return to justify the offensive. For example, a primary weakness of major automobile manufacturers is their inability to produce truly "one-of-a-kind" cars. Many attempts have been made world-wide to capitalize on this "weakness," but only a handful have realized any success.

Timing

The timing of the selected strategy should be appropriate in two important ways. First, the length of time that will be necessary to implement the strategy should be appropriate given the company's present resources or the time it will take to get them. For a simple example, a firm's cash flow position can be deteriorating faster than its management's ability to retrench by collecting receivables, arranging a loan, or cutting expenses. Second, the strategy must be timely in terms of environmental circumstances. When Chrysler decided during the early 1970s to try to strengthen its position in the large-car market, the oil embargo of 1974-1975 left it with a huge inventory of suddenly unpopular autos.

Flexibility

The selected strategy should allow sufficient maneu-verability so that management can respond to competitors' reactions and minor environmental changes while still maintaining the integrity of the strategy. One way to build in flexibility is to develop several contingency strategies, each of which applies to a somewhat different set of likely environmental assumptions. Then if the environmental assumptions begin to come true, the appropriate modifications can be made, having already been analyzed and pondered for their effects and requirements. The same sort of contingency strategy set can be developed around likely competitor reactions.

Management Commitment

The selected strategy should have the commitment of all levels of management. In some organizations top management's advocacy of a strategy will soon lead to its support. In others, however, factions for and against a strategy will develop. With such division present, successful implementation of the strategy becomes difficult. "Successful strategies require commitment, not just acceptance. How can the commitment of individuals be developed? Staw explains that commitment to a course of action is a function of the extent to which the action (strategy) is perceived as satisfying three needs: the need to justify past decisions (retrospective rationality), the need for consistency, and the need for positive subjective expected utility (prospective rationality).

To generate maximum commitment, the selected strategy in some way should confirm the correctness of decisions already made. Presumably managers at each level of the organization will react or proact to overall strategy with their own respective strategies. The more their responses can be seen as justifications of their past decisions, the greater will be the chances that they will sense commitment to, rather than merely acceptance of, the selected overall strategy, as well as their role in it.

Then, there are both cultural and organizational norms for consistency that apply to strategy selection as well as other decisions. According to Staw, Motivation to justify decisions can be seen as a function of responsibility for negative consequences as well as both internal and external demands for competence... Responsibility for negative consequences leads to a motivation to justify previous decisions, if there is a need to demonstrate competence to oneself or others. In other words some degree of consistency between the past strategy and the selected one is important in developing commitment because the similar new one demonstrates the correctness of the past one. This may at least partially explain why it tends to be difficult to get all the key actors in an organization to dedicate themselves to a radically new strategy. It may also explain why some boards of directors seem to replace CEOs when they feel that a strategy change is necessary.

Finally, the higher the prospective rationality of the selection, the more commitment is facilitated. Prospective rationality is the product of the perceived probability of future outcomes and the perceived value of those outcomes. It is roughly equivalent to the expected value of the strategy. A manager who feels that the selected strategy has a high expected value will be more committed to it than one who feels the expected value is low. Thus for commitment to develop, all participants should be convinced that the organization has the resources, skills, time, and other attributes necessary to reach goals successfully with the new action plans, which together constitute a new strategy.

COMPETITIVE (BUSINESS LEVEL) STRATEGY MANAGEMENT

In this second aspect of a company's strategy, the focus is on how to compete successfully in each of the lines of business the company has chosen to engage in. The central thrust is how to build and improve the company's competitive position for each of its lines of business. A company has competitive advantage whenever it can attract customers and defend against competitive forces better than its rivals. Companies want to develop competitive advantages that have some sustainability. Successful competitive strategies usually involve building uniquely strong or distinctive competencies in one or several areas crucial to success and using them to maintain a competitive edge over rivals. Some examples of distinctive competencies are superior technology and/ or product features, better manufacturing technology and skills, superior sales and distribution capabilities, and better customer service and convenience.

- Competitive strategy is about being different. It means deliberately choosing to perform activities differently or to perform different activities than rivals to deliver a unique mix of value.
- The essence of strategy lies in creating tomorrow's competitive advantages faster than competitors mimic the ones you possess today.

We will consider competitive strategy by using Porter's four generic strategies as the fundamental choices, and then adding various competitive tactics.

PORTER'S FOUR GENERIC COMPETITIVE STRATEGIES

He argues that a business needs to make two fundamental decisions in establishing its competitive advantage:

- Whether to compete primarily on price or to compete through providing some distinctive points of differentiation that justify higher prices, and
- How broad a market target it will aim at. These two choices define the following four generic competitive strategies. which he argues cover the fundamental range of choices.

Overall Price (Cost) Leadership

Overall Price (Cost) Leadership appealing to a broad cross-section of the market by providing products or services at the lowest price. This requires being the overall low-cost provider of the products or services. Implementing this strategy successfully requires continual, exceptional efforts to reduce costs—without excluding product features and services that buyers consider essential. It also requires achieving cost advantages in ways that are hard for competitors to copy or match.

Some conditions that tend to make this strategy an attractive choice are:

- The industry's product is much the same from seller to seller
- The marketplace is dominated by price competition, with highly price-sensitive buyers
- There are few ways to achieve product differentiation that have much value to buyers
- Most buyers use product in same ways—common user requirements
- Switching costs for buyers are low
- Buyers are large and have significant bargaining power

Differentiation

Differentiation appealing to a broad cross-section of the market through offering differentiating features that make customers willing to pay premium prices, *e.g.*, superior technology, quality, prestige, special features, service, convenience. Success with this type of strategy requires differentiation features that are hard or expensive for competitors to duplicate. Sustainable differentiation usually comes from advantages in core competencies, unique company resources or capabilities, and superior management of value chain activities.

Some conditions that tend to favour differentiation strategies are:

- There are multiple ways to differentiate the product/service that buyers think have substantial value
- Buyers have different needs or uses of the product/service
- Product innovations and technological change are rapid and competition emphasizes the latest product features
- Not many rivals are following a similar differentiation strategy

Price (Cost) Focus

Price (Cost) Focus a market niche strategy, concentrating on a narrow customer segment and competing with lowest prices, which, again, requires having lower cost structure than competitors.

Some conditions that tend to favour focus are:

- The business is new and/or has modest resources
- The company lacks the capability to go after a wider part of the total market
- Buyers' needs or uses of the item are diverse; there are many different niches and segments in the industry
- Buyer segments differ widely in size, growth rate, profitability, and intensity in the five competitive forces, making some segments more attractive than others
- Industry leaders don't see the niche as crucial to their own success
- Few or no other rivals are attempting to specialize in the same target segment

Differentiation Focus

Differentiation Focus a second market niche strategy, concentrating on a narrow customer segment and competing through differentiating features.

Best-Cost Provider Strategy

Best-Cost Provider Strategy This is a strategy of trying to give customers the best cost/value combination, by incorporating key good-or-better product characteristics at a lower cost than competitors. This strategy is a mixture or hybrid of low-price and differentiation, and targets a segment of value-conscious buyers that is usually larger than a market niche, but smaller than a broad market. Successful implementation of this strategy requires the company to have the resources, skills, capabilities to incorporate up-scale features at lower cost than competitors. This strategy could be attractive in markets that have both variety in buyer needs that make differentiation common and where large numbers of buyers are sensitive to both price and value. Porter might argue that this strategy is often temporary, and that a business should choose and achieve one of the four generic competitive strategies above. Otherwise, the business is stuck in the middle of the competitive marketplace and will be outperformed by competitors who choose and excel in one of the fundamental strategies. His argument is analogous to the threats to a tennis player who is standing at the service line, rather than near the baseline or getting to the net. However, others present examples of companies who seem to be able to pursue successfully a best-cost provider strategy, with stability.

COMPETITIVE TACTICS

Although a choice of one of the generic competitive strategies provides the foundation for a business strategy, there are many variations and elaborations. Among these are various tactics that may be useful.

Timing Tactics

When to make a strategic move is often as important as what move to make. We often speak of first-movers, second-movers or rapid followers, and late movers. Each tactic can have advantages and disadvantages.

Being a first-mover can have major strategic advantages when:

- Doing so builds an important image and reputation with buyers;
- Early adoption of new technologies, different components, exclusive distribution channels, etc. can produce cost and/or other advantages over rivals;
- First-time customers remain strongly loyal in making repeat purchases; and
- Moving first makes entry and imitation by competitors hard or unlikely.

However, being a second- or late-mover isn't necessarily a disadvantage. There are cases in which the first-mover's skills, technology, and strategies are easily copied or even surpassed by later-movers, allowing them to catch or pass the first-mover in a relatively short period, while having the advantage of minimizing risks by waiting until a new market is established. Sometimes, there are advantages to being a skillful follower rather than a first-mover, *e.g.*, when:

- Being a first-mover is more costly than imitating and only modest experience curve benefits accrue to the leader
- The products of an innovator are somewhat primitive and do not live up to buyer expectations, thus allowing a clever follower to win buyers away from the leader with better performing products;
- Technology is advancing rapidly, giving fast followers the opening to

leapfrog a first-mover's products with more attractive and full-featured second- and third-generation products; and
- The first-mover ignores market segments that can be picked up easily.

Market Location Tactics

These fall conveniently into offensive and defensive tactics. Offensive tactics are designed to take market share from a competitor, while defensive tactics attempt to keep a competitor from taking away some of our present market share, under the onslaught of offensive tactics by the competitor.

Some offensive tactics are:

- *Frontal Assault*: Going head-to-head with the competitor, matching each other in every way. To be successful, the attacker must have superior resources and be willing to continue longer than the company attacked.
- *Flanking Maneuver*: Attacking a part of the market where the competitor is weak. To be successful, the attacker must be patient and willing to carefully expand out of the relatively undefended market niche or else face retaliation by an established competitor.
- *Encirclement*: Usually evolving from the previous two, encirclement involves encircling and pushing over the competitor's position in terms of greater product variety and/or serving more markets. This requires a wide variety of abilities and resources necessary to attack multiple market segments.
- *Bypass Attack*: Attempting to cut the market out from under the established defender by offering a new, superior type of produce that makes the competitor's product unnecessary or undesirable.
- *Guerrilla Warfare*: Using a "hit and run" attack on a competitor, with small, intermittent assaults on different market segments. This offers the possibility for even a small firm to make some gains without seriously threatening a large, established competitor and evoking some form of retaliation.

Some Defensive Tactics are:

- *Raise Structural Barriers*: Block avenues challengers can take in mounting an offensive
- *Increase Expected Retaliation*: Signal challengers that there is threat of strong retaliation if they attack
- *Reduce Inducement for Attacks*: *e.g.*, lower profits to make things less attractive. Keeping prices very low gives a new entrant little profit incentive to enter.

The general experience is that any competitive advantage currently held will eventually be eroded by the actions of competent, resourceful competitors. Therefore, to sustain its initial advantage, a firm must use both defensive and offensive strategies, in elaborating on its basic competitive strategy.

COOPERATIVE STRATEGIES

Another group of "competitive" tactics involve cooperation among companies. These could be grouped under the heading of various types of strategic alliances, which have been discussed to some extent under Corporate Level growth strategies. These involve an agreement or alliance between two or more businesses formed to achieve strategically significant objectives that are mutually beneficial. Some are very short-term; others are longer-term and may be the first stage of an eventual merger between the companies. Some of the reasons for strategic alliances are to: obtain/share technology, share manufacturing capabilities and facilities, share access to specific markets, reduce financial/political/market risks, and achieve other competitive advantages not otherwise available.

SOCIETAL STRATEGY MANAGEMENT

Societal strategy consists of goals and action plans of which the overall purpose is to guide the ways in which management intends the organization to respond to the major social demands placed on it. It is an explicit definition of the organization's social responsibilities: how it is expected to react to the demands of particular groups of external constituents. The recent emergence of this level deserves further explanation.

The idea of isolating social responsibility in a separate (from corporate, business, and functional) strategy level was introduced in 1979 by Ansoff and modified by Schendel and Hofer. Ansoff presented it as follows. The original concept of product/market strategy appears as only one component of a much broader concept. We might call it *enterprise strategy*, which is needed to integrate and relate the new dimensions of the strategic problems.

The development of societal legitimacy (or enterprise) strategy is Ansoff's proposed solution to the increasing importance of... socio-political variables in the life of the firm. Included in these variables are "new consumer attitudes, new dimensions of social control and, above all, a questioning of the firm's role in society."

In other words, Ansoff suggests concentrating managers' attempts to deal with new liberal views about the social role of business, growing egalitarianism, and the proliferation of constrictive regulation, among other social demands, in a societal legitimacy strategy that specializes in matters of social responsibility. Actually Ansoff's proposal for enterprise strategy goes beyond social responsibility issues to include other substrategy areas. Schendel and Hofer limit its contents to social-legitimacy concerns because of their belief that the other strategy areas are effectively addressed within prevailing definitions of corporate-business-and functional-level strategies.

Thus they recommend, Enterprise strategy attempts to integrate the firm with its broader non-controllable environment, not in terms of product/market matches in a narrower economic sense, but in the sense of the overall role that business, as one of society's important institutions, should play in the everyday affairs of society... More explicit attention will have to be given to (societal legitimacy strategy) in the future, just as Ansoff suggests, just as it has been necessary to separate corporate and business strategy considerations from the problems of functional area interpretation, over the past two decades.

However, some strategists may prefer not to institute this new strategy level, for reasons explained by Dill: "There has been less turbulence in the environment for companies which have spent time over the years listening to and assessing what various internal and external constituencies have to say about the powers they are and are not willing to delegate to corporations and corporate management."

Stated differently, some managers may prefer to address *all* social legitimacy issues within the rubric of existing strategy levels. For them social responsibility concerns would be addressed within the fabric of goals and action plans at the corporate, business, and functional levels. Our conclusion about the usefulness of enterprise strategy is that it should be employed by organizations that have particularly sensitive relationships with the environment.

Firms such as utility companies, toy manufacturers, and educational institutions, for which an especially sharply focused public scrutiny has devolved, would be well suited for development of separate social-legitimacy goals and action plans. For others, whose society interaction is less controversial, matters of social responsibility might be handled more efficiently, and even effectively, within goals and action plans at the corporate, business, and functional levels alone. However, the advisability of their formulation for a given firm as a distinct activity is intended to be a matter of judgement depending upon whether or not sufficiently poignant social issues either confront the firm at present, or are expected to do so in the future.

Corporate-Level Strategy

A corporation's portfolio of business units (SBUs) can vary in its desirability just as a financial manager's portfolio of investments can. The acceptability of a particular*business portfolio* is determined by assessing whether it reflects mission and expected strengths, weaknesses, threats, and opportunities (determined through environmental, industry, and internal analyses of each business unit) as well as values and political exigencies.

Additions to and deletions from the present portfolio would then be expressed in merger and/or divestment strategy. Finally, these strategies would be implemented by the appropriate organizational units and the machinery would thus be activated to adjust the present portfolio. The content of corporate-level strategy is a set of action plans and corresponding corporate-level goals expressed in terms of the firm's collection of subsidiaries. By comparison, business strategy focuses on expected operational results of a business unit. However, it also consists of action plans that relate to goals (at the business level).

The substance of corporate-level goals and action plans can be summarized as follows:

- *Corporate-level goals*: The desired portfolio of business units by the end of the firm's planning period.
- *Corporate-level action plans*: How to get from the present portfolio to that targeted in terms of:
  - Business unit strategies to be retained.
  - Additions of business units expressed as either growth strategy parameters (for "home grown" units) or merger and acquisition strategy.
  - Business units to be divested.

Business-Level Strategy

The content of business-level strategy is also a combination of goals and action plans. Business-level goals should be stated in such a way that for each one, the following four components are evident:

- *Identifying, characteristics* of each objective or target.
- Each target's *substantive threshold value;* that is, the hurdle value upon reaching which the target will be considered attained (often stated as a specific value of the evaluative criteria).
- *Evaluative criteria* to be monitored in order to measure the firms progress towards the target.
- *Time frame threshold value;* that is, the date by which, or the elapsed time during which, the substantive threshold value would be reached.

Business-level action specifications should be devolved so that collectively they define the following elements:

- The firm's *product market scope;* that is, the nature of the products or services provided and the markets served by the firm.
- *Input-output transformations* in which the firm is engaged; that is, the nature of the activities with which the firm adds value to its labour and material inputs and what those inputs are.
- What *synergies* are sought in the operation of the firm.

Whether a strategy is being analyzed from within or outside the firm, these characteristics should be present. The outside analyst may use them as dimensions along which a firm's strategy can be described. The inside analyst or strategist may use them as guidelines for determining the comprehensiveness of strategy. When taken together, these elements of business-level strategy should combine uniquely to:

- Define the business of the SBU or firm,
- Describe its competitive edge.

Thus strategy aligns the strategic business unit or firm relative to its competitors, distinguishes it from them, and hopefully propels it beyond them.

Functional-Level Strategy

In contrast with the other levels of strategy, functional strategies serve as guidelines for the employees of each of the firms's subdivisions. Which ones of these segments or functional areas are included in a firm's functional strategy set is itself a matter of strategy. For example, whether to have an R&D department or not in the first place is a strategic decision.

Functional goals and action plans are developed for each of the functional parts of the firm to guide the behaviour of people in a way that would put the other strategies into motion. If part of a firm's business-level strategy were a target of a 10 per cent increase in sales to be brought about by market penetration, for example, marketing strategy might include a change in compensation policy for salespersons and a specified increase in the advertising budget.

In that way marketing strategy would provide some detail about how the marketing aspects of the market penetration action plan would be implemented. Similarly, financial strategy would consist of a set of guidelines on how the financial elements of the firm would be put into effect. Personal strategy, production strategy, research and development strategy, and appropriate other functional strategy areas would do the same.

Nature of Strategic Decisions And Strategic Thinking

Although the process of creating strategy is often discussed as if it were an unconstrained design process, keep in mind that while strategists evaluate strategy, the firm is operating.

This evaluation involves assessing the extent to which present strategy is meeting expectations. It may be the case that only a small part of, say, marketing strategy would have to be changed to correct a problem. In effect, then, such a change would constitute an acceptance of corporate- and business-level strategy, and also of the firm's functional strategy set. Marketing strategy would be all that was rejected. When a firm's performance is less than satisfactory, the reason often is a functional strategy shortcoming. One might say that a "good" business-level strategy would have been poorly implemented by part of its functional strategy set. For this simple example, a change in marketing strategy could improve performance while other levels of strategy would remain unchanged.

Alternatively, a problem with the nature of a firm's or SBU's business brought about by a major environmental opportunity or threat, a change in that level's goals set, or the development of some internal capability or weakness could necessitate a business-level strategy change. The new strategy would probably include vestiges of the old along with some unfamiliar elements. In most cases a whole new functional strategy set would likely have to be designed and put into effect to implement the new business-level strategy.

More generally, one could conceivably change parts of a firm's functional strategy set without changing business-level strategy. However, rarely would one expect to encounter the case in which a change in business-level strategy did not trigger the necessity to alter functional-level strategy in some way, at least not in a successfully managed business.

There is a risk of incorrectly identifying the strategy level at which a problem exists. A tendency exists in business to change functional-level strategies or organizational structure in a attempt to remedy any problem.

Of course, if the problem existed within the firm's corporate-or business-level strategy, for example, changing functional-level strategy would not correct it. In fact, this move would most likely aggravate the situation. The reason for this tendency is probably that functional strategy changes are potentially less disruptive than changes in the other levels. They certainly would affect fewer people than modifications at the corporate or business levels. The results of trying to solve a business-level strategic problem with a functional-level solution is well illustrated by the "big four" U.S. automobile companies.

With overseas competitors exporting fuel-efficient automobiles to the United States, and with widely acknowledged shrinkages of fossil fuel supplies, they still stubbornly tried to retain their old business and corporate strategies, well into the 1970s, by changing market strategy only. A set of major environmental threats, particularly at the business level, was met by minor model changes and increased efforts to convince the car-buying public that big autos were what we all really wanted. During the 1970s and early 1980s, these companies finally began to respond to their business strategy problems with business strategy changes—major philosophical alterations in the nature of their businesses.

If U.S. auto firms were to rely on small cars instead of traditional American big cars as their primary sources of growth, far-reaching changes in their functional strategy sets were also necessary. New growth rates, profit targets, market-share goals, and the like, along with related broad action plans that centered around contraction in many forms, were implemented along with new functional strategy.

They included such things as cash rebates, Chrysler's government-guaranteed loan, employee layoffs, close cooperation with UAW officials, R&D efforts focused on producing smaller, less powerful engines as a primary effort rather than as an inconvenience. The U.S. auto firms' strategy changes were finally implemented during a period of chaos. However, by then they were all in the red, and the doomsayers were having a heyday.

South claims that the key to successful strategic decisions is the creation of competitive advantage—selection of competitive areas within which success is clearly achievable. The Japanese have taught us that there are really two very different forms of competition: Reciprocal and strategic. Reciprocal competition is the traditional form in which companies in mature industries compete with other firms having similar strategic positions while attempting to distinguish themselves on the basis of operations.

Many colleges and universities offer similar programmes, with traditional facilities and are significantly different only in terms of the geographical areas within which they operate. Strategic competition, on the other hand, involves competing primarily by establishing superior strategic position. That is, the main concern of strategists is selection of a strategically advantageous posture which affords their organization a position of strength from which to do battle. Lincoln Electric Company has successfully differentiated itself on the basis of price and quality.

Their industrial welding equipment is regarded as the top quality product of its kind and the firm has consistently passed along cost savings to customers in the form of low prices. As a result, Lincoln is very difficult to compete with because of its strong price position. Following this set of ideas, then, strategic decisions are those which involve "clear and favorable differentiation from competitors," so that one's competitive advantage is tangible, measurable, and preservable.

Defining strategic thinking is made especially difficult by the absence of a consensus on what strategic management is. On the latter point, Gluck, et al commented, "hardly anyone yet fully understands what strategic management is, knows exactly how to do it, or can clearly define its benefits." Their explanation of strategic management is that it is an approach to management which fuses strategic planning (plan development through analysis of environment, competition, and strategy choices) and the firm's system of operational decision making. This process has five dimensions.

First, strategic management requires a widely understood strategic planning process tightly interwoven with a strategically centered organization structure. Second, it requires widely discussed, analyzed and negotiated goal choices from which are culled out the ones that are not adoptable. Third, strategic management relies on the shared ability to think strategically by managers throughout the company.

Fourth, a performance evaluation system is necessary that focuses top level evaluators' attention on critical positive and negative strategic factors. Finally, it requires a strategy supportive motivational system and value orientation among managers. These qualities, they say, define a strategically managed organization. Four of these qualities are readily understandable. But still subject to question is what is meant by the ability to think strategically.

Strategic thinking is that which generates:

- Creative, environmentally relevant ideas
- Concepts about how to turn them into systematically managed action plans.

It has the following prerequisites:

- Input information is based on facts and logical data.
- Previously unquestioned assumptions are sought out and examined.
- A burning desire for resource conservation, and
- Indirect, spontaneous, and unexpected thought processes which are hard for competitors to predict.

These requirements of strategic thinking set it apart from other kinds of decision making. First, strategic thinking requires factual and logical input data because it is competitively dangerous to base strategy formulation on erroneous information. The stakes are too high to "hoof it." Second, long-held assumptions should be identified and analyzed to make sure they still apply. This is especially true about goals which are in force, understandings about the environment and competitors, market acceptance and image, etc.

Third, the manager attempting to think strategically should be committed to conservation of the organization's resources rather than expecting that a good idea will precipitate a cornucopia of funds, people, and support. It is easy to be creative while assuming that most resource requirements can be taken care of. A greater degree of creativity is required when one must conserve resources. Finally, strategic thinking must be done without setting patterns which competitors can identify and anticipate. The problems of predictable strategic thinking are analogous to the football coach sending in plays to his quarterback using hand signals that are understood by the opposing team's coaches.

MARKETING STRATEGY MANAGEMENT

Marketing goals and action plans should address matters of product/service, price, distribution, communication, and the process of new product development.

Product/Service

Product/service strategy would be set to:

- Define the key characteristics of the product or service.
- Locate it within the organization's product/service hierarchy,
- Select the quality level,
- Outline product/service support programmes. This information would be specified when an old product/service is to be changed or a new one, or several, added.

These characteristics of a firm's product/service are determined by finding the best fit between the organization's various internal factors and its external factors as they relate to product/service.

Thus a university college might introduce an evening programme to broaden its asset utilization and extend its instructional capabilities (internal factors) in the face of increased numbers of non-traditional students with heightened demand for education (external factors), to help implement a product (service) development action plan to reach a goal of increased revenue.

Price

Strategy regarding product/service price would be set to accomplish one or some combination of four fundamental things:

- Change in profitability,
- Change in sales level or growth rate,
- Change in net cash flow,
- Maintenance of present sales, profit, or cash flow level.

Marketing goals and action plans deal with price by specifying the planned-for impact on company performance (as measured by the income statement) desired of a strategy. The task of actually setting price to yield that impact is normally the responsibility of the firm's marketing director where marketing is decentralized. In cases where a profit impact is expected, marketing goals can set a target return on assets, net cash flow, return on sales, or some other evaluative criterion that would have been determined to justify the higher-level strategy. In small sole proprietorships or partnerships, the targeted return might be a dollar amount required to cover the spending needs of the owner/manager.

Some managers prefer to have prices set so as to generate a certain targeted dollar amount of sales, rate of change of sales, or market share. Although sales are more immediately measurable than profit, their use as a focus can lead to earnings or cash flow slippage that go undetected in the short term.

For example, a firm could allow progressively more liberal receivables policy and thus attract sales to meet a rigid sales growth or market share goal. Yet by increasing payables commitments, the firm could suddenly find itself placed on the cash basis by suppliers and unable to meet delivery requirements. Obviously sales and profitability would then be threatened.

Firms can also set a net cash flow target, which, when coupled with normal credit terms for an industry or geographical area, can dictate within narrow limits what price would be most appropriate. here a strong need for cash might require a relatively low price. This would be the case if buyers were unwilling to pay a higher price on short credit terms and the seller needed cash inflow to meet required outflows.

Finally, a strategist may feel that prices should be set so that competitive attention is not drawn to the firm or that risk is minimized. This equilibrium or "status quo"maintenance goal could be effective for a firm with stable returns on sales, for example, which is trying to avoid competitive retaliation.

Distribution (Place)

As with other marketing variables, the details of distribution system structure and selection are the province of the marketing director in a decentralized firm. Yet the corporate strategist's input to distribution system design is critical in that it sets the limits for subsequent distribution decisions.

The primary element of distribution goals and action plans is a definition of planned-for coverage or exposure of products addressed at higher levels of strategy.

Intended product exposure is a function of:

- The extent to which the firm is integrated forward or backward,
- Whether the output of intermediate steps in the production process will be marketed or retained only as components,
- Desired coverage, usually in geographical terms, of the items marketed.

To illustrate, a fully integrated home microcomputer manufacturer could limit distribution to sales of computers, the final products, to consumers. In so doing the firm would have foregone potential sales of separate intermediate products such as electronic components, individual hardware units, and software.

In this case distribution decisions would be a function of how wide a market area the strategist plans to cover with the finished product. If, alternatively, business strategy called for marketing the output of each step in the production process, then distribution strategy would address the coverage of variables for components, hardware, and software. Each one could have different coverage requirements, depending upon the density in the market area of potential buyers for each product class.

Promotion

The strategist's primary concern with promotion, or, more generally, communication, is to provide guidance to the firm's marketing specialists so that product communication assumes a form consistent with overall strategy.

There are four types of communication methods:

- *Personal sales presentations*: Direct communication between sellers and potential buyers.
- *Sales promotion*: Displays, exhibitions, demonstrations, and trade shows to complement other commu-nication techniques.
- *Mass advertising*: Communication with large aggregates of potential buyers simultaneously.
- *Public relations*: Free non-personal communication.

In a decentralized firm, the job of selecting a particular combination of communication methods is usually the responsibility of marketing specialists. To optimize congruence between communication methods and overall strategy, the strategist sets communication strategy in four areas to guide the specialist's decisions. First, a set of quantitative communication goals specifies expectations of the programme ultimately designed. These goals are the planned-for results of the communication programme and are not necessarily the same as overall strategic goals.

Communication goals should be segment-specific such that the net effect of several communication efforts (say, one for each of several segments or markets served by the firm) is attainment of one overall growth rate in sales, market share, or profit. These goals should also clarify whether the purpose of communication is to educate, persuade, or remind. Second, communication activities are aimed at either one or a combination of target market segments. A segment description is normally part of all marketing strategy subsets but has specific implications for communication specialists.

Third, while analyzing the firm's environmental circumstances, competitive position, and internal characteristics, strategic analysis (the process that would have led to the development of a new product or maintenance of an existing one) would have revealed a selection of possible selling points for the product or product mix. A selling point is the collection of product or service attributes that constitute the primary message of the firm's communication programme; it is the information conveyed in the communication effort. Fourth, communication strategy should include the amount to be budgeted for the communication programme expressed in either dollars or percentage of sales or gross profit.

New Product Development

As products reach the decline stage of their life cycles, they must be replaced by new products in order for the firm to grow and prosper. Thus an integral part of a business strategy that stresses product development is a marketing strategy defining the way in which new product ideas will be generated. The product development process is summarized by Rabino and Moskowitz as four chronologically ordered stages as follows:

- *Formulation of product goals*: These may be thought of as the organization's requirements for new products; what must it "get out of" new product entries and therefore what are its purposes for generating new product ideas.
- Search, discovery, and evaluation of new product proposals. Procedures are developed and implemented to identify and screen new product ideas which may potentially heed product goals.
- *Product development and testing*: The number of new product ideas is reduced to the few tangible ones that have the highest chance of meeting goals and which fall within the company's strategic capability.
- *Market entry*: The commercialization phase is typically the province

of the rest of the marketing function and requires expertise which resides there.

The rudiments of marketing strategy can be laid out by setting goals and action plans for each element above. For analysis of cases, students who formulate marketing strategy should follow the guidelines above for each element at a minimum.

FINANCE STRATEGY

The management of a firm's financial resources is intricately connected to the upper-level strategies of the firm. That enterprise-, corporate-, and business-level goals normally include explicit financial performance criteria attests to the fundamental strategic nature of higher-order financial matters. So too financial resources thread through all the operational components of an enterprise in a manner that either enhances or constrains their contribution to overall performance. As such financial concerns are both directive and supportive in a strategic context.

Finance strategy is generally concerned with the acquisition and allocation of financial resources for the purpose of achieving goals at an acceptable level of risk. Thus the setting of goals and action plans for finance can be viewed as a problem relating the sources and uses of capital that is constrained, at least in part, by stockholders' wealth goals. In this section financial goals and action plans are treated from capital acquisition and allocation perspectives, though this distinction is only for expository purposes. Rarely are capital acquisition decisions made in isolation from those relating to how funds would be allocated, and vice versa. Indeed the familiar cost-of-capital notion has meaning in both regards.

On the matter of risk, we will find that it enters into both sources and uses problems. It is manifest primarily through the notions of financial leverage, operating leverage, liquidity, and working capital management. All are discussed in the present section.

Capital Allocation

Higher-level strategies normally involve certain current and fixed asset investments that represent short- and long-term applications or uses of funds. Specifications describing these investments are outlined in terms of capital budgeting techniques, cost-benefit analysis, and a cash budget, which serve:

- To determine the financial characteristics of strategic investments
- As evaluative criteria for monitoring the operation of the firm under the business-level strategy.

Of course, to determine the financial impact of strategic investments, a comprehensive financial analysis (explained earlier) of the firm is necessary to define its preimple-mentation financial structure.

All subsequent changes can then be evaluated according to their expected effect on this financial profile. Business-level strategy will necessitate selection from among various expenditure choices. Finance goals and action plans are needed to establish the expected outcomes and methods to be followed in such evaluations. Related decisions involve the relative amounts of capital diverted to dividends versus reinvestment in the firm (the dividend payout ratio or its opposite, the earning retention ratio).

Investment Project Categories

Investment projects can be classified as follows:

- *Cost reduction*: Expenditures to increase the efficiency of labour or equipment would fall into this category. They commonly would be part of a retrenchment strategy or one targeting increased profitability.
- *Maintenance*: These expenditures are for replacement of worn-out or damaged equipment or facilities where no strategic change is intended.
- *Market development or penetration*: Expenditures for action plans requiring expansion into new markets or increased penetration of existing markets are included here. They would be for advertising campaigns, market research, geographical expansion, and so on.
- *Product development*: When expenditures are for the production of new or modified products, they fall into this category.
- *Compliance*: Expenditures are often required by government regulations, labour contracts, or insurance terms.
- *Miscellaneous*: Projects that do not fall into the other five categories are classified as miscellaneous. Examples include office facilities and some employee benefit programmes.

Authorization hierarchies: To evaluate investment alternatives, most managements establish expenditure authorization hierarchies by type of investment project, functional department, and/or division. Thus market development investments might have to be reviewed by the sales manager, the vice-president of marketing, a vice-presidential expenditure committee, the CEO, and ultimately the board of directors.

A dollar limit is usually established for each level. An expenditure above that limit has to be forwarded to the next highest level for authorization until it is either approved or denied. The magnitude of these limits and where they are applied depends upon the type of business, style of management, track records of individuals involved, and other factors, and should reflect the sensitivity of the firm's financial position involved, and other factors, and should reflect the sensitivity of the firm's financial position to losses. Authorization limits and the way they are administered become prime (though inconclusive) indicators of the type and degree of decentralization in an organization.

Project Selection Criteria

In all instances the capital allocation process becomes a budgetary matter therefore, we have the term "capital budgeting." But it is as much a process of selection as it is of submission. Compliance and most miscellaneous projects, which usually involve no cash inflows, are evaluated by level of necessity and dollar amount. The other types of projects involve both cash inflows and outflows and can be evaluated by various measures of net return as well as size of outflow (or investment).

Most common among the various methods are the payback period, average rate of return, net present value, internal rate of return, and profitability index models. The model to be used to evaluate projects is specified by finance strategy along with the project selection criterion (or cutoff point) for approval. Capital budgeting models allow the strategist to rank investment alternatives by profitability (or other bases). Establishing a cutoff point for selection from among the ranked alternatives is another strategic decision.

Two popular ways to determine the cutoff point are:

- To use the firm's cost of capital
- To compute other hurdle rates of return. Of course, some expenditures are simply necessary regardless of their return and would be selected accordingly. Compliance investments, for example, often fall into this category.

Cost of Capital. If investments are made in projects with returns below the rate paid to obtain capital, the earnings available to common shareholders will be reduced accordingly. The cost of capital for a firm is thus the rate of return on projects that is necessary to prevent changes in the earnings available to common shareholders and can be used as an evaluative criterion for selection from among strategic investment choices.

This definition does not imply that the concern is only with the cost of equity financing (which includes new common share issues as well as retained earnings). Debt and preferred stock are also sources of investment funds, both of which normally have different component costs from common equity sources taken alone. But the focus of cost of capital as an investment criterion is on the returns generated for common shareholders. Establishing the firm's cost of capital is important to ensure that investments are not made with expected returns that are less than the amount the firm pays for capital. Thus the cost of capital can be used as a "hurdle" rate of return. This estimate is also used as the discount rate in computing net present value, internal rate of return, and the profitability index for projects.

Operating Leverage and Risk. All strategic investment decisions are going to involve some degree of risk. Risk entails not only the profitable versus unprofitable dichotomy, but also the variability in earnings or losses emanating from an investment project. One dimension of the risk-management question is captured in the concept of operating leverage. Operating leverage is the degree of magnification of earnings or losses (expressed as cash flows or profits) set off by different levels of output. The magnification results from the variable cost versus fixed cost mix in an investment period. Generally the higher the level of fixed commitment in relation to variable costs, the greater is the leverage (and magnification). This, of course, is the central notion in the familiar break-even analysis, where concern is given not only to the break-even point, but also the levels of earnings or losses around it.

Operating leverage becomes a strategic issue because it affects such things as variability of anticipated sales, competitive strategy, and the degree to which the firm can absorb or tolerate variations in earnings. The fact that differences exist across companies in their relative amounts of operating leverage may be largely a function of the industry in which each of them competes. The fashion apparel industry, for example, tends to display a good deal more demand volatility than does the tobacco industry.

The first, therefore, tends to be more labour (variable cost) intensive than the latter in its production processes (though there are other explanations for this difference as well). It is much more difficult to reduce fixed than variable commitments than in the short term to address temporary demand shortfalls. Second, a firm's fixed versus variable cost mix is often a function of the competitive advantage it is trying to achieve. A firm choosing a technological leadership role would likely have comparably large fixed commitments to research and development.

This would raise its relative break-even point and magnify the levels of losses or earnings at other output levels. Or a firm trying to maintain a price leadership position might require automated (capital-intensive) production systems. Here lower total costs at higher output levels allow the competitive price advantage and magnify earnings above break-even volume. Below break-even volume, the reverse is true. Finally, the tolerance for, or ability to absorb, earnings fluctuations affects the operating leverage profile. A marginal firm, intolerant of losses, would probably make as few fixed commitments as possible. Though this might impair its upside earnings capability, the firm's primary concern would be with downside risk.

Managers are also concerned with the degree of operating leverage when confronted with vertical integration decisions, since they usually represent the conversion of variable costs to fixed costs. One reason for integrating vertically is to capture the margins realized by suppliers or downstream distributors.

But in the process, additional fixed costs are normally incurred that alter the degree of operating leverage the integrator experiences. Any resulting variations in earnings or loss potential must be consistent with overall financial performance goals. If not, the new acquisition might operate at a loss (below break-even). Losses could be avoided by margin/cost trade-offs between integrated units (absorption), or additional fixed-cost commitments may be simply insignificant in the grand scheme of things. In any case the operating leverage profile of a firm and that of individual investments pose risk, as well as profitability, questions.

Capital Acquisition

The second aspect of financial goals and action plans is determining the sources of capital to be invested in assets needed to carry out a higher-level (usually business-level) strategy. Long-term sources will affect primarily the firm's debt/equity structure; short-term sources its liquidity position. But, as we shall see, they are interrelated.

Financial choices will be made to optimize the firm's overall financial profile while also maximizing the likelihood that a new set of higher-level strategies will be implemented as planned. Making these choices is a decision process fraught with trade-offs. Using equity to raise funds may improve debt/equity position, but will dilute ownership. Use of short-term debt will preserve ownership but will threaten liquidity. Using internally generated funds will prevent interest expense increases, but may threaten dividend payout ability. Thus the strategist's primary concern is with setting limits or guidelines for key financial criteria within which a higher-level strategy's financial requirements must fit.

Considerations in the Capital Mix. Financing for strategic investments falls generally into two classes; short term and long term. For both the strategist must select the optimal type of financing—optimal in terms of cash/return trade-offs, relative costs, and control as indicated by the firm's mission and master strategy. For example, if stockholders through the board of directors were to oppose further dilution of holdings, the strategist probably would not consider equity financing, even if it was considered optimal for another reason.

Next the impact of the selected mix of financing sources is assessed on:

- The firm's liquidity position
- The firm's debt/equity structure.

In the process of selecting sources of funds and capital, managers have the opportunity to affect the firm's financial profile. They can take advantage of financial strengths such as strong liquidity or a relatively low debt-to-equity position. Conversely they can, within reasonable limits, strengthen financial weaknesses.

Weak liquidity can be at least partially ameliorated by generating cash through tightening credit collection policies, improving inventory control, or controlling operating expenses. These are largely working capital management matters. Dividend Policy. In deciding between long- and short-term financing, the strategist must evaluate the firm's dividend policy. The proportions of earnings allocated to dividends and retained earnings can materially affect the firm's ability to meet debt repayment schedules with cash. Over-commitment to debt could necessitate reducing, or not increasing, dividend payments, and thus lessening cash flows to stockholders.

Dividend policy generally will be one of three major types: stable dollar amount per share, constant payout ratio, or low regular dividend plus extras. Which of these is appropriate for an individual firm is a function of a financial interpretation of shareholder goals, including expectations of returns and risk. It is therefore a matter of highest-level concern, and normally is treated by the board of directors. Decisions regarding dividend policy also eventually affect the liquidity and debt structure of the firm, as well as stockholder relations. Consequently, students should carefully enunciate the potential impact of proposed changes in dividend policy of companies they are analyzing in cases by explaining how they will alter the firm's liquidity position, debt structure, and stockholder relations. Financial Leverage and Risk. In addition to dividend policy, the strategist will be particularly concerned with financial leverage. Not to be confused with operating leverage, financial leverage involves the use of debt in the firm's financial structure.

Though it may be operationally defined and measured in a variety of ways, it essentially entails the use of debt to extend the earning power of funds committed by the firm's shareholders. When used properly financial leverage magnifies returns on committed funds. Because of the nature of financial leverage, it carries within it not only the general types of risk associated with operating leverage, but also two others that have rather specific implications. First, there is the risk of default—the inability to meet debt obligations as they come due. By definition, as financial leverage increases, cash flow requirements necessary to service additional debt increase as well. The risk of inadequate cash flow is, therefore, a primary concern in strategic decisions regarding financial structure. This, of course, suggests that liquidity and leverage are intricately intertwined in decisions of that kind.

Second, the informed strategist not only must consider the risk of default and the involuntary actions that failure may lead to, but also the priority of claims that attend a given financial structure. In the case of liquidation, voluntary or involuntary, shareholders normally hold a claims position subordinate to that of debt holders. Thus increased leverage can have a deteriorating effect on the assets available for distribution to shareholders upon liquidation. Therefore, this component of risk enters financial structure decisions as well.

Cost of Capital. The cost of capital is of major importance in investment decisions (as a discount rate or hurdle rate of return), but it also has strategic importance in capital mix decisions. Since a firm's cost of capital represents the combined influence of all of its individual components, it can serve as a useful criterion for evaluating the capital structure itself. That is, the lower the overall cost of capital, generally the more "optimal" is the capital structure for a given risk profile. In planning the capital mix, the finance strategist is concerned with minimizing the combined cost of funds so that the funding of future growth can be accomplished most economically. Thus if the addition of long-term debt to the capital structure ends up reducing the combined cost of capital (through a marked increase in the price of common stock, for example), then the increased-leverage decision can be partly justified on that basis. Similarly increases in common shares issued may have a disproportionately negative influence on the cost of debt. In these cases the cost-of-capital concept offers a useful framework for establishing capital mix objectives. Further, it forces the analyst to consider the interactive effects of different forms of financing, rather than simply examine the individual component costs of the various forms of debt and equity available.

Long-Term Financing Instruments

The major classes of long-term financing are common stock, preferred stock, various forms of debt, and convertible securities. Selection from among these choices is a function of the firm's dividend policy, leverage position, cost of capital, and earnings per share; target values for each of these, in turn, are a function of higher-level goals and strategy. The strategist can set financial goals for each of these risk/return variables so as to guide the selection of long-term financing instruments.

Leasing

Increasingly popular as a method of financing, leasing is loosely a form of leverage. Because of the debt characteristics of leasing, which normally extend beyond one year, it is included in our discussion of long-term sources of funds. One author refers to leases as "soft debt." The Internal Revenue Service normally allows an income tax deduction for the full amount of a lease (annualized, of course, by the payment schedule). This amount is often greater than that resulting from an asset purchase where depreciation and related interest expenses are deductible. Leases may also prove a more expeditious method of obtaining assets than by an outright purchase, and may allow for greater flexibility in asset management and financial planning. The viability of leasing instead of purchasing an asset is largely a function of cash outflows and the cost of funds. Although there are several ways to analyse the lease-or-buy decision, the internal rate of return approach is straightforward and reasonably comprehensive. The internal rate of return of leasing is compared with the after-tax cost of debt to determine which has the lower cost.

EVOLUTION OF BUSINESS STRATEGIC MANAGEMENT

Such information may provide additional insight into the operation of the firm and help understand the degree of strategic management progress made by managers. More importantly, however, it may be useful in helping students understand strategic management as the highest level of a hierarchy of management activities.

The McKinsey analysis discovered four quite distinct phases of strategic management evolution. In Phase 1, financial planning, management focuses on the preparation of budgets with an emphasis on functional operations. Most organizations have a budgeting process, in at least rudimentary form, as a way of allocating resources among functional units, subsidiaries, or projects. The second, forecast-based planning, follows naturally from the first as managers project budget requirements beyond the one-year cycle.

This phase represents an effort to extend managers' attention beyond the immediate future as scenarios are developed which describe their expectations about future time periods. Budgets are often constructed for several years at a time and are rolled over annually so that the appropriateness of a budgeted amount can be reviewed several times before it is operationalized. Phase 2 planning is very "now" oriented.

Current operations and characteristics are stressed in analyses of the firm and there is little attention to or patience for considering operational options or development of strategic changes. The business portfolio of a Phase 2 firm is often viewed as the final expression of strategy rather than as an input to the strategy formulation process. Current structure and business activities may be considered fixed, not as strategic variables. Planners are required to adopt an external orientation and tools and procedures for environmental and internal assessment.

Concern centers on understanding the organization's environment and competitive position and generating ideas about how the company might better fit its environment. Several choices, contingency plans, are often devised for how the company might fit its environment. Lower level planners and managers are often involved in the process of generating choices, an activity that soon puts top management in the position of choosing a plan in which it had little involvement in developing. Strategic management, evolves as top management senses the need to more heavily invest in the planning process because of its lack of understanding of or involvement in the details of earlier plan development. Strategic management is the meshing of Phase 3 planning and operational management into one process. It is analysis and conclusion that takes place year-round and ties performance evaluation and motivational programmes to strategy.

Deliberateness of Strategy

Sometimes outsiders impute strategy to the behaviour of firms. Obviously, students analyzing case studies are placed in this position when they impute strategy from the data they are able to generate on the firm's operations.

Similarly, journalists and the managers of competing firms may impute strategy to a firm's behaviour; and it may or may not accurately reflect the real strategy in place. Outsiders may also imply intent to an imputed strategy. That is, they assume not only that the strategy they imputed from the firm's behaviour is the real strategy its employees are implementing, but they imply that this strategy is the one intended for the firm by its management. Seldom is this the case.

Mintzberg developed a taxonomy which is useful for discussing the realism and deliberateness of strategy. First, he distinguished between strategy that is the result of a plan, and of a pattern of behaviour. He referred to them as "strategy as plan" and "strategy as pattern," respectively. Strategy as plan is a chosen course of action; it could be a real strategy (one intended for implementation) or a ploy (a tactical move whereby a competitor may be influenced into making a mistake). Some people think that Coca-Cola's rumored change in Coke's formula in the mid-1980s was such a ploy.

The implication is that Coca-Cola had not intended to really change the formula. Instead, it is thought, they publicized their plan to change formula, intoduced a new product with a different formula that tasted a lot like a competitor's product, and finally graciously conceded to continue producing the old formula product when the public demonstrated a preference for it over the new—"similar to a competitor's—" formula.

Incidentally, if this was in fact a ploy, it has to rank among the top marketing moves ever attempted by any business. Coca-Cola reaped an immediate increase in market share of about 15 per cent that thrust them once again into unquestioned dominance in the huge U.S. softdrink market. Strategy as plan, when implemented, may or may not be what the firm ends up with. That is, the planned strategy could ultimately be either realized or unrealized.

If it is realized, then the entire process would be a textbook case of strategy formulation and implementation in the sense that the firm successfully implemented what was intended. But what happens if the planned strategy is implemented and, for some reason, the strategy that is realized is not the intended one? We might say that the planned strategy was unrealized, and the realized strategy (the one that seems to describe what the company is actually doing) arises out of some consistency in the behaviour of the company.

Mintzberg and Waters call this unintended realized strategy, "strategy as pattern," or a pattern in a series of actions by the organization. Strategy as pattern is what you will end up with when you impute strategy to the behaviour of a company you are analyzing in a case study, or what journalists produce when they attribute a strategy to a company based only on its actions.

Thus, a realized strategy could be either a deliberate strategy as plan, or an "undeliberate" strategy as pattern. If the realized strategy was planned and also accurately described the firm's actions, then strategy as pattern and strategy as plan would be synonymous. However, when realized strategy is not intended strategy (that is, it was either not what was intended by management when they drafted a planned strategy, or they drafted no strategy at all), then it simply "grew" out of the activities of the company. In Mintzberg's terms, it "emerged" as a pattern of behaviour in the absence of intension, or despite unrealized intentions. A realized strategy is what a company is actually doing. If it is the one intended by management, then it is deliberate If not, then the intended strategy wasunrealized, and the realized strategy is emergent. An emergent strategy is, by definition, not deliberate.

However, a manager may choose not to consciously formulate strategy and, instead, "go with" the emergent one. But even here, the resultant emergent strategy would not have been deliberate in the same way an intended strategy would have been. Often it is convenient to distinguish between intended and emergent strategies. When management performs no strategic management at all, they still will have a realized strategy that is emergent. This emergent strategy could be recognized by outsiders (and insiders for that matter) even though it may not have been intended my management.

Contingency Strategies

Managers may develop several versions of strategy, each of which is intended to fit a different environmental scenario. An environmental scenario consists of a set of environmental characteristics that describe a firm's external circumstances.

By structuring external variables into sets of related variables, different scenarios result. Thus several scenarios (usually three) can be arrayed on a probability distribution for which the horizonal axis is a measure of the extent to which they are viewed as "good" or "bad"—supportive or not supportive—to the firm.

In the scenarios that fall on the left side of the distribution are considered pessimistic (undesirable but only a small probability that they might have to be dealt with); those on the right as optimistic (desirable but probably will not materialize either); and those in the middle as most likely to occur and having some good and bad features.

Next a strategy set is established for each scenario. These could be entirely different strategies or variations of one. Evaluative criteria then are formulated for each scenario. These are variables to be monitored in order to figure out which of the scenarios is going to apply in the future.

Actually this is a matter of deciding whether the present scenario will continue to be the best description of the firm's environment or, instead, if one of the others seems to be emerging as most correct. By identifying critical values for evaluative criteria, the strategist knows beforehand under what set of conditions to switch from the present strategy set to the pessimistic or optimistic set.

Summary

This chapter serves to familiarize the reader with the underlying principles of strategic management and to outline the path through that field taken by the chapters. First, the history of strategic management as an academic discipline is reviewed to provide perspective on its current stage of development. Next, summarizes the results of some of the major studies conducted to answer the question "Does strategic management pay off?" Also discussed in this section are the primary methodological problems encountered in doing such research.

The mission statement is considered an input to the strategy formulation process, which is outlined in the next section. Strategy at four organizational levels comprise the focus of this section and the book's text. They are the enterprise, corporate, business, and functional levels.

9

Corporate Communication

To understand communication in a corporate setting, one can explore any of several defining characteristics. One characteristic has to do with time: Communicative acts are embedded within a flow of prior and subsequent interaction. Indeed, in a business setting, a document may not have any more intrinsic importance to that community than the process that created it; that is, the real value in the process may come from negotiating a consensus for the final text. Another characteristic relates to form, as the ideas constructed over time may move through many communicative forms: Informal discussion may lead to an agenda item in a meeting, which may result in a request for a document, which may in turn be presented orally in another meeting.

An almost endless variety of forms are possible — from formal documents to review comments, from hallway conversations to lengthy presentations, from scrawled notes to multimedia. Not only is the relationship between oral and written texts important, but also the plethora of technology-mediated forms that confound traditional definitions of text. Even with so many possibilities, form is a relatively straightforward characteristic in describing communication after the fact.

Form, on the other hand, is considerably more complex for the individual doing the communicating. In a business setting, individuals choosing the form of a communicative performance must balance a whole range of contextual factors from access to timeliness to appropriateness. In short, the flow of communication over time and the form communicators choose to give it are embedded within a social framework a set of cultural expectations — that largely define how the individuals within a particular setting interact.

CONTEXT AND NON-ACADEMIC WRITING

The connection between context and non-academic writing has been fruitful territory for research. Nonetheless, it is a difficult concept to generalize. Write presents a useful definition of context not tied to a specific research site, which (to paraphrase mightily) focuses on the writer's projected self in light of the writer's understanding of external reality. Context and the social perspective have much to offer in understanding the role of texts in constructing meaning, but they also raise challenging questions when applied to non-academic research sites. The essential difficulty can be stated briefly: How can we know an unfamiliar context?

Returning to the ideas of flow and form help emphasize this difficulty. As a researcher, we can fairly easily characterize the form of a text; we can also, through various means, explore its flow in terms of precedents and antecedents. Thus, we can describe what a communicative performance is and where it fits into the overall conversation. But context, in one simple word, embraces the localized social complexity of communication and all that suggests in terms of what is knowable and what transformations take place in representation. The crux of the difficulty may lie in moving from the familiar to the unfamiliar. In researching writing in the classroom, a familiar setting for many researchers, the barriers to understanding context may not be insurmountable to the extent that we can really understand the context of classroom communication from external points of view. But in many non-academic settings, writing researchers may find themselves on alien turf.

Context in a business setting may involve anything from the competitive climate for an entire industry to relations among employees assigned to the same project; from the formal power relationships defined by organizational charts to informal power hierarchies based on information distribution; from managerial attempts to create unified corporate cultures to the unique aspirations of individual employees. Context, in any setting, is layered: The difficulties in its characterization are exacerbated by unfamiliar value systems and distinctly different institutional goals. Yet context can charge texts-even fairly mundane business texts such as memos and meeting minutes — with subtle ironies, implied put-downs, challenges, celebrations, and humour — all difficult to detect for the cultural outsider. For the purposes of this study, however, we chose to impose some boundaries on the idea of context.

Non-academic writing researchers have most often used qualitative research methods to understand context, generally focusing on individuals or relatively small groups of employees. My own approach is similar but perhaps foregrounds the sources of contextual knowledge to a greater extent in that we asked employees specific questions about context (defined as three layers of corporate culture), supplemented with research into the history of the corporation, where the research took place, and the industry in which it competes. It may be that making explicit the sources of contextual knowledge and relying where possible on the words of cultural insiders to describe their perceptions of context reduces some of the difficulties with representing an unfamiliar culture. This approach, of course, has its limitations: Perceptions of context will differ among any set of cultural informants so that any claim for an overall characterization of context becomes suspect; the selection of which details to present, although in informants' own words, reflect the researcher's institutional biases. Still, as cultures are dynamic, context may be best described as a phenomenon based in individual perception. Construction of meaning ultimately begins in the interaction among and between individuals and small groups.

TECHNOLOGY AND CONTEXT

The balance focuses on the relationship between context and technology (a major influence on both form and flow), providing a socio technological perspective on communication at a specific site. We chose this focus for several reasons. First, as noted earlier, connections between text and context are well established, as are links between context and texts over time. Connections between context and use of technology — from a communications point of view — are not as well understood. Third, choice of technology provides a useful site to emphasize a relationship between context defined as perceptions of corporate culture and decision making about communication. Many decisions about communication are fleeting, recoverable only through means such as protocol analysis.

Decisions about choice of technology, on the other hand, are observable and recordable, and other means of gathering information still apply. Finally, like understanding context in unfamiliar settings, understanding the use of technology in a corporate setting presents its own challenges. In composition and other fields concerned with communication, researchers have tended to study technologies as discrete entities, starting with a focus on personal computers and word processing software in the early and mid-1980s, through recent scholarship focusing on new or emerging technologies such as electronic mail over local area networks, hypertext, and multimedia.

In many workplaces, and in contrast to the college or university computer lab, employees often choose among many available computer-based technologies to communicate a particular message. In terms of technology, then, this research had two goals: first, to explore how people chose among many technological options; and second, to investigate links between employees' perceptions of their context and their use of technology to interact with other employees. And there were links. At the corporate site where we conducted my research, social factors defined the use of communication technologies. Specifically,

- Communication technology options were determined by contextual factors at the organizational level. That is, technology deployment echoed the organization's goals, values, and conflicts.
- Choice among the options reflected local culture. For example, widely held perceptions of uncertainty or distrust of management affected which technologies employees used to communicate.
- Not surprisingly, individual factors, such as an employee's interest

in new technology, a need for control, or a dislike of writing further affected choice among communication media.

RESEARCH METHODOLOGY

Research for this study took place at the NetCon Division of Computer Corporation. (All names are fictitious at the request of the corporation.) The research site within NetCon Division was a project team that had just begun working on the development of a new product (Product X), which was based on a technology in which NetCon had little expertise. The purpose of this project team, like other teams at NetCon, was to coordinate the various departments that took part in the product development effort.

Team members included representatives from the areas of software, hardware, and performance engineering, product management, marketing, technical publications, technical customer support, and manufacturing. With Product X, coordination was particularly important, as the product combined hardware and software components. Most products at NetCon are one or the other: These two development areas within NetCon have rarely collaborated directly in developing a new product. Within the project, several individual participants were selected as "cases." They represented a range of job descriptions, departments, and levels in the corporate hierarchy. It is important to note that the research results emphasize the relationships of context and technology among these individuals at this particular site; we do not intend them to be generalizable to all corporate settings.

TECHNIQUES FOR GATHERING INFORMATION

I used a multiphase, qualitative research design, similar to that employed by Spilka in her study, "Orality and Literacy in the Workplace: Process and Text-Based Strategies for Multiple-Audience Adaptation." Like Spilka, we used several information gathering strategies, allowing for both methodological triangulation and the broadest coverage of group and individual communicative activities within the 6-month period of the study.

PROJECT TEAM MEETINGS

With one exception, we attended all project team meetings over a 6-month period. We particularly noted any discussions that related to the activities of my participants, particularly any "texts" (presentations, memos, formal reports, manuals, etc.) they were involved in preparing, any comments about the work environment, and any discussion concerning technology use.

QUESTIONNAIRE AND INITIAL INTERVIEW

We administered a detailed questionnaire to the four research participants to meet several goals. First, we used it to collect simple demographic information about the participants. Second, we asked them through a series of questions to assess their communicative behaviour. We included these questions to establish a baseline of their own perceptions; we later collected information on the same topics through other means.

Questions in this series asked them:

- How much of their time at work they spent writing, what kinds of documents they produced, and how they felt about writing;
- How much of their time at work they spent reading, and how much they read as a reviewer, how much for their own information;
- How much of their time at work they spent in meetings, formal and informal; and
- How they used different communication technologies (including e-mail, voice mail, telephone, and fax).

Another set of questions asked them to describe the corporate culture of their department, of NetCon Division, and of Computer Corporation as a whole. These were general questions and provided a useful springboard for questions in a follow-up, audiotaped interview with each participant.

LOGGING AND SHADOWING

Two weeks after the initial interview, We asked each participant to keep a log of their communicative activities for one week. The goal was to capture a snapshot of their communicative activities that could be compared to their self-assessment and to gain insight into each participant's mix of oral, written, and technology-mediated communicative activity.

Detailed log forms were provided to each participant to record and describe acts of reading, writing, and speaking, noting start and end times for each event. However, the logs proved impractical for two of the participants. For these participants, we supplemented their log entries with additional interviews and "shadowing," where we followed these participants as they performed their jobs, asking questions and taking notes.

CORPORATE STRATEGY

A number of models exist which may help us to understand the relationship between corporate strategy and career systems. Slocum and Cron (1988) have focused on the two types of business strategies known as defenders and analyzers. Defenders protect their niche in relatively stable environments. They rely on internal efficiency to competitively price their existing products or services.

They generally utilize formalized, centralized control systems. There is often functional organisation and managers are specialists who are promoted within their specialized areas. Because of the strategic orientation towards low cost, efficient production or operations, the powerful functions in such firms are the financial, accounting, and production areas. Analyzers operate like defenders in some product markets but also are poised to move quickly to take advantage of new opportunities. There is a greater need for marketing expertise and scanning of the external environment. The firm must be organized to allow for flexibility as well as efficiency.

In the defender firm there is more stability and an emphasis on carefully developing those who are in the critical areas of production and accounting/finance. These firms use extensive on-the-job training and detailed succession planning programmes. They typically hire into lower level positions and promote from within. They are likely to rely on early predictors of management potential. Although most managers move up within their functional areas, those who have been identified as high potential employees may have the opportunity to learn various functions.

Because the analyzers are looking for new opportunities as well as trying to protect established areas, the human resource practices and career patterns are different. Some individuals are brought in at entry level and trained within specific functions, but others are recruited from outside to provide immediate expertise. The areas of marketing, engineering, and production are all important. There is more of an emphasis on movement across functions and products as a means of learning about the various departments.

The opportunities for upward mobility varied in relation to strategy within a sample of seven mature industrial products manufacturers studied by Slocum and Cron. The career phenomenon of plateauing occurs when the probability of further promotion in a company becomes very low.

By considering both the perceived likelihood of future promotion and the current level of performance, we may classify employees into four categories. "Stars" are employees who are doing well and who are expected to continue to move up in the organisation. "Comers" have been identified as having the potential to move up but are currently performing below their potential. "Solid citizens" are performing well but are unlikely to move any farther.

And finally, "deadwood" are employees who are performing below standard and have little chance of moving up. Both solid citizens and deadwood are considered plateaued employees. In the defender firms, 66 per cent of the employees were plateaued as compared to 27 per cent in the analyzer firms. Fifty per cent of the employees in the analyzers were considered comers compared to 19 per cent in the defender firms, and 23 per cent were seen as stars in an analyzer situation in contrast to 15 per cent in the defender scenario.

Despite the plateauing, defender employees were less likely to leave the firm but more willing to relocate for another job in the company. They were more concerned about immediate promotions than were the employees of the analyzer firms. Employees in the defender firms also reported less challenge and involvement with their work, less satisfaction, and less visibility and influence to senior managers. In analyzer firms, employees are generally more motivated both by the challenge of their work and by the greater opportunities for advancement.

In the studies that we have reviewed earlier, the firms in which sponsored or tournament mobility systems were the norm appear to be those with a defender strategy: the Bell System companies before deregulation, the established firm studied by Rosenbaum, and the public utility in the Sheridan study. The study in which a horse race was found to describe the promotion pattern was in an analyzer mode. This company's business was changing; it was looking for new opportunities to supplement its traditional strengths; it was looking outside for new managerial and professional talent. The very early identification and development of higher level management candidates was not consistent with the strategy being adapted at this point in time.

The nature of career opportunities can be thought of as part of the organization's reward system. The relationships among business strategy, reward systems, and corporate culture have been studied recently by Kerr and Slocum. This in-depth study of 14 companies focused on their corporate growth strategies. The authors used the steady state versus evolutionary dichotomy. Steady state firms are primarily internally focused. They may grow as the result of internally developed new products or through increased penetration of existing markets. On the other hand, evolutionary firms actively pursue new products and markets through mergers and acquisitions. Kerr and Slocum found that all but one firm with a steady state strategy had adapted what they called a hierarchy-based reward system. All of the firms with an evolutionary strategy used a performance-based reward system.

In a hierarchy-based reward system, performance evaluation is subtle and subjective. Performance is defined qualitatively as well as quantitatively. Superiors have a great deal of control over evaluation and, consequently, mobility within the firm. A close relationship with superiors and other mentors is essential in order to be successful. Parenthetically, this type of vertical exchange was found to be very important in the study of upward mobility in the Japanese firm discussed earlier. The reward system motivates more cooperative effort and long-term commitment. Managers are promoted from within and promotions are often given to an employee more for developmental reasons than for business reasons.

There are many lateral and diagonal moves designed to help the employee understand the whole company and build stronger internal relationships. The system performs the function of completely socializing the younger manager into a strong corporate culture. As Kerr and Slocum point out, this type of system has been described by Ouchi as a "clan culture." A clan culture fosters long-term loyalty and commitment through this lengthy, sometimes arbitrary, socialization process. The performance-based system is more objective.

Rewards are based upon clearly defined expectations. The employee is much less dependent on the superior for evaluation or development.

In fact, there is generally little concern with employee development. Socialization is not a primary purpose of the performance-based reward system. Neither cooperation with others nor learning the whole system were emphasized. Promotions were not necessarily from within—many top managers were brought in from outside. Kerr and Slocum describe the situation as a "mutually exploitive relationship." This is consistent with a "market culture" in which relationships are clearly spelled out and there is little need for loyalty or long-term commitments. There is an emphasis on individual initiative and accomplishment, however. Each reward system seems to fit the needs of the firms in which they were found.

The steady state firms were mature capital-intensive operations such as aluminum, forest products, power generation, pharmaceuticals, and machine tools. It was felt that successful managers would have a long-term commitment to the firm and be able to function well in a highly integrated organisation. The hierarchy-based reward system develops such managers. The firms with an evolutionary strategy were generally conglomerates whose success depends on the management of a portfolio of businesses. In this situation, commitment to a particular business is of less value (and some might argue is actually a liability).

Such firms are successful when the various businesses or divisions are given a high level of autonomy and are evaluated as objectively as possible. Loyalty and commitment are not a concern in a system where the possibility of divestment of businesses is a part of the corporate strategy. Again, the reward system promotes the type of behaviour that is most compatible with the corporate strategy. Returning again to our studies of career mobility, those firms with sponsored or tournament mobility appear to have been following a steady state strategy and therefore used these promotion systems to ensure an adequate supply of well trained, well socialized managers who understood the entire system and appreciated the subtleties of getting things done in a clan culture.

This was the case in the utilities, Rosenbaum's firm, and of course in the Japanese firm. A more open system of competition was found in the oil and gas firm, which in fact was attempting to diversify and acquire new products and markets through acquisition. Here there was a great deal of emphasis on individual entrepreneurial ability and relatively little concern for loyalty or cooperation. The firm was looking for the most capable managers and was not terribly concerned about their earlier socialization, their networks, or even their early record of promotions.

At this point, we will discuss one more system for classifying career systems. While similar to those described above, this model introduces additional categories and further refinements that may prove helpful for our understanding of managerial careers. This model of career systems, developed by Sonnenfeld and Peiperl (1988), is based on two dimensions: supply flow and assignment flow. Supply flow refers to the degree to which personnel may easily move into and out of the firm. An internal supply flow implies promotion from within. External supply means that the firm actively recruits managerial and professional personnel from external sources. Assignment flow describes the bases for making job assignment and promotion decisions.

These are seen within this model as being based primarily on either individual performance or on the degree of contribution to the group effort. Combining these two career properties results in four cells, some of which are very similar to the categories discussed previously. When an internal supply flow is combined with assignment based on contribution to the group, we have the career system that Sonnenfeld and Peiperl call the "club." Internal supply combined with assignment based on individual contribution is referred to as the "academy." External supply plus individual assignment criteria results in the "baseball team" and external supply with a group assignment basis is known as the "fortress."

The club recruits new employees primarily at the entry level and develops them slowly and carefully. The socialization of those selected into the trainee programme in the public utility described by Sheridan et al. would be typical of club practice. There is an emphasis on fair treatment of members and loyalty to the organisation is expected. Assignments and promotions are based on contribution to the group, not just individual performance. Members see their firm as providing important services—as having an important mission. An employee's perceived value (and consequently his opportunity for advancement) is influenced by status attainment prior to joining the firm. Those who have the right background or schooling may enjoy what we have called sponsored mobility.

Strategically, clubs are likely to be "defenders," trying to perform efficiently and effectively within a limited domain. They are often monopolies or in regulated industries. Examples given by Sonnenfeld and Peiperl include utilities, airlines, banks, surface common carriers, as well as the military and government agencies. Firms where internal supply flow is combined with assignment based on individual contribution are the "academies." Here the emphasis is on recruiting employees early in their career and developing them in house. There is more emphasis on differentiating among employees based on their individual contributions according to Sonnenfeld and Peiperl (1988). Large, well established firms such as IBM, Kodak, and Exxon are typical examples of academies. The authors note how sharply career paths differ across different types of firms: At IBM, point of entry is restricted to early career positions. An employee entering any given management group has an 80 per cent chance of staying with IBM through to retirement. At a major New York City bank that same individual would have an 80 per cent chance of quitting by the end of his or her first decade of employment. Within the academy there are often sophisticated career development practices: assessment centers, management development programmes, career tracking and sponsorship of high potential employees, and dual career ladders. The system is designed to develop and retain in-house talent. As a result, employees are oriented towards personal growth and career development.

Strategically, firms using the academy career system are likely to be analyzers. They are protecting established core businesses but are also constantly looking for new products and services.

They try to combine stability and innovation. They need employees who are motivated to learn new things and take moderate risks while remaining loyal to the firm. Sonnenfeld and Peiperl state that the following types of firms use the academy system: office products, pharmaceuticals, electronics, automobiles, and consumer products. The concept of tournament mobility fits nicely in this type of setting. There is an orientation towards longterm development of talented personnel; however, advancement is a function of individual performance which is evaluated on a regular basis. There are, in fact, likely to be multiple tournaments ongoing in various functions and divisions.

A number of forces dictate against the adherence to a strict tournament in which only early winners succeed. These include the nature of the business—multiple existing products or services plus the constant search for new opportunities—and the nature of the career system—long-term commitment plus lots of lateral movement. Where more uncertainty exists early predictions are much tougher to make with any accuracy. Future needs are unknown. It is better to delay selection and develop many people and give them opportunities to prove themselves in many different settings.

The third type of career system described by Sonnenfeld and Peiperl is the "baseball team." As the name suggests, the orientation here is towards obtaining the best available talent in the labour market. These firms are looking for proven individual performers and are open to external labour markets at all levels.

There is little concern with employee training and development. High turnover is expected and therefore there is no point in succession planning. The firm is often looking for high levels of creativity and innovation, and would be categorized as a "prospector." Successful employees are highly, motivated people who see themselves as minor celebrities. Examples here include broadcasting, advertising, law firms, consulting firms, investment banks, and software development. The competition is very open, with employers continually searching for new talent and at the same time discarding those who are no longer that useful.

The last category is the "fortress" or the "institution under siege." This organisation is struggling to survive and its needs take precedence over any individual concerns. They are hiring and firing in reaction to immediate market conditions. They may be in highly competitive businesses or in a crisis or turnaround scenario.

The firm may be reacting to a change in the external business environment and/or may have changed its business strategy. Such "reactor" firms are often out of control as a result of poor management or due to the nature of their business. Examples given by Sonnenfeld and Peiperl are hotels, retailing, textiles, and natural resources. Unsuccessful baseball teams become fortresses very quickly. Here neither the firm nor the individual are concerned about career paths, immediate survival is the only issue.

As we have noted above, the career paths adapted by a firm seem to be a means for dealing with its particular business environment. The club, in a stable and often regulated environment, attempts to identify top management talent very early. Therefore, we see evidence of sponsored or strict tournament mobility. To get ahead, you need the appropriate background and education and/or you need to prove your ability very early through outstanding performance. As we saw, this pattern existed in the Bell operating companies as well as another public utility. It was also seen in a Japanese firm and was originally identified in the well established firm studied by Rosenbaum.

Which did not find strong tournaments in effect, was done in an oil and gas company undergoing a change in business strategy. The firm was becoming a major producer of crude oil, having previously been a regional refiner and marketer. It was moving from a defender strategy towards an analyzer strategy and also from a steady state position with respect to growth towards an evolutionary strategy. Developing and selecting people according to the rules of clubs or clans would no longer serve all of its needs.

During this transition period, the firm was operating in many respects like a baseball team—seeking new talent in the external labour market and sending some existing players down to the farm. There was also evidence of a market culture with respect to the treatment of the new stars who were brought aboard and with respect to decisions concerning acquisitions and divestments. However, within the core business of this firm there were strong traditions, and loyalty and acceptance of corporate values were rewarded. Strategically, acquisitions were considered only if related to the core business. The career system would best be described as an academy which had entered the external labour market in order to cope with change.

Other factors affecting career paths were also operating in this case. The delayed promotion patterns found in this firm were at least partially due to changes in the profitability and size of the company. During the early portion of this longitudinal study, the company invested heavily in a very risky joint venture. The venture proved to be very successful with the payoffs coming towards the end of the period studied. Therefore, more opportunities for upward mobility were created in the later years. Different career patterns were found for those entering into different functional areas. This can be explained by again considering the firm's ability to deal with its external environment.

Particular functional areas gain in power, influence, and upward mobility if they possess the skills needed to deal with critical environmental demands. In this firm, technical expertise was certainly related to the most critical tasks: exploration, production, processing, distribution, and research and development. Non-technical administrative skills seem to have been less important. This is similar to the finding of Slocum and his colleagues (1985). Sales personnel were more likely to be plateaued when they worked in a defender firm in which financial and production issues were more critical than were marketing issues such as growth and new products.

The pattern of slower promotion for technical personnel may apply beyond this firm and industry. Veiga (1985) data on managers in manufacturing firms showed slower rates of movement were associated with what he called intensive technology—activities like research and development and engineering. Perhaps it takes longer to evaluate the managerial potential of technical personnel, or perhaps their skills are too valuable to lose by early promotion into managerial positions. Our study spanned 11 years and we concluded that a strict tournament was not in effect because early promotions did not make that much difference. However, perhaps in this case the "early" contests take longer—possibly up to seven years. If this were the case, then a tournament may have been in effect, but employees, especially technical employees, were given longer to prove themselves.

The corporate strategy approach described above is useful in understanding how career patterns evolve or are developed in order to help the organisation achieve its objectives. This does not just happen as if by magic, although it may appear that way to many people within the firm as well as to the more distant observer.

A firm's success depends on the availability of competent human resources. Without the correct career system in place, the firm will not be able to accomplish its strategic objectives. Therefore it is essential that top managers and human resource professionals be aware of the strong connection between strategic planning and human resource planning—especially with regard to the design of the entire career system.

A key issue here is the promotion decision—what criteria are being used to choose those who move up and into contention for top executive positions? Following Rosenbaum's lead, we believe that human decision makers often rely on a small number of simple cues or in this case "signals." Academicians may infer the existence of different career systems by identifying the signals used in making promotion decisions. Practitioners may change existing career systems or develop new ones by influencing the choice of these signals. For example, if derision makers, consciously or unconsciously, look for signals such as socioeconomic background or the right education, then sponsored mobility will occur. If they believe that early performance and promotion are important indicators of ability, then we will see tournament mobility.

Other signals that we have seen in the studies discussed here have included university status, assessment centre evaluation, entry into a special trainee programme, entry into a powerful department, early functional area, and a high level of lateral intrafirm mobility. Many of these signals serve a useful purpose in the organisation. However, often career paths become institutionalized. That is, the use of a signal that seemed to make sense in the past leads to many powerful decision makers with similar backgrounds. These high level managers assume that the firm needs more of the same type of person and therefore select people just like themselves for promotion. Of course in a changing environment this practice can be disastrous.

ADVANTAGES AND DISADVANTAGES

So far we have discussed different career paths primarily from the organization's point of view. We have seen that many firms use early upward mobility as a signal indicative of management potential. Other firms that do not seem to emphasize early upward movement, such as the oil and gas company that we studied, still prefer those employees who have held a larger number of different jobs when making promotion decisions. At this point we will take a closer look at the advantages and disadvantages of such fast tracks—both for the organisation and for the individual.

ADVANTAGES

In addition to being a step in an individual's career, job changes, both promotions and transfers, serve many other organizational purposes. Open positions are constantly being created in any organisation. They are created by normal attrition and by growth and change in the organizational structure.

Of course, someone must be found to fill these positions and the most obvious choices are people dose to the open position—that is, those in the same function and at the same level or slightly below. Often, however, the firm will choose to move employees across functions or divisions. This strategy allows cross-fertilization. The person being moved has a chance to learn much more about the range of activities and opportunities within the organisation. This is, of course, valuable experience for the employee who aspires to further upward mobility. The practice also may enrich those who have the opportunity to interact with the person from a different area. They may learn to appreciate the problems and issues faced by other functions and divisions by communicating with outsiders. Frequent movement may also be an organizational tactic that helps create and maintain a strong corporate culture. Those who make frequent geographic moves come to identify more with the organisation than with any particular community. Those who frequently change functional area will also identify more strongly with the company than with any specific professional groups. This is seen clearly in the military and in companies like IBM, where many employees believe the firm's initials stand for "I've been moved."

For the individual, job change is generally an opportunity for new learning and growth. Even lateral moves expose the employee to new challenges and allow them to develop new skills. Promotions are a natural progression as the employee gains experience and acceptance within the organisation. People expect that they will be given more authority and responsibility as they mature in the job. They also expect that their status and financial position in life will improve with time on the job. The firm that does not satisfy these expectations will lose valued employees.

DISADVANTAGE

From the organization's perspective, moving employees is very costly. There are the obvious costs of physically relocating the employee plus the somewhat hidden costs of reduced productivity both before and after the move. There is also a domino effect in which the first move creates another vacancy that must be filled, which creates another, and so on, thus multiplying the costs. Training costs must also be considered, as well as the possibility that the employee will refuse the move and may even leave the company.

Because fast track employees realise that they will be moved within a year or two, and that short-term performance is essential for their career progress, they tend to focus on immediate results. They may abandon useful programmes initiated by predecessors and replace them with their own inventions in order to gain more visibility and credibility. They may not support long-term efforts involving needed organizational change and development because they will not pay off quickly enough. Frequent job change can be a frustrating and stressful experience for the individual. Feldman (1988) has listed the many costs to the individual. These include increased demands for high performance with little training. They are expected to "hit the floor running" with a minimum of assistance from anyone else. Sometimes employees are moved so rapidly that they never learn the job. Feldman (1988) reports that: One employee in production management had been promoted from plant manager to director of national operations to vice president, international operations in 18 months. At first, such quick promotions leave managers feeling exhilarated. Later, though, these managers feel frightened and out of control as they realise they are responsible for products or services about which they know virtually nothing.

The fast track manager may be learning to adapt strategies that will hurt both them and their companies in the long run. They may never be satisfied with any job because all they care about is the next position and getting to it as quickly as possible. They may never master the technical aspects of any function. They may ignore their families and never develop any interests outside of work. Finally, they may burn out at a relatively early age as a result of the stress of this type of career.

Geographical relocation brings with it additional problems. Many employees do not want to move but are afraid of the possible negative impact of refusing. Economic hardship may accompany a move. This may come about as the result of higher costs of living or the difficulty of the spouse finding employment in the new location. Social relationships, both at work and outside, tend to suffer. Finally, there is the disruption of the lives of the spouse and children, however, recent research indicates that most families adapt rather well to moving.

POLICY IMPLICATIONS

James Rosenbaum, who first proposed the concept of tournament mobility, has also been the most articulate critic of this system. They minimize the number of employees in whom the firm must invest and they maximize the amortization time for the investment. This efficiency, however, assumes three preconditions according to Rosenbaum: "(1) they must use appropriate selection criteria, (2) they must increase amortization time, and (3) they must not reduce productivity by their selections". With regard to the first point, the tournament model makes selections based upon short-term performance. Employees who demonstrate successful short-term results, perhaps even at the cost of long-term performance, will be promoted. As we noted above, the employees within such systems quickly learn the rules of the game and attend only to outcomes that will help them in the short run.

The system seems to be well designed to catch and correct errors of inclusion. If an individual with little true managerial ability wins the early contest, this may be discovered in the next competition. Ideally this would be the case. However, we feel that given the emphasis on short-term performance evaluations and the strong signals sent by early promotion, the lack of ability may not be detected until late in the career. Errors of exclusion are virtually undetectable. There are no second chances. Those who are not selected early are out of the running. This is an even more serious problem in sponsored systems. In these programmes, identification of talented people occurs before any real performance evaluation can occur.

Once the selection is made, many forces come into play to reinforce and validate the decision. Those selected receive special socialization and developmental experiences, often promotion opportunities are created for these "high potential" employees, and before too long, everyone, including the top management candidate, begins to believe in their ability. This may have worked effectively in many situations in the past and may still work well enough in stable regulated industries (which, in fact, were where we saw the strongest evidence of this practice); however, in the fiercely competitive world of the 1990s and beyond we should be trying harder to make the very best selections.

Rosenbaum's second criterion for efficient selection was that amortization time will be increased. It seems obvious that earlier decisions would allow this to occur. However, that assumes that everyone stays with the organisation. In fact, selection of an employee for a fast track management development programme may increase the chances that he or she will leave the firm. Younger people in general are more likely to change employers, and when they have been through some early managerial development their value in the external labour market increases. Investing in older employees may actually result in a greater return to the firm.

Lastly, Rosenbaum proposed that tournaments must not reduce productivity. On this point he argues persuasively that a tournament system is a major contributor to the mid-career crises experienced by many employees: The career system may be instrumental in building up the skills, status, and expectations of high-potential people, and it may be powerful in its destructive force in lowering the skills, status, and expectations of employees who have been eliminated from further competition. It withholds further investments from them, it attributes low-ability status to them, and it creates the expectation that these individuals are not going any further in their careers.

In addition to contributing to mid-career crises, Rosenbaum expresses concern over the level of early career stress generated by the tournament system. The timing of this pressure is also unfortunate because it forces many young employees to choose between their careers and the high demands of a young family. This is particularly troublesome for women in the workplace and is often used as justification for discrimination against young women. Rosenbaum concludes that the "economic justifications of early selections require rethinking" and recommends that tournament mobility systems be replaced by more open systems that allow for delayed selections. This should result in more accurate selection decisions and eliminate many of the negative consequences of the tournament model. We agree and feel that changes in the business environment, in organizational structures, and in demographics are combining to make this a feasible and practical alternative.

CORPORATE CULTURE AND TECHNOLOGY USE AT NETCON DIVISION

The follow provide a description and commentary on the use of communications technologies by the four cases. To put this use in its organizational context-and to explore the impact of context on use.

We provide a brief historical description of NetCon based on articles in the trade press, reviews of company archives (including company newsletters and press releases), and interviews with public relations employees. This description sheds some light on the current work climate and value system at NetCon. The second, presents results from the cases, first presenting summaries of perceptions of corporate culture and then examining each person's use of communication technologies, as reported in interviews and as observed through logging/shadowing.

THE LAYERED CULTURES OF NETCON DIVISION

NetCon Division, at one time an independent company in the computer industry, had been acquired a number of years previous to the study by Computer Corporation. Shortly after the takeover, like many companies in the computer industry, Computer Corporation laid off significant numbers of employees. These reductions hit NetCon particularly hard. In addition to the impact of takeover, it appears that significant cultural shifts have taken place during the 20 years or so of NetCon's existence. Its initial entrepreneurial culture was, in Morgan's terms, solidly "organic". The organizational chart was relatively flat (by later standards), and work was accomplished in a project-oriented environment that consisted of teams from many departments.

It appears from internal company publications that product innovation and achieving aggressive development schedules were highly valued. However, the culture of Computer Corporation, as evidenced after the purchase, was quite different. Computer Corporation, although viewing itself as an innovative, adaptable organization, was larger, more bureaucratic — and to use Morgan's terms — more "mechanistic" than NetCon. What followed the acquisition was a difficult mix of Computer Corporation's dominantly mechanistic culture overlaying NetCon's organic one.

Although daily work continued to follow established patterns (*i.e.*, project-oriented work teams), a pervasive atmosphere of process control and budgetary accountability began to change interactions within those groups. This conflict is quite apparent in information gathered from research participants.

CASE ONE: KENT

CORPORATE CULTURES

Kent did not offer strong opinions about the parent company, Computer Corporation. He described it simply as "conservative": "I guess they do things the way that you expect. Pretty hierarchical. People have been here a long time, have done things a certain way. They listen to the same things." Kent had more to say about the culture of NetCon Division. Although he thought current upper management were more "upbeat" than the other participants, he noted that the workforce at NetCon was "mature, dominated by old-timers," and that the division was "struggling to find a new road to travel."

Although fairly consistent with the other participants in his views on culture at the corporate and division levels, Kent described a more positive departmental culture, noting the mood of the group that he manages as "fairly loose and upbeat." He said that *"it's better than it was.*

I think people are interested in the [current] project," and in comparing that to recent history at NetCon, noted that, "it's rather bizarre, actually."

TECHNOLOGY USE: DISPARATE NETWORKS AND VOICE MAIL

Kent's department uses a sophisticated CASE (computer-aided software engineering) system. This system, beside providing an online environment for writing, compiling, integrating, and testing computer programmes, offers an e-mail facility.

But this e-mail system has limited usefulness. Kent explained: "There are a lot of e-mail systems here, but they aren't connected. We're on the Internet side of the house. Then there's the Novell side. Basically, I e-mail stuff to my people. I can't, like, e-mail stuff to hardware engineering." Question: "Do you ever converse over e-mail?" Kent: "No. It's one-ended.

We don't even get a message every day. It's not as important as voice mail for me. We don't have any surveillance anyway." As Kent noted, he makes heavy use of voice mail: "I hate the telephone. We really do. So voice mail frees me a lot. We can pick up messages when we want, and we can leave messages for people when they aren't there, we love voice mail, but we hate the telephone. One I'm in control, the other I'm not in control."

NetCon's voice mail system, unlike the disparate e-mail systems, is company-wide, requires very little effort to learn, and for those who are interested, offers a fairly wide range of features, including broadcasting to a specified user list, forwarding messages with comments, and storage of up to an hour's worth of messages. In many ways, it offers all of the advantages of e-mail without the effort of entering text on a keyboard. Kent's comments about "surveillance" and "control" are interesting in this context. He indirectly associated e-mail with surveillance.

By contrast, the idea that he was in control of the voice mail system makes it appear a more comfortable site for Kent to communicate, and more effective when compared to the ordinary telephone and the limited connectivity of his departmental e-mail system.

In composing voice mail messages, Kent was observed to follow generally the same pattern:

- Establish the purpose;
- Provide context and background (*e.g.*, reason for request; allusion to a previous call, conversation, or document);

- Give his own perspective (*e.g.*, a guess about the answer to his question, a possible source for the answer, a possible procedure); and
- Request an action (typically, a return call). This pattern is similar to inductive memo formats where the text builds towards a request for an action. Revision also had a role in Kent's use of voice mail. He noted: *"I guess if I'm doing a group delivery, we think about what I'm going to say, and then I record it. I listen to it, and then do it again. About one out of four times I record it again."*

ANALYSIS

The communication technology options facing Kent reflect recent history at NetCon. At the time of the study, Kent could not communicate electronically with Computer Corporation, highlighting the slow integration of NetCon into Computer Corporation and, perhaps, the latter's conservative approach to conducting business.

The lack of e-mail connectivity among departments is more puzzling. Given NetCon's tradition of interdepartmental project teams, one would expect that management would facilitate cooperation among departments with universal e-mail. Yet e-mail system installation occurred after NetCon's acquisition; thus, its insular configuration may not reflect tradition but more recent influences — specifically Computer Corporation's more hierarchical culture.

Connecting workers across (not up) the hierarchy -enabling workers to communicate without managerial mediation — may not have seemed desirable to management. That left voice mail, at least for Kent, as the communication technology that best fit his professional and personal needs (*i.e.*, the need to communicate asynchronously and the need to feel in control of his own communicative activities).

It is interesting that for someone who indicated that he did not like writing, his composition of voice mail messages almost appeared to be writing in a different medium.

USE OF TECHNOLOGY: TRADITIONAL TEXT AND VOICE MAIL

Mary spends about half of a typical work day in meetings, about a quarter of her time reading and writing, and the final quarter on the phone. Her responses to questions about communications technologies were very similar to Kent's not surprising in that they worked in the same department for many years and have similar professional profiles. While working in software development, Mary used the same e-mail system as Kent.

However, the product management department, after years of repeated requests from its workers, had just recently installed a departmental local area network with e-mail capabilities. Like the system in development, the product management system is supposed to communicate with the Computer Corporation system, but otherwise fits NetCon's pattern of incompatible networks. Mary noted: *"It [the system] does go to other departments, but I couldn't tell you who right now."*

Mary expressed the opinion that this defeated the purpose of e-mail: *"I think we should have a company system. I should be able to send a memo to anybody in this building, you know. To a janitor if I want to. The phone's a lot easier right now."* Mary's use of the phone includes both the traditional, including at least one conference call a week, and voice mail. To Mary, the major benefit of voice mail is its convenience for asynchronous communication. She described composing a voice mail message in the same language she used to describe composing a memo: *"For me, it's like a little letter. I think that is the format that people go through mentally."*

ANALYSIS

Overall, Mary spends most of her work time in meetings, in verbal interaction, not with computer-based communications technologies. Even her use of voice mail is somewhat limited. And outside of meetings, most of her communicative activity centres on traditional texts. This reflects her job duties, which focus on the production of planning, marketing, and competitive analysis documents and the fact that product management has been slow in adopting e-mail.

Yet, Mary's responses highlight the "ease of use" factor for the different technologies. With technical difficulties in installing the local area network, with procedural difficulties in sending e-mail to anyone outside of the department, the default technology for distance communication becomes the familiar telephone and the relatively straightforward enhancement of voice mail. Also, one senses in Mary's responses, as in the other cases, a certain reluctance to pursue electronic communication with Computer Corporation. This has its roots in the cultural context, in NetCon Division's sense of separate identity. It is likely that in a more culturally integrated company, the technical obstacles in establishing company-wide e-mail connectivity would seem less significant.

CASE THREE: SCOTT

CORPORATE CULTURES

Like Kent, Scott found the culture of Computer Corporation conservative, but also commented on the power structure. He described Computer Corporation as "a very bureaucratic feudal oligarchy, prone to high level re-orgs that reflect shifts in power." In terms of the culture of NetCon Division, Scott contrasted the current culture with that of NetCon Division in the past: "It's different than it was. There used to be certain movers and shakers who, whether you agreed with them or not, they certainly put their stamp on things. And now that they are gone.... People have a strong notion that [business] is declining. Being part of something declining is really a bummer." Scott described his own department as one that used to be very cohesive, but because he and other technical communicators had been "colocated" with product development groups instead of being located with other technical communicators, Scott thought much of this had changed: *"It is easy to see how our own practices have gotten diffuse, when people don't use the same tools, or use them in the same way. They don't necessarily have the same standards applied to everybody, and we don't seem to have anybody who can bring that together."*

TECHNOLOGY USE: REFLECTIONS ON THE USE OF E-MAIL

Scott has nearly the same technology options as Kent: outside of face-to-face conversation, Scott can communicate with coworkers via e-mail or voice mail. For Scott, a computer network provides a unifying force for a department physically scattered throughout the building, although the network is rarely used as a site for the exchange of important ideas: "I use e-mail to get messages... primarily about department business, notices about both personal things -going away lunches — and business stuff — there's a new virus, check your PC.

Sometimes [his manager] puts a message out there that he wants you to respond to.... It's useful from a business point of view, and also a social point of view, too. It helps to have something unifying." However, Scott noted that there were "no real conversations" over e-mail. The network, like most others at NetCon, has limited connection to those in other departments. However, according to Scott what really prevents electronic communication between departments may be rooted in social factors rather than technical ones:

One of the things that [a previous senior manager] wanted to implement was [a special e-mail system], which is very much a conversational thing, attaching notes and comments to this data base of ideas. It pretty much just sat there. People used it to send mail, but I don't think anybody used it in the way it was intended for a kind of development way of collecting data. Someone would have an idea, and then you could attach everyone's comments to that idea.... I'm sure it could work, but not sure it would work here. It would take a certain culture — it would probably work great at Lotus or someplace else that's more open.

Scott attributed the lack of success for this system to several factors. First, it was implemented among a large group of engineers whose project was in jeopardy. With the uncertainty of possible reassignment or even job loss in the air, people did not want to express opinions or complain in so public a forum. Second, Scott said that he and others noticed that management did not use the system. Finally, although presented in a positive light by management, employees felt the system might be used to monitor them. Indeed, Scott, unlike the other participants, did not favour a division-wide e-mail capability.

But like the other participants, Scott thought highly of voice mail. He noted that it can be used to prompt people to attend meetings, by using the broadcast list feature: *"It's a good, thorough thing to do." Further, Scott stated: "Voice mail is good for, well, it prevents information from getting lost. You can leave a message and the message will be there.... From that standpoint, it's pretty useful. You can call someone and be pretty much assured that they'll pick up the phone at some point. I think it's just primarily more certain."* The voice mail system at NetCon really is not that permanent; unless a user takes special actions, the system erases stored messages at regular time intervals. However, as Kent noted, the voice mail system does provide convenient asynchronous communications, one of the major benefits reported for e-mail by researchers such as Sproull and Kiesler.

When asked to comment on composing for voice mail in comparison to composing text, Scott, in contrast to Kent, does not see voice mail as a medium to convey substantive messages: *"I would never leave a voice mail message that is too complex to express verbally.... I'll say 'Call back.' If I were trying to convince somebody of something, I wouldn't do that on the phone."*

ANALYSIS

Scott, a technical communicator, enjoys writing. He feels more comfortable submitting more complex ideas or requests in written text. Kent finds writing "tedious" and definitely uses voice mail more extensively than Scott. Part of this may be owing to differences in job responsibilities and time constraints, but part, I think, is due to their quite different perceptions of their strengths as communicators. While many other factors may affect technology use, Scott's and Kent's choices among similar media options may be due in part to their differences as individuals.

However, corporate culture enters into Scott's technology use at another level. Scott perceives the various levels of corporate culture in somewhat more negative terms than Kent, particularly upper management. Whereas he sees e-mail as a unifying force for his department and views a sense of cohesiveness within the department as desirable, he is suspicious both of broader e-mail connectivity and of use of e-mail for substantive exchange of ideas. It could be that a certain level of distrust for corporate management has coloured his view of technologies that could link employees across departments — that this kind of network, despite its stated purpose, might be a tool for management control.

USE OF TECHNOLOGY: HIERARCHICAL NETWORKS AND FAX

Cara's job is very different from those of the other participants. Their jobs, in one way or another, concern the development of new products for NetCon. Cara supports NetCon's existing products; that is, she identifies solutions to errors (programme or human) in NetCon's software products. A brief description of this support process is necessary here. When customers experience a problem, they first contact a local support representative. If the local person cannot solve the problem, that support person, or the customer, calls NetCon Division directly for a higher level of technical support.

Cara provides this kind of support for international customers. As problems arrive, they are logged into a problem tracking database implemented on a mainframe-based, hierarchical network. It is 15- or 20-year-old technology. Cara's department does have e-mail capability that is accessible even to customers, but it is not heavily used. She noted: "I know we have e-mail. Every time I turn on my PC in the morning it says 'you have no e-mail.' It definitely is not used much internally."

However, although there are no real conversations over e-mail, support engineers have learned to use the problem tracking database as a kind of forum where people can reference each other's work and exchange ideas more actively than on any of the e-mail systems I observed at NetCon. This is not an easy system to use for this purpose: They have adopted a single response area for this, an assigned field for providing problem descriptions that permits the entry of free-form text.

They refer to this internally as the status text. The system does not allow status text entries to be specifically addressed to individuals; however, individual support engineers locate status texts that interest them by referencing problem numbers. They can then enter additional comments to the status text if they wish.

Some exchanges I reviewed in status text fields went on for several days with a variety of support and development engineers involved. In these written conversations, they reference past solutions, documentation, and common experiences. It can become an even larger conversation. Some local support engineers and large customers have access to the problem tracking system but do not have the system security clearance to add to the status text. They read the status text and join the discussion through phone calls, memos, or faxes; often, summaries of their comments are included by engineers who have the required level of clearance.

Fax is another important technology of communication to Cara and the other support engineers — much more important, it appeared, than to the other research participants. In dealing with international customers, Cara must deal with language barriers and significant time differences: Some people seem to use the phone [to communicate with customers].

It's hard enough just to hear someone long distance on the phone, with the accent on top of that. In talking to places in Africa, you have to be careful taking turns. When I talk, he can't; and when he talks, we have to wait. We have a tendency to interrupt. I had to curb that, and to laugh! I'd lose half a sentence because I laughed. I'm just not polite. So I just send a fax, especially with the time differences. You can fax anytime.

Fax permits virtually instantaneous communication, but minimizes, among other things, the possible pitfalls of different cultural styles of conversation. Voice mail could overcome the time differences, but the need of both engineer and customer in this setting is for highly detailed technical information. Cara noted that fax communication allows the support engineers to specify exactly what kind of information they need from customers.

ANALYSIS

Cara's case is particularly illuminating for two reasons. First, in a department where she feels marginalized in everyday interaction, Cara contributed regularly to the "status text" conversations, where her technical insight was valued in group problem solving.

Cultural norms shifted in this context: instead of gender, common background, or a shared "us against them attitude" that characterized the support department, technical expertise is what counted in the problem tracking system. This is not so much a case of a communications technology masking cues to culture, ethnicity, or gender, as a case of a shift in the value system within the world of the computer system.

Also, the use of the system itself is interesting. It was so dated, had such a complex user interface, and seemed so inflexible that, in my original research plan, I almost ignored it. However, the support engineers felt a strong need to collaborate, an important need to share technical information. The problem tracking system provided a means to accomplish this — between adjacent offices as well as geographically dispersed sites. It provided a site for communication that was all their own as employees in other departments had no interest in using the system, and it was unlikely that management outside of the department, who are viewed with some distrust, would go to the trouble of reviewing status text entries. In contrast to the e-mail system, where electronic communication was possible between NetCon and Computer Corporation but nobody really wanted to communicate, the users here adapted a very difficult computer system to become a vehicle for the vital exchange of ideas.

In short, what the problem tracking system emphasizes is that:

- A real need must exist to use the technology,
- The system has to connect the people necessary to carry on the conversation, and
- A technology can reinforce a sense of community insofar as it is not likely to be monitored. This use of the problem tracking system was not part of overall corporate communication planning, not an anticipated use of technology; yet, it emphasizes how important contextual factors become in choice of technology.

Another reason Cara's case is interesting centres on the use of fax technology. Here the contextual factors are not based in perceptions of corporate culture but in the realities of international business. Extensive use of fax with international customers allows Cara and her coworkers to simplify potential language problems, accurately transfer technical information, avoid the time zone difficulties of phone conversation — and still, when required, have virtually instantaneous communication. Fax combines the familiarity of paper with the speed of synchronous phone lines.

VIRTUES OF CORPORATE LIFE

The bottom line of the Aristotelian approach to business ethics is that we have to get away from bottom-line thinking. What is essential to a good life in business is not just results and accomplishments as measured by financial gain but what is above (not beyond) the bottom line, the whole package of cooperative as well as competitive effort, personal integrity as well as contribution to the community. Wanting too much without regard to one's character or reputation is a myopic form of stupidity, evident in Midas-like individuals throughout history, no doubt, but peculiar as a generally approved consciousness in our time.

Aristotle saw quite clearly that greed (or "grasping," *pleonexia*) was a kind of pathology, a defect of character so serious that it was beyond redemption. Not that he was against wealth and comfort (no ascetics, those Athenians), but in the quest for the good life it was at most a favorable precondition, not something worth worrying about at the expense of one's soul. To this we might reply, of course, that in Athenian society aristocrats and their favorite philosophers didn't have to worry about such matters, but we do. Socrates provides a clear counterexample, however, and Aristotle, like almost all philosophers, recognised the nobility of Socrates' virtue even in his poverty.

The point is not that Americans should stop worrying about money or that we can or should try to discourage our students from their current career-obsessive paths. It is a question of proper perspective, and the truth is that our concept of happiness is a lot more Aristotelian than we would think. Students and job-hoppers (and, let me say, even professors of the humanities) who accept positions on the basis of salary alone and then hate their jobs (and often their luxurious lives, as well) miss the obvious: what makes for happiness is not money to spend but a respected place in a decent and prosperous community and time in which to enjoy it.

Success is not salary but respect and love and admiration. As John Steinbeck wrote in *East of Eden*, "A living, or money.... Money's easy to make if it's money you want. But with a few exceptions people don't want money. They want luxury and they want love and they want admiration." What the Aristotelian approach to business ethics demands is that we enlarge this common-sense observation and apply it not only to people in their so-called personal lives (even that notion is the symptom of an enormous sociological problem) but to business and people in business, for much of the problem of business ethics and its faulty myths and metaphors has to do with the artificial and problematic walling off of business practices and business life from the larger arena of people, communities, and society. (The new and welcome concept of the "stakeholders" in a business, which pointedly includes community and the larger society, still tends to retain too much of the cloistered business imagery even while expanding the scope and vocabulary of social responsibility.)

The Aristotelian approach to business ethics ultimately comes down to the idea that, while business life has its specific goals and distinctive practices and people in business have their particular concerns, loyalties, roles, and responsibilities, there is ultimately no business world but only people working in business as part of their life in society. It is an obvious point, perhaps, but to read much if not most of what gets written about business and to listen to managers and executives on the job talk about what they do is to realise that it is a point readily lost in the obsessive pressure to satisfy the bottom line.

That line, after all, is only a measure, and what it measures — often falsely or misleadingly — is the quality and efficiency of an organization and its output, which in turn is the product of hundreds or thousands of individuals and how well they work together. The Aristotelian approach is not antibusiness and certainly not antisuccess but only anti-*pleonexia,* antigreed. Aristotle's central ethical concept is "happiness" (more accurately, *eudaimonia,* perhaps better translated as "flourishing" or "doing well"). "Happiness," therefore, has what we would call "success" built into it, and success in a consumer society necessarily entails a certain level of financial success.

Let's remember, however, that we "consume" art and music, books and ideas, as well as cars and kitchenware, and the dollar costs of such consumption may not be considerable at all. What Aristotle's conception excludes is mediocrity and isolation — especially the mean-spirited competition that too many people in business abstractly confuse with free enterprise. Moreover, it is not enough to be a subjectively contented or even blithe failure; it is what one actually accomplishes, with and for others as well as by and for oneself that counts. It would be a crass vulgarization to suppose that doing well is to be understood, in our society, as just a matter of "making it."

Most Americans, when not engaged in business conversation, would rather readily admit that the only bottom line that counts is how happy we are, as individuals, as families, as employees, as a people. Happiness may include success, but it is not wholly defined by success, and while an excellent company will almost always do well in the market, it is not doing well that makes them excellent. Tom Peters's incessant insistence on the "satisfied customer" and the "contented employee" highlights an extremely important Aristotelian measure. The rather banal equation between happiness and having fun too readily blinds us to the idea that our work ought to be satisfying and rewarding (only occasionally "fun"). The familiar image of the harried manager, on the other hand, is a symptom of something very wrong, in a career, in a company, in the market itself. Happiness (for us as well as for Aristotle) is a holistic concept, and it is one's character, not one's bottom line, that is the ultimate determinant and beneficiary of happiness. This is equally true, I want to insist, for giant corporations as it is for the individuals who work for them. I want to use Aristotle to attack a popular misconception of what this notion of character and the related notion of social-mindedness entails.

One of the worst philosophical dichotomies to have worked itself through the ranks of the hoi polloi is the false antagonism between selfishness on the one hand and what is called altruism on the other, but for the properly constituted social self the distinction between self-interest and social-mindedness is all but unintelligible and what we call selfishness is guaranteed to be self-destructive as well. And altruism is too easily turned into self-sacrifice, for instance by that self-appointed champion of selfishness, Ayn Rand. But altruism isn't self-sacrifice; it's just a more reasonable conception of self as tied up intimately with community, with friends and family who may, indeed, count at times for more than we do. What the Aristotelian approach to business ethics demands isn't self-sacrifice or the submerging of oneself to the interests of the corporation, much less voluntary unhappiness. What it does say is that the distinctions and oppositions between self and society that give rise to these wrongheaded conceptions are themselves the problem, as well as the cause of so much unhappiness and dissatisfaction. To get beyond the bottom line is not just to give up an overly narrow conception of the good or, at least, the good in business. It is also to reject a certain kind of "hard-headed" thinking, so evident in the sophisticated games of game theory and in much of the discussion of ethics and business ethics.

It is that obsession with quantification, with precise comparisons of options and strategies. Aristotle famously commented at the beginning of his *Nicomachean Ethics* that a person should not demand more precision of a subject than it is capable of providing. He might have been warning us against late-twentieth century ethics. Somewhere along the line, we lost sight of ethics as one of the humanities and got into our heads the idea that it was one of the social sciences. Granted, there is no paucity of candidates to shoulder the blame, especially among the various defenders of *Wissenschaft* in the last century.

And there are some rich sociological accounts of this transformation, as one would expect in the annals of the social sciences plotting their own progress. But when I ask my philosophical students and colleagues who is to blame or praise for this atomization of business thinking (no pun intended), the name that comes up most frequently is Adam Smith. I think that Smith is innocent of the charge. I would rather point the philosophical finger at the particularly utility-minded ethics, rendered ever more refined and sophisticated by decision theory and the social sciences, called utilitarianism. But the charge of bottom-line thinking seems to me as unfair to the leading proponent of utilitarianism, John Stuart Mill, as it is to Adam Smith.

Given the current climate, however, these claims require a long defence, which I will not attempt even to summarise here. The virtue of the Aristotelian approach to business ethics, I have argued, is its focus on the character of the individual and not just on impersonal policies and abstract principles and theories. A related virtue, however, points us in just the opposite direction, towards the enlargement of the self as a thoroughly social self and not an isolated Hobbesian or Lockean self whose place in society is up for negotiation.

The Aristotelian approach must be understood in terms of a certain concept of self, an expanded self that is constituted by and identifies itself with the larger community or society. The self is, as I have argued elsewhere, first of all a matter of emotions, and so one might suspect that a special set of emotions will be particularly concerned with this enlarged sense of self. Too often it is assumed without argument or discussion that the emotions are merely personal, whether this means that they are merely subjective, exclusively of concern to the emotee, or merely physical and of no real importance. But emotions can be "about" all sorts of things and of varied significance to both the individual and the society.

Some emotions are not only "about" society (as their "object") but involve society in the very identity of their subject. They are emotions that would be unintelligible without this larger sense of self. I should like to end this brief essay, therefore, with an even more brief outline of a few of the emotional virtues that it is the aim of the Aristotelian approach to business to cultivate. Of particular interest here is a mixed set of emotions that, with the rise of radical individualism and the loss of a sense of Aristotelian virtue, the emphasis on policies and principles and the neglect of the person, has all but dropped out of business ethics. They include *loyalty, honour,* and a sense of *shame.* (Guilt is quite different from shame and is not part of the set.)

All three emotions tie into the central notion of *integrity,* the first two by way of definition, the latter in the breach. Loyalty is a kind of integrity, not within oneself (conceived of as a self-sufficient, integral whole), but rather with oneself conceived as a part of a larger self, a group, a community, an organization or institution. As Josiah Royce wrote in his *Philosophy of Loyalty*, "Loyalty has its domestic, its religious, its commercial, its professional forms, and many other forms as well. The essence of it, whatever forms it may take, is... this: Since no man can find a plan of life by merely looking within his own chaotic nature, he has to look without, to the world of social conventions, deeds and causes." Business ethics too often ignores loyalty in favour of the more abstract and universal concepts of rights. It is as if to say that, so long as we respect contracts, we need not be concerned with a superfluous and perhaps childish emotion like loyalty. Of course, loyalty (like patriotism, one special variant of it) can be a refuge from responsibility or a forum for venal self-righteousness, but it does not follow — as many people seem to think it does — that it is an emotion that has lost its place in the corporate world and that one's loyalties should always be first and foremost to oneself, to one's conscience, or to some set of "higher" standards.

Every employer wants the loyalty of the employees, of course, but the objection to such loyalty is that the employees will thereby lose sight of their own best interests and perhaps find themselves bound to plans or policies that they find unethical or even illegal. The argument here, however, is not against loyalty but rather in support of the need for critical selfawareness of one's loyalties. It is not an argument against loyalty any more than the dangers of love are an argument against love. (Loyalty would not be wrongly conceived as a variety of love, appropriate to groups and institutions as well as to individuals.)

Against the recent "work-for-hire" approach to employer-employee relations, I want to argue that an Aristotelian emphasis on loyalty — and that means loyalty in both directions — has a lot to offer to business ethics that too often gets dismissed with the usual stories of uncritical loyalty and gross corporate malfeasance. Honour is a second grand emotion of the Aristotelian self, an essential ingredient in integrity (some people would equate the two) and another emotion that is an endangered species in radical individualist thinking. Honour, when we use the term at all, usually means pride — a very different emotion — or even vanity, a very different and hardly flattering emotion indeed.

As Hume argued in his *Treatise*, pride has mainly to do with a sense of personal accomplishment. Its focus is typically the individual self, but through loyalty and affiliation it can be expanded to encompass one's community and corporation. Pride, however, tends to be too personal and too concerned with accomplishment. Honour, by contrast, need not involve accomplishment at all (although it certainly may and often does), and it makes very little sense as a purely personal notion. (That is why, when people say that they are defending their honour but are obviously nursing their pride, we find such behaviour not only foolish but pretentious as well.)

Honour requires a sense of belonging, a sense of membership, a sense of self that incorporates one's corporate identity. It also involves living up to the expectations of the corporation, whether these are spelled out as a code of honour or set of moral rules or are simply implicit in the practices and goals of the group. (It is not obeying moral rules that makes a person honourable, however; it is obeying the rules because they are the rules of his or her corporation — very un-Kantian).

A person's honour, in other words, is never his or her honour alone. It is the honour of the community or corporation that he or she represents, and standing up for honour necessarily entails defending it as a representative of that community or corporation. In business ethics, this sense of honour helps clarify both the role of the individual employee or executive in the corporation and, even more important, the role of both the individual and the corporation in society. (Tragedy in business ethics, one might add, does not usually consist of a conflict of interests but a rather a conflicting sense of honour, a sense of being torn between one membership and another — as an employee of the company, as the friend of one's immediate supervisor or as the member of the greater community.) Honour should not be thought of as a set of personal constraints defined by membership in a group.

The notion of constraints is appropriate rather to a group of which one is not a member or, perhaps, is a member only by chance or because one was a member even though one now desperately wants to extricate oneself. One's sense of honour is, if not voluntary, at least personally acceptable, part and parcel of one's sense of self. It is, in this sense, a species of merit, but this is very different from any sense of desert or what one has achieved. Merit in the context of honour has to do with who one is — namely, a member of the group in good standing — and not particularly with anything that one has done (or not done) except insofar as such acts are part of one's membership in the group. So, too, there is a natural affinity between honour and self-esteem; one's selfesteem depends on one's sense of honour (though not vice versa), and one's standing in the group becomes the criterion of self-esteem.

One cannot be much of a member if one can be humiliated in the group and nevertheless have a solid sense of self-worth. So, too, the contemporary idea that one's main objective after public humiliation is to "get over it" makes impossible any sense of honour — which pre- supposes that one doesn't just "get over it." One might note that one symptom of our collective loss of honour is the fact that no one seems to believe in the concept of a "ruined life" anymore.

One just moves to another town or gets another job or sets up another company and "starts over." In practical terms, what this means is that the business community is notoriously poor in sanctioning its own rules and punishing even the most flagrant offenders of those rules. Business failure is neither adequate nor sufficiently dependable as a measure or a punishment for unethical business practices. It is a person's sense of honour that must be put into play, and for those who don't understand or who scoff at this notion the old tribal practice of exile (federal minimum security prisons will do) serves an extremely necessary function in the survival of the business community. The opposite of honour is *shame.* Aristotle lists, with some discomfort, shame as one of the virtues, not because it is good to be ashamed but rather because, as in that Ethiopian proverb, "where there is no shame, there is no honour." Thus,

John Rawls is not entirely wrong when he insists that shame is the opposite of selfesteem, since honour can be the criterion for self-esteem.

Not all societies are honour societies, however, and not everyone's self-esteem is tied to a sense of honour. Shame is not, as Rawls says, failing to live up to one's potential; it is, much more specifically, failing to live up to the standards of the group through which one gains one's selfidentity and one's standards. Shame is, in other words, a loss of integrity, a breach of the commitments or principles one accepts and knows that one should accept. Of course, in the Aristotelian approach to business ethics, failing to live up to one's potential may well be equivalent to failing to live up to the standards of the group, perhaps because one has made a commitment that cannot be kept or set a goal that cannot be met. But personal achievement and failure as such are not essential and often not relevant to honour and shame.

What one fails to be is acceptable to the group and, accordingly, acceptable in terms of one's own essential sense of identity. To feel shame (not quite the same as "being ashamed") is quite literally to fail oneself, but only in the context of one's larger self. It is in this sense that shame is contrasted to guilt, for it is guilt, not shame, that defines the appropriate attitude in our non-honour society. Shame is always defined in a group context; guilt is borne by one alone. It is not surprising that the Scriptures talk mainly of sin and guilt when discussing an individual's wrongdoing before God. Guilt is an emotion that permeates the personal self, but other people, one's peers, play no clear role in its workings.

We feel guilty, not shamed, for failing to live up to our own goals and standards. We feel guilty, not shamed, for breaking the rules or committing a moral infelicity. Guilt is appropriate to isolated individuals; shame is possible only in groups. Guilt ties in nicely with the traditional concept of the individual soul; shame is essentially a tribal emotion. It has often been said (by Nietzsche and Freud most famously) that there is too much guilt in our society. I would like to suggest that, while this is probably true, there isn't nearly enough shame. Indeed, the payoff for public humiliation in current-day America seems to be a fat book advance and profitable public appearances, not repentence, apology, and retribution.

We may have more guilt than we ought to have, but part of the reason may be that we don't have enough room for honour — or shame. What all of this amounts to is the idea that business ethics is at once more personal and more social than it is usually thought to be.

It is not enough to teach principles and policies, much less the theories of the great, dead, mostly white male philosophers. Business ethics requires the cultivation of the civic virtues, not something possible in an isolated business ethics course — on this, at least, the critics are correct — but nevertheless, as Aristotle himself surely would have argued, something absolutely necessary for the health and well-being of the business world itself.

What business ethics does and what business ethics courses do is not to "teach" ethics to business students and managers. Instead, they remind us all that there are standards and virtues at issue in business without which an enterprise (no matter how "free") will not and does not deserve to survive.

It is in the humanities that the personal dimension of ethics gets cultivated (not inculcated, perhaps — that comes long before), but the current myths and metaphors of business convince me that most of the obstacles to ethics in business are not the result of inadequate upbringing but rather of corporate cultural illiteracy and moral myopia.

Business students are steeped in business lore and too rarely exposed to those broader human issues and concerns that are the stuff of literature and philosophy. They learn the ins and outs of game theory and strategic planning but are taught to think very little about their lives or the values they are pursuing with such enthusiasm. They learn techniques of finance, theories of management, and maybe even some public policy, but they get little chance to exercise their imaginations or their emotions, much less to experience (one can hear them scoffing) their "humanity." I have argued elsewhere that the subjects and disciplines of the humanities — in particular, reading books — are essential and not merely marginal in the cultivation of the moral imagination and emotions.

It is a tragedy — albeit one that can be easily explained and rationalised — that business and the humanities have drifted so far apart. The price of the resulting gap between them is not only uncultivated executives and unworldly scholars; it is an enormous gap in business ethics, not just the study but the actual ethics of business. So long as ethics gets deferred and appealed to government policies, so long as ethics remains formalised in rules and codes and abstract principles and isn't taken seriously and personally by the individual businessman and -woman, it will continue to appear as something foreign, something imposed on if not opposed to the aims and ambitions of business. The humanities, whatever else they may be, are serious and personal.

The great books allow us to get involved in and to live vicariously through the difficulties and dilemmas of life, and those difficulties and dilemmas are, to a large extent, ethical quandaries, predicaments of loyalty and honour, or occasions for shame. The tragedies of *King Lear* and *Macbeth*, the comedies of Moliére and Tom Stoppard, the rude advice of Rousseau and Machiavelli — these may not contain the precise situations faced by every middle manager and executive, but it takes very little imagination to see how those grand tragedies, farces, and philosophical essays stretch the mind and open up our awareness for the more pedestrian dilemmas that we do face daily.

Humanitas is ultimately not a subject matter but a certain attitude towards life, an attitude of "humanity" and a broad perspective in which it is the whole of life that comes into focus, not just the office problem of the moment, in which the whole of community and even the whole of humanity is within our scope, not just the boardroom or the stock report or one's immediate superiors and subordinates. It is, in other words, just that larger sense of self that Aristotle talked about so long ago. The Aristotelian approach to business ethics is, ultimately, just another way of saying that people come before profits, and before a great deal of what is often called ethics, too.

NEW TRENDS IN MARKETING COMMUNICATION

In 2010 is poised to be an exciting year for marketers; trends that have been taking shape over the course of the past decade are creating new opportunities for business owners. The first 10 years of the 21st century brought economic problems, corporate collapses and environmental disasters, but it was also a decade defined by a shift in communications from traditional media to a worldwide conversation that flows faster and farther than anyone could have imagined. Thanks to the tools of the social web, such as Twitter, Facebook, blogs, online video and so on, news and information travels instantaneously, and that means marketers have new and exciting opportunities to reach consumers.

With those economic, cultural, political and environmental events, as well as the advances in technology and the global online conversation in mind, following are 10 trends that affect all areas of marketing, from advertising to branding and everything in between, and will shape marketing strategy throughout 2010 and beyond.

- Transparency and trust are paramount.
- Consumers have lived through a variety of negative events throughout the past decade, and they're no longer willing to accept anything businesses tell them. Brands that embrace the loss of naïveté and make a concentrated effort to be honest and open in their marketing communications will generate positive consumer responses, which can lead to brand loyalty and brand advocacy. Building trust is the most important thing in 2010, and once you've earned it, you need to make sure you keep it. In other words, transparency and trust are not a one-time thing. They're an ongoing effort.
- Less interruption, more enhancement and value-add.
- The days when ads and marketing messages were developed for the sole purpose of getting the attention of consumers are over. People expect more from businesses and brands. Give them more by ensuring your marketing communications and efforts deliver useful and meaningful value.
- Speaking of value...
- The economic downturn that occurred in the latter part of the past decade

stopped many consumers in their tracks. Rather than spending money frivolously, consumers began seeking out deals, using coupons and actively looking for the biggest bang for their buck. When the economy recovers, that behaviour will not disappear immediately. Be prepared for the consumer focus on value to continue well beyond 2010, and build marketing campaigns with that consumer demand in mind.

- Show it, don't tell it.
- Consumers don't believe everything they hear. Indeed, consumers are more skeptical than ever, and you need to prove your marketing claims. Don't just tell consumers about your product, business or services, show them what's in it for them if they pull out their hard-earned money and buy from you.
- Social media is not going away, and engagement is critical.
- Twitter, Facebook, blogs, YouTube, and other tools of the online social community are not going anywhere. Instead, these tools are being adopted by more and more people around the world. If you thought you could avoid joining the bandwagon, you were wrong. In 2010, it's critical that your business joins the social web conversation, and you must engage consumers on the social networking sites. Give them amazing content and interact with them to fully leverage the power of the social media.
- Peace-of-mind messages prevail.
- Consumers have lived through a wide variety of negative events over the past several years, from economic turmoil to environmental disasters and more. They're actively seeking marketing messages that give them a feeling of peace of mind. Try to communicate a feeling of security in your marketing efforts to meet this need.
- Relationships rule.
- With the growth of web-based social networks and a desire for transparency, trust and peace-of-mind messages, it shouldn't be surprising that relationships rule in 2010 and beyond. Leverage the social web to interact with people around the world and build relationships that wouldn't have been possible a decade ago. When you build relationships with consumers, you also build a band of brand loyalists that can become your most powerful source of word-of-mouth marketing, brand advocacy and brand guardianship.
- Online video and mobile marketing are hot.
- Both online video and mobile marketing are set to explode, and we'll really start to see that happen in 2010. You can create your own online video content or mobile content, or you can invest in online video or mobile advertising. The choice is yours, but there is no better time to jump in than right now!

- Focus, focus, focus!
- Don't try to be everything to everyone in 2010. The strongest brands are focused brands. As the first decade of the 21st century unfolded, marketers and social media professionals began using the term *niche* more and more to identify highly focused products, web sites, blogs and so on. Today, that strategy is even more important. Build your core and keep it as strong as possible before you try to extend your brand and branch out into new areas.
- Integrated marketing trumps stand-alone tactics.
- It is absolutely essential that you surround consumers with your marketing messages in 2010. The number of marketing communications that people see each day is overwhelming, so it's important that your messages don't get lost in the clutter. You can make your brand, your business and your messages stand out by surrounding consumers with branded experiences and allowing them to choose which of those experiences they want to consume. For example, use online advertising, online video, custom content, point-of-sale collateral, and ads with consistent messaging to engage consumers in different parts of their lives. If you're consistent and persistent, your messages are more likely to connect with your target audience—raising brand awareness, recognition, purchases and loyalty.

INTEGRATED MARKETING COMMUNICATION

The evolution of this new perspective has two origins. Marketers began to realise that advertising, public relations, and sales were often at odds regarding responsibilities, budgets, management input and myriad other decisions affecting the successful marketing of a brand. Executives in each area competed with the others for resources and a voice in decision making. The outcome was inconsistent promotional efforts, wasted money, counterproductive management decisions, and, perhaps worst of all, confusion among consumers.

Secondly, the marketing perspective itself began to shift from being market oriented to market driven. Marketing communication was traditionally viewed as an inside-out way of presenting the company's messages. Advertising was the dominant element in the promotional mix because the mass media could effectively deliver a sales message to a mass audience. But then the mass market began to fragment.

Consumers became better educated and more skeptical about advertising. A variety of sources, both controlled by the marketer and uncontrolled, became important to consumers. News reports, word-of-mouth, experts' opinions, and financial reports were just some of the"brand contacts" consumers began to use to learn about and form attitudes and opinions about a brand or company, or make purchase decisions. Advertising began to lose some of its luster in terms of its ability to deliver huge homogeneous audiences. Companies began to seek new ways to coordinate the multiplicity of product and company messages being issued and used by consumers and others.

Thus, two ideas permeate integrated marketing communication: relationship building and synergy. Rather than the traditional inside-out view, IMC is seen as an outside-in perspective. Customers are viewed not as targets but as partners in an ongoing relationship. Customers, prospects, and others encounter the brand and company through a host of sources and create from these various contacts ideas about the brand and company.

By knowing the media habits and lifestyles of important consumer segments, marketers can tailor messages through media that are most likely to reach these segments at times when these segments are most likely to be receptive to these messages, thus optimizing the marketing communication effort.

Ideally, IMC is implemented by developing comprehensive databases on customers and prospects, segmenting these current and potential customers into groups with certain common awareness levels, predispositions, and behaviours, and developing messages and media strategies that guide the communication tactics to meet marketing objectives. In doing this, IMC builds and reinforces mutually profitable relationships with customers and other important stakeholders and generates synergy by coordinating all elements in the promotional mix into a programme that possesses clarity, consistency, and maximum impact.

Practitioners and academics alike, however, have noted the difficulty of effectively implementing IMC. Defining exactly what IMC is has been difficult. For example, merely coordinating messages so that speaking"with one clear voice" in all promotional efforts does not fully capture the meaning of IMC. Also, changing the organization to accommodate the integrated approach has challenged the command and control structure of many organizations. However, studies suggest that IMC is viewed by a vast majority of marketing executives as having the greatest potential impact on their company's marketing strategies, more so than the economy, pricing, and globalization.

ADVERTISING

Advertising has four characteristics: it is persuasive in nature; it is non-personal; it is paid for by an identified sponsor; and it is disseminated through mass channels of communication. Advertising messages may promote the adoption of goods, services, persons, or ideas. Because the sales message is disseminated through the mass media—as opposed to personal selling—it is viewed as a much cheaper way of reaching consumers. However, its non-personal nature means it lacks the ability to tailor the sales message to the message recipient and, more importantly, actually get the sale.

Therefore, advertising effects are best measured in terms of increasing awareness and changing attitudes and opinions, not creating sales. Advertising's contribution to sales is difficult to isolate because many factors influence sales. The contribution advertising makes to sales are best viewed over the long run. The exception to this thinking is within the internet arena. While banner ads, pop-ups and interstitials should still be viewed as brand promoting and not necessarily sales drivers, technology provides the ability to track how many of a web site's visitors click the banner, investigate a product, request more information, and ultimately make a purchase.

Through the use of symbols and images advertising can help differentiate products and services that are otherwise similar. Advertising also helps create and maintain brand equity. Brand equity is an intangible asset that results from a favourable image, impressions of differentiation, or consumer attachment to the company, brand, or trademark. This equity translates into greater sales volume, and/or higher margins, thus greater competitive advantage. Brand equity is established and maintained through advertising that focuses on image, product attributes, service, or other features of the company and its products or services.

Cost is the greatest disadvantage of advertising. The average cost for a 30-second spot on network television increased fivefold between 1980 and 2005. Plus, the average cost of producing a 30-second ad for network television is quite expensive. It is not uncommon for a national advertiser to spend in the millions of dollars for one 30-second commercial to be produced. Add more millions on top of that if celebrity talent is utilized.

Credibility and clutter are other disadvantages. Consumers have become increasingly skeptical about advertising messages and tend to resent advertisers' attempt to persuade. Advertising is everywhere, from network television, to daily newspapers, to roadside billboards, to golf course signs, to stickers on fruit in grocery stores. Clutter encourages consumers to ignore many advertising messages. New media are emerging, such as DVRs which allow consumers to record programmes and then skip commercials, and satellite radio which provides a majority of its channels advertising free.

PUBLIC RELATIONS

Public relations is defined as a management function which identifies, establishes, and maintains mutually beneficial relationships between an organization and the publics upon which its success or failure depends. Whereas advertising is a one-way communication from sender to the receiver, public relations considers multiple audiences and uses two-way communication to monitor feedback and adjust both its message and the organization's actions for maximum benefit. A primary tool used by public relations practitioners is publicity. Publicity capitalizes on the news value of a product, service, idea, person or event so that the information can be disseminated through the news media. This third party "endorsement" by the news media provides a vital boost to the marketing communication message: credibility.

In the media are perceived as being more objective than advertisements, and their messages are more likely to be absorbed and believed. For example, after the CBS newsmagazine 60 Minutes reported in the early 1990s that drinking moderate amounts of red wine could prevent heart attacks by lowering cholesterol, red wine sales in the United States increased 50 per cent. Another benefit publicity offers is that it is free, not considering the great amount of effort it can require to get out-bound publicity noticed and picked up by media sources.

Public relations' role in the promotional mix is becoming more important because of what Philip Kotler describes as an "over communicated society." Consumers develop "communication-avoidance routines" where they are likely to tune out commercial messages. As advertising loses some of its cost-effectiveness, marketers are turning to news coverage, events, and community programmes to help disseminate their product and company messages.

Some consumers may also base their purchase decisions on the image of the company, for example, how environmentally responsible the company is. In this regard, public relations plays an important role in presenting, through news reports, sponsorships, "advertorials" and other forms of communication, what the company stands for.

DIRECT MARKETING AND DATABASE MARKETING

Direct Marketing

Direct marketing, the oldest form of marketing, is the process of communicating directly with target customers to encourage response by telephone, mail, electronic means, or personal visit. Users of direct marketing include retailers, wholesalers, manufacturers, and service providers, and they use a variety of methods including direct mail, telemarketing, direct-response advertising, online computer shopping services, cable shopping networks, and infomercials.

Traditionally not viewed as an element in the promotional mix, direct marketing represents one of the most profound changes in marketing and promotion in the last 25 years. Aspects of direct marketing, which includes direct response advertising and direct mail advertising as well as the various research and support activities necessary for their implementation, have been adopted by virtually all companies engaged in marketing products, services, ideas, or persons. Direct marketing has become an important part of many marketing communication programmes for three reasons. First, the number of two-income households has increased dramatically. About six in every ten women in the United States work outside the home. This has reduced the amount of time families have for shopping trips. Secondly, more shoppers than ever before rely on credit cards for payment of goods and services. These cashless transactions make products easier and faster to purchase. Finally, technological advances in telecommunications and computers allow consumers to make purchases from their homes via telephone, television, or computer with ease and safety. These three factors have dramatically altered the purchasing habits of American consumers and made direct marketing a growing field worldwide.

Direct marketing allows a company to target more precisely a segment of customers and prospects with a sales message tailored to their specific needs and characteristics. Unlike advertising and public relations, whose connections to actual sales are tenuous or nebulous at best, direct marketing offers accountability by providing tangible results. The economics of direct marketing have also improved over the years as more information is gathered about customers and prospects. By identifying those consumers they can serve more effectively and profitably, companies may be more efficient in their marketing efforts. Whereas network television in the past offered opportunities to reach huge groups of consumers at a low cost per thousand, direct marketing can reach individual consumers and develop a relationship with each of them.

Research indicates that brands with strong brand equity are more successful in direct marketing efforts than little-known brands. Direct marketing, then, works best when other marketing communication such as traditional media advertising supports the direct marketing effort.

Direct marketing has its drawbacks also. Just as consumers built resistance to the persuasive nature of advertising, so have they with direct marketing efforts. Direct marketers have responded by being less sales oriented and more relationship oriented. Also, just as consumers grew weary of advertising clutter, so have they with the direct marketing efforts. Consumers are bombarded with mail, infomercials, and telemarketing pitches daily. Some direct marketers have responded by regarding privacy as a customer service benefit. Direct marketers must also overcome consumer mistrust of direct marketing efforts due to incidents of illegal behaviour by companies and individuals using direct marketing. The U.S. Postal Service, the Federal Trade Commission, and other federal and state agencies may prosecute criminal acts. The industry then risks legislation regulating the behaviour of direct marketers if it is not successful in self-regulation. The Direct Marketing Association, the leading trade organization for direct marketing, works with companies and government agencies to initiate self-regulation. In March of 2003 the National Do Not Call Registry went into affect whereby consumers added their names to a list that telemarketers had to eliminate from their out-bound call database.

Database Marketing

Database marketing is a form of direct marketing that attempts to gain and reinforce sales transactions while at the same time being customer driven. Successful database marketing continually updates lists of prospects and customers by identifying who they are, what they are like, and what they are purchasing now or may be purchasing in the future.

By using database marketing, marketers can develop products and/or product packages to meet their customers' needs or develop creative and media strategies that match their tastes, values, and lifestyles. Like IMC, database marketing is viewed by many marketers as supplanting traditional marketing strategies and is a major component of most IMC programmes.

At the core of database marketing is the idea that market segments are constantly shifting and changing. People who may be considered current customers, potential customers, and former customers and people who are likely never to be customers are constantly changing. By identifying these various segments and developing a working knowledge of their wants, needs, and characteristics, marketers can reduce the cost of reaching non-prospects and build customer loyalty. Perhaps the most important role of database marketing is its ability to retain customers. The cumulative profit for a five-year loyal customer is between seven and eight times the first-year profit.

Since database marketing is expensive to develop and complex to implement effectively, companies considering database marketing should consider three important questions. First, do relatively frequent purchasers or high dollar volume purchasers for the brand exist? Secondly, is the market diverse enough so that segmenting into subgroups would be beneficial? Finally, are there customers that represent opportunities for higher volume purchases?

SALES PROMOTION/SPONSORSHIPS/EXHIBITIONS

Sales Promotion

Sales promotions are direct inducements that offer extra incentives to enhance or accelerate the product's movement from producer to consumer. Sales promotions may be directed at the consumer or the trade. Consumer promotions such as coupons, sampling, premiums, sweepstakes, price packs, low-cost financing deals, and rebates are purchase incentives in that they induce product trial and encourage repurchase. Consumer promotions may also include incentives to visit a retail establishment or request additional information. Trade promotions include slotting allowances, allowances for featuring the brand in retail advertising, display and merchandising allowances, buying allowances, bill back allowances, incentives to salespeople, and other tactics to encourage retailers to carry the item and to push the brand. Two perspectives may be found among marketers regarding sales promotion. First, sales promotion is supplemental to advertising in that it binds the role of advertising with personal selling. This view regards sales promotion as a minor player in the marketing communication programme. A second view regards sales promotion and advertising as distinct functions with objectives and strategies very different from each other. Sales promotion in this sense is equal to or even more important than advertising. Some companies allocate as much as 75 per cent of their advertising/promotion dollars to sales promotion and just 25 per cent to advertising. Finding the right balance is often a difficult task. The main purpose of sales promotion is to spur action. Advertising sets up the deal by developing a brand reputation and building market value. Sales promotion helps close the deal by providing incentives that build market volume.

Sales promotions can motivate customers to select a particular brand, especially when brands appear to be equal, and they can produce more immediate and measurable results than advertising. However, too heavy a reliance on sales promotions results in "deal-prone" consumers with little brand loyalty and too much price sensitivity. Sales promotions can also force competitors to offer similar inducements, with sales and profits suffering for everyone.

Sponsorships

Sponsorships, or event marketing, combine advertising and sales promotions with public relations. Sponsorships increase awareness of a company or product, build loyalty with a specific target audience, help differentiate a product from its competitors, provide merchandising opportunities, demonstrate commitment to a community or ethnic group, or impact the bottom line.

Like advertising, sponsorships are initiated to build long-term associations. Organizations sometimes compare sponsorships with advertising by using gross impressions or cost-per-thousand measurements. However, the value of sponsorships can be very difficult to measure. Companies considering sponsorships should consider the short-term public relations value of sponsorships and the long-term goals of the organization. Sports sponsorships make up about two-thirds of all sponsorships.

Exhibits

Exhibits, or trade shows, are hybrid forms of promotion between business-to-business advertising and personal selling. Trade shows provide opportunities for face-to-face contact with prospects, enable new companies to create a viable customer base in a short period of time, and allow small and midsize companies that may not be visited on a regular basis by salespeople to become familiar with suppliers and vendors. Because many trade shows generate media attention, they have also become popular venues for introducing new products and providing a stage for executives to gain visibility.

PERSONAL SELLING

Personal selling includes all person-to-person contact with customers with the purpose of introducing the product to the customer, convincing him or her of the product's value, and closing the sale. The role of personal selling varies from organization to organization, depending on the nature and size of the company, the industry, and the products or services it is marketing. Many marketing executives realise that both sales and non-sales employees act as salespeople for their organization in one way or another.

One study that perhaps supports this contention found that marketing executives predicted greater emphasis being placed on sales management and personal selling in their organization than on any other promotional mix element. These organizations have launched training sessions that show employees how they act as salespeople for the organization and how they can improve their interpersonal skills with clients, customers, and prospects. Employee reward programmes now reward employees for their efforts in this regard. Personal selling is the most effective way to make a sale because of the interpersonal communication between the salesperson and the prospect. Messages can be tailored to particular situations, immediate feedback can be processed, and message strategies can be changed to accommodate the feedback. However, personal selling is the most expensive way to make a sale, with the average cost per sales call ranging from $235 to $332 and the average number of sales calls needed to close a deal being between three and six personal calls.

Sales and marketing management classifies salespersons into one of three groups: creative selling, order taking, and missionary sales reps. Creative selling jobs require the most skills and preparation. They are the "point person" for the sales function. They prospect for customers, analyse situations, determine how their company can satisfy wants and needs of prospects, and, most importantly, get an order. Order takers take over after the initial order is received. They handle repeat purchases and modified rebuys. Missionary sales reps service accounts by introducing new products, promotions, and other programmes. Orders are taken by order takers or by distributors.

INTERNET MARKETING

Just as direct marketing has become a prominent player in the promotional mix, so too has the Internet. Virtually unheard of in the 1980s, the 1990s saw this new medium explode onto the scene, being adopted by families, businesses and other organizations more quickly than any other medium in history. Web sites provide a new way of transmitting information, entertainment, and advertising, and have generated a new dimension in marketing: electronic commerce. E-commerce is the term used to describe the act of selling goods and services over the Internet. In other words, the Internet has become more that a communication channel; it is a marketing channel itself with companies,

CDNow, eBay, and others selling goods via the Internet to individuals around the globe. In less than 10 years advertising expenditures on the Internet will rival those for radio and outdoor. Public relations practitioners realise the value that web sites offer in establishing and maintaining relationships with important publics. For example, company and product information can be posted on the company's site for news reporters researching stories and for current and potential customers seeking information. Political candidates have web sites that provide information about their background and their political experience.

The interactivity of the Internet is perhaps its greatest asset. By communicating with customers, prospects, and others one-on-one, firms can build databases that help them meet specific needs of individuals, thus building a loyal customer base. Because the cost of entry is negligible, the Internet is cluttered with web sites. However, this clutter does not present the same kind of problem that advertising clutter does. Advertising and most other forms of promotion assume a passive audience that will be exposed to marketing communication messages via the mass media or mail regardless of their receptivity. Web sites require audiences who are active in the information-seeking process to purposely visit the site. Therefore, the quality and freshness of content is vital for the success of the web site.

THE FUTURE OF MARKETING COMMUNICATION

Marketing communication has become an integral part of the social and economic system in the United States. Consumers rely on the information from marketing communication to make wise purchase decisions. Businesses, ranging from multinational corporations to small retailers, depend on marketing communication to sell their goods and services.

Marketing communication has also become an important player in the life of a business. Marketing communication helps move products, services, and ideas from manufacturers to end users and builds and maintains relationships with customers, prospects, and other important stakeholders in the company. Advertising and sales promotion will continue to play important roles in marketing communication mix. However, marketing strategies that stress relationship building in addition to producing sales will force marketers to consider all the elements in the marketing communication mix. In the future new information gathering techniques will help marketers target more precisely customers and prospects using direct marketing strategies. New media technologies will provide businesses and consumers new ways to establish and reinforce relationships that are important for the success of the firm and important for consumers as they make purchase decisions. The Internet will become a major force in how organizations communicate with a variety of constituents, customers, clients, and other interested parties.

Bibliography

A C Gupta: *Business Economics*, Rawat Publication, Delhi, 2003.

Argenti: *Digital Strategies for Powerful Corporate Communications*, Tata McGraw-Hill, Delhi, 2009.

B. Rameshwaran: *Consumer Behaviour and Promotional Strategies*, Serials Publications, Delhi, 2011.

B.K. Tejpal: *Business Economics : Modern Methods and Techniques*, Ritu Publications, Delhi, 2012.

Dhires Bhattacharyya and Pranab Chakrabarti: *Fundamentals of Business Economics*, BS Publication, Delhi, 2008.

G.L. Jain: *Business Economics : New Trends & Practices*, Shree Niwas Publication, Delhi, 2007.

Jagdish Chandra: *Business Economics in Corporate Sector*, Alfa Publication, Delhi, 2007.

Jaishri Jethwaney: *Corporate Communication : Principles and Practice*, Oxford University Press, Delhi, 2010.

James L.T. Thanga: *Consumer Behaviour in North East India*, Anshah Publication, Delhi, 2010.

Joseph Fernandez: *Corporate Communications : A Twenty-first Century Primer*, Response Books, Delhi, 2004.

Lalata Keshari Pani, M.K. Nabi and Kishore C. Raut: *Consumer Behaviour*, Sonali Publications, Delhi, 2010.

M.S. Narasimha Murthy and S. Nagendra: *Business Economics*, Mohit Publication, Delhi, 2010.

Meenu Agrawal: *Consumer Behaviour and Consumer Protection in India*, New Century Publication, Delhi, 2006.

Prakash Vohra and Rakesh Mehta: *Business Economics*, Commonwealth Publication, Delhi, 2007.

Premananda Pradhan and S.N. Tripathy: *Business Economics*, Anmol Publication, Delhi, 2006.

R.C. Gupta and T.C. Jain: *Consumer Behaviour*, Alfa Publication, Delhi, 2011.

Ravi Chaddha: *Business Economics*, Sumit Enterprises, Delhi, 2011.

Ravi Jyee and Avinash Chiranjeev: *Consumer Behaviour*, Jnanada Prakashan, Delhi, 2010.

Robert East, Malcolm Wright and Marc Vanhuele: *Consumer Behaviour Applications in Marketing*, Sage Publications, Delhi, 2009.

S H H Kazmi: *Consumer Behaviour and Marketing Communication*, Excel Books, Delhi, 2003.

Sajeevan Rao Arigela and Vikas Indoria: *Consumer Behaviour*, Wisdom Press, Delhi, 2013.

Sandeep Saxena: *A Textbook of Business Economics*, Dominant Publication, Delhi, 2013.

Santosh Mehrotra: *Business Economics : Modern Methods & Techniques*, ABD Publication, Delhi, 2006.

Seema Tak: *Business Economics*, DND Publications, Delhi, 2012.

Shailendra Mohan: *Capital Markets and Business Economics*, Swastik Publication, Delhi, 2011.

Soma Sen Gupta: *Consumer Behaviour : Dynamics of Building Brand Equity*, New Century Publication, Delhi, 2005.

Veena Tewari Nandi: *Consumer Behaviour in Service Marketing*, Enkay Publishing House, Delhi, 2012.

Yashwant Khatarkar: *Business Economics*, Adhyayan Publication, Delhi, 2007.

Index

A

Acquisition 247, 255, 258, 259, 282, 284
Allocation 142, 255, 257
Alterations 109
ASP 30
Assumes 141, 186
Authorities 205, 206, 207, 210, 211
Average Variable 144

B

Bargaining 166
Bond Investment 83
Brainstorming 118
Break-even 163, 164
Budgets 262
Business-level 106, 247, 248, 249, 254, 259

C

Capabilities 127, 128, 129, 131, 132
Capital Controls 77, 78
Capital Formation 70, 71
Capital Market 69, 70, 71, 72, 73, 74, 75, 76, 77, 78, 81, 82, 89
CEO 31
Circumstances 205, 209
Commercial Paper 71, 88, 91
Company Debentures 88, 90
Compulsiveness 29
Conservative 282, 284, 285
Consumerism 21, 22, 25, 26, 27, 28, 29
Contingency 239, 262, 264
Corporate Cultures 267, 282, 285
Corporate Life 290
Corporate-level 246, 247
Customer Value 124

D

Deliberateness 262, 263
Demand Analysis 166, 168, 170, 171, 177
Demand Forecasting 185
Demand Terminology 176
Design Process 111, 112, 113
Dimensions 245, 247, 250
Dramatically 43

E

Effectiveness 238
Elements 109, 237, 247, 248, 249
Engage 100
Environmental Analysis 237
Equity Shares 85, 86, 87
Estimation 177
Extroversion 29

F

Finance Strategy 255, 257
Financial Analysis 255

Financial Institutions 70, 88, 89
Financial Intermediaries 69, 70
Flexibility 237, 239, 261
Forecasting 185, 186, 235
Forecasting Methods 186
Formulation 246, 251, 254, 262, 263, 265
FTC 28
Functional-level 245, 248, 249

G

Goals 106, 107, 108, 233, 237, 238, 240, 245, 246, 247, 248, 249, 251, 252, 253, 254, 255, 256, 258, 259, 260, 261

H

Hierarchical Networks 287
Hierarchy 236, 251, 262

I

Implementation 30, 48, 128, 132, 303
Initial Interview 269, 270
Insurmountable 267
Internal Analyses 246
Investment Banks 75, 76, 77
Investment Returns 80, 81

L

Laboratory Research 130
Leadership 124, 125
Legislation 304

M

Machinery 209, 211
Managing Existing Products 128
Market Theory 73, 74, 75, 79
Market Transactions 75, 76, 77, 78
Marketing 15, 16, 17, 52, 53, 54, 55, 56, 57, 58, 64, 67, 68
Marketing Research 125
Marketing Strategy 127

N

Necessary 204, 207, 214
Nonacademic Writing 266, 267

O

Occurrence 174
Offensive 239
Opportunity Cost 141, 142, 144
Organisation 142

P

Predict 140, 142, 166, 168, 169, 185
Price 235, 250, 251, 252, 258, 261
Product Decisions 130
Product Design 111, 112, 113, 131
Production System 98
Public Policy 297

Q

Qualitative Forecasting 186

R

Raising Capital 71
Reconceptualized 130
Repositioning 128
Research Methodology 269
Retained Earnings 257, 259

S

Sas 26, 298, 299
Secondary Markets 71, 76, 77, 81
Security Receipts 78, 83
Semi-Variable 165
Social Responsibility 291
Societal Strategy 245
Stock Market 72, 79, 81, 82

T

Targeting 16
Technological 109, 258
Timing 237, 239
Transfer Pricing 204, 205, 206, 207, 208, 213, 214